NeXTSTEP® Programming
Concepts and Applications

Alex Duong Nghiem
Object Lesson Inc.

P T R Prentice Hall
Englewood Cliffs, New Jersey 07632

Nghiem, Alex Duong.
  NeXTSTEP programming : concepts and applications / Alex Duong Nghiem.
      p. cm.
  Includes bibliographical references and index.
  ISBN 0-13-605916-3
  1. NeXT (Computer)--Programming. 2. NeXTSTEP. I. Title.
ZA76.8.N4N497 1993
005.4'3--dc20   93-13033
                                                                CIP

Editorial/production supervision: *Ann Sullivan*
Buyer: *Mary Elizabeth McCartney*
Acquisitions editor: *Gregory G. Doench*
Editoral Assistant: *Tara Dawn Mahon*
Cover Illustration: *Jean-Francois Podevin/The Image Bank*

©1993 by Alex Duong Nghiem

Published by P T R Prentice-Hall, Inc.
A Simon & Schuster Company
Englewood Cliffs, New Jersey 07632

The publisher offers discounts on this book when ordered in bulk quantities. For more information, contact: Corporate Sales, PTR Prentice Hall, 113 Sylvan Avenue, Englewood Cliffs, NJ 07632; Phone: 201-592-2863; FAX: 201-592-2249

NeXT, the NeXT logo, NeXTSTEP, NeXTSTEP486, Application Kit, Project Builder, Interface Builder, 3DKit, DBKit, ISDN Kit, PhoneKit, NeXTStation, NeXTMail, Workspace Manager, Digital Librarian, Edit, Terminal and Header Viewer are registered trademarks of NeXT Computer Inc. PostScript, Display PostScript and Encapsulated Post Script are registered trademarks of Adobe Systems Incorporated. Create is a registered trademark of Stone Design Incorporated. Diagram! is a registered trademark of Lighthouse Design Ltd. WriteNow is a registered trademark of T/Maker Company. FrameMaker is a registered trademark of Frame Technology Corporation. VT100 is a trademark of Digital Equipment Corporation. UNIX is a registered trademark of UNIX System Laboratories.

All rights reserved. No part of this book may be reproduced, in any form or by any means, without permission in writing from the publisher.

Printed in the United States of America
10 9 8 7 6 5 4 3 2

ISBN 0-13-605916-3

Prentice-Hall International (UK) Limited, *London*
Prentice-Hall of Australia Pty. Limited, *Sydney*
Prentice-Hall Canada Inc., *Toronto*
Prentice-Hall Hispanoamericana, S.A., *Mexico*
Prentice-Hall of India Private Limited, *New Delhi*
Prentice-Hall of Japan, Inc., *Tokyo*
Simon & Schuster Asia Pte. Ltd., *Singapore*
Editora Prentice-Hall do Brasil, Ltda., *Rio de Janeiro*

To my family for all their sacrifices.

Alex

Preface xxiii
   Audience xxiv
   Prerequisites xxiv
   Hardware and Software xxv
   Interface Tools: To Use or Not? xxvi
   Organization xxvii
   Conventions xxix
   Tools Used to Create This Book xxx
   Obtaining the Source Code xxxi
   Author's Biography xxxi
   Contacting the Author xxxi
   Acknowledgments xxxii

Chapter 1 NeXTSTEP Components 1
   1.1 Mach and UNIX 2
   1.2 The Window Server 3
   1.3 The Application Kit 4
   1.4 Objective-C 5
   1.5 The Workspace Manager 5
   1.6 ProjectBuilder 5
   1.7 InterfaceBuilder 6
   1.8 Summary 6

Chapter 2 OOP and Objective-C 7
   2.1 Goals 7
   2.2 Object-Oriented Programming 8
      2.2.1 Encapsulation 9
      2.2.2 Classes 10
      2.2.3 Instances 10
      2.2.4 Subclasses 13
      2.2.5 Messages 17
      2.2.6 Polymorphism 18
   2.3 Objective-C 21
      2.3.1 Support for Abstract Data Types 23
      2.3.2 Messages 24
      2.3.3 Naming Conventions 25

    2.3.4 Objective-C Comments 26
  2.4 A Sample Objective-C Application 27
    2.4.1 Defining Classes 31
    2.4.2 Class Methods and Instance Methods 35
    2.4.3 Messaging Mechanisms 36
    2.4.4 Methods and Functions 40
    2.4.5 Self and Super 41
    2.4.6 Instantiating Classes 44
    2.4.7 Initializing Instances 45
    2.4.8 Freeing Objects 46
  2.5 Suggestions 50
    2.5.1 Printing the Indices of the List's Contents 50
    2.5.2 Freeing the List and its Contents 51
  2.6 Summary 51

Chapter 3 Object-Oriented Design 53
  3.1 Goals 53
  3.2 Methodology 54
    3.2.1 Identifying the Objects 55
    3.2.2 Determining What Each Object Does 57
    3.2.3 Identifying the Relationships Between the Objects 59
    3.2.4 Modeling the Flow of the Application 60
  3.3 Designing ShapeArea 61
  3.4 Tools and Techniques 62
    3.4.1 CRC Cards 62
    3.4.2 Class Summary Tables 66
    3.4.3 Message Diagrams 68
    3.4.4 Hierarchy Graphs 70
  3.5 Implementing ShapeArea 70
    3.5.1 Implementation Pass I 72
    3.5.2 Implementation Pass II 80
    3.5.3 Implementation Pass III 89
  3.6 Common Pitfalls in OOD 94
  3.7 Suggestions 96
  3.8 Summary 96

Chapter 4 The Application Kit 99
4.1 Goals 99
4.2 The Application Kit Classes 99
4.3 The Common Classes 102
4.4 A NeXTSTEP Application vs. an Objective-C Application.........................103
4.5 A Minimal NeXTSTEP Application 104
    4.5.1 Design 105
    4.5.2 Implementation Pass I: Displaying a Window 111
    4.5.3 Implementation Pass II: Adding a Quit Menu Option 117
4.6 Suggestions 121
4.7 Summary 121

Chapter 5 ProjectBuilder and InterfaceBuilder 123
5.1 Goals 124
5.2 The Development Cycle..124
    5.2.1 Starting a Project...126
    5.2.2 Adding the Objects 133
    5.2.3 Inspecting the Objects...134
    5.2.4 Making the Connections 138
    5.2.5 Testing the Interface 141
    5.2.6 Compiling the Application..142
    5.2.7 Launching the Application..144
    5.2.8 Decomposing a NeXTSTEP Application 146
5.3 Summary 148

Chapter 6 Processing Events 149
6.1 Goals 149
6.2 Event-Driven Programming 150
6.3 The Target-Action Paradigm...153
    6.3.1 The Button Class...154
    6.3.2 The Slider Class 161
    6.3.3 The TextField Class 165
    6.3.4 The Form Class 168
6.4 The Delegation Paradigm..172
6.5 Designing Money 180
6.6 Implementing Money 186

6.7 Walking Through the Code 196
6.8 Suggestions 197
    6.8.1 Adding Another Menu Option 197
    6.8.2 Setting a Window's Minimum Size 198
    6.8.3 Autosizing 203
6.9 Troubleshooting 205
6.10 Summary 207

Chapter 7 Drawing With PostScript 209

7.1 Goals 209
7.2 The View Class 209
    7.2.1 Creating a View 210
    7.2.2 Adding Subviews 213
    7.2.3 Displaying the Views 214
7.3 Mouse Events 218
7.4 Converting Coordinates 220
7.5 PostScript 222
    7.5.1 PostScript Primer 224
    7.5.2 PostScript Special Effects 229
    7.5.3 Interfacing to Objective-C Using Single Operators 232
    7.5.4 Interfacing to Objective-C Using pswraps 234
7.6 Instance Drawing 237
7.7 Designing Shapes 241
7.8 Implementing Shapes 252
7.9 Walking Through the Code 269
7.10 Suggestions 274
    7.10.1 Adding Support for Printing 274
    7.10.2 Drawing Shadows 274
    7.10.3 Adding a Triangle Class 275
    7.10.4 Detecting Mouse Clicks 275
7.11 Troubleshooting 276
7.12 Summary 278

Chapter 8 Customizing NeXTSTEP Applications 279

8.1 Goals 279
8.2 The Defaults Database 279
    8.2.1 Reading Defaults with dread 280

  8.2.2 Registering Defaults 281
  8.2.3 Writing Defaults with dwrite 288
 8.3 Using Multiple .nib Files 289
  8.3.1 Setting the File's Owner 290
  8.3.2 Initializing Outlets 292
 8.4 Redesigning Money: Adding a Preferences Panel 296
 8.5 Implementing Money 309
 8.6 Examining the Code 324
 8.7 Suggestions 333
  8.7.1 Implementing the Quit Prompt 333
  8.7.2 Adding Support for Significant Figures 333
  8.7.3 Implementing Dynamic Conversion Rates 334
  8.7.4 Adding an Info Panel 334
 8.8 Troubleshooting 334
 8.9 Summary 336

Chapter 9 Processing Text 337
 9.1 Goals 337
 9.2 Creating the Text 338
 9.3 Selecting the Text 339
 9.4 Cutting and Pasting the Text 341
 9.5 Setting the First Responder 343
 9.6 Scrolling the Text 345
 9.7 Saving the Text 350
  9.7.1 Using the SavePanel 351
  9.7.2 Writing the Text to a File 354
 9.8 Loading the Text 357
  9.8.1 Using the OpenPanel 357
  9.8.2 Loading the Text From a File 361
 9.9 Adding a Text Delegate 362
 9.10 Designing Words 364
 9.11 Implementing Words 374
 9.12 Walking Through the Code 387
 9.13 Suggestions 397
  9.13.1 Enabling the Menu Options 398
  9.13.2 Updating the OpenPanel and SavePanel 398

- 9.13.3 Adding Printing Support 398
- 9.13.4 Saving Part of a Document 400
- 9.13.5 Adding a Preferences Panel 400
- 9.13.6 Opening Files from the Workspace 402
- 9.14 Troubleshooting 408
- 9.15 Summary 409

Chapter 10 Implementing On-Line Help 411
- 10.1 Goals 411
- 10.2 The On-Line Help System 411
- 10.3 Using Links 413
- 10.4 Using Markers 415
- 10.5 Adding On-line Help to Words 417
- 10.6 Troubleshooting 424
- 10.7 Suggestions 426
  - 10.7.1 Adding the Help Entries to the Index 427
  - 10.7.2 Creating More Help Entries 427
  - 10.7.3 Adding Graphics to the Help Files 427
- 10.8 Summary 427
- 10.9 Epilogue 428

Appendix A A NeXTSTEP Tutorial 431

Appendix B Tools of the Trade 447
- B.1 Edit 447
  - B.1.1 Using the Implicit Expansion Dictionary 447
  - B.1.2 Customizing the Expansion Dictionary 449
  - B.1.3 Contracting and Expanding the Listing 452
- B.2 Digital Librarian 453
  - B.2.1 Expanding the Search String 456
  - B.2.2 Limitations of Digital Librarian 457
- B.3 HeaderViewer 458
  - B.3.1 Language Elements 459
  - B.3.2 Using the Find Controls Options panel 460
  - B.3.3 HeaderViewer vs. Digital Librarian 463
- B.4 Terminal 465
  - B.4.1 Copying Text 465

Contents   xi

    B.4.2 Messaging the Workspace 468
    B.4.3 Messaging HeaderViewer 469
    B.4.4 Messaging Digital Librarian 470
  B.5 The make Utility 470
    B.5.1 The Makefile 470
    B.5.2 Removing Files: make clean 474
    B.5.3 Installing the Application: make install 474
    B.5.4 Deinstalling the Application: make deinstall 475
    B.5.5 Makefiles for the Applications 476
    B.5.6 Error Messages in make 480

Appendix C Common NeXTSTEP Mistakes 483
  C.1 Runtime Errors 483
  C.2 Warnings 486

Appendix D Debugging 491
  D.1 Tracing the Program 491
    D.1.1 Tracing a Non-Event Driven Application 492
    D.1.2 Tracing an Event-Driven Program 493
    D.1.3 Implicit and Explicit Message Sending 498
    D.1.4 Reverse-engineering an Application 501
  D.2 Debugging with gdb 504
    D.2.1 Compiling for Debugging 504
    D.2.2 Setting BreakPoints 508
    D.2.3 Running the Application 509
    D.2.4 Printing Variables 510
    D.2.5 Single-Stepping 512
    D.2.6 Browsing Objects 514
    D.2.7 Continuing the Execution 518
    D.2.8 Setting Variables 519
  D.3 Suggestions 521
  D.4 Summary 521

Appendix E Resources 523
  E.1 Bundled Documentation and Source Code 523
  E.2 Books 524
    E.2.1 NeXTSTEP 524

- E.2.2 Object-Oriented Design and Technology 525
- E.2.3 Object-Oriented Programming and Objective-C 525
- E.2.4 PostScript...526
- E.2.5 C 527
- E.2.6 UNIX 527
- E.2.7 User-Interface Design..528
- E.2.8 Miscellaneous 528
- E.3 Magazines and Journals..529
- E.4 Internet Archives 530
  - E.4.1 Using anonymous ftp...531
  - E.4.2 Using the Mail Server..532
  - E.4.3 Unpacking the Data..533
- E.5 NeXTAnswers 534
- E.6 Newsgroups 534
- E.7 Users Groups 535
- E.8 Special Interest Groups Mailing Lists 571
- E.9 Bulletin Boards...572
- E.10 Associations...573
- E.11 Conventions 573

Appendix F Porting to NeXTSTEP/Intel 575

- F.1 Hardware Considerations..576
  - F.1.1 The Screen 576
  - F.1.2 The Mouse 578
  - F.1.3 The Keyboard...578
  - F.1.4 Sound 580
- F.2 Data Representation Considerations..580
  - F.2.1 Datum Size...580
  - F.2.2 Byte Alignment...581
  - F.2.3 Byte Order...581
  - F.2.4 Datum Format..582
  - F.2.5 Argument Passing 582
  - F.2.6 External Data 583
    - F.2.6.1 Reading and Writing Structure Bitfields 584
    - F.2.6.2 Reading Existing Files 588

F.2.7 Internal Data 593
F.2.8 Memory-mapped Data 594

Index 597

Figures

Figure 1.1	The layers of NeXTSTEP	1
Figure 2.1	In procedural programming, the functions are kept separate from the data they operate on	8
Figure 2.2	An object is a collection of data (instance variables) along with the functions (methods) that can access the data	9
Figure 2.3	Accessing an instance variable through one of the methods	9
Figure 2.4	Once a class is defined, it can be used to create instances	11
Figure 2.5	A subclass inherits the methods and instance variables defined in the superclass	14
Figure 2.6	A message expression has two parts	18
Figure 2.7	Polymorphism allows identically named methods in more than one class	19
Figure 2.8	The higher classes are more generalized than the lower classes	21
Figure 2.9	The interface file declares the instance variables and methods which the class contains	31
Figure 2.10	The implementation file contains the code for the methods defined in the class' interface file	34
Figure 2.11	The class object has two message dispatch tables that contain the addresses of the instance and class methods	37
Figure 2.12	Objective-C searches for the appropriate method in the dispatch table	39
Figure 2.13	Dynamic binding defers associating the receiver to the method until runtime	40
Figure 2.14	**self** is the current object and **super** is the superclass	43
Figure 2.15	Objective-C starts at the **Object** class to allocate the memory for a newly created instance	45
Figure 2.16	The contents of **theWindow** and **name** are completely external to **theDocument**	48
Figure 2.17	An object should free the memory block an instance variable is pointing to before freeing the instance variable	50
Figure 3.1	Object-oriented design is composed of activities rather than steps	55
Figure 3.2	**AbstractShape** has no collaborators	64
Figure 3.3	The **Rectangle** class has no collaborators	65
Figure 3.4	The **Square** class has no collaborators	65
Figure 3.5	The **List** class has no collaborators	66
Figure 3.6	In a message diagram, the classes are depicted as boxes, and the lines and their directions depict the messages	69
Figure 3.7	The **Object** class is always the root class of an Objective-C application	70
Figure 4.1	The major classes in the Application Kit	100
Figure 4.2	The Common Classes hierarchy	102
Figure 4.3	The CRC card for the **Menu** class	106
Figure 4.4	The CRC card for the **Window** class	107
Figure 4.5	The CRC card for the **Application** class	107

Figures

Figure 4.6	The message diagram for **AppKitDemo**	111
Figure 4.7	**AppKitDemo** in execution	114
Figure 4.8	**AppKitDemo** with a **Quit** option	119
Figure 5.1	The NeXTSTEP development cycle	125
Figure 5.2	Creating a new project with ProjectBuilder	127
Figure 5.3	The Files accessory view of ProjectBuilder	127
Figure 5.4	The Attributes accessory view of ProjectBuilder	129
Figure 5.5	The Build accessory view	129
Figure 5.6	The initial screen in InterfaceBuilder	130
Figure 5.7	The File Window contains the resources	131
Figure 5.8	The Palettes Window contains more than one palette	132
Figure 5.9	InterfaceBuilder automatically creates menu options for the Main Menu	132
Figure 5.10	Adding a menu option to the Main Menu	133
Figure 5.11	Adding a panel to the application	134
Figure 5.12	Placing a textfield in the Info panel	134
Figure 5.13	Displaying the Attributes Inspector for the Info panel	135
Figure 5.14	Editing the title of a panel	136
Figure 5.15	Editing the text of a textfield	137
Figure 5.16	Editing the text of a menu option	137
Figure 5.17	Making a connection to the Main Window	139
Figure 5.18	Displaying an already existing connection.	140
Figure 5.19	Switching to **Test Mode** in InterfaceBuilder	141
Figure 5.20	Building an application in ProjectBuilder	144
Figure 5.21	The components of an application	147
Figure 6.1	The framework for a NeXTSTEP application	151
Figure 6.2	Clicking on the **Hide** menu option sends a **hide:** message to **NXApp** (the target)	153
Figure 6.3	Some sample buttons	155
Figure 6.4	**ControlDemo** during execution	158
Figure 6.5	The components of **ControlDemo**	159
Figure 6.6	Some sample sliders	161
Figure 6.7	The granularity of a slider	162
Figure 6.8	**ControlDemo** with a slider and a button	164
Figure 6.9	Some sample textfields	165
Figure 6.10	A converter application with two textfields	166

Figures xvii

Figure 6.11	**ControlDemo** with a button, a slider, and a textfield	167
Figure 6.12	The slider is the textfield's target and the textfield is the slider's target	168
Figure 6.13	A sample form	169
Figure 6.14	**ControlDemo** with all the controls	171
Figure 6.15	**ControlDemo** with the button as the form's target	172
Figure 6.16	The **windowWillClose:** method in action	180
Figure 6.17	**Money** with six textfields and a button	182
Figure 6.18	The CRC card for the **MoneyConverter** class	184
Figure 6.19	The message diagram for **Money**	185
Figure 6.20	The hierarchy graph for **Money**	185
Figure 6.21	Adding fields to a form	186
Figure 6.22	Labeling the form with the appropriate fields	187
Figure 6.23	Subclassing **Object** to create **MoneyConverter**	188
Figure 6.24	Adding the **moneyForm** outlet to the **Converter** class	189
Figure 6.25	Adding the **convert:** method	190
Figure 6.26	Instantiating the **MoneyConverter** class	191
Figure 6.27	Connecting the objects in **Money.nib**	191
Figure 6.28	Connecting to the form instead of to the formcell	192
Figure 6.29	Adding an arrow icon to the button	194
Figure 6.30	Generating the template files with the **Unparse** command	194
Figure 6.31	Setting the moneyconverter as the delegate of the Main Window	198
Figure 6.32	Determining the size of a window with the Size Inspector	199
Figure 6.33	Parsing in a class updates the outlets and actions for the class in InterfaceBuilder	200
Figure 6.34	Setting the moneyconverter as the delegate of the application object	201
Figure 6.35	Using the autosizing features in the Size Inspector	204
Figure 6.36	Setting the autosizing characteristics of the button and the form	205
Figure 7.1.	Coordinates in the base system and screen system	210
Figure 7.2.	A view's location inside its window	213
Figure 7.3.	Drawing order of views in a window	215
Figure 7.4.	A view's frame rectangle can be outside of its superview's	216
Figure 7.5.	Drawing a shape with PostScript	224
Figure 7.6.	Execution of a typical PostScript command	225
Figure 7.7.	Execution of **square_outline.ps**	226
Figure 7.8.	Execution of **black_square.ps**	227

Figure 7.9.	Execution of **circle.ps** 228	
Figure 7.10.	Rotating the axes 230	
Figure 7.11.	Producing a shadow effect in PostScript 231	
Figure 7.12.	How **pswraps** fits in the program structure 235	
Figure 7.13.	A sample wraps function 236	
Figure 7.14.	An example of instance drawing 238	
Figure 7.15.	Correct and incorrect use of instance drawing 241	
Figure 7.16.	Updating a view in response to the user's actions 244	
Figure 7.17.	A preliminary interface for **Shapes** 245	
Figure 7.18.	A more refined interface for **Shapes** 246	
Figure 7.19.	The CRC card for the **ShapeView** class 247	
Figure 7.20.	The CRC card for the **SquareView** class 247	
Figure 7.21.	The CRC card for the **CircleView** class 248	
Figure 7.22.	The message diagram for **Shapes** 251	
Figure 7.23.	The hierarchy graph for **Shapes** 252	
Figure 7.24.	Instantiating the **SquareView** class 254	
Figure 7.25.	Creating a matrix of two sliders 255	
Figure 7.26.	The user interface with the sliders labeled 256	
Figure 7.27.	Grouping objects with a box 257	
Figure 7.28.	The user interface with the controls defined 259	
Figure 7.29.	Making the connections in **Shapes.nib** 260	
Figure 8.1	The precedence order for building the registration table 285	
Figure 8.2	Using **NXUpdateDefault**() to update a default's value in the registration table 288	
Figure 8.3	The views in a Preferences panel is controlled by a popuplist 289	
Figure 8.4	InterfaceBuilder doesn't allow connections between **.nib** files since this would violate encapsulation 291	
Figure 8.5	An object can appear as an instance in one **.nib** file and as the **File's Owner** in another **.nib** file 291	
Figure 8.6	A switchbutton is more appropriate than a textfield for options that only have two possible values 298	
Figure 8.7	The CRC card for the **PrefsController** class 304	
Figure 8.8	The CRC card for the **SwitchView** class 304	
Figure 8.9	The updated CRC card for the **MoneyConverter** class 305	
Figure 8.10	The message diagram for **Money** 308	
Figure 8.11	The updated class hierarchy graph for **Money** 309	

Figures xix

Figure 8.12	Adding header files to a project by dragging them from the Workspace	311
Figure 8.13	Setting the class of the **File's Owner**	311
Figure 8.14	Editing the entries in a popuplist	312
Figure 8.15	The Preferences panel with the switchview	313
Figure 8.16	Connecting all the objects in **Prefs.nib**	313
Figure 8.17	Enabling the **Preferences** menu option	315
Figure 8.18	Connecting the objects in **Money.nib**	316
Figure 8.19	Centering a view in its superview's coordinate system	329
Figure 8.20	Drawing a bezeled line	330
Figure 9.1	A regular coordinate system vs. a flipped coordinate system	338
Figure 9.2	The key window and the main window may or may not be the same window	343
Figure 9.3	The search order when a target is not explicitly set	345
Figure 9.4	A text object can grow beyond the boundaries of its superview	346
Figure 9.5	The components of a scrollview	347
Figure 9.6	A typical savepanel	351
Figure 9.7	A typical openpanel	357
Figure 9.8	Retrieving the selected filename(s)	360
Figure 9.9	A preliminary interface for **Words**	368
Figure 9.10	The CRC card for the **Document** class	369
Figure 9.11	The CRC card for the **TextController** class	370
Figure 9.12	The CRC card for the **SavePanel** class	370
Figure 9.13	The CRC card for the **OpenPanel** class	371
Figure 9.14	The CRC card for the **Window** class	371
Figure 9.15	The message diagram for **Words**	374
Figure 9.16	The hierarchy graph for the custom classes in **Words**	374
Figure 9.17	Adding a **Command-w** keyboard alternative to the **Close** menu option	375
Figure 9.18	Making the connections in **Words.nib**	379
Figure 9.19	Adding a scrollview to **Document.nib**	381
Figure 9.20	Connecting the objects in **Document.nib**	382
Figure 9.21	Double-clicking on a file from the Workspace sets off a complex series of events	403
Figure 9.22	Adding an icon and changing the extension for an application's documents	405
Figure 9.23	Changing the application's icon	406
Figure 9.24	Setting **Words** as the default application for **.word** documents	407
Figure 10.1	The on-line help for the keyboard in the Preferences application	412

Figures

Figure 10.2	Enabling **Developer Mode** in Edit	413
Figure 10.3	Inserting a link in a document	414
Figure 10.4	Displaying and editing a link	415
Figure 10.5	Inserting a marker in a file	416
Figure 10.6	The **New.rtf** file after it has been modified	420
Figure 10.7	The **New.rtf** file with the links and marker	421
Figure 10.8	The **Open.rtf** file with the links and marker	422
Figure 10.9	The **Save.rtf** file with the links and marker	423
Figure 10.10	Attaching help to the **New** menu option	424
Figure A.1	The NeXTSTEP login window	431
Figure A.2	The initial screen after logging in	432
Figure A.3	NeXTSTEP windows and icons	433
Figure A.4	Displaying a submenu	434
Figure A.5	Miniaturizing a window	435
Figure A.6	Display the contents of a folder and selecting a file	436
Figure A.7	Scrolling through the **README.rtf** file	437
Figure A.8	The title bar contains the filename and the path	438
Figure A.9	To close a window, click on the close button, located in the upper right hand of the title bar	439
Figure A.10	Double-click a word to select it	440
Figure A.11	Copying and pasting the text	440
Figure A.12	To get our attention, NeXTSTEP places the alert panel above the other windows	441
Figure A.13	Edit displays a savepanel to ask us where to save the file	442
Figure A.14	To recycle a folder, drag the folder to the Recycler icon	443
Figure A.15	Displaying the contents of the Recycler	443
Figure A.16	Renaming the folder from **NewFolder** to **JunkContainer**	444
Figure A.17	Recovering the **junk** folder from the Recycler	445
Figure B.1	Using the implicit Expansion Dictionary	448
Figure B.2	Adding an entry to the Expansion Dictionary	450
Figure B.3	Using an entry from the Expansion Dictionary	450
Figure B.4	Edit displays only the name of the method when the method is contracted	453
Figure B.5	Indexing an unindexed target in Librarian	455
Figure B.6	The initial screen of HeaderViewer (the Browser view)	458
Figure B.7	The Find Control Options panel of HeaderViewer	461

Figure B.8	The List view of HeaderViewer 462	
Figure B.9	Appending the current directory in Terminal by dragging from the Workspace 469	
Figure D.1	Searching an entire folder for a given string 503	
Figure D.2	Including debugging information in ProjectBuilder 505	
Figure D.3	Clicking on the **Debug** button in ProjectBuilder produces a gdb shell window 506	
Figure D.4	The Gdb panel in Edit 507	
Figure D.5	Click on **self** to display its contents 515	
Figure D.6	The value of **popUpButton**'s and **switchView**'s **window** outlets should be identical since they refer to the same window 516	
Figure D.7	Comparing the value of **switchView**'s **accessoryView** outlet against **truncateSwitch** 517	
Figure D.8	Checking the values of the **rate** array in the moneyconverter 520	

Preface

NeXTSTEP is the most complete object-oriented environment on the market today. As a user interface, it offers ease-of-use without sacrificing the flexibility of its powerful underlying operating system, UNIX (which sits on top of a Mach kernel, but we are getting ahead of ourselves here). As a development environment, NeXTSTEP offers developers unparalleled tools for creating powerful applications rapidly.

Since NeXTSTEP is designed to offer an intuitive interface, learning to use it is fairly straightforward. However, learning to program in it is a different story: NeXTSTEP is composed of many new—radical by some standards—ideas, and learning to program in this environment effectively requires you to learn many new skills (such as object-oriented programming, Objective-C, et al.) and tools (ProjectBuilder, InterfaceBuilder, et al.) before you can even finish your first NeXTSTEP application. The learning curve may seem steep at first ("I have to learn all that to get something to work?!"), but the trick is to recognize that you only need to learn a little of each skill and then combine them to get a project off the ground. That is the primary purpose of this book: to introduce these skills and tools so you can write NeXTSTEP applications to conform to the NeXTSTEP user-interface guidelines. Once you have learned these skills, you can apply them to any project whether it is in NeXTSTEP or not.

The book is written in a tutorial style and is more of a programmer's guide than a reference manual. Each chapter groups related NeXTSTEP concepts and demonstrates these concepts through a complete application. Each application is fully functional, and each chapter offers suggestions for extending the application. You are encouraged to expand the applications and experiment because the more you explore alternatives, the more you will learn. For each application, the book will present alternative designs that explore the advantages and disadvantages of each design. Once a design is chosen, you will construct the interface using InterfaceBuilder and implement the application using Objective-C (an object-oriented version of C) and the Application Kit, the standard NeXTSTEP toolkit.

While you may not be a NeXTSTEP wizard when you are finished, working through these examples should provide you with a solid foundation of how to write programs in this powerful environment and with enough knowledge to know where to look for further help.

Audience

This book is for programmers interested in writing NeXTSTEP programs at the application level; it covers how to use InterfaceBuilder (and ProjectBuilder) and the various classes in the Application Kit to produce applications. This book does not devote much time to the Mach kernel or the Digital Signal Processor (DSP). Additionally, though the book covers NeXTSTEP 3.0, it does not cover the newly bundled kits such as the 3DKit, the Phone Kit, etc.

The book is suitable as an introductory text to a course on NeXTSTEP programming and/or as a user-interface design course. The text emphasizes learning by doing. You should work through each example and compare your results with those given in the text to insure that your application is implemented correctly.

Prerequisites

This book assumes the following prerequisites:

- basic NeXTSTEP knowledge such as how to launch applications, how to dock an application, etc. For an introduction to NeXTSTEP, consult the tutorial in Appendix A or the *NeXTSTEP User's Guide*.
- some experience with the C programming language since the source code in this book is in Objective-C, a hybrid language that adds object-oriented programming (OOP) support to C. NeXTSTEP supports other languages, but this book focuses on Objective-C because it is the primary language used in NeXTSTEP development.

- some knowledge of basic UNIX terminology such as what a directory is, how to change to a different directory (using the **cd** command), etc.

Appendix E lists books that cover these topics in further detail.

Hardware and Software

This book covers NeXTSTEP on the NeXT platforms and Intel-based platforms. Unless otherwise noted, NeXTSTEP is hardware-independent, and we will generically refer to all versions of NeXTSTEP as simply NeXTSTEP.

Before proceeding, verify that you have the following hardware and software:

- Hardware
    - a computer capable of running NeXTSTEP
    - a monitor, monochrome or color
    - a hard drive with at least 300 megabytes (MB).
- Software
    - NeXTSTEP 3.0 (or later) Extended Edition—this contain the programming tools necessary to implement the examples in this book. These tools include:
        - Project Builder
        - InterfaceBuilder
        - Application Kit
        - Objective-C compiler
        - GNU debugger
        - On-line programming documentation.

A quick way to determine if you have the Extended Edition installed is to check the **/NextDeveloper/Apps** directory. If you can't find InterfaceBuilder, you probably do not have the Extended Edition installed. Contact your NeXT dealer for more information. The full Extended Edition requires about 300 MB of disk space.

The source code examples have been tested on a NeXTStation Turbo and on a Compaq 50M running NeXTSTEP/Intel. All examples in this book, with the exception of those in Appendix F, are completely hardware-independent.

Interface Tools: To Use or Not?

There has been considerable debate about whether a programmer should produce the user interface from scratch or by using a tool like InterfaceBuilder. Anti-tools programmers argue that a programmer who relies on such a tool as a crutch never truly understands how to write the code to create the interface while others argue that developing an interface from scratch is too cost and time prohibitive. There is evidence to support the latter claim because studies have shown that as much as 60 percent (conservatively) of a project's development time is taken up by the interface alone.

Both viewpoints seem to have some merit. This book has taken the hybrid approach of creating a subset of the interface programmatically at the start of each chapter and then using InterfaceBuilder to complete the interface. This approach offers two advantages:

- you gain some insight to how the interface truly works. However, we limit these examples to only small interfaces, since implementing an entire interface programmatically is extremely time-consuming and error-prone.
- you learn how to use InterfaceBuilder. The examples that you will encounter (including those distributed by other authors and those included with the NeXTSTEP Extended Edition) will have been constructed using InterfaceBuilder. Bear in mind that even though InterfaceBuilder is a powerful tool, it has limits: except for truly trivial applications, you always need to write code.

Organization

The book can be divided into main parts. Part I, composed of Chapters 1 through 5, discusses fundamental concepts including object-oriented programming, object-oriented design, and Objective-C. Even if you are already familiar with these topics, you should at least skim over these chapters before continuing.

Chapter 1 covers the major components of NeXTSTEP from a programmer's viewpoint and explains how these components work together to provide a rich programming environment.

Chapter 2 introduces the terminology of object-oriented programming and Objective-C, the primary language used in NeXTSTEP programming. A small application is introduced to highlight the ideas from object-oriented programming and Objective-C.

Chapter 3 introduces object-oriented design and tools for managing a design.

Chapter 4 shows how to write a minimal NeXTSTEP application using the Application Kit.

Chapter 5 is a tutorial on ProjectBuilder and InterfaceBuilder.

Part II, Chapters 6 through 10, forms the heart of the book. Each chapter starts by explaining the goals, proceeds through program and interface design, and concludes with suggestions for extending the application after it has been tested. The interfaces are designed to conform to the NeXTSTEP interface guidelines, and the programs are designed for code reusability.

Chapter 6 discusses event-driven programming and controls and illustrates these concepts with a universal money converter.

Chapter 7 discusses the **View** class and explains how to interface Objective-C with PostScript, a

	device-independent language used for drawing in NeXTSTEP.
Chapter 8	explains how to customize a NeXTSTEP application with the **dread** and **dwrite** commands and how to use multiple **.nib** (NeXT InterfaceBuilder) files to implement a front-end to these commands.
Chapter 9	discusses the **Text** class and demonstrates its uses in a minimal word processor. The **OpenPanel** and **SavePanel** classes are used to build the interface for loading and saving documents.
Chapter 10	discusses the on-line help system and provides a tutorial on how to use HelpBuilder to incorporate on-line help into an application.

The appendices list information that does not belong to any particular chapter such as debugging techniques and how to correct common Objective-C mistakes.

Appendix A	is a tutorial on how to perform rudimentary NeXTSTEP tasks such as logging in, launching applications, etc.
Appendix B	discusses how to use other development tools including Terminal, Digital Librarian, HeaderViewer, and **make** and their limitations.
Appendix C	points out common mistakes in Objective-C and NeXTSTEP and how to correct them.
Appendix D	explains how to trace NeXTSTEP applications and how to debug them using **gdb** (the GNU Debugger) from the **Gdb** panel in Edit.
Appendix E	lists various sources of technical information that may prove useful to aspiring programmers: these range from books to the archive sites on Internet to the various NeXT-related news forums on Usenet.

Appendix F discusses issues encountered when porting applications from NeXTSTEP to NeXTSTEP/Intel.

Conventions

The following conventions and fonts are used throughout the book.

- Times-Roman is used for text body like this paragraph.
- **Bold Times-Roman** is used for specifying folder names and file names (such as select the **Document.m** file in **/NextApps**), UNIX utilities (**emacs**, **make**, etc.), menu options (such as click on the **OK** button), class names (such as the **Window** class), and method names (such as the **initFrame:** method). Note that:
    - standard NeXTSTEP applications such as InterfaceBuilder are not in bold.
    - the standard bundled documentation does not use the bold typeface for class names and method names.
- *Italics* are for a variable value like the following: The **setTitle:** method sets the title of the button to *string*.
- ***Italics bold*** are for introducing new terms like the following: An ***object*** is a package of data bundled with its associated ***methods***.
- `Courier` is for the code listings. For example:
    ```
    for (x=0; x<10; x++)
       {
       printf("This is sample code\n");
       }
    ```
- **Courier bold** indicates input that should be typed verbatim such as (the **%** indicates the C shell prompt from the Terminal application and should be not be typed):
    ```
    % cc -g -c -o Document.o Document.m
    ```
- A menu structure is indicated with a right arrow: **Menu ⇒ Submenu1 ⇒ Submenu2**. Thus, to indicate the **Open** menu option under the **Document** menu, we would use: **Document ⇒ Open**.

- To indicate a modifier key should be typed with a regular key, we use the modifier followed by a dash and then the key itself. For example, **Command-h** means to hold down the **Command** key and then type the **h**. To indicate we need to hold down the **Command** key and the **Shift** key while typing another key (assume **a**), we will not use **Command-Shift-a**: we will use **Command-A** instead. Note that only **Command** key combinations are case-sensitive. **Control** key combinations are not: **Control-Z** is the same as **Control-z**.
- The **Return** key generically refers to the carriage return key on various systems. Some keyboards label this as **Enter** and others (most notably the European-style keyboards) use an L shaped arrow.

At many points throughout the book, we make use of tech blocks. A tech block either discusses the current topic in greater detail or addresses orthogonal issues. If you feel comfortable reading them, feel free to do so; if not, skip them on the first pass and return to them later. A tech block looks like this:

> This is a sample tech block.

A summary block shows the paragraph's key point

Additionally, we make use of summary blocks like the one on this page. These summary blocks summarize the key point of a paragraph and allow you to quickly scan a chapter.

Tools Used to Create This Book

This book was created on a NeXT workstation using FrameMaker, Diagram!, Create, and Grab

The entire book was laid out and published using FrameMaker 3.1 on a NeXT workstation. All screen shots were captured with the Grab application in **/NextApps**. Most of the illustrations were created using Stone Design's **Create** and Lighthouse's **Diagram!**. These illustration were then imported into FrameMaker as Encapsulated PostScript (EPS) files. The final manuscript was delivered in PostScript format to Prentice Hall for typesetting.

Obtaining the Source Code

The source code for this book is available through Internet and Usenet. For more information on how to obtain the code for the examples, see Appendix E; it explains how to download using **anonymous ftp** (file transfer protocol), and the **sonata** mail server at Purdue University.

The source code is available on Internet and Usenet

Author's Biography

Alex Duong Nghiem is the Founder and President of Object Lesson Inc., a company that specializes in mentoring and object-oriented solutions; the list of clients includes Fortune 500 companies and major universities in North America and Europe. He was formerly an employee at IBM and at Pencom Software, and he has been working with NeXTSTEP since the 0.9 release.

This book is his third publication to date. While attending college, he co-published two fantasy computer games with Gary Scott Smith, *Realms of Darkness* and *Tangled Tales*; both were nominated for Best Fantasy Game of their respective years.

When he's not working or writing, he is performing with the JAMZ SQUAD, a street dance team that has performed with major celebrities including Whitney Houston, Kid-n-Play, Marky Mark and the Funky Bunch, and, of course, the Dallas Cowboys Cheerleaders. His other claim to fame is an exciting (albeit brief) comedy career as a semi-finalist in a ShowTime comedy special.

Contacting the Author

Please send your comments and suggestions to either of the following e-mail addresses.

- **alex@oolesson.com** (preferred)—NeXTMail is OK at this address, but please try to limit the message to under 100K. If this address bounces, try the address in an alternate format, **oolesson!alex@uunet.uu.net**.

- 75040.3647@compuserve.com—if the UUNET address bounces, please try the Compuserve address. Do not send NeXTMail to this address.

Acknowledgments

Thanks to my editor, Greg Doench, Tara Mahon and the rest of the staff at Prentice-Hall

This book resulted from a simple conversation between myself and my editor, Greg Doench. I approached him at the Usenix 1990 conference in Anaheim and, thinking he was one of the salesmen, asked whether Prentice Hall carried any NeXTSTEP books. He replied by asking if I knew anyone who would be interested in writing one. Many (many!) months later (and after an excessive number of missed deadlines) this book is finally done. Thank you, Greg, for believing in this book enough to publish it. By the way, has your son finished my game Tangled Tales yet? ☻ Kudos to Tara Mahon for her help and thanks to all the folks at Prentice Hall for putting this book together.

Thanks to my brother, Hoang, and my family

Writing a book is never a one-person affair: many people contributed through various means, and I would like to thank them for believing in me through this long process. I would like to first thank my brother Hoang ("Richard") for offering support when I needed it and for taking care of me (and our apartment) while I wrote this book (you're one in a million, Hoang) and my family for not disowning me for visiting them less than once a year. ☻

Thanks to Pencom Software, especially Ed Taylor and Chris Chauvin

Although this book is not affiliated with Pencom, the powers-that-be were kind enough to allow me to use the facilities until I could purchase my personal NeXTstation. Special thanks to Ed Taylor, founder of Pencom Software, for giving me the freedom to pursue this book; Ricardo Parada for proofreading the work and offering many suggestions for the examples; Tim Heap for his encouragement and help in preparing the index; Bill Dudney for offering many comments on the source code and proofreading (as well as taking that fateful assignment); Chris Chauvin for being a wonderful (and very understanding) technical lead and an awesome programmer dude; the co-Xist team (Pam O'Neal, Matthew Waters, Jan Falcona, Dwight Flinkerbusch, and Mile's O'Neal) for making it a joy to work so that I could still muster enough energy to write after-hours; Tom McLellan for allowing me to back down from all those out-of-town trips so that I could concentrate on this book; Kari Karhi for softening the culture shock when I first arrived at Pencom; Cindy Berrier for taking care of the loan so that I could purchase my own Turbo NeXTStation; the system administrators, Lisa Gerlich and David Bryant, for helping me set up my home machine; Christine Kungl, Sarah Brandmire, Mike Sanford, Cindy Castillo, and all the other folks at Pencom for keeping the place silly and happy.

People I can't forget include: Sam Griffith for teaching me to believe in myself and for being a wonderful friend and mentor—many of the ideas and illustrations in this book are a direct result of our conversations; Bruce Webster of Pages Inc. (and author of *The NeXT Book*) for his many valuable comments and insights; Professor Meinhard "Hardy" Mayer of the University of California at Irvine for many pages of comments (and for a refresher in calculus); Joe Grace of Tetrasoft and his students for their feedback from using the book in their NeXTSTEP class; Ali Ozer of NeXT Inc. for all the corrections; Glenn Reid of RightBrain Software for his comments; Lisa Farwell for producing many of the fine illustrations throughout the text; Professor Claude Anderson at the Rose Hulman Institute of Technology for suffering through an early draft of this book; Gary Scott Smith for introducing me to computers back in the Apple II days and for publishing our computer games together; Scott Shattuck of DBSA for setting up the UUNET account so I can keep in touch with my readers; Bill Edney of FirstSoft for loaning me extra equipment during a critical phase of the book; Michael McFall for his awesome reading speed; Carl Sturmer of Sturmer Hauss Corporation for giving me a chance; Wilson Gee, Matt Accapadi, Umesh Khatwani, and Daniel Mak for their invaluable friendship and for all the good times (and honest criticisms, although they are not always easy to deal with).

Added thanks to Gino Johnson for teaching me cardio-funk and street dancing (wonderful for relieving stress!); David "Special K" Kellough for being a friend and for continuing my street dance career ("You go, girl"); the JAMZ SQUAD (Hello to Darrell, Julianna, Melinda, Clara, Garrett, Larissa, Rana, Robin, Diane,

Thanks to Sam Griffith, Bruce Webster, Professor Mayer, Joe Grace, Ali Ozer, Glenn Reid, Lisa Farwell, Professor Anderson, Gary Scott Smith, Scott Shattuck, Bill Edney, Wilson Gee, Matt Accapadi, Umesh Khatwani, and Daniel Mak

Thanks to Gino, David Kellough, the JAMZ Squad, Mariselle Marshall, Ricardo Moncada, Shari Black, and the Dallas Cowboys Cheerleaders

Stacey, and Amber) for our rehearsals and performances, especially at the Texas Stadium and Austin Convention Center—I will treasure these memories for years to come; Mariselle Marshall (née Mary Isabella Drattlo) for never allowing me to do less than my best in class and for the stimulating discussions (especially the sisterly advice); Ricardo Moncada ("The other left foot!") and his assistant, Shari Black, for introducing me to—and continually teaching—so many dance styles and for showing me all the joy that dancing brings; and the Dallas Cowboys Cheerleaders for allowing me to teach them and experience what it feels like to perform with them in front of 60,000 people.

Thanks to Steve Jobs and all the people at NeXT

Finally, thanks to Steve Jobs and all the folks at NeXT for giving us NeXTSTEP, a wonderful environment without which this book would not have been possible.

Alex Duong Nghiem
April 15, 1993

Chapter 1
NeXTSTEP Components

For our purposes, NeXTSTEP is composed of the following layers:

- Mach and UNIX
- the Window Server
- the Application Kit and Objective-C
- the Workspace Manager
- ProjectBuilder and InterfaceBuilder.

Figure 1.1 shows how each of these layers form the NeXTSTEP environment. Each of these layers is further explored in the following section.

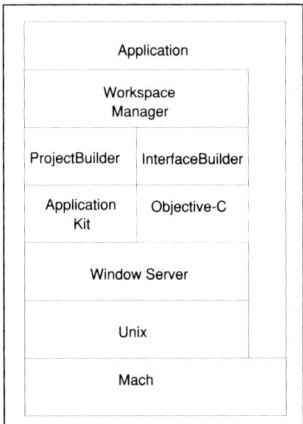

Figure 1.1 The layers of NeXTSTEP

In addition to the Application Kit, NeXTSTEP 3.0 includes several other kits:

- the 3DKit—classes that interact with the rendering language, RenderMan.
- the Database Kit (DBKit)—classes that allow database access and retrieval.
- the Phone Kit—classes that take advantage of the **ISDN** (Integrated Services Digital Network) and **POTS** (Perfectly Ordinary Telephone Services) facilities.
- the Indexing Kit (IXKit)—classes that provide indexing functionality.

We will concern ourselves only with the Application Kit, however.

> Why is the operating system considered part of NeXTSTEP? Unlike most environments, NeXTSTEP is closely tied to its operating system (Mach). For example, the interprocess communication in NeXTSTEP is implemented on top of Mach messaging. One example of this interprocess communication is when we click on a document to launch an application: the Workspace Manager sends a message to the application requesting it to launch. However, this is totally transparent to the application since NeXTSTEP handles most of these details.

1.1 Mach and UNIX

NeXTSTEP is built on Mach

NeXTSTEP is built on top of Mach, a multi-tasking operating system that was pioneered at Carnegie-Mellon University. The multi-tasking feature of Mach allows us to switch between multiple applications and sessions. Mach has many exotic features including object-based messaging (not to be confused with the messaging facilities of the Objective-C runtime system) and sophisticated virtual memory management.

To maintain compatibility with other systems, the creators of NeXTSTEP added support for UNIX, a multi-tasking operating system that was invented at AT&T. Many of the concepts in NeXTSTEP, such as folders, are actually derivatives of UNIX concepts (directories). There are many variants of UNIX including SystemV and BSD (Berkeley Standard Distribution); NeXTSTEP uses BSD 4.3.

NeXTSTEP supports BSD 4.3

Most of the discussions will not be at the operating system level (Mach or UNIX) since our main goal is to write NeXTSTEP applications at the Application Kit level. NeXTSTEP does an admirable job of hiding the operating system level details, but we sometimes have to deal with UNIX to point out some of the whys and wherefores of NeXTSTEP.

1.2 The Window Server

NeXTSTEP is based on a *client-server model*, i.e., there is a server to handle requests made by a client. The client is our application, and the server is the Window Server, a process that is always executing "behind the scenes" (in UNIX jargon, "in the background").

NeXTSTEP uses a client-server model

> Note that NeXTSTEP uses the term *server* and *client* in an unconventional manner. Typically, a server is a machine that provides services to other machines, its clients. In NeXTSTEP, both the server and client are programs: the server is the Window Server, which provides services to our application, the client.

The following are the Window Server's main responsibilities:

- determining which application owns a given window since the user's actions (keypresses and mouse actions) are always associated with a window. The Window Server must route the actions to the appropriate application so it can process the action.
- performing all drawing to the monitor or other medium such as the printer, fax, etc.

NeXTSTEP uses Display PostScript to perform drawing

All the applications we write communicate with the Window Server to perform their tasks and to display themselves on the screen.

The Window Server includes an interpreter for Display PostScript, a powerful two-dimensional imaging language. Unlike other environments, NeXTSTEP uses PostScript for displaying as well as printing. This ***unified imaging model*** results in a ***what-you-see-is-what-you-get*** (abbreviated as **WYSIWYG** and pronounced *wizzywig*) environment. The only difference is the resolution since the print medium tends to have a much higher resolution than the monitor. PostScript is resolution independent and displays at whatever resolution the medium is capable of supporting.

1.3 The Application Kit

The Application Kit insulates us from low-level details

Writing applications in a graphical environment like NeXTSTEP can be a daunting task. NeXTSTEP facilitates this by providing the Application Kit. The Application Kit provides objects for constructing interfaces (such as windows, buttons, etc) and a framework that insulates us from handling events (such as mouse-clicks and keypresses) at the hardware level. Consequently, building interfaces and dealing with events are relatively painless in NeXTSTEP.

1.4 Objective-C

The entire Application Kit is implemented in *Objective-C*, a powerful language that adds object-oriented programming syntax to ANSI-C. Objective-C is fairly easy to learn since it adds little new syntax to C. We will discuss this language in greater detail in Chapter 2.

Objective-C is fairly easy to learn

> Objective-C was invented by StepStone Incorporated. Rather than license the compiler from StepStone, NeXT Inc. took the C compiler that was developed by the Free Software Foundation (FSF) and added support for Objective-C. There are differences between the implementation of Objective-C in NeXTSTEP and Objective-C on other platforms. However, these differences are subtle and will not be discussed in any great detail.

1.5 The Workspace Manager

The *Workspace Manager* (hereafter referred to as the Workspace for brevity) allows us to conveniently manage our files and folders as well as launch applications. Like the Window Server, the Workspace is started automatically as soon as we log in. The Workspace can communicate with other applications, which allows us to launch an application by simply double-clicking on a document created by the application. We will explore how to implement this functionality in Chapter 9. For more information on how to use Workspace, consult the NeXTSTEP tutorial in Appendix A.

The Workspace allows us to easily manage our files

1.6 ProjectBuilder

ProjectBuilder helps us to coordinate development tasks (such as compiling, linking, and debugging) by managing the many files involved in a NeXTSTEP application:

- the project file

ProjectBuilder is used mainly for project management

- interface file(s)
- class files
- help files.

We will be using this tool extensively starting with Chapter 5.

1.7 InterfaceBuilder

InterfaceBuilder is used to graphically create and test user interfaces

InterfaceBuilder allows us to graphically design and test interfaces as well as create and inspect objects. Typically, we use InterfaceBuilder to build the interface and we use Objective-C with the Application Kit to implement the application. To construct an interface with InterfaceBuilder, we simply drag the desired object from a predefined palette and place it in our application. For example, to place a button in our window, we simply drag the button from a palette and place it in the window. An Inspector panel allows us to inspect and modify many of the attributes of the objects in the interface. For example, to modify the size of the button, we can use the Button Inspector (the Inspector panel updates to the currently selected object) or directly manipulate the button.

InterfaceBuilder has a Test Mode for testing an interface without a lengthy compilation cycle. This feature allows us to quickly refine the interface.

1.8 Summary

These tools work together seamlessly to provide us with a powerful programming environment. To take advantage of these features, we must first learn object-oriented programming and Objective-C. The two tools we will be using the most, the Application Kit and InterfaceBuilder, are built using these concepts.

Chapter 2
OOP and Objective-C

Object-oriented programming (OOP) is a concept that has been around since the 1960s but has not been widely used until the recent advent of window-based environments like NeXTSTEP. Object-oriented programming is regarded by many as a more productive way to write software because it is easier to write reusable and maintainable code. In this chapter, we first introduce some object-oriented programming concepts without concern for the syntax of a language. Once we have introduced the concepts and terminology, we proceed to Objective-C, a powerful language that adds object-oriented programming extensions to C.

Object-oriented programming allows us to produce more reusable code

Object-oriented programming is a complex topic and involves a lot of new terminology. Unfortunately, this terminology is not consistent among different texts: the topic may be named one thing in theory (object-oriented programming) and another in practice (in our case, Objective-C). If the two terms diverge, we choose the Objective-C terminology since our ultimate goal is to program in Objective-C. Fortunately, these incidents are rare.

Object-oriented programming includes some inconsistent terminology

Additionally, there are some concepts of object-oriented programming that are not supported by Objective-C like multiple inheritance and operator overloading. Again, since our goal is to learn Objective-C, we will not deal with any object-oriented programming concepts not present in the language.

Objective-C does not implement some ideas of OOP such as operator overloading

Once we have covered object-oriented programming and Objective-C, we proceed to implement a simple application that demonstrates the key concepts in this chapter.

2.1 Goals

In this chapter, we will:

- discuss basic object-oriented programming terminology.
- explain basic Objective-C syntax.
- explain how to implement classes in Objective-C.

- illustrate how to compile and link an application.

2.2 Object-Oriented Programming

In procedural programming, the data is kept separate from the functions

The most common way to produce software is *procedural programming*. A program is viewed as a collection of procedures and functions that can manipulate a collection of data that is kept separate from the functions (from this point, on, we will use the term *function* to be synonymous with *procedure*). Typically, the data is global, and functions can share the data. Therefore, even a simple change made to the data can have undesirable side effects on any function that accesses it. Figure 2.1 illustrates the procedural programming model.

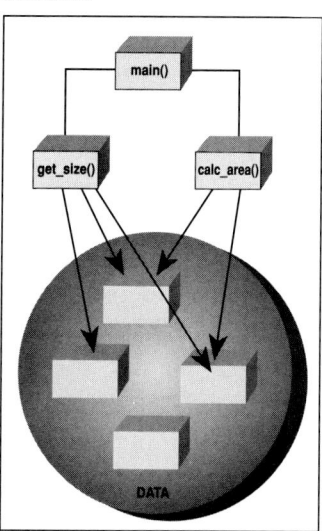

Figure 2.1 In procedural programming, the functions are kept separate from the data they operate on

In OOP, the data is grouped with the functions that manipulate the data

In object-oriented programming, the view is quite different. The data are grouped with the functions which can exclusively manipulate the data. The data are called *instance variables*, and the functions that manipulate the instance variables are called the *methods*. Each collection of data and its associated methods produce an *object*, a term for a generic abstract data type and its associated methods. Figure 2.2 shows the object-oriented programming model.

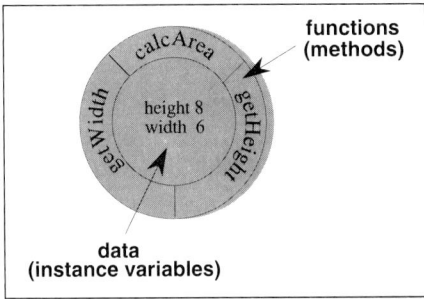

Figure 2.2 An object is a collection of data (instance variables) along with the functions (methods) that can access the data

2.2.1 Encapsulation

Since an object's instance variables are private to the object, the only way for one object to access *another* object's instance variables is through the methods bundled with the object (an object can refer to its *own* instance variables by simply referring to them by name). Figure 2.3 illustrates one object accessing another's **height** instance variable.

An object's instance variables can only be accessed through its methods

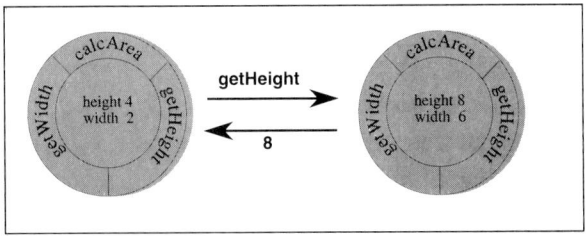

Figure 2.3 Accessing an instance variable through one of the methods

Another key characteristic of object-oriented programming is that the implementation details of the methods are private to each object. Packaging the data with the methods and hiding the implementation details of the methods produce a form of ***encapsulation***.

Encapsulation hides the implementation details

For example, assume there is a list object that can contain other objects. An application that makes use of the list simply inserts

A list object demonstrates encapsulation

the object into the list, and the list then contains the object. The application does not care how the list is implemented, be it with arrays, pointers, hash tables, etc. All the application knows is that it can insert objects into the list. In short, the implementation details are encapsulated in the list and completely hidden from the application that uses the list.

2.2.2 Classes

A class is a template of code that is meant to be reused

To promote code reusability, object-oriented programming introduces the concept of a *class*, a template of code meant to be reused and to create objects. For example, assume we are implementing an application which has to calculate the area of many rectangles. Each rectangle declares a **height** and **width** (both instance variables are of type **float**), and each rectangle needs a method to calculate the area (call this the **calcArea** method). It would be grossly inefficient if we had to declare **height** and **width** as well as a **calcArea** method for each rectangle. We should be able to define the instance variables and method once in a template and then reuse the template to create many rectangles. In short, we can create a **Rectangle** class that can then be used to create rectangles.

> The capitalization of certain words (such as **Rectangle** class and rectangle object) may seem arbitrary at this point. However, Objective-C actually encourages a fairly straightforward capitalization convention, which we will cover shortly.

2.2.3 Instances

Instantiating a class is creating an instance from the class

Once we have created the **Rectangle** template (class), we can create one or more *instances* (instance is synonymous with object) of the class, which are the individual rectangles. Creating an instance of a class is referred to as *instantiating* the class.

Assign variable names to the instances

To differentiate between the instances, we can name them, just as we name variables. For example, if we have two rectangle instances, we can name the first **rectangle1** and the second

rectangle2. Because the **Rectangle** class defines two instance variables (**height** and **width**) with a **calcArea** method, and **rectangle1** and **rectangle2** are instances of the **Rectangle** class, we can conclude the following things about **rectangle1** and **rectangle2**:

- each has a **height** and **width**. Of course, the *values* of **height** and **width** can be different between the two instances. For example, the values for **rectangle1**'s **height** and **width** could be **8** and **6**, respectively, and the values for **rectangle2**'s **height** and **width** could be **4** and **2**, respectively.
- each has a **calcArea** method.

Figure 2.4 shows the relationships between a class and its instances.

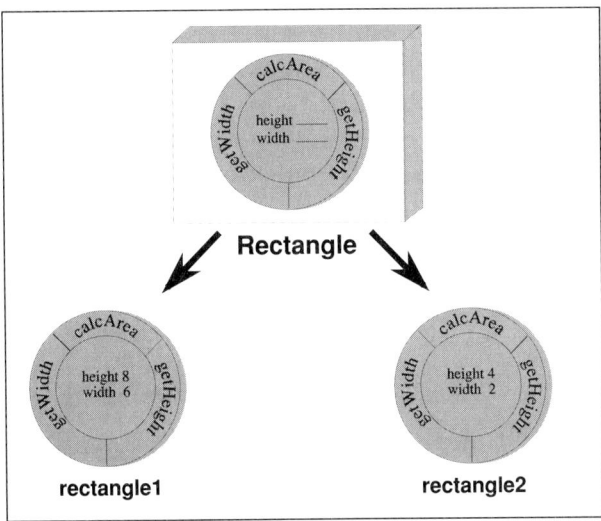

Figure 2.4 Once a class is defined, it can be used to create instances

Since it is cumbersome to constantly refer to an instance of a class as such, it is quite common to shorten this term and use the class name itself. For example, most object-oriented literature would refer to an instance of the **Rectangle** class as a rectangle. When we use the term to refer to a class, we capitalize it (**Rectangle** or we explicitly say the **Rectangle** class), and when we use the term to refer to an instance, we do not capitalize it (a

"An instance of a Rectangle class" is often shortened to "a rectangle"

rectangle). The following sentences are equivalent (recall that object is synonymous with instance):

- This object's width is 5.
- This instance's width is 5.
- This rectangle's width is 5.

An object "knows" how to perform methods

The instance variables are defined in each instance, but the methods are defined only once (for more information, see "Class Methods and Instance Methods" on page 35). Since each instance of the class has access to these methods, it is quite acceptable to say the instance has the methods, or the instance "knows" how to perform a particular method. For example, each rectangle instance knows how to calculate its area. That is, we consider each instance to have a rudimentary intelligence. In procedural programming, we would say, "Call this function to calculate the area of the circle." In object-oriented programming, we tend to say, "Tell the circle to calculate its area." In object-oriented programming, it becomes quite natural to view a system as a collection of classes and instances that knows how to perform tasks instead of a collection of functions that processes data: this phenomenon is a form of *abstraction*.

> Classes promote code reusability for the programmer and provide consistency for the user since applications with objects constructed from the same class have a more consistent behavior. For example, a button in the Mail application looks and behaves like a button found in the Webster application because the two buttons were instantiated from the same **Button** class.
>
> The recent popularity of graphical user interfaces (***GUI***) is the primary reason object-oriented programming has received so much publicity. One of the greatest benefits of GUI's over the command-line interface (i.e., we issue commands by typing them rather than by manipulating icons with a mouse) is the consistency of the interface between applications. Classes allow us to easily maintain this consistency.
>
> In the NeXTSTEP environment, these user interface classes are collected in a kit, the Application Kit. The Application Kit will be discussed in Chapter 4 in greater detail.

2.2.4 Subclasses

A key theme in programming is to reuse as much code as possible. In procedural programming, this idea is usually enforced by reusing functions or libraries. With object-oriented programming, we reuse code by finding existing classes that implement the functionality we need. If we need to modify or extend the behavior of a class, we simply *subclass*. Subclassing is defining another class in terms of an existing class. The existing class is called the *superclass*, and the newly defined class is the *subclass* of its superclass.

Subclassing is defining a new class in terms of an existing class

The subclass can access the methods and instance variables of its superclass through *inheritance*; the common terminology is to say that the subclass *inherits* from the superclass. For example, assume we need an object that behaves like a rectangle but we also need this object to have **color**. In this case, we would sub-

A subclass inherits instance variables and methods from its superclass

Subclasses

class **Rectangle** to create **ColoredRectangle**. In **ColoredRectangle**, we can add a **color** instance variable to store the **color**. Likewise, we can add a **getColor** method to access the **color**. Figure 2.5 shows the relationship between the **Rectangle** class and its hypothetical subclass, **ColoredRectangle**.

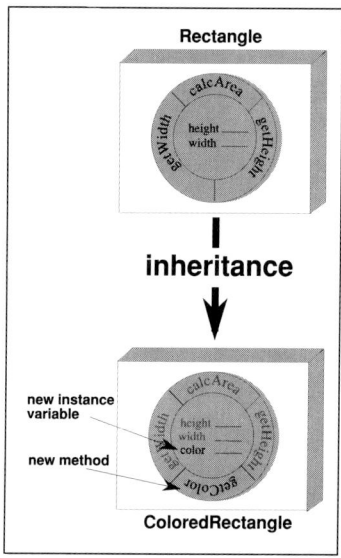

Figure 2.5 A subclass inherits the methods and instance variables defined in the superclass

Inheritance increases productivity and reduces errors

Inheritance reduces the code we need to write because the subclass already has access to the instance variables and methods that were written for the superclass. This increases productivity and reduces errors because we can reuse code that has (hopefully) been tested.

> An object can be composed of several other objects. For example, a standard openpanel is composed of, among other things, three buttons, a textfield, and a browser. This is illustrated in the following diagram.
>
>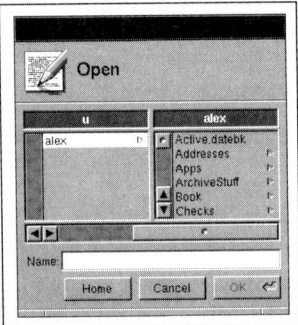
>
> This is an example of code reuse without inheritance since the openpanel is not derived from the same superclass as the other classes. An object composed of other objects is a ***composite object***.

To illustrate an example of subclassing and inheritance, assume we are writing an application to calculate the area of two types of shapes: rectangles and squares. Two suitable classes would be the **Rectangle** class and the **Square** class. However, a square is simply a rectangle with an equal **height** and **width**. Thus, we can make the **Square** class a subclass of the **Rectangle** class; the **Square** class will then be able to access to the methods and instance variables that are defined in the **Rectangle** class.

> Objective-C also allows a class to be extended through a ***category***. A category can add methods but not instance variables to a class. We will not be covering categories in our examples.

A subclass cannot choose what it inherits from its superclasses

A subclass cannot choose which methods and instance variables it wants to inherit from its superclass. It inherits all of the methods and instance variables. A subclass can do the following:

- modify inherited methods
- add new methods
- add instance variables.

A subclass can override methods inherited from the superclass

The subclass cannot redefine the type of the superclass' instance variables. That is, if a superclass defines an **x** variable as a **float**, the subclass cannot redefine the same variable to be an **int**. The subclass can modify the implementation of an identically named method it inherits from its superclass; this is known as *overriding a method*. A subclass overrides a method to:

- extend the functionality of the method. For example, the **Square** class inherits the **calcArea** method from the **Rectangle** class. However, we may decide at some point that in addition to printing the **area**, each square should print its **height** and **width**. The easiest way to accomplish this is for the **Square** class to override the **calcArea** method and:
    - inherit the code to calculate the area from the **Rectangle** class.
    - add code to print the **height** and **width** of each square.
- completely change the functionality of the method since the implementation is not appropriate for this class. For example, if we add a **Circle** class to the application, it would inherit the **calcArea** method from the **Rectangle** class. However, the **Circle** class would have to override the **calcArea** method because the

Rectangle class assume the area is simply **height** times **width**. For a circle, the area is calculated as the **radius** squared times π.

> Placing the **Rectangle** class as the root class introduces some problems since the class defines two instance variables, **height** and **width**, that do not apply to other shapes, such as triangles and circles. Our current design is not very elegant because we cannot easily modify it to accommodate other shapes. This flaw was intentionally included to show that designing classes is an iterative process much like the other stages of software development. We will address this limitation in an improved design at the end of the section.

Table 2.1 shows what a subclass can do with the inherited characteristics. Note that a subclass cannot remove method definitions or instance variables.

	Operation allowed	Description
Instance variables	add	add new instance variables
Methods	override	extend or replace the inherited method
	add	add new methods

Table 2.1   What a subclass can do with its inherited characteristics

2.2.5 Messages

To request an object (an instance or a class) to perform a method, *send a message* to the object. A message is composed of two parts: an object and the method the object should perform. The receiving object is referred to as the *receiver* and the method is

Send a message to the object to request it to perform a method

the *selector*. For example, to request **rectangle1** to perform its **calcArea** method, send a **calcArea** message to it. Figure 2.6 shows the syntax of a message expression.

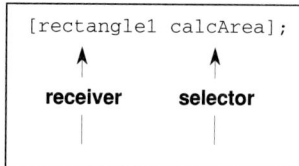

Figure 2.6 A message expression has two parts

2.2.6 Polymorphism

Polymorphism allows different classes to have identically named methods

Another key feature of object-oriented programming is *polymorphism*, which allows identically named methods to exist in different classes. Returning to the earlier example, one of the methods we need is one that calculates the area of a shape. Without polymorphism, we would have to name one method **square_calcArea** (for the **Square** class) and the other **rect_calcArea** (for the **Rectangle** class) just to differentiate between the two. This can easily become unmanageable if we add a third class, say a **Circle** class, and we wanted the instances to be able to calculate their areas. We would have to create a method called **circle_calcArea** to differentiate it from the other two methods.

With polymorphism, we tell an object what to do, not how to do it

With polymorphism, we can simply define the methods as **calcArea** and change the way the area is actually calculated. Instead of telling the object how it should do something, we simply tell it what to do. If we want a shape to calculate its area, we simply send a **calcArea** message to the shape, and it will calculate its area in the appropriate manner. For example, a circle would calculate its area by squaring its radius times π whereas a rectangle would calculate its area as its height times its width. Polymorphism reinforces the idea of encapsulation, which is to hide the implementation details. Figure 2.7 shows the benefits of polymorphism.

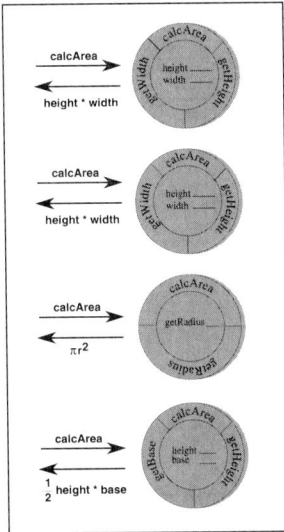

Figure 2.7 Polymorphism allows identically named methods in more than one class

Let us recap our original problem, which is to design an application to calculate the area of rectangles and squares. We specified two classes: **Rectangle** and its subclass, **Square**. The **Rectangle** class defines two instance variables (**height** and **width**) and one method (**calcArea**) that are inherited by the **Square** class. This design is too restrictive because the root class, **Rectangle**, defines two variables, **height** and **width**, that do not apply to other shapes such as circles and triangles. Therefore, it would be difficult to extend the design to add other shapes.

The only characteristic which these shapes (rectangles, squares, circles, and triangles) share is not their dimensions but rather the need to calculate their area. A key in object-oriented programming is to recognize common functionality and then abstract it in a class. Thus, we can define the area calculation once in a new superclass and let all the shape classes inherit the functionality. For now, let us call this class **AbstractShape**. We never actually instantiate the **AbstractShape** class: it simply groups methods and instances variables as a class for other classes to inherit from (our abstract superclass, **AbstractShape**, only defines a method,

Adding the AbstractShape class makes the design more flexible

An abstract superclass groups methods and instance variables for its subclasses to inherit from

calcArea, and no instance variables). Such a class is called an *abstract superclass*. We never instantiate an abstract superclass directly: rather, we create subclasses from the abstract superclass and then instantiate these classes instead. For example, from the abstract superclass (**AbstractShape**), we created four subclasses (**Rectangle**, **Square**, **Circle**, and **Triangle**), and we then instantiated these subclasses.

> For a more thorough example and discussion of an abstract superclass, see the **ShapeView** example in Chapter 7.

We leave the dimensions (**height** and **width**) defined in the **Rectangle** class for its subclass, **Square**, to inherit. For the **Circle** class, we can define **radius**, and for the **Triangle** class, we can define **base** and **height**. Each class would need to implement a **calcArea** method, but how this method is implemented depends on the class since each shape has its own way of calculating its **area**.

Leaving the calcArea method defined in the AbstractShape class improves the design

Adding the **AbstractShape** class improves the design because:

- we can look at the **AbstractShape** class alone and know what it and its subclasses are trying to do, namely calculate the **area**. Of course, each subclass of **AbstractShape** (**Rectangle** and **Square** as well as **Circle** and **Triangle**) has to override the **calcArea** method to calculate the **area**.
- each subclass knows what methods it must override to work correctly in the framework defined by the superclass.

The classes in an application form a hierarchy tree

The classes in an application form a hierarchy with the more generalized classes near the root of the tree, and the more specific classes as the leaves of the tree. The class at the root of the hierarchy tree is referred as the *root class*. In this example, **AbstractShape** is the root class, although as we will shortly see, Objective-C has a special class which will be used at the root class for the entire class hierarchy. Figure 2.8 illustrates these concepts.

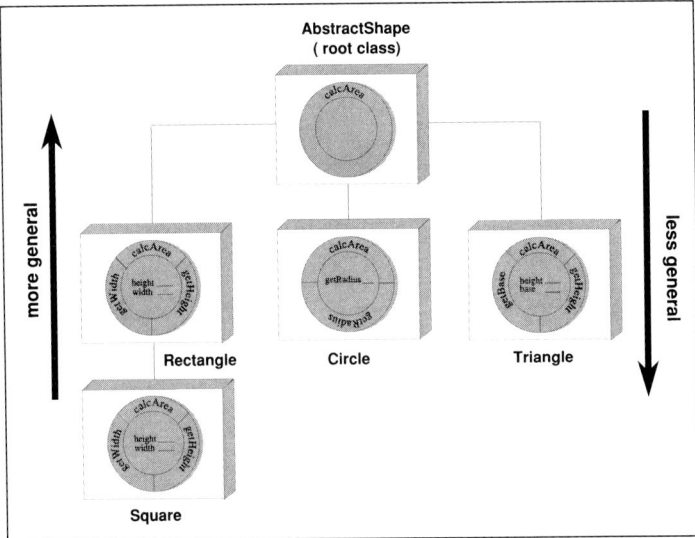

Figure 2.8 The higher classes are more generalized than the lower classes

2.3 Objective-C

Object-oriented programming is a technique that can be applied in any conventional language such as C or Pascal. However, the lack of polymorphism (and dynamic binding, which will be explained shortly) makes it more difficult to program in this manner than would be the case with an object-oriented language. Even though NeXTSTEP supports several object-oriented languages (including C++, Smalltalk, and Objective-C), we will concentrate on Objective-C for two reasons:

- the programming interfaces to the Application Kit and the Common classes (these two collections of classes collectively form all of the classes in NeXTSTEP) and almost all the source code we will encounter—in this book and elsewhere—are in Objective-C.
- InterfaceBuilder, the primary tool for building NeXTSTEP applications, uses the dynamic binding features of Objective-C.

Object-oriented programming is a technique rather than a language

Objective-C is fairly easy to learn because it add little new syntax to C

Objective-C supports the entire C language and adds support for object-oriented programming. Objective-C does not introduce a totally new syntax but adds only a few keywords to the C language. Thus, a C programmer can easily learn Objective-C. Because Objective-C merely adds a few new features to an otherwise procedural language (C), it is classified as a *hybrid language* instead of a *pure object-oriented language* such as Smalltalk. In Smalltalk, even an integer is an object!

> Objective-C uses some of the concepts pioneered by Smalltalk:
> - dynamic binding
> - the inclusion of the colon in the method names
> - the syntax of a message expression, i.e., *receiver method*. In Smalltalk, the [ ] indicates a block and is not necessarily related to the message expression.

Among other things, Objective-C offers the following features:

- complete compatibility with ANSI-C including function prototyping
- support for abstract data types
- static typing and dynamic binding
- single inheritance
- categories
- distributed objects
- protocols.

> We will not be discussing the last three topics since they are fairly advanced nor will we discuss what constitutes ANSI-C. For a more complete reference on Objective-C, consult **/NextLibrary/Documentation/NextDev/Concepts/ObjectiveC.rtfd**.

2.3.1 Support for Abstract Data Types

Objective-C adds one new type, **id**. The default return type for an Objective-C method is **id** instead of **int**, as is the case for a function in C. An **id** can be used to identify any object regardless of its class.

To declare a variable of type **id**, use:

```
id theRect;
```

> Declaring **theRect** as type **id** means the object will not be bound to its class until the object is actually instantiated (during runtime). Therefore, the compiler cannot perform type checking during compilation. Objective-C does allow an object to be declared as a pointer to a class (for example, **Rectangle *theRect;**) to enforce stronger type checking: this form of typing is known as *static typing*.

To declare a method, use:

```
-display;
```

As mentioned earlier, the default return type for a method is **id**. Therefore, the **display** method will return an **id**. The dash (-) before the method name indicates that this is an instance method. This will be explained shortly.

Another typical method declaration is:

```
-(float)getHeight;
```

Since the default return type is an **id**, a method must use typecast to force the method to return another type. In this case, the **getHeight** method returns a **float**.

Objective-C defines a new type, id, for object identifier

The default return type for a method is id

2.3.2 Messages

To request **theRect** to perform its **calcArea** method, send it a message as follows:

```
[theRect calcArea];
```

In this message, the receiver is **theRect** (an instance of the **Rectangle** class) and the selector is **calcArea**. The method name in the message expression is also referred to as the *selector*.

A message expression ultimately resolves to a single value

A message expression ultimately resolves to a single value and can therefore be used like any C expression. In the following example, an Objective-C message returns a value (presumably a **float**), which is then passed as an argument to the standard **printf()** C function:

```
printf("The area of the rectangle is %f",
    [theRect calcArea]);
```

Messages are often embedded in other messages, as follows:

```
id theDocument;
id theWindow;
   .
   .
[[theDocument window] setTitle];
```

This sequence works because:

- the return type for the **window** method is an **id.**
- messages are evaluated from the innermost level outward just as in C functions. In this case, the object returned by **window** method is sent the **setTitle** method. In English, the statement reads, "Get the window of **theDocument** using **window** and then set the window's **title** with **setTitle**."

A message expression can also include parameters, such as:

```
[theCircle setRadius];
[theCircle setRadius:30];
```

```
[theCircle doWithThis:50 andThat:100];
```

Table 2.2 shows the components of a message expression.

Message Expression	Selector	Parameters
[theCircle setRadius]	setRadius	NONE
[theCircle setRadius:30]	setRadius:	30
[theCircle doWithThis:50 andThat:100]	doWithThis:andThat:	50 100

Table 2.2 The components of a message expression

Notice that the first selector is **setRadius** and the second selector is **setRadius:** (notice the colon). These two methods are not equivalent because the first does not expect a parameter and the second does. The colons are actually part of the *method names* which Objective-C resolves to addresses during execution.

The colons are an integral part of the method names

2.3.3 Naming Conventions

So far, it may appear that the naming conventions have been haphazard, but the naming conventions in Objective-C and NeXTSTEP are actually quite straightforward:

- for a class name, the first letter of every word should be capitalized. Thus, the **Window** class is **Window** and the buttoncell class is **ButtonCell**. Some classes start with **NX**, and this is prepended to the class name as in **NXImageRep**.
- for an instance variable, the first letter of every word except the first is capitalized. Some examples are **rectangle**, **theRect**, and **myCustomRect**.
- for a method, the convention is the same as for an instance variable. However, a method name can consist of several phrases, each phrase ending with a colon. These follow the same convention as for instance variables. Some examples are:
  - **display**
  - **appDidInit:**
  - **getSubstring: start: length:**

• **readRichText: atPosition:**.

We will follow this convention because the entire Application Kit, InterfaceBuilder, and all the Objective-C code we are likely to encounter will follow this practice.

> There is one exception that is so common it needs to be addressed: the application object of each application. This object is always named **NXApp** to indicate it is a global variable, meaning it can be accessed by any object in the application. The **NXApp** variable is not related to the **NX** classes (**NXBrowser, NXImage, NXCursor**, etc.). **NXApp** is an instance of the application class, whereas the **NX** classes are classes that were introduced with NeXTSTEP 2.0 and 3.0. The designers of the Application Kit used the **NX** prefix to avoid possible name conflict with the classes that have been distributed by other NeXTSTEP programmers since the introduction of the original NeXTSTEP distribution.

2.3.4 Objective-C Comments

Objective-C can use either // at the beginning of a line or the traditional C style /* */ for comments as shown in the following code fragment:

The two comment styles in Objective-C

```
/*
  This comment style can span
  more than one line
*/

// This comment cannot span more than one line
// but it is easier to type
```

2.4 A Sample Objective-C Application

We have now covered enough Objective-C to implement a sample application, **Sample**. **Sample** basically creates one object and then inserts it into a list, a general container that can hold other objects, regardless of their class. The **List** class already exists in NeXTSTEP and is used extensively.

NeXTSTEP provides three different editors for editing source code: Edit, **emacs** and **vi**. Edit is an editor that supports the NeXTSTEP user interface, whereas the other two editors use fairly cryptic commands. For more information on how to use Edit, consult **/NextLibrary/Documentation/NextDev/DevTools/04_Edit** and Appendix B. For more information on **vi** and **emacs**, use the UNIX **man** (for manual page) command:

```
% man vi
% man emacs
```

For a list of books that deal with the **vi** and **emacs** editors, consult Appendix E. Using any of the available editors (Edit, **vi**, or **emacs**), type in the following file:

Listing for Sample.m

```
// import the header files for all the classes
// which we will be using: appkit.h contains
// the header files for all the classes

#import <appkit/appkit.h>

// minimal Obj-C program to insert some objects
// into a list

main()
{
  // declare the objects
  id theList, aSampleObject;

  // instantiate the List class using alloc
  // and initialize the list using init
  theList = [[List alloc] init];
```

We will now implement a small Objective-C application

NeXTSTEP provides three editors: vi, emacs, and Edit

```
    // create an object
    aSampleObject = [[Object alloc] init];

    // insert the objects into the list;
    [theList addObject:aSampleObject];

    // print how many objects are in the list
    printf("There are %d object(s) in the list\n",
      [theList count]);

    // demonstrate polymorphism by sending the
    // name method to theList and aSampleObject
    printf("theList is an instance of %s\n",
      [theList name]);
    printf("aSampleObject is an instance of %s\n",
      [aSampleObject name]);

    // exit the application
    exit(0);
}
```

> In most cases, we would never instantiate the **Object** class since it is an abstract superclass. However, this sample application is intended to mainly illustrate how easy it is to use Objective-C rather than demonstrate good design: this will come a little later.

NeXTSTEP refers to each application as a project

NeXTSTEP defines an application as a *project*. Before proceeding, create a folder in our home directory to store our project. Name the folder **Sample**, and save this file as **~/Sample/Sample.m** (~ refers to our home directory; for more information on the home directory, see Appendix A). Using the name of the application as the folder name is another NeXTSTEP naming convention. **Sample** only has one file, but as we will shortly see, most applications usually involves many files: creating a separate folder for each application allows us to manage the files associated with the application.

> To create a new folder in the current folder, use either **mkdir** *foldername* or click **File** ⇒ **New Folder** in the Workspace.

Using the following command, compile the **Sample.m** source code to produce the **Sample** executable:

```
% cc -g -o Sample Sample.m -lNeXT_s
```

The flags passed to **cc** (the C compiler) are as follows:

- **-g**—include debugging information in the executable. This increases the size of the executable, but the debugging information is useful when we need to debug the application.
- **-o**—take the next parameter to be the name of the executable (**Sample**).
- **-l***filename*—link the application with the library specified by *filename*. All our application will be using the functions defined in the standard library, **NeXT_s**.

> Since compiling and linking an application can be fairly tedious, consider using the **Makefile** for the **Sample** application from Appendix B.

Thus, the above command basically compiles the **Sample.m** source file and produces a **Sample** executable in the current directory. If it doesn't, verify the source code against the listing and for further help, consult Appendix C.

If there are errors, refer to Appendix C

> Typically, we compile the source file into an object file and then link it with a library before we produce an executable. However, we combined these two steps here since there is only one source file.

Run the application by either double-clicking on **~/Sample/Sample** or by opening a shell in Terminal and then typing in the following command:

```
% ~/Sample/Sample
```

In either case, the output should be:

```
There are 1 object(s) in the list
theList is an instance of List
aSampleObject is an instance of Object
```

The starting point of execution for an Objective-C program is main()

Similar to a C program, the starting point of execution for an Objective-C program is the **main()** function. This creates a list and then inserts an object into the list. Afterwards, **main()** sends a message to the list to ask it how many objects are in the list. Afterwards, **main()** sends a message to the list and to the object requesting them to print their classes. As a final step, **main()** exits with a **0** to indicate that the application executed successfully.

Even though **Sample** is quite trivial, it does illustrate many of the key concepts which we have covered:

- code reusability—we used an existing class, **List**.
- encapsulation—to use the **List** class, our application simply accessed the list through its methods; our application did not depend on or even care how the **List** class is implemented.
- classes and instances—**Sample** instantiated the **List** class using **alloc** and then initialized the resulting instance using **init**. We will return to this topic shortly.
- messages— **main()** sent messages to the objects to request them to perform their methods such as when **main()** requested the list to add an object with the following message expression, **[theList addObject:objectA];**. In this case, the receiver is **theList**, the selector is **addObject:**, and the parameter to the selector is **objectA**.
- polymorphism—both the list and the object implement a **name** method.
- naming conventions—using Objective-C's naming conventions, the first word in the variable names are in lower cases and the

second (and succeeding) words are in upper case. Two examples are **theList** and **aSampleObject**.
- Objective-C comments—**Sample** uses // as the comment style rather than /* */.

In the upcoming sections, we will explore how classes are declared and implemented.

2.4.1 Defining Classes

In Objective-C, a class is defined in two files: the *interface file* and the *implementation file*. The interface file lists the superclass, the instance variables, and the methods the class understands; the implementation file contains the code for the methods themselves. This separation of implementation details from the programming interface reinforces the idea of encapsulation, i.e., we should be able to use a class from just the method declarations. In practice, this is not always the case since the method declarations are often too sparse to be of much use. In addition to the interface file, we often need a specification sheet describing what the methods do. Figure 2.9 shows the components of a typical interface file; the mandatory components are in bold.

Each class has an interface file and an implementation file

```
#import "Superclass.h"

@interface ClassName:Superclass
{
  // optional
  instance variables
}
// optional
method declarations

@end
```

Figure 2.9 The interface file declares the instance variables and methods which the class contains

The interface file:

- is identified by a **.h** extension appended to the class' name as in **Square.h**.

- includes the superclass' header file by using the **#import** directive.
- identifies the current class and the superclass with the **@interface** directive.
- declares instance variables, if any, between the curly braces ({}).
- declares methods, if any, and their return types after the curly braces.
- terminates with the **@end** directive.

#import guarantees a file is never included more than once

Like the **#include** directive in C, the Objective-C **#import** directive includes the named file. However, **#import** guarantees the same file is never included more than once. If we wish to use a class in our application, we must include the header file of the class.

A sample interface file is as follows (we will explain what the - preceding each method name means shortly):

Listing for **Rectangle.h**

```
#import "AbstractShape.h"

@interface Rectangle:AbstractShape
{
  float height;
  float width;
}

-initHeight:(float)h width:(float)w;
-(float)calcArea;
```

```
-free;

@end
```

> Note that Objective-C uses the colon to mean two different things, depending on the context:
> - on the **@interface** line in an interface file, the colon is a separator between the class and its superclass such as **Square:Rectangle**.
> - in a message expression, the colon is part of the method name and is used to separate the method name from the associated parameter such as **initHeight:(float)h width:(float)w;**

As mentioned earlier, a class is always defined in terms of a superclass. This is true with one exception, the **Object** class. Unlike some object-oriented languages (one example is C++), Objective-C requires the root class to be **Object**. **Object** defines methods for memory management and other miscellaneous tasks. The method most used is the **alloc** method, which allocates memory for an instance. **Object** is an abstract superclass from which all other classes are defined, and as such, we never instantiate the **Object** class; we create subclasses from it then instantiate the subclasses.

Every class, except for Object, has a superclass

Whereas the interface declares the methods and their return types, the implementation file contains the code that actually implements the methods. The implementation file:

- is identified by a **.m** extension (**m** for methods) appended to the class' name as in **Square.m**.
- imports its own interface file.
- identifies itself as such to the compiler with the **@implementation** directive.
- contains the code for the methods defined in the interface file.
- terminates with the **@end** directive.

Figure 2.10 shows the components of an implementation file; the mandatory components are shown in bold.

```
#import "ClassName.h"

@implementation ClassName

method definitions

@end
```

Figure 2.10 The implementation file contains the code for the methods defined in the class' interface file

A sample implementation file is as follows:

Listing for **Rectangle.m**

```
#import "Rectangle.h"

@implementation Rectangle

-initHeight:(float)h width:(float)w
{
  [super init];
  height = h;
  width = w;
  return self;
}

-(float)calcArea
{
  return height * width;
}

-free
{
  return [super free];
}

@end
```

2.4.2 Class Methods and Instance Methods

Typically we do not work with the class itself but with the instances created from the class. Creating an instance in Objective-C is a two-step process:

- first, send an **alloc** method to the *class object*. Objective-C defines a class object for each class and uses it to determine how much memory to allocate for an instance. The name of the class object for a given class is the name of the class.

The name of the class object is the name of the class

> A class object is sometimes called a factory object. Likewise, a class method is sometimes called a factory method.

- once the instance is created, initialize it. Each class has a *designated initializer method* for initializing an instance. The name of the designated initializer method varies for each class, but it usually starts with **init**, as in **initFrame**:, **initFrame:text:alignment**, etc.

After the instance is created, initialize it with the designated initializer method

Afterwards, we assign the instance to a variable so we can refer to it later as shown in the following fragment:

Instantiating a class and initializing an object

```
id theRect;
// allocate memory for a new Rectangle instance
// initialize the instance and assign it
// to theRect
theRect = [[Rectangle alloc]
  initHeight:8 width:6];
[theRect calcArea];
```

Since the **alloc** method is sent to the class object, it is a *class method*. Since the **initHeight:width:** method is sent to the instance, it is an *instance method*. For a given class, there are usually more instance methods than class methods. The **alloc** message is defined in the **Object** class and is accessible to all other classes since all classes ultimately inherit from **Object**.

A class method is used with a class object, and an instance method is used with an instance

Note that the characteristics of **theRect** are not determined (i.e., **theRect** is not associated with its class) until it is created and initialized at the **alloc** and **initHeight:width:** statement.

> Classes that should only have a single instance per application (such as **Application**, **OpenPanel**, **SavePanel**, and **PrintPanel**) use **new** instead of **alloc** and **init** to enforce the idea that the instance will always be initialized with default values by NeXTSTEP. For more information on using **new**, see Chapter 9.

There are two simple ways of determining if a method is an instance method or a class method:

- if the receiver in a message expression is the name of a class (the class object), the method is a class method. If the receiver is an instance, the method is an instance method.
- if the method declaration in the implementation file is preceded by a dash (-), it is an instance method. If the method is preceded by a plus (+), it is a class method.

> A useful mnemonic is to remember we typically use a class object to create an instance, which increases the number of instances by 1. Therefore, the + means to create one more instance.

2.4.3 Messaging Mechanisms

An object's isa pointer links to its class

Every object in Objective-C has an *isa* instance variable that serves as a link to its class. The **isa** variable is pronounced "is a," i.e., "**theRect** is a rectangle." The class object contains two *mes-*

sage dispatch tables, one containing the addresses of the instance methods and one containing the addresses of the class methods. Figure 2.11 illustrates these concepts.

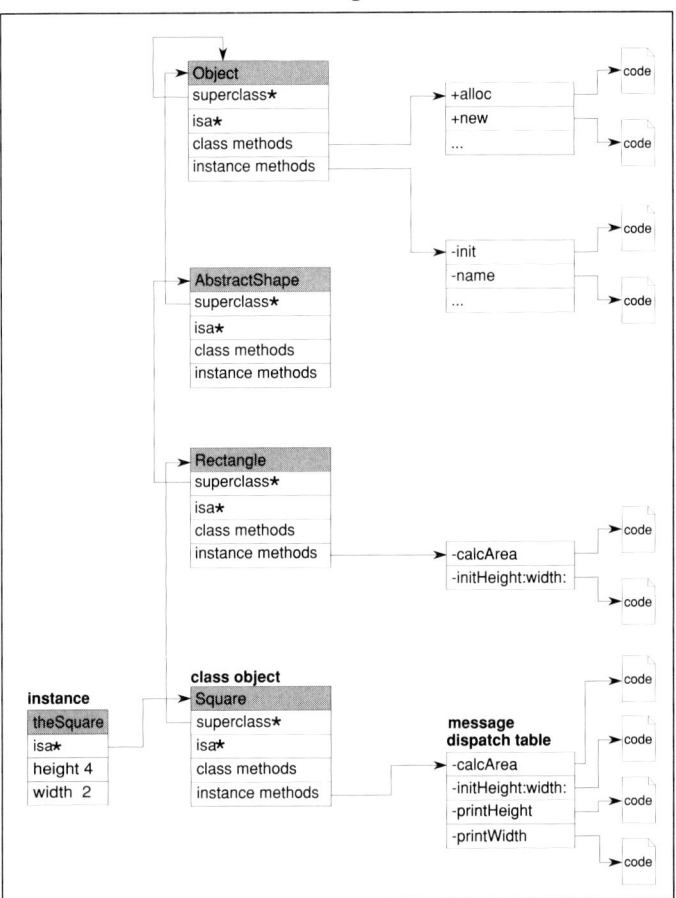

Figure 2.11 The class object has two message dispatch tables that contain the addresses of the instance and class methods

The **isa** pointer of the class object actually points to the *metaclass*, which contains the message dispatch table for the class methods. However, for the sake of simplicity, we have omitted the metaclass from our discussions.

When an instance receives a message, Objective-C uses the instance's **isa** pointer to find the class object. Then, Objective-C

Objective-C uses an object's isa pointer to find the class object

searches the class object's message dispatch table of the instance methods to locate the instance method. If Objective-C cannot find the method in the current class object, it uses the class object's **superclass** pointer to traverse up to the superclass. This sequence repeats until one of two things happen:

- the method is found in a superclass and is executed as is usually the case.
- the method is not found even after searching the **Object** class object. At this point, the application will crash and produce an error message similar to: *anObject* **cannot respond to** *selector*. This can happen in one of three cases:
    - an instance received a class method or vice versa. This produces an error because it is not sensible. For example, it is meaningless to send an **alloc** message to an instance because it is impossible for an instance to create another instance.
    - the method name is misspelled. For example, the selector in the message expression is **calc_Area** whereas it should be **calcArea**.
    - the method does not exist. For example, the rectangle receives a **calcVolume** message, and there is no such method.

Figure 2.12 illustrates what happens when an object receives an instance method.

```
                    ┌─────────────────┐
                    │ Object          │───┬──► +alloc  ───► code
                    │ superclass★     │   │   +new
                    │ isa★            │   │   ...        ───► code
              ⑥     │ class methods   │   │
                    │ instance methods│   │   FOUND!
                    └─────────────────┘ ⑦    ▼
                                           ─init        ───► code
                                           ─name
                    ┌─────────────────┐    ...          ───► code
                    │ AbstractShape   │
                    │ superclass★     │
              ⑤     │ isa★            │
                    │ class methods   │
                    │ instance methods│
                    └─────────────────┘

                    ┌─────────────────┐
                    │ Rectangle       │
                    │ superclass★     │
              ③     │ isa★            │
                    │ class methods   │ ④
                    │ instance methods│───► -calcArea      ───► code
                    └─────────────────┘    -initHeight:width:
                                                            ───► code

                        class object
 instance           ┌─────────────────┐                     ───► code
┌──────────┐        │ Square          │
│ theSquare│ ①      │ superclass★     │    message
│ isa★     │        │ isa★            │    dispatch table
│ height 4 │        │ class methods   │ ②   -calcArea       ───► code
│ width  2 │        │ instance methods│───►-initHeight:width:
└──────────┘        └─────────────────┘    -printHeight    ───► code
                                           -printWidth
                                                            ───► code
```

[theSquare name];

1. Objective-C follows the object's **isa★** pointer to find the **Square** class object.
2. since the receiver is an instance, Objective-C searches the instance message dispatch table for the **name** method.
3. Objective-C then uses the **superclass★** pointer to find the instance's superclass, **Rectangle**.
4. Objective-C searches the instance message dispatch table for the **name** method.
5. Objective-C then uses the **superclass★** pointer to find the instance's superclass, **AbstractShape**.
6. Objective-C then uses the **superclass★** pointer to find the instance's superclass, **Object**.
7. Objective-C searches the instance message dispatch table to find the **name** method.

Figure 2.12 Objective-C searches for the appropriate method in the dispatch table

The search sequence described above also holds true when a class object receives a class message: the only difference is that Objective-C searches for the selector in the message dispatch table for the class methods instead of the one for the instance methods.

2.4.4 Methods and Functions

The address of a method is not determined until runtime

At this point, we may be asking ourselves "What is the difference between sending a message in object-oriented programming and calling a function in procedural programming?" The primary difference is the memory address of a function is resolved at compile time whereas the memory address of a method is resolved at runtime (that is, while the application is executing): the former is known as ***static binding*** (or ***early binding***) and the latter is ***dynamic binding*** (or ***late binding***).

Dynamic binding is needed since it may not be possible to determine the class until runtime

Dynamic binding is useful because we may not always know what the current receiver of the message is until execution. For example, assume we have a graphic editor with a **Cut** menu option. Ideally, we should be able to select an object and then select **Cut** to cut the currently selected object. In this message expression, the selector is the **cut** method, but it is impossible to determine what the currently selected object is until runtime: it could be a square, a circle, or another object such as text. In short, this is an example of polymorphism and dynamic binding since:

• each object must implement a **cut** method.

• the receiver of the message is not determined until runtime.

Figure 2.13 illustrates an example of dynamic binding.

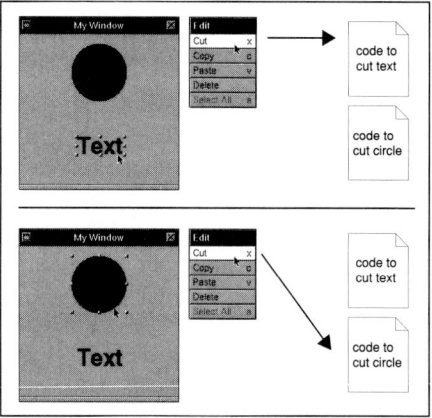

Figure 2.13 Dynamic binding defers associating the receiver to the method until runtime

2.4.5 Self and Super

The **Square** class already inherits the **calcArea** (from the **Rectangle** class) to calculate its **area**. Now assume that we want to extend **Square**'s **calcArea** method to also print the **height** and **width** of each square. One way to do this is to add two methods, **printHeight** and **printWidth**, to print these variables. The receiver of these messages should be the same object that received the **calcArea** method. However, it is impossible to determine what the receiver is until the application is executing since Objective-C does not bind the object to the method until runtime. How then do we solve this problem? Objective-C provides a keyword, **self**, which serves as a placeholder to refer to the original receiver of the message expression. This is useful if the object needs to refer to itself again in another method, as illustrated in the following code fragment:

self refers to the receiver in the original message expression

Square.m with modifications

```
#import "Square.h"

@implementation Square

-printHeight
{
  printf("The height is %.2f\n", height);
  return self;
}

-printWidth
{
  printf("The width is %.2f\n", width);
  return self;
}

-(float)calcArea
{
  // use self to refer to the same object
  // that received the calcArea method
  [self printHeight];
  [self printWidth];
  // calculate the area
  return height * width;
```

```
}
@end
```

[self calcArea] in the calcArea method would produce an infinite loop

However, the last line of Square's **calcArea** method presents a less than ideal situation because the method should be able to access the existing functionality already defined in **Rectangle**'s **calcArea** method. How can the square accomplish this? At first, we may consider something like **[self calcArea]**. However, this would create an infinite loop since **calcArea** would then be sending a **calcArea** message!

super allows an object to refer to its superclass' implementation of the method in which super appears

This situation creates a dilemma because the newly created **calcArea** method (in **Square**) needs to access the existing **calcArea** method (in **Rectangle**). How do we accomplish this without copying the code over from the existing method? Objective-C provides a keyword, **super**, to allow an object to refer to its superclass' implementation of the method in which **super** appears. The code in bold shows how the square calculates its **area** by using **super** to access the **calcArea** method defined in the **Rectangle** class:

Listing for Square.m

```
-(float)calcArea
{
  // use self to refer to the same object
  // that received the calcArea method
  [self printHeight];
  [self printWidth];
  // use super to access the superclass'
```

```
    // implementation
    return [super calcArea];
}
```

Remember that an object can access its *own* instance variables by simply referring to them, as is the case in **printHeight** and **printWidth**. An object only needs to send a message if it is trying to access *another* object's instance variables.

Figure 2.14 shows how Objective-C uses **self** and **super**.

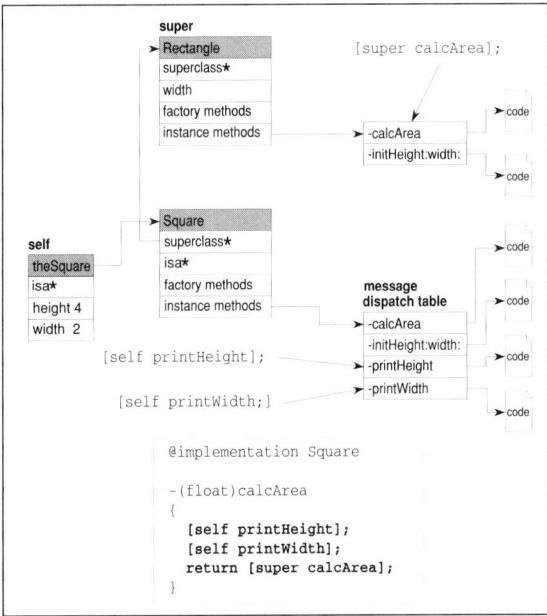

Figure 2.14 **self** is the current object and **super** is the superclass

Note that **super** refers to the superclass of the method in which **super** appears rather than the superclass of the selector of the message expression. In this case, that distinction is moot since both the method where **super** appears and the selector are **calcArea**. However, as we will see in "Initializing Instances" on page 45, that is not always the case.

Typically, a method returns **self** because the default return type is an **id**. For example, the following convention is quite common:

An Objective-C method typically returns **self**

```
-printHeight
{
  printf("The height is %.2f\n", height);
  return self;
}
```

2.4.6 Instantiating Classes

Objective-C allocates memory for the instance variables starting at Object

To instantiate a class, Objective-C allocates memory for the instance variables defined in the superclass(es) and the current class. Objective-C allocates memory starting at the **Object** class, proceeds to the next immediate subclass of **Object**, and ends at the class to be instantiated. For example, the **Rectangle** class defines two instance variables, **height** and **width**. To instantiate the **Rectangle** class, Objective-C:

- uses **Rectangle**'s **superclass** pointer to find the superclass. This process is repeated until Objective-C reaches the **Object** class.
- Objective-C then allocates memory for the instance variables defined in the **Object** class; the only instance variable defined for the **Object** class is the **isa** pointer.
- Objective-C then proceeds to allocate memory for the instance variables defined in **Object**'s subclass, **AbstractShape.** Since **AbstractShape** doesn't define any instance variables, Objective-C then descends to the next subclass, **Rectangle**, which defines two instance variables, **height** and **width**.

This sequence explains why a class cannot redefine the type of its inherited instance variables: the types are already set by its superclass. Figure 2.15 illustrates this sequence.

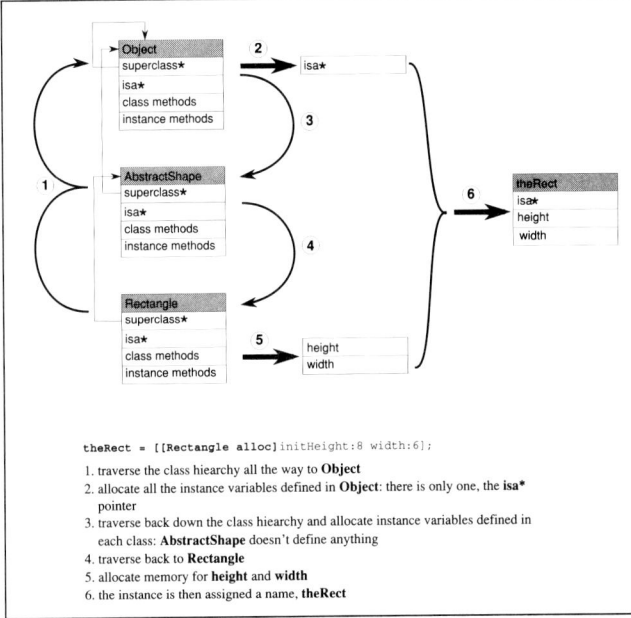

Figure 2.15 Objective-C starts at the **Object** class to allocate the memory for a newly created instance

2.4.7 Initializing Instances

Once Objective-C allocates the memory for the instance, it proceeds to initialize the instance variables. This sequence is almost identical to the memory allocation process. Returning to our earlier example, Objective-C uses **Rectangle**'s **superclass** pointer to traverse the class hierarchy all the way to **Object**. Objective-C starts the initialization process by initializing the instance variables starting at the **Object** class and finishes initialization with the instance variables defined in the current class (**Rectangle**). The designated initializer method for the **Rectangle** class would look like the following example:

The initialization sequence is similar to the allocating sequence

The designated initializer method for **Rectangle**

```
-initHeight:(float)h width:(float)w
```

```
{
  [super init];
  height = h;
  width = w;
  return self;
}
```

Use [super init] to initialize the inherited instance variables

In the designated initializer method, the class should first use **super** to ensure that it is initializing the instance variables inherited from its superclass and then proceed to initialize its own instance variables. In this example, the **Rectangle** class uses **super** to initialize the instance variables which it inherits from **AbstractShape**. The **Rectangle** class then proceeds to initialize **height** and **width** to **h** and **w**, respectively.

In this example, super refers to AbstractShape instead of Object

Note that **super** refers to the superclass of the method where **super** appears (**initHeight:width:**) rather than the superclass of the selector in the message expression (**init**). Thus, **super** refers to the superclass of the class that implements **initHeight:width:**, (**Rectangle**) instead of the superclass of the class that implements **init** (**Object**). **Object** implements **init** and **Object** is its own superclass.

2.4.8 Freeing Objects

Objective-C does not provide automatic garbage collection

Each time an application creates an object, it dynamically allocates some memory to accommodate the object. Some languages—one example is Smalltalk—can automatically reclaim memory that an application allocates but no longer references during execution: this task is known as *automatic garbage collection*. With Objective-C, however, an application is responsible for freeing (deallocating) all memory it *dynamically* allocates.

Use the free method to free an object

The application usually sends an object a **free** message to request the object to deallocate itself. The **free** method should free all dynamically allocated memory in the current class and then free the object. For example, assume we have a subclass of **Object**, **Document**. This class defines three new variables:

- **theWindow**—the **id** of the window the document displays in.

- **saved**—a **Boolean** flag indicating whether the document has been saved or not (**YES** or **NO**).
- **name**—a **char** pointer (a string) representing the name of the file the document is associated with.

In C, a string is a series of characters with a *null terminator*. A null terminator is a character that indicates the end of a string and is represented as \0. Even though it looks like two characters, the null terminator occupies only one byte in memory. In allocating memory for a string, we must allocate enough memory for the characters in the string plus one more byte for the null terminator. To allocate memory for a string, use the **malloc()** system call. NeXTSTEP defines **NX_MALLOC()**, a macro for the **malloc()** system call, for dynamically allocating memory for anything other than objects (use **alloc** to allocate memory for objects). For example, to allocate memory for a string of fifty characters, allocate fifty-one bytes (fifty characters plus one for the null terminator) as in the following example:

Use NX_MALLOC() to allocate memory for everything other than objects

Allocating memory using **NX_MALLOC()**

```
// allocate memory for 50 characters and
// the null terminator
NX_MALLOC(name, char, 51);
```

Since the **Document** class is now dynamically allocating **name**, it must free **name** in its **free** method as follows (**NX_FREE()** is a macro for the **free()** system call):

Freeing memory with **NX_FREE()**

```
- free
{
  [theWindow free];
  NX_FREE(name);
```

```
        return [super free];
}
```

> The classes in the Application Kit usually know how to free themselves and their dynamically allocated instance variables. For example, sending a **free** message to a window frees the memory allocated to the window as well as the contents of the window such as the views, buttons, etc.

An object only needs to explicitly free its dynamically allocated instance variables

An object doesn't need to *explicitly* free all of its instance variables, only those it dynamically allocates. For example, a document doesn't need to free its **saved** instance variable since it is intrinsic to the document and will be freed when the document is freed. However, the document needs to free its **theWindow** and **name** instance variables because they reference memory blocks that are completely external to the document. To facilitate our discussions, we say that **theWindow** and **name** *point* to other memory blocks. Figure 2.16 illustrates these ideas.

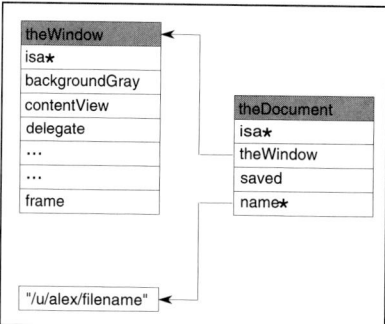

Figure 2.16 The contents of **theWindow** and **name** are completely external to **theDocument**

NX_FREE() only frees the memory blocks which the instance variable is pointing to

Note that the statements **[theWindow free]** and **NX_FREE(name)** only free the memory blocks that the variables are pointing to. In the former case, the application is freeing the memory block **theWindow** is pointing to and in the latter case, the application is freeing the memory block **name** is pointing to. However, the memory occupied by the variables themselves (**theWindow** and **name**) are not freed until the object that contains these variables (**theDocument**) is freed. The document is freed with the **[super free]** statement; this traverses all the way to **Object**, which then frees the object and its instance variables.

An object should always free the memory block a dynamic instance variable points to *before* freeing the variable itself; if an application frees the dynamic instance variable—thereby invalidating it—the application would not be able to determine what memory block the dynamic instance variable was originally pointing to. The memory block would still be allocated but it would be impossible to retrieve the reference to the memory block.

Free the memory block the dynamic instance variable points to before freeing the dynamic instance variable

> The object that owns the memory (that is, allocates the memory for its dynamic instance variables) should be the one that frees the same memory. An application still works even if its objects do not free themselves or their dynamically allocated instance variables. However, the application tends to grow in size the longer it executes. NeXTSTEP, with its virtual paging system, can accommodate the increasing memory which the application demands. However, eventually, these *memory leaks* tend to make an application less efficient since it demands more system resources than necessary.
>
> Once an object is freed, do not send any messages to it or the application will most likely crash because a freed object typically contains invalid data. Sending a message to a freed object is a common mistake in NeXTSTEP.

Figure 2.17 shows the sequence of steps which **theDocument** uses to free itself.

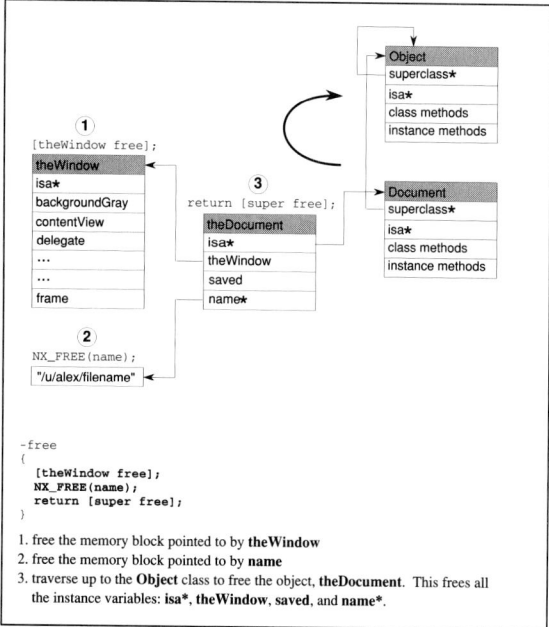

Figure 2.17 An object should free the memory block an instance variable is pointing to before freeing the instance variable

2.5 Suggestions

Consider extending the **Sample** application in the following manners to learn more about Objective-C.

2.5.1 Printing the Indices of the List's Contents

Add some code to insert more objects into the list and then printing out the indices of each of these objects. To print the index of a given object, use **indexOf:** and pass the **id** of the object. The following code fragment demonstrates how to use the **indexOf:** method.

Printing the index of an object in a list

```
printf("The index of aSampleObject is %d\n",
    [theList indexOf:aSampleObject]);
```

2.5.2 Freeing the List and its Contents

Consider freeing the list and its contents. First, free the contents by sending the list a **freeObjects** message and then free the list itself by sending it a **free** message. The **freeObjects** method will send a **free** message to each object in the list.

2.6 Summary

The fundamental element in object-oriented programming is an object, a package that encapsulates the data (instance variables) with their corresponding functions (methods). This model views a system as a collection of cooperative objects that communicate by sending messages to each other. To create an object, we must first define a class and then instantiate it. To extend or modify the behavior of a class, we can create a subclass to inherit the instance variables and methods from its superclasses. A subclass extends or modifies the behavior inherited from its superclass by overriding an identically named method.

These object-oriented ideas are implemented in Objective-C, a hybrid language based on C with support for object-oriented programming. Objective-C is fairly easy to learn since it adds little new syntax to C. The primary feature of Objective-C is dynamic binding (late binding), which allows more flexibility than static binding by not associating a method with its receiver until runtime.

With this background in Objective-C, we will proceed to another topic in the object-oriented model: object-oriented design.

Summary

Chapter 3
Object-Oriented Design

The **Sample** application from Chapter 2 is simple enough that we could implement it without having to first design the application. However, we rarely have the luxury of depending completely on existing classes. Typically, we have to at least create some classes ourselves. In many ways, it is more difficult to determine what classes to implement than it is to implement the classes. Determining what classes to implement for a given system is known as *object-oriented design*. Although we typically design an application before implementing it, we have deferred this topic until now because the design model tends to be more abstract and thus more difficult to grasp than the programming model.

It is often more difficult to design classes than it is to implement them

Even a simple application tends to involve many classes and as this number grows, we need a more systematic way of determining what classes to create and documenting what each class does. In this chapter, we explore how to determine what classes to create (what instance variables should the class contain and what methods should the class implement) and how to use various tools to manage the classes in an application.

Object-oriented design allows us to design classes systematically

Afterwards, we will implement a more ambitious Objective-C application, **ShapeArea.** Before implementing the application, we will design and document all the custom subclasses using the tools and techniques which we will learn.

3.1 Goals

In this chapter, we will:

- introduce object-oriented design.
- describe some of the tools used in the object-oriented design stage of application development.
- illustrate how to create custom subclasses.
- introduce another Objective-C application, **ShapeArea**.

3.2 Methodology

Object-oriented design is as much an art as a science

Although the object-oriented paradigm has been around since the 1960s, the techniques that have been proposed rely as much on intuition as on formal methodologies; producing a good object-oriented design is still as much an art as a science. However, some major activities are common to most of the proposed techniques. These activities include:

- identifying the objects
- determining what each object does
- establishing the relationships between the objects
- modeling the flow of the system.

In most cases, we will use the term object to mean the class and its instances

Since the design stage precedes the implementation stage, we will not concern ourselves with minute details such as how a method is implemented and what its return type is, etc. At this point, we will not attempt to differentiate between a class and its instance(s) since we are trying to model the application at a fairly abstract level. All discussions at this stage will use the term "object" for generality.

Object-oriented design does not proceed linearly

Keep in mind that the methodology is based on *activities* rather than *steps*. This means we do not proceed through the design stage in a completely linear manner. Often, we need to change some decisions made at an earlier stage because of the feedback from users. Designing an object-oriented solution is an iterative process of refinement, much like designing in any other discipline. Figure 3.1 illustrates the activities of object-oriented design.

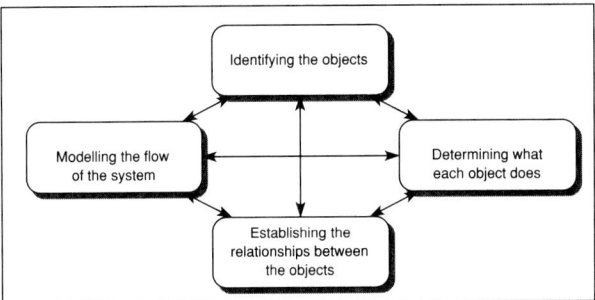

Figure 3.1 Object-oriented design is composed of activities rather than steps

Because of its flexibility, object-oriented design is often used for *rapid prototyping*. This is a technique that allows us to create a prototype quickly to demonstrate to the users how the finished system will behave. Rapid prototyping is possible through the encapsulation of objects: since most of the functionality of a system is enclosed in the objects, we can implement only a minimum set of objects to demonstrate the system and then add the other objects later as needed to "flesh out" the system. Often, after seeing a prototype of the system, users will be able to provide much better feedback than they could at the analysis or design stages. We can then change the design (and requirements, as necessary) to accommodate the feedback. However, for the sake of simplicity, we will assume that our design proceeds linearly.

> Object-oriented design is often used for rapid prototyping

3.2.1 Identifying the Objects

Unlike conventional design techniques, which tend to focus on the processes in a system, object-oriented design focuses on the data and how they interact in the system. In short, object-oriented design focuses on the objects.

The first activity in object-oriented design is to identify the data in the problem. There are many ways of doing this, but the simplest way is to look at the specifications of the problem, and mark the nouns in the specifications: these are the *things*, which imply that

> To identify the objects, look for the nouns in the specifications

they are objects. For example, assume that we are given the following specifications for an application named **ShapeArea**:

> ShapeArea is an application that calculates the areas of rectangles and squares. The user is allowed to specify which shape to create and what the dimensions of each shape are. As each shape is created, it is inserted into a list. When the user quits the application, ShapeArea prints the area of all the shapes in the list again.

Now, mark the nouns in bold. This produces the following specifications:

> **ShapeArea** is an **application** that calculates the **areas** of **rectangles** and **squares**. The **user** can specify which **shape** to create and what the **dimensions** of each shape are. As each shape is created, it is inserted into a **list**. When the user quits the application, ShapeArea prints the area of all the shapes from the list again.

Some nouns may only be characteristics of other nouns

Of course, this only produces the likely candidates for objects since it is quite possible that some of the nouns are actually characteristics of other nouns. For example, **area** is a noun but it is not an object. Rather, it is a characteristic of each of the shapes. A quick way to determine whether a noun is an object or simply a characteristic of another object is to ask the following question: *does the object have only one characteristic and if so, is that characteristic the noun itself?* For example, the only characteristic of **area** is **area**. This noun would probably not qualify as an object since the definition of an object is a grouping of the data with the operations which can manipulate them. Compare the noun **area** with one of the shapes such as a **rectangle**. A **rectangle** has a **height** and **width**, and it needs to calculate its **area**. Since the noun **rectangle** has characteristics other than itself as well as operations it needs to perform, it is most likely an object.

> Additionally, some objects necessary to the application may not appear in the specifications because they are contained in other objects. For example, a window usually has a close button. We do not consider this a separate object since it is completely private to the window.
>
> Finally, some objects in the specifications do not need to be modeled as software. For example, the specifications may mention that we need to use the mouse to initiate an action: the mouse is a hardware object and does not belong in the software model.

Now that we have a good idea of how to identify objects, we need to determine what the objects can do in order to produce the methods to implement.

3.2.2 Determining What Each Object Does

An object must have some operations to perform. It is fairly intuitive to determine these operations from the specifications since all we need to do is locate the verbs and mark them. The verbs will be marked in bold italics to differentiate them from the nouns, which are in bold. Using the **ShapeArea** specifications and marking the verbs in bold italics produces the following:

> **ShapeArea** is an **application** that *calculates* the **areas** of **rectangles** and **squares**. The **user** *can specify* which **shape** to *create* and what the **dimensions** of each shape are. As each shape is created, it is *inserted* into a **list**. When the user *quits* the application, ShapeArea *prints* the area of all the shapes from the list again.

Although determining the operations of a system is fairly straightforward, determining which object an operation belongs to is not always obvious. For example, consider the verb **inserted**. What

To find the actions, look for the verbs

The difficulty lies in trying to determine which object is responsible for a given action

object will insert these shapes? Will another object insert these shapes into the list, or will the shapes insert themselves into the list? We may not be able to answer these questions until we model the flow of the application, which is one the last activities of this process.

Most actions can be grouped into one of three major categories:

- derive a result—in **ShapeArea**, calculating a shape's **area** is an example of deriving a result. Deriving a result is by far the most common action which most objects perform.
- monitor or update the state of another object—for example, every NeXTSTEP application maintains a list of windows for which it is responsible. If we close a window, the application needs to remove the closed window from its list.

> As we will learn in Chapter 6, NeXTSTEP initializes certain objects whenever an application is started. However, an application often needs to perform additional initialization, and it can only accomplish this by creating another object whose main purpose is to initialize (update) and monitor other objects.

- display—since NeXTSTEP is a graphical environment, most applications will perform some drawing. Fortunately, the classes in the Application Kit have been meticulously designed so that all classes that need to display themselves already include the necessary code. If we design a custom object and we wish it to draw to the screen, we must implement our own drawing code. We will explore this further in Chapter 7.

Do not centralize the functionality into one object

A common mistake when designing objects is to centralize all the intelligence into a single object. This defeats the purpose of object-oriented design (and programming), which is to distribute functionality across various objects. Distributing the intelligence throughout the objects allows each one to know as little about its environment as possible. The more generalized an object is, the more reusable it will be.

3.2.3 Identifying the Relationships Between the Objects

With all the objects defined, the next activity is to determine the relationships between them: this produces a hierarchy of objects and the messages they use to communicate with each other. Keep the following points in mind when determining these relationships:

- if several objects share a similar characteristic, create an abstract object and then move that characteristic into the parent object rather than define it in each of the child objects. For example, in the **ShapeArea** application, **area** is common to all the shapes. Therefore, instead of defining it in each of the shapes, we should create an abstract object and define **area** in that object. The upcoming **ShapeArea** application will demonstrate this point.
- instead of creating a single monolithic object, consider building an object from existing objects, i.e., a composite object. For instance, an openpanel (this panel appears whenever we attempt to open a file) is composed of, among other things, three buttons, a textfield, and a browser.
- determine whether manipulating one object affects another one in the application. For example, clicking on the **Quit** menu option quits an application. Therefore, there must be some relationship between the **Quit** menu option and the application. As we will see in Chapter 6, manipulating one object to control another is one of the two control paradigms in the NeXTSTEP environment.
- determine whether updating the state of an object will update the status of another object. For example, in the **Sample** application from Chapter 2, each time the **main()** function inserts a shape into the list, it is increasing the list's size by one.

Determining the relationships between the objects produces a hierarchy and the list of messages

At this point, we need to determine the order in which the objects will message to each other.

3.2.4 Modeling the Flow of the Application

Modeling the flow of the application allows us to determine when the objects should be created and initialized

Although object-oriented programming views an application as a system of autonomous objects that communicate by sending messages to each other, there is still a need for an initialization stage when the objects are created and initialized. The lifetime of each object also needs to be determined to maximize system resources. When an object is no longer needed, it needs to be deallocated to free system resources. Since Objective-C is based on C, the starting point of program execution is the **main**() function. The **main**() function typically creates the minimum number of objects to allow the application to launch. For maximum efficiency, an application should create objects only as they are needed.

To maximize system resources, do not create objects until necessary and free the objects when they are no longer needed

For example, every application has an Info panel, a panel that contains the name of the application, the name of author(s), etc. However since the Info panel is rarely accessed, the application should not create the panel until the user clicks on the **Info** menu option. Or consider a word processor that has to manipulate multiple documents, each one displayed in a separate window. The application should only create a window and a document each time the user opens a file. Similarly, the application should free the document and window immediately after the user closes the window. We will explore these scenarios more closely in Chapter 9.

After the object is created, we need to determine what happens when certain actions are performed:

- what happens when the user saves a document?
- what object should process this message?
- what happens when the user closes the document but it has not been saved? Should the application prompt the user or quietly close the document?

These questions simply determine how an object should process each action as it is initiated by the user. Now that we have covered some techniques, we will apply them to a sample application.

3.3 Designing ShapeArea

At this point, we will design a new application, **ShapeArea**. Our specifications (with the nouns and verbs already marked) are as follows:

> **ShapeArea** is an **application** that *calculates* the **areas** of **rectangles** and **squares**. The **user** *can specify* which **shape** to *create* and what the **dimensions** of each shape are. As each shape is created, it is *inserted* into a **list**. When the user *quits* the application, ShapeArea *prints* the area of all the shapes from the list again.

ShapeArea calculates the area of an arbitrary shape

To find all the objects, list all the nouns first:

- ShapeArea—the name of the application.
- application—this is the entire collection of objects rather than a single object.
- areas—as explained in "Identifying the Objects" on page 55, area is simply a characteristic of each shape and is therefore not an object.
- rectangles—this is an object since it has some actions (calculate its own area) and it has some characteristics, namely its dimensions.
- squares—same as above.
- shape—a synonym for either a rectangle or a square.
- dimensions—like area, the dimensions are characteristics of the shapes. For rectangles and squares, the dimensions are the height and width.
- list—as we learned in Chapter 2, this is an object which can contain other objects.

Thus, we have at least three nouns (candidate objects) so far: rectangle, square, and list. We will return to the nouns shortly, but for now, let us explore the verbs to determine what methods the objects are capable of performing. The list of verbs include:

- calculate—this is the responsibility of each shape since the formula for calculating the shape's area is dependent on what type of shape it is. For example, for a rectangle (and a square), the area is defined as the height times the width, but for a triangle, the area would be one-half of its base times its height.
- allow—this is simply a helping verb in the specifications.
- (can) specify—this implies a list of choices from which the user can specify which shape to create and also what the dimensions of each shape are. This responsibility can rest either with the object or with the **main**() function. We will return to this responsibility shortly.
- insert—each shape will be inserted into the list, but the object which will be responsible for inserting the shapes has yet to be determined.
- print—ideally, this would be a method which each shape understands. However, to keep the design simple, we will implement the print action in the **main**() function through **printf**() rather than define a **print** method for each shape.

As we have seen, even a simple object can have many responsibilities. Therefore, unless we use some tools to document these objects, an application can easily become unmanageable.

3.4 Tools and Techniques

Now that we have explained what classes and methods are in the application, we need to explore tools to concisely communicate all this information. We will explore four such tools: Class/Responsibility/Collaborator (CRC) cards, class summary tables, message diagrams, and hierarchy graphs.

CRC cards are used with responsibility-driven design

3.4.1 CRC Cards

CRC is an acronym for Class/Responsibility/Collaborator. CRC cards are used to document the classes, their *responsibilities*, and the other classes they need to communicate with to perform these responsibilities: these classes are called the ***collaborators***. This type of design is known as ***responsibility-driven design*** since the focus is to determine the responsibilities of the various objects in the system.

> Of course, it is not the classes that are communicating with each other, it is the instances. However since this technique is called the Class/Responsibilities/Collaborator, we will use the term class.

CRC cards are often implemented using index cards and they are most effective in group situations: the technique encourages the participants to think in an object-oriented manner because each card contains information about only one class, which promotes the idea of encapsulation.

CRC cards are implemented using index cards

To produce the CRC cards:

- list the name of the class and its superclasses in the upper left-hand corner of the card.
- list and number the responsibilities the class implements on the left side of the index card.
- list the collaborator(s) this class needs to depend on to carry out each of its responsibilities. To determine if a class requires a collaborator to carry out a given responsibility, ask these questions:
  - is an instance of this class capable of performing this responsibility by itself?
  - if not, from what other instance (of another class) does this instance need help? The current instance must be able to send messages to another instance (from this other class) in order to collaborate with it. For example, consider the **Document** class from Chapter 2. If the document has to set the title of its associated window, then the window must be a collaborator of the document. Why? The document must be able to message to the window in order to set its title. However, the document is not necessarily a collaborator of the window since the window may never need to message the document.

Let's apply this technique to the **ShapeArea** application. There are four main classes:

- **AbstractShape**
- **List**
- **Rectangle**
- **Square**.

The **AbstractShape** class is an abstract superclass that defines the **calcArea** method for its subclasses to override. Figure 3.2 shows the CRC card for this class.

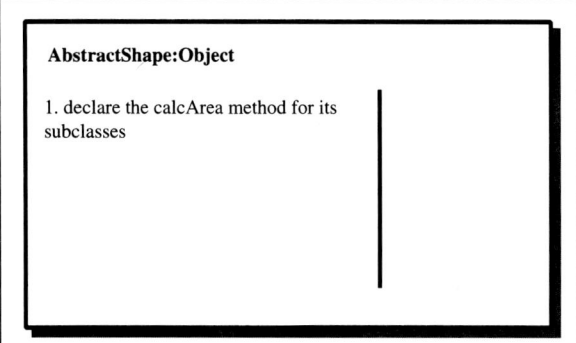

Figure 3.2 The **AbstractShape** class has no collaborators

> Notice that the CRC cards do not list the instance variables which the class declares. That is a detail we can safely ignore at this stage of the design since we are more interested in what each class does.

The **Rectangle** class defines three methods (**initHeight:width:**, **calcArea**, and **free**) it can accomplish on its own. Thus, the

Rectangle class has no collaborators. Figure 3.3 shows the CRC card for the **Rectangle** class.

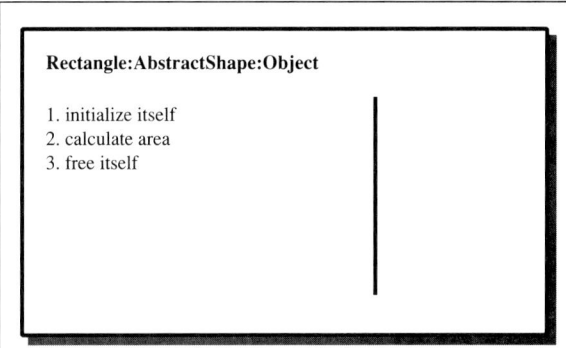

Figure 3.3 The **Rectangle** class has no collaborators

The **Square** class overrides the **calcArea** method inherited from the **Rectangle** class. Although the **Square** class depends on the **Rectangle** class for the **calcArea** method, we don't list the **Rectangle** class as a collaborator since this dependency is intrinsic in the definition of inheritance. Figure 3.4 shows the CRC card for the **Square** class.

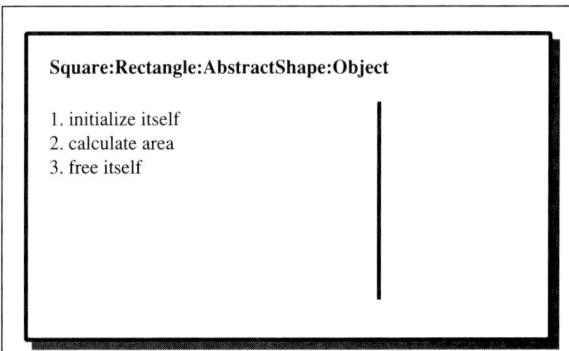

Figure 3.4 The **Square** class has no collaborators

The **List** class is primarily responsible for collecting the shapes. To collect each shape, the **main()** function sends the list an **addObject:** message.

Figure 3.5 shows the CRC card for the **List** class.

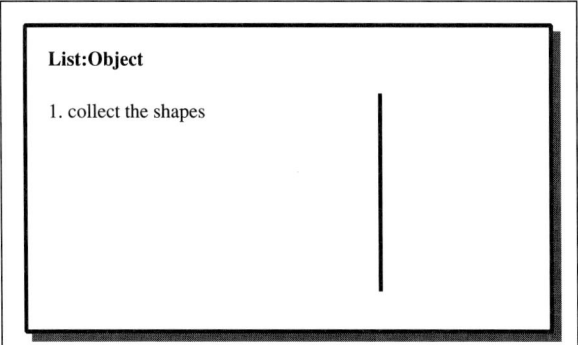

Figure 3.5 The **List** class has no collaborators

3.4.2 Class Summary Tables

A class summary table summarizes the methods and the instance variables of the class

While a CRC card documents the functionality of a class and lists the collaborators, a *class summary table* lists the various methods a class implements and a short description of what the method does. The title of the table lists the inheritance all the way to the **Object** class. Table 3.1 shows the class summary table for the **AbstractShape** class.

AbstractShape:Object		
	Name	**Description**
Instance Variables	N/A	N/A
Methods	(float)calcArea	does nothing; a subclass should override this to calculate the area appropriate for the shape

Table 3.1 Class summary table for the **AbstractShape** class

Table 3.2 shows the class summary table for the **Rectangle** class.

Rectangle:AbstractShape:Object		
	Name	**Description**
Instance Variables	height	the height of the rectangle
	width	the width of the rectangle
Methods	initHeight:(float)h width:(float)w	initializes the rectangle's height to *h* and width to *w*
	(float)calcArea	calculates the area of the rectangle
	free	frees the rectangle

Table 3.2 Class summary table for the **Rectangle** class

Table 3.3 shows the class summary table for the **Square** class.

Square:Rectangle:AbstractShape:Object		
	Name	**Description**
Instance Variables	height	inherited from Rectangle
	width	inherited from Rectangle
Methods	initHeight:(float)h width:(float)w	initializes the square's height to *h* and width to *w*
	(float)calcArea	calculates the area of the square and prints its dimensions
	free	frees the square

Table 3.3 Class summary table for the **Square** class

Table 3.4 shows the class summary table for the **List** class.

List:Object		
	Name	Description
Instance Variables	N/A	N/A
Methods	addObject:anObject	adds *anObject* at the end of the list
	objectAt:(unsigned int)index	returns the object at slot *index*
	freeObjects	frees each object in the list
	free	frees the list

Table 3.4 Class summary table for the **List** class

3.4.3 Message Diagrams

A message diagram documents the messages the objects send to each other

Once we have produced the CRC cards and the class summary tables for the objects in an application, the next step is to show the messages the objects send to each other. Producing a *message diagram* provides a broad picture of the application and allows us to determine if all the responsibilities which are listed on the cards are being used. In an object-oriented environment, all responsibilities must be accounted for.

In a message diagram, the objects are depicted as boxes, and the boxes are connected by lines with arrowheads. The box at the end of an arrowhead is the receiver in the message expression. Note that the messages are sent between the instances rather than the classes. Since the squares and rectangles are never named in the code, we generically name them as **square** and **rectangle**. Figure 3.6 shows the message diagram for **ShapeArea**.

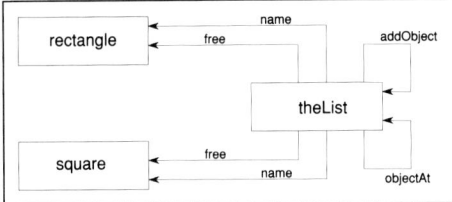

Figure 3.6 In a message diagram, the classes are depicted as boxes, and the lines and their directions depict the messages

A group of classes that provide a single functionality can also be grouped as a *subsystem*. For example, assume we produced a group of classes that, when used in unison, provide animation capability. An application that uses this (for example, a game) can view the entire collection of classes as a subsystem since the game does not care how all the classes interact to animate an object. Ideally, the game should be able to pass the object to the subsystem, and the object will be animated.

3.4.4 Hierarchy Graphs

A hierarchy graph shows the class hierarchy of the classes in an application

As an application tends to grow in complexity, so does the number of classes. To manage these classes and to determine their inheritance, use a *hierarchy graph*. Since the root class is always **Object**, include this at the top of the hierarchy. Figure 3.7 shows the hierarchy graph for the **ShapeArea** application.

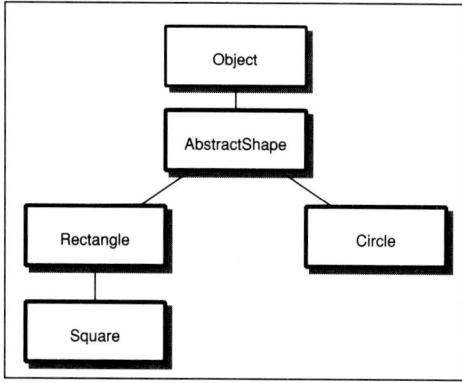

Figure 3.7 The **Object** class is always the root class of an Objective-C application

Now that we have covered the design techniques and the tools to document the design, we will actually implement the application.

3.5 Implementing ShapeArea

ShapeArea initially contains only four classes

ShapeArea initially contains only four classes: **AbstractShape**, **Rectangle**, **Square**, and **List**. To keep the task manageable, we will implement **ShapeArea** in three passes:

- in the first pass, we will implement the event processing loop in the **main()** function.
- in the second pass, we will implement the **Rectangle** class, add code which inserts the rectangles into the list and then traverses the list to calculate each rectangle's **area**.
- in the third pass, we will add the **Square** class. We leave the addition of the **Triangle** class and the **Circle** class as an exercise.

The classes will have only new instance methods (for initialization and for calculating the area) since they are already inheriting the class methods like **alloc** from the **Object** class.

This example illustrates:

- using object-oriented design techniques.
- creating and implementing custom classes
- adding classes to an application.
- freeing objects.

> Note that this application violates two fundamental concepts in NeXTSTEP:
>
> - instead of using the event-dispatching mechanism provided by NeXTSTEP (more specifically, the Application Kit), we are writing our own processing loop. This was done intentionally to illustrate how difficult it is to write an event processing loop even for a simple application. As we will learn in Chapter 4, it is trivial to use the event processing loop that is already in the Application Kit.
> - the user interface does not respond to mouse events. Again, the mouse support was intentionally omitted to illustrate how difficult it is to write even a simple user interface.
>
> In short, this application is written in Objective-C and does not implement the NeXTSTEP "look and feel." We will explore that topic more closely when we explore the Application Kit in Chapter 4.

Unlike **Sample** from Chapter 2, **ShapeArea** will involve many files since it is creating custom subclasses (recall that each class has two files, an interface file and an implementation file). As mentioned in Chapter 2, to keep all the files associated with a project manageable, create a separate folder for each project under the home directory. Name the folder after the name of the application. Thus, this folder would be named **~/ShapeArea**.

ShapeArea consists of many files

3.5.1 Implementation Pass I

In the first pass, implement only the event processing loop in the main program, **ShapeArea_main.m**.

Listing for **ShapeArea_main.m**

```
#import <appkit/appkit.h>

// a program that demonstrates dynamic binding

// function prototypes
void createObjects(void), run(void);
void calculateAreas(void), freeAll(void);
void main(void);
BOOL readInput(void);

// global variable
id theList;

void createObjects(void)
{
  // create list to hold shapes
  theList = [[List alloc] init];
}

void run(void)
{
  // stay in loop until Q is pressed
  BOOL done = NO;
  while (!done)
    {
    done = readInput();
    }
}

BOOL readInput(void)
{
  char inputString[10];
  unsigned int choice;
  float width, height;

  // print the menu
  printf("\nShapeArea calculates the ");
  printf("areas of various shapes\n");
```

```c
  printf("==============\n");
  printf("Select a shape\n");
  printf("Type Q to quit\n\n");
  printf("1 rectangle\n");
  printf("2 square\n");
  printf("==============\n");
  // get input
  scanf("%s", inputString);
  if (strcmp(inputString, "Q") != 0)
    {
    choice = atoi(inputString);
    switch (choice)
      {
      case 1:
        // get width and height
        printf("Enter the height\n");
        scanf("%f", &height);
        printf("Enter the width\n");
        scanf("%f", &width);
        // create rectangle and init it
        break;
      case 2:
        // get height for square
        printf("Enter the height\n");
        // since a square's height
        // is equal to its width,
        // get only one value
        scanf("%f", &height);
        // create square and init it
        break;
      default:
        // invalid choice
        printf("No such shape!\n");
        printf("Please try again!\n\n");
        break;
      }
    // return NO to stay in while loop
    // of run() function
    return NO;
    }
  else
    // return YES to abort while loop
    return YES;
}
```

```
void main(void)
{
  createObjects();
  run();
  exit(0);
}
```

Compile the main program as follows:

```
$ cc -c -g -o ShapeArea_main.o ShapeArea_main.m
$ cc -g -o ShapeArea ShapeArea_main.o -lNeXT_s
```

The new flag passed to **cc** (the C compiler) is:

- **-c**—compile the application only but do not link it with a library yet. If we don't use this flag, then **cc** will complain about unresolved references when we compile the main program (**ShapeArea_main.m**). We need to compile each source file into an object file and then link all the object files to form the executable.

Thus, the previous command basically:

- compiles the **ShapeArea_main.m** source file to create a **ShapeArea.o** object file.
- links the **ShapeArea_main.o** file to **NeXT_s** to form the final executable, **ShapeArea**.

> Note that the **Makefile** in Appendix E for **ShapeArea** assumes all three passes have been implemented. Thus, before we can use this **Makefile**, we have to implement all the classes and the main program.

Now execute the application:

Executing the **ShapeArea** application

```
$ ShapeArea

ShapeArea calculates the areas of various shapes
==============
Select a shape
```

```
Type Q to quit

1 rectangle
2 square
===============
```
1 *(Create a rectangle)*
```
Enter the height
```
5 *(Specify the height)*
```
Enter the width
```
4 *(Specify the width)*
```

ShapeArea calculates the areas of various shapes
==============
Select a shape
Type Q to quit

1 rectangle
2 square
===============
```
2 *(Create a square)*
```
Enter the height
```
5 *(Specify the height for the square)*
```

ShapeArea calculates the areas of various shapes
==============
Select a shape
Type Q to quit
```

```
1 rectangle
2 square
===============
```
Q *(Quit the application)*

Don't place **ShapeArea** in the background (with **&**) since the application is waiting for input from the keyboard. Doing so will produce the following message:

```
% ShapeArea &
[1] 647
%
ShapeArea calculates the areas of various shapes
===============
Select a shape
Type Q to quit

1 rectangle
2 square
===============
```
1 *(Create a rectangle)*
```
1: Command not found.
[1]    + Stopped (tty input)    ShapeArea
```

NeXTSTEP (more specifically, the C shell) is trying to interpret **1** as a command and issues an error. To rectify this, bring the application to the foreground using the **fg** command and then proceed as normal.

```
% fg
```

Now that we are finished with the application, let's examine it to see what we have implemented. Since **ShapeArea** will be using the methods defined in the **List** class, it needs to import the header file for the appropriate classes.

Importing the header files

```
#import <appkit/appkit.h>
```

The **<appkit/appkit.h>** file contains the method declarations for every class in NeXTSTEP including the **List** class. **ShapeArea** then declares the function prototypes for the functions. The function prototypes are as follows:

The function prototypes

```
// function prototypes
void createObjects(void), run(void);
void calculateAreas(void), freeAll(void);
void main(void);
BOOL readInput(void);
```

Function prototyping is used to declare:

- the type of a function's return value
- how many parameters the function expects, if any
- the type of each parameter, if the function expects one or more parameters.

The **void** keyword, depending on the context, means one of two things in function prototyping:

- **void** preceding the function name specifies that the function does not return a value.
- **void** in the parameter list specifies that the function does not expect any parameters.

Thus, **void main(void)** means that the **main()** function does not return a value, and it does not expect any parameters. Function prototyping allows the compiler to perform stricter type checking since it can compare the function's declaration (in the class' interface file) against the function's implementation (in the class' implementation file).

Instead of returning **void** like the other functions, **readInput()** returns a *Boolean* value, **YES** or **NO**.

> The **BOOL** type is newly defined under NeXTSTEP and is used when there are only two possible values for a return type, **YES** or **NO**. For example, the **isBordered** method of the **Button** class is a **Boolean** function since a button is either bordered (**YES**, it is covered with a border) or it is not (**NO**, it is not).

ShapeArea proceeds to declare a global variable, **theList**, which will contain the shapes during execution.

The global variable, **theList**

```
// global variable
id theList;
```

As mentioned previously, the starting point of execution for an Objective-C program is at the same point as that of a C program, namely the **main()** function:

The **main()** function

```
void main(void)
{
  createObjects();
  run();
  exit(0);
}
```

ShapeArea first calls the **createObjects()** function to create a list, which will be used to contain the shapes, and assigns the object a global variable, **theList**.

Creating a list to contain the object

```
void createObjects(void)
```

```
{
  // create list to hold shapes
  theList = [[List alloc] init];
}
```

ShapeArea then enters a loop in the **run()** function. The **run()** function repeatedly calls the **readInput()** function until the user types **Q** in **readInput()** to quit the application.

Reading the input

```
void run(void)
{
  // stay in loop until Q is pressed
  BOOL done = NO;
  while (!done)
    {
    done = readInput();
    }
}
```

In the **readInput()** function, the only valid input are:

- **1**—create a rectangle. The **readInput()** function then prompts for **height** and **width**.
- **2**—create a square. The **readInput()** function then prompts only for **height** since **width** will be the same value.
- **Q**—quit the application.

Although we can specify the dimensions for the shapes, we have not added the functionality to actually create the shapes and insert them into the list yet. That will be the purpose of the next pass.

> This may seem like a lot of work to produce such simple output. Fortunately, NeXTSTEP includes tools to facilitate this process, and the one we will be using the most is InterfaceBuilder. However, this example covers a lot of fundamental ideas we need to understand before we can learn InterfaceBuilder.

The second pass adds the AbstractShape and the Rectangle class

3.5.2 Implementation Pass II

At this point, we need to implement two more classes, **AbstractShape** and **Rectangle**. Why do we need to implement both classes? Because the main program uses **Rectangle**, and **Rectangle** inherits from **AbstractShape**. The changes we need to make are as follows:

- **#import** the header file for the **Rectangle** class because the main program (**ShapeArea_main.m**) uses this class. Since **ShapeArea_main.m** does not refer to **AbstractShape**, it does not need to **#import AbstractShape**'s header file.
- modify the **readInput()** function so that it actually creates the shapes and inserts them into the list.
- add a **calcAreas()** function that requests each shape to calculate its area.
- add a **freeAll()** function that frees all the shapes in the list and then frees the list itself.
- declare both functions as **void** since neither function returns any value.

First, add this statement after the **#import <appkit/appkit.h>** statement in **ShapeArea_main.m**.

Importing **Rectangle**'s *header file*

```
#import "Rectangle.h"
```

Now, modify the **readInput()** function in **ShapeArea_main.m** with the changes in bold:

A modified **readInput()** *function*

```
BOOL readInput(void)
{
  char inputString[10];
  unsigned int choice;
  float width, height;
  id object;
```

```
// print the menu
printf("\nShapeArea calculates the ");
printf("areas of various shapes\n");
printf("==============\n");
printf("Select a shape\n");
printf("Type Q to quit\n\n");
printf("1 rectangle\n");
printf("2 square\n");
printf("==============\n");
// get input
scanf("%s", inputString);
if (strcmp(inputString, "Q") != 0)
  {
  choice = atoi(inputString);
  switch (choice)
    {
    case 1:
      // get width and height
      printf("Enter the height\n");
      scanf("%f", &height);
      printf("Enter the width\n");
      scanf("%f", &width);
      // create rectangle and init it
      object = [[Rectangle alloc]
        initHeight:height
        width:width];
      // add rectangle to list
      [theList addObject:object];
      printf("The area of this shape is %.2f\n",
        [object calcArea]);
      break;
    case 2:
      // get height for square
      printf("Enter the height\n");
      // since a square's height
      // is equal to its width,
      // get only one value
      scanf("%f", &height);
      // create square and init it
      break;
    default:
      // invalid choice
      printf("No such shape!\n");
      printf("Please try again!\n\n");
      break;
```

```
            }
         // return NO to stay in while loop
         // of run() function
         return NO;
         }
      else
         // return YES to abort while loop
         return YES;
   }
```

Add the two new functions, **calculateAreas()** and **freeAll()**.

The calculateAreas() and freeAll() functions

```
void calculateAreas(void)
{
  int i;
  // traverse the list and request each
  // instance to perform its calcArea method
  // this demonstrates dynamic binding
  // since it impossible to determine
  // the class of each instance until runtime
  for (i=0; i < [theList count]; i++)
    {
    printf("\nThis shape is an instance of %s\n",
      [[theList objectAt:i] name]);
    printf("The area of this shape is %.2f\n",
      [[theList objectAt:i] calcArea]);
    }
}

void freeAll(void)
{
  // free the objects in the list
  // freeObjects sends a free message
  // to each object in the list
  [theList freeObjects];
  // free the list itself
  [theList free];
}
```

Declare both of these functions as **void** at the top of the main program as follows:

Declaring the **calculateAreas()** and **freeAll()** functions

```
// function prototypes
void createObjects(void), run(void);
void calculateAreas(void), freeAll(void);
void main(void);
BOOL readInput(void);
```

Modify the **main()** function so that it calls these two functions:

A modified **main()** function

```
void main(void)
{
  createObjects();
  run();
  calculateAreas();
  freeAll();
  exit(0);
}
```

At this point, implement **AbstractShape** by typing in **AbstractShape.h** and **AbstractShape.m**. Since this is an abstract superclass, it only declares instance variables and methods for its subclasses to inherit.

Listing for **AbstractShape.h**

```
#import <objc/Object.h>

@interface AbstractShape:Object
{
}

-(float)calcArea;

@end
```

Listing for **AbstractShape.m**

```
#import "AbstractShape.h"

@implementation AbstractShape

-(float)calcArea
{
}

@end
```

Now, type in **Rectangle.h** and **Rectangle.m** and save them.

Listing for **Rectangle.h**

```
#import "AbstractShape.h"

@interface Rectangle:AbstractShape
{
  float height;
  float width;
}

-initHeight:(float)h width:(float)w;
-(float)calcArea;
-free;

@end
```

Listing for **Rectangle.m**

```
#import "Rectangle.h"

@implementation Rectangle

-initHeight:(float)h width:(float)w
{
  [super init];
  height = h;
  width = w;
  return self;
```

```
}

-(float)calcArea
{
  return height * width;
}

-free
{
  return [super free];
}

@end
```

Compile the main program, the **AbstractShape** class, and the **Rectangle** class. Since we want to create all the object files and then link them together to form the executable, we must use the **-c** option, which tells **cc** to only compile and not link.

```
% cc -c -g -o ShapeArea_main.o ShapeArea_main.m
% cc -c -g -o AbstractShape.o AbstractShape.m
% cc -c -g -o Rectangle.o Rectangle.m
```

With all the object files created, link them together to form a single executable, **ShapeArea**:

```
% cc -g -o ShapeArea ShapeArea_main.o AbstractShape.o Rectangle.o -lNeXT_s
```

If everything proceeded perfectly, this command should link all the object files together and form a **ShapeArea** executable in the current directory. Execute the application by typing the following command. The sample session shows a 4 by 5 rectangle being created. Note that creating a square at this point is fairly pointless since we have not implemented the **Square** class yet.

Executing the **ShapeArea** application

```
$ ShapeArea

ShapeArea calculates the areas of various shapes
==============
Select a shape
Type Q to quit
```

```
1 rectangle
2 square
===============
1 (Create a rectangle)
Enter the height
4 (Specify the height)
Enter the width
5 (Specify the width)
The area of this shape is 20.00

ShapeArea calculates the areas of various shapes
===============
Select a shape
Type Q to quit

1 rectangle
2 square
===============
2 (Create a square)
Enter the height
8 (Nothing happens since the Square class is not implemented yet)

ShapeArea calculates the areas of various shapes
===============
Select a shape
Type Q to quit

1 rectangle
2 square
===============
Q (Quit the application)

This shape is an instance of Rectangle
The area of this shape is 20.00
```

In the **readInput()** function, the only valid input is **1** (create a rectangle), **2** (create a square), or **Q** (quit). If we specify a rectangle, **readInput()** then prompts for **height** and **width**. With these values, **readInput()** instantiates a rectangle and initializes it by sending it an **initHeight:width** message, as follows:

The initHeight:width method for the Rectangle class

```
-initHeight:(float)h width:(float)w
{
  [super init];
  height = h;
  width = w;
  return self;
}
```

The **readInput()** function then proceeds to add the rectangle to the list and prints the rectangle's **area** by sending it a **calcArea** message. Afterwards, **readInput()** returns **NO** to the **run()** method to indicate that the loop should continue. This cycle of fetching a rectangle, inserting it into a list, and printing the **area** continues until we press **Q**. At this point, **run()** exits from its loop, and **ShapeArea** calls the **calculateAreas()** function to traverse the list and calculate the area of each shape accordingly.

Calculating the areas of the shapes in the list

```
void calculateAreas(void)
{
  int i;
  // traverse the list and request each
  // instance to perform its calcArea method
  // this demonstrates dynamic binding
  // since it impossible to determine
  // the class of each instance until runtime
  for (i=0; i < [theList count]; i++)
    {
    printf("\nThis shape is an instance of %s\n",
       [[theList objectAt:i] name]);
    printf("The area of this shape is %.2f\n",
       [[theList objectAt:i] calcArea]);
    }
}
```

The **calculateAreas()** function demonstrates dynamic binding since it is impossible to determine the class of a shape at a given slot in the list until runtime. In this case, the point is moot since there is only one shape class, **Rectangle**. However, as we will see shortly, we won't have to modify **calculateAreas()** even if there are more shape classes.

To deallocate the memory used by the objects, **main()** calls the **freeAll()** function to free the objects which have been allocated. First, **freeAll()** sends a **freeObjects** message to **theList**. The **freeObjects** method then sends a **free** message to each object in the list. Afterwards, the **freeObjects** method returns to the **freeAll()** function, which frees the list itself.

Freeing all the shapes and the list

```
void freeAll(void)
{
  // free the objects in the list
  // freeObjects sends a free message
  // to each object in the list
  [theList freeObjects];
  // free the list itself
  [theList free];
}
```

Since the **Rectangle** class does not dynamically allocate any instance variables, it only needs to free itself and not the instance variables.

The **free** method for the **Rectangle** class

```
-free
{
  return [super free];
}
```

After **freeAll()** frees the contents of the list and the list, it returns to **main()**. At this point, **main()** then terminates the process with a return value of **0** to indicate a normal exit.

> Technically speaking, the **Rectangle** class (and the upcoming **Square** class) do not need to implement a **free** method since neither class defines any dynamic instance variables. We are implementing these methods as a matter of completeness since we may add dynamic instance variables in the future.

3.5.3 Implementation Pass III

With the base functionality implemented, add the **Square** class to the application. To differentiate this class from the **Rectangle** class, print out the dimensions (**height** and **width**) of each square and calculate its **area**. The easiest way to implement this is to override **calcArea** from the **Rectangle** class. The **calcArea** method of the **Square** class will:

The third pass adds the Square class

- print out each square's **height** and **width** by invoking its **printHeight** and **printWidth** methods. Since each square needs to invoke methods defined in its class, it uses the **self** keyword.
- use the **Rectangle** class' implementation to calculate the area by using the **super** keyword.

To implement these changes, modify the **readInput()** function of **ShapeArea_main.m** to support the **Square** class (the changes are in bold).

A modified readInput() function

```
BOOL readInput(void)
{
  char inputString[10];
  unsigned int choice;
  float width, height;
  id object;

  // print the menu
  printf("\nShapeArea calculates the ");
```

```
printf("areas of various shapes\n");
printf("===============\n");
printf("Select a shape\n");
printf("Type Q to quit\n\n");
printf("1 rectangle\n");
printf("2 square\n");
printf("===============\n");
// get input
scanf("%s", inputString);
if (strcmp(inputString, "Q") != 0)
  {
  choice = atoi(inputString);
  switch (choice)
    {
    case 1:
      // get width and height
      printf("Enter the height\n");
      scanf("%f", &height);
      printf("Enter the width\n");
      scanf("%f", &width);
      // create rectangle and init it
      object = [[Rectangle alloc]
        initHeight:height
        width:width];
      // add rectangle to list
      [theList addObject:object];
      printf("The area of this shape is %.2f\n",
        [object calcArea]);
      break;
    case 2:
      // get height for square
      printf("Enter the height\n");
      // since a square's height
      // is equal to its width,
      // get only one value
      scanf("%f", &height);
      // create square and init it
      object = [[Square alloc]
        initHeight:height
        width:height];
      // add square to list
      [theList addObject:object];
      printf("The area of this shape is %.2f\n",
        [object calcArea]);
      break;
```

```
      default:
        // invalid choice
        printf("No such shape!\n");
        printf("Please try again!\n\n");
        break;
      }
    // return NO to stay in while loop
    // of run() function
    return NO;
    }
  else
    // return YES to abort while loop
    return YES;
}
```

Add the following line after the **#import <appkit/appkit.h>** statement in **ShapeArea_main.m** to import the header file for the **Square** class:

Importing **Square**'s header file

```
# import "Square.h"
```

Implement the class files for the **Square** class:

Listing for **Square.h**

```
#import "Rectangle.h"

@interface Square:Rectangle
{
}

-(float)calcArea;
-printHeight;
-printWidth;
-free;

@end
```

Listing for **Square.m**

```
#import "Square.h"

@implementation Square

// override method to print the width and height
// as well as the area
-(float)calcArea
{
  // use self to refer to the same object
  // that received the calcArea method
  [self printHeight];
  [self printWidth];
  // use super to access the superclass'
  // implementation
  return [super calcArea];
}

-printHeight
{
  printf("The height is %.2f\n", height);
  return self;
}

-printWidth
{
  printf("The width is %.2f\n", width);
  return self;
}

-free
{
  return [super free];
}

@end
```

Recompile **ShapeArea_main.m** again to incorporate the additional functionality:

```
% cc -c -g -o ShapeArea_main.o ShapeArea_main.m
```

Compile the **Square** class to produce an object file:

```
% cc -c -g -o Square.o Square.m
```

Link the new class to produce a new executable:

```
% cc -g -o ShapeArea ShapeArea_main.o
AbstractShape.o Rectangle.o Square.o -lNeXT_s
```

Execute the program again to verify that it works (this session assumes that we create a 4 by 5 rectangle and a 6 by 6 square).

Executing the **ShapeArea** application

% **ShapeArea** *(Start the application)*

```
ShapeArea calculates the areas of various shapes
==============
Select a shape
Type Q to quit

1 rectangle
2 square
==============
```
1 *(Create a rectangle)*
```
Enter the height
```
4 *(Specify a height of 4)*
```
Enter the width
```
5 *(Specify a width of 5)*
```
The area of this shape is 20.00

ShapeArea calculates the areas of various shapes
==============
Select a shape
Type Q to quit

1 rectangle
2 square
==============
```
2 *(Create a square)*
```
Enter the height
```
6 *(Specify a height of 6)*
```
The height is 6.00
The width is 6.00
The area of this shape is 36.00

ShapeArea calculates the areas of various shapes
```

```
==============
Select a shape
Type Q to quit

1 rectangle
2 square
==============
```
Q *(Quit the application)*

```
This shape is an instance of Rectangle
The area of this shape is 20.00

This shape is an instance of Square
The height is 6.00
The width is 6.00
The area of this shape is 36.00
```

readInput() is an example of tight coupling and calcAreas() is an example of loose coupling

Notice that by using dynamic binding in **calcAreas()**, we avoid having to modify it to accommodate other shapes. With this design, we can add as many shape classes as we want, as long as each shape knows how to calculate its area. Compare the **calcAreas()** function with the **readInput()** function. The primary difference between these two functions is where the control decision is made. With **calcAreas()**, the control decision lies in the objects themselves (the list and its contents); with **readInput()**, the control decision lies in the function. Thus, **readInput()** has to be modified each time we add a new shape class. The **calcAreas()** function is an example of *loose coupling*, and the **readInput()** function is an example of *tight coupling*. Loose coupling is more flexible and facilitates code maintenance.

3.6 Common Pitfalls in OOD

There are a lot of pitfalls in object-oriented design

By now, we have covered the basics of object-oriented design. Although there is no standardized methodology for object-oriented design, there are pitfalls that should be avoided if possible, regardless of the methodology used. These traps include (at this point, we have to be more specific in our terminology, so we will differentiate between a class and its instances):

- an object directly modifying the instance variables of another object—this is commonly done in procedural programming, but it should be avoided in object-oriented programming since it violates encapsulation. If **thisObject** needs to modify **otherObject**'s instance variables, **thisObject** should send a message to **otherObject** requesting it to do so.
- a class that has too many responsibilities—the more responsibilities a class has, the more complete it is and ultimately, the less reusable it is. Remember that one of the themes of the object-oriented model is code reusability. A complex class is also much more difficult to debug than a simpler one.
- a class that has no responsibility—in an object-oriented system, every responsibility must be accounted for. If a class has no responsibility, it probably should not be an object because it is most likely an attribute of another object. For example, in the **ShapeArea** application in Chapter 2, area should not be an object since it has no function: it is simply an attribute of each of the shapes.
- two classes that have redundant responsibilities—if two classes have an identical responsibility, move the responsibility to the superclass, if possible. For example, in the **ShapeArea** application, the **calcArea** method was defined once in the **AbstractShape** class. Although each of the subclasses overrides this method, declaring **calcArea** once in the abstract superclass improves the design because we can then look exclusively at the **AbstractShape** class only to determine the framework of the application.
- a class that has a misleading name—this is a subtle problem since it is difficult to determine what is a good name. Consider naming the class after its functionality or its description. For example, the main classes in **ShapeArea** were named after the shapes (**Square**, **Circle**, etc.) and the **AbstractShape** was named after its functionality; the class served an as abstract superclass for the other shape classes.

3.7 Suggestions

Extend the **ShapeArea** application to add other shapes like triangles and circles. To do so, create two new classes, **Triangle** and **Circle**. In each class, define an appropriate designated initializer method.

For the **Triangle** class, name the designated initializer method **initBase:(float)b height:(float)h** or something similar since a triangle has a **base** and **height**. The area of a triangle is calculated as one-half the **base** times the **height**. For the **Circle** class, call the designated initializer method **initRadius:(float)r** or something similar. The area of a circle is defined as the **radius** squared times π.

When implementing each class, keep the following points in mind:

- compile each class without linking (use the **-c** option) or the linker will complain.
- once all the object files for the classes are created, link them to form the executable.

To keep the task manageable, add the first class and verify that it works before adding the second. Also, consider rewriting the **readInput()** function so it uses dynamic binding. In this case, each type of shape would need a **readInput** method to prompt for the appropriate input. **ShapeArea** would then be able to accommodate as many shapes as needed without requiring us to modify **ShapeArea_main.m**.

3.8 Summary

In this chapter, we explored another stage in developing an application, object-oriented design. This technique consists of the following activities:

- identifying the objects
- determining what each object does
- establishing the relationships between the objects

- modeling the flow of the application.

We rarely perform these activities in a completely linear manner since many decisions at a current activity depend on decisions that can only be made in a later activity. Object-oriented design is quite powerful and is often used for rapid prototyping.

To aid us during the object-oriented design stage, we introduced four tools: CRC cards, class summary tables, message diagrams, and hierarchy graphs. Each of these tools allows us to view the design from a different perspective.

With this background in Objective-C and object-oriented design, we are ready to proceed to the Application Kit, the predefined collection of classes in NeXTSTEP.

Summary

Chapter 4
The Application Kit

This chapter introduces the Application Kit, a collection of more than fifty classes bundled with the NeXTSTEP environment and the Common Classes. Since these classes provide a framework common to all applications such as drawing to the screen, processing events, and displaying windows, we need only to write code that is unique to our application. Before we can program effectively in NeXTSTEP, we must learn some of the classes in the Application Kit and their characteristics. We will not cover every one of the classes because the majority of them are derived from a few abstract superclasses.

The Application Kit includes more than fifty classes

Once we have covered some of the fundamental classes, we will implement a minimal application that displays a window along with a **Quit** option in a menu. The application is barely functional, but it illustrates the basic framework of a NeXTSTEP application and points out the differences between an Objective-C application and a NeXTSTEP application.

4.1 Goals

In this chapter, we will:

- describe the Application Kit and the Common Classes.
- describe the general framework of a NeXTSTEP application.
- list the minimal requirements of a NeXTSTEP application.

4.2 The Application Kit Classes

NeXTSTEP includes a library of more than fifty classes, collectively called the *Application Kit* (AppKit for short). Most of what we see on the screen is created from the Application Kit: this includes the windows and menus of each application, the text inside a word processor or a spreadsheet, the panels, etc.

Most of the classes in the AppKit provide support for building interfaces

Most of the Application Kit classes provide support for implementing a user interface and dealing with user input. Some examples of these classes include: **Button**, **View**, **Window**, **Menu**, etc. NeXTSTEP also includes another collection of classes that provide more general functionality such as storage and memory allocation: these classes are called the *Common Classes*, and we will discuss them in further detail in the next section. Rather than cover every class in the hierarchy, we will limit ourselves to the classes we will be using the most. Figure 4.1 shows the major classes in the Application Kit.

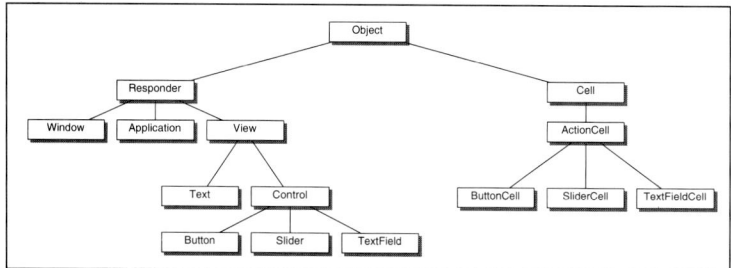

Figure 4.1 The major classes in the Application Kit

To see the entire Application Kit hierarchy, consult
**/NextLibrary/Documentation/NextDev/GeneralRef/
02_ApplicationKit/IntroAppKit.rtfd**

Starting at the top, the list of classes which we will cover include:

- **Object**—an abstract superclass that is the root of both the Common Classes and the Application Kit. Among other things, the **Object** class defines methods for allocating and freeing objects.
  - **Cell**—an abstract superclass that provides methods for displaying text and icons. A cell often works with a control (see the upcoming **Control** class for more details) to provide user interface objects.
    - **ActionCell**—another abstract superclass that defines a framework for processing events. This class defines many subclasses:

- **ButtonCell**—this class works with the **Button** class to provide the functionality of a button.
- **SliderCell**—this class works with the **Slider** class to provide the functionality of a slider.
- **TextFieldCell**—this class works with the **TextField** class to provide the functionality of a textfield.

• **Responder**—an abstract superclass with methods to interpret user events such as mouse and keyboard events. The events are dispatched and processed in a particular order: this is the subject of Chapter 6.

- **Application**—this class provides the framework for a NeXTSTEP application. Every NeXTSTEP application must have an application object to connect to the Window Server. Through this connection, the application can receive events and draw to the screen. The application object also maintains a list of the windows that belong to the application.
- **Window**—the **Window** class defines objects that can contain other objects (such as buttons and sliders) and can draw to the screen (the class is much more complex than this, but this is enough for now). Among other things, each window maintains a hierarchy of views and defines a delegate that can extend the functionality without subclassing. Delegates are further explored in Chapter 6 along with event processing.
- **View**—an abstract superclass that defines a framework for drawing to the screen. The **View** class is further explored in Chapter 7. Most of the classes we will encounter are subclasses of **View**.
  - **Text**—this subclass of **View** defines all of the functionality which we are likely to need for text processing. If fact, we can easily write a simple word processor by instantiating the **Text** class, as we will see in Chapter 9.
  - **Control**—an abstract class that works with the **Cell** subclasses to provide user interface objects such as

buttons. Controls are explored more closely in Chapter 6. Some examples of controls include:

- **Button**—provides an object that sends the action message to a target each time the button is pressed.
- **Slider**—provides an object with a sliding knob that sends an action message when the knob is moved.
- **TextField**—provides an object that allows us to enter or display a single value.

> Since a subclass inherits the behavior of its superclass, the instance of the subclass can also be thought of as an instance of the superclass. For example, a button is also a control because **Button** inherits from **Control**.
>
> For more information on these and other classes, use the HeaderViewer and Digital Librarian applications as explained in Appendix B.

4.3 The Common Classes

The classes in the Common Classes provide support for tasks not related to the user interface such as memory allocation

While the Application Kit provides classes to implement a user interface, the *Common Classes* provide classes for other tasks such as memory allocation, instance initialization, etc. These classes include the **Object** class, the abstract superclass from which all other classes are derived. This section briefly describes some of the Common Classes we will be using. Figure 4.2 shows the hierarchy for the entire Common Classes hierarchy.

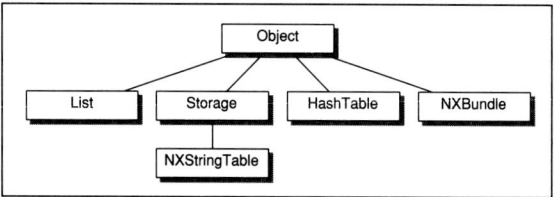

Figure 4.2 The Common Classes hierarchy

We will concentrate on the following two classes:

- **Object**—an abstract superclass that is the root of both the Common Classes and the Application Kit. Among other things, the **Object** class defines methods for allocating and freeing memory for objects.
- **List**—a miscellaneous class that can store other objects. For example, every application maintains a list that contains the **id**'s of the windows for which the application is responsible.

4.4 A NeXTSTEP Application vs. an Objective-C Application

We can write an entire application without using the Application Kit. Although the application would be functional, it would be an Objective-C application rather than a NeXTSTEP application. Consider the **ShapeArea** example. Although this application is fully functional, it is not a NeXTSTEP application because:

ShapeArea is not a NeXTSTEP application

- it did not use the Application Kit and therefore did not have a mouse-driven interface from which we can make selections. An application needs to follow certain guidelines before it can be considered a NeXTSTEP application: one of the requirements is a **Quit** option.

> An easy test to determine whether the application is a NeXTSTEP application (one conforming to the NeXTSTEP user interface guidelines) is to ask the following question: can all the features of the applications be accessible from the keyboard? If so, the application is probably not a NeXTSTEP application: applications that don't use the mouse tend to be menu-driven (from the keyboard) like **ShapeArea**. Note that terminal emulators such as Terminal, are an exception to this test because the entire purpose of terminal emulators is to allow us to type commands to the system. The UNIX utilities that are accessible from Terminal such as **vi**, **emacs**, are definitely not NeXTSTEP applications. We will discuss this topic more thoroughly in Chapter 6.

- it did not use an application object to establish a connection to the Window Server to receive events from the mouse and to draw to the screen. Recall that **ShapeArea** does not perform any drawing to the screen nor is it mouse driven.

From this point on, we will be writing applications that conform to the NeXTSTEP user interface guidelines.

4.5 A Minimal NeXTSTEP Application

To explore the differences between an Objective-C application and a NeXTSTEP application, we will use the Application Kit to implement a minimal NeXTSTEP application, **AppKitDemo**. The specification is as follows:

> Upon start-up, **AppKitDemo** *displays* a **window** and a **menu** with a **Quit option**. Using the **mouse**, the **user** can *move* the window or menu. The user can *miniaturize* the window by *clicking* on its **miniaturize button**. The window and menu display until the user clicks the Quit option

at which point the **application** *terminates* and *removes* the window and menu from the **screen**.

4.5.1 Design

The candidate objects are as follows:

- AppKitDemo—the name of the application and therefore not an object.
- window—the window object provided by the Application Kit.
- menu—the menu object provided by the Application Kit.
- Quit option—a menu option, actually a separate object, but we will consider it part of the menu for simplicity.
- mouse—a hardware object that does not belong in the software model.
- user—does not need to be modeled.
- miniaturize button—a component internal to the window object that does not need to be considered.
- application—the application object, also provided by the Application Kit.
- screen—a hardware object that does not belong in the software model.

The list of actions include:

- display—the window and menu perform this action.
- move—the window performs this by redrawing itself.
- miniaturize—the window performs this by redrawing itself.
- click—this does not need to be simulated because it is the start of every user action.
- terminate—the application performs this function and in turn removes all the objects (the menu and the window) from the screen.
- remove—see above.

There are three main classes for this application: **Menu**, **Window**, and **Application**. Consider the **Menu** class. It has two primary responsibilities: displaying itself and terminating the application

There are three main classes in AppKitDemo

when the **Quit** option is selected. The menu can display itself without any help, but in order to terminate the application, the menu object needs to send a **terminate:** message to the **Application** class. Hence the **Application** class is a collaborator of the **Menu** class. Figure 4.3 shows the CRC card for the **Menu** class.

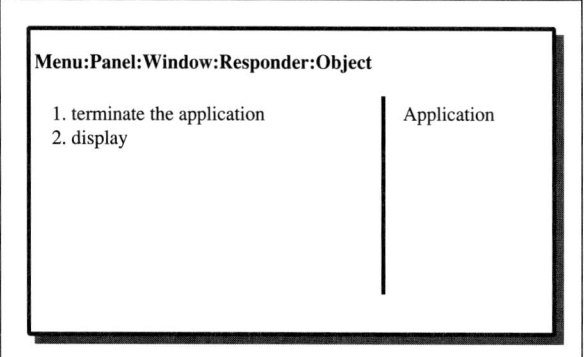

Figure 4.3 The CRC card for the **Menu** class

We are intentionally omitting messages which are needed to create the objects such as references to the **alloc** message. Why? Because we must assume that these objects exist, or we would not be able to message them.

Additionally, every NeXTSTEP application includes instances from two other classes, **Speaker** and **Listener**. These classes allow an application to send and receive messages from other applications. However, since we will not be doing this, we can ignore these classes.

The **Window** class needs to move, display, and miniaturize itself; it can perform these responsibilities on its own and therefore, it has no collaborators. Figure 4.4 shows the CRC card for the **Window** class.

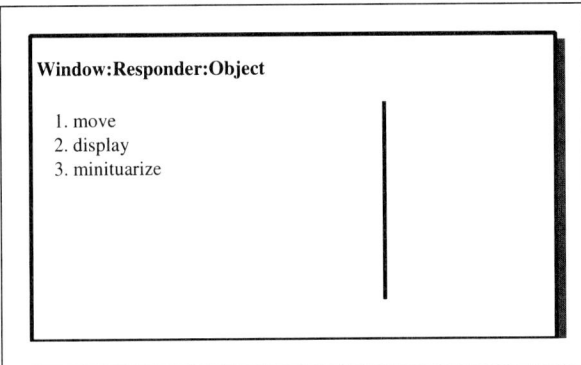

Figure 4.4 The CRC card for the **Window** class

The responsibilities of the **Application** class include retrieving/dispatching events and setting a menu for the application. The **Application** class can perform the first responsibility by itself but it needs the help of the **Menu** class for the second. Figure 4.5 shows the CRC card for the **Application** class.

The Application class collaborates with the Menu class to display the menu

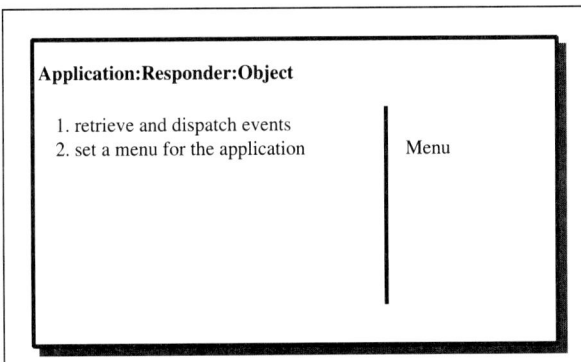

Figure 4.5 The CRC card for the **Application** class

From this point on, we will consider **Window**, **Application**, and **Menu** to be *core classes*: that is, they are assumed to exist in every application. Therefore, we will not prepare CRC cards for them in the succeeding applications unless other objects specifically message them.

Window, Application, and Menu are considered core classes

Now that we have prepared the CRC cards, we need to consider the relationships between the objects in the application. The ideas are introduced here but they will be covered in more detail in Chapter 6.

The miniaturize button sends a miniaturize: message to its window

When we click on the miniaturize button, it sends a **miniaturize:** message to the window. However, since this relationship is private to the window—the miniaturize button, if present, is an integral part of the window—we do not need to consider it. The other relationship is between the menu option and the application object. When we click on the **Quit** menu option, it sends a **terminate:** message to the application. This effectively terminates the application and removes the window and menu from the screen.

Instantiating the Application class creates a connection to the Window Sever

Now consider the flow of the application. The **main**() function first instantiates **Window**, **Menu**, and **Application**. To create a connection to the Window Server, **main**() instantiates the **Application** class. Once the application object exists, it needs a designated menu. To associate a menu with the application, the application object sends a **setMainMenu:** method to the menu object. The **setMainMenu:** method automatically displays the menu.

main() sends makeKeyAndOrderFront: to the window to display it

In order to display the window, **main**() explicitly sends the window a **makeKeyAndOrderFront:** message that brings the window to the front of other windows to receive events. Once the window and menu are displayed, the application needs to retrieve events. To do this, **main**() sends a **run** message to the application object, which starts the application object's main event loop. This loop continues until the application receives a **terminate**: message (which is sent when we click on the **Quit** menu option).

The application only receives the events it asks for

The Window Server forwards each event to our application, and the application processes only the events that it is interested in. By default, every window (and menu, since the **Menu** class inherits from the **Window** class) can respond to move-related events. Therefore, we do not need to write any code to move the window. To make the window respond to miniaturize events, we must create the window with a miniaturize button; this will be specified as a parameter when we create the window.

As the final step, **main()** creates the **Quit** menu option and then specifies that, when clicked, it should send a **terminate:** message to **NXApp**. Afterwards, **main()** resizes the menu with a **sizeToFit** method to accommodate the new menu item after inserting it. The relationship between the application and the menu option is established when the menu is created with the **addItem:action:keyEquivalent:** method.

> **There is a relationship between the Quit menu option and NXApp**

With the design completed, we need to prepare the class summary tables. Table 4.1 shows the class summary table for the **Menu** class. Since every class in the Application Kit contains too many instance variables and methods to document in the class summary table, we only document those instance variables and methods used in our application.

	Menu:Panel:Window:Responder:Object	
	Name	**Description**
Instance Variables	N/A	N/A
Methods	addItem:(const char*)aString action:(SEL)aSelector keyEquivalent:(unsigned short)charCode	adds a menucell with the specified string, action, and key equivalent
	sizeToFit	resizes and displays the menu to accommodate the menu entries

Table 4.1 Class summary table for the **Menu** class

Table 4.2 shows the class summary table for the **Window** class.

Window:Responder:Object		
	Name	**Description**
Instance Variables	N/A	N/A
Methods	initContent:(const NXRect*)contentRect style:(int)aStyle backing:(int)backingType buttonMask:(int)mask defer:(BOOL)flag	initializes the window with the specified size, style, backing store, buttonmask, and defer style. The *defer* flag specifies whether to immediately create a window device to correspond to the window object
	makeKeyAndOrderFront:sender	orders the window to the front and displays it

Table 4.2 Class summary table for the **Window** class

Table 4.3 shows the class summary table for the **Application** class.

Application:Responder:Object		
	Name	**Description**
Instance Variables	N/A	N/A
Methods	run	places the application in an polling loop and starts receiving events
	terminate:sender	terminates the application and frees the application object

Table 4.3 Class summary table for the **Application** class

Figure 4.6 shows the message diagram for **AppKitDemo**. Note that since **main()** is not really an object, we use a circle instead of a box.

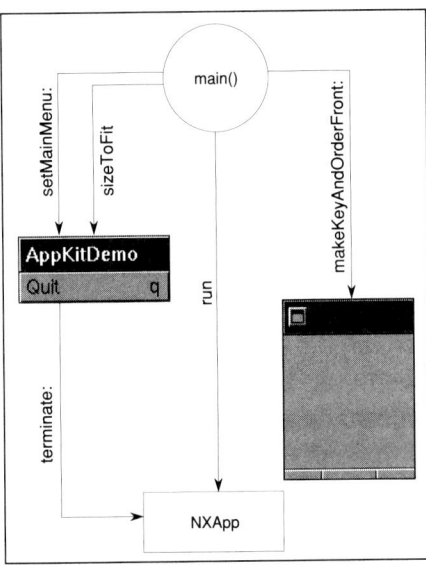

Figure 4.6 The message diagram for **AppKitDemo**

Again, we will be implementing the application in more than one pass. We will first display a window, and then we will add a menu with a **Quit** option.

> Note that we have to include **main()** in our message diagram since it creates the objects. However, as we will see in Chapter 5, these core classes are instantiated and initialized in the **.nib** (NeXTSTEP InterfaceBuilder) file.

4.5.2 Implementation Pass I: Displaying a Window

The first thing we need to do is type in the main program, **AppKitDemo.m**.

Implementation Pass I: Displaying a Window

Listing for **AppKitDemo.m**

```objc
#import <appkit/appkit.h>

// a program to demonstrate how to display
// a window and a menu with a Quit option

void main(void)
{
    // create an application object
    // to establish connection to
    // Window Server
    id NXApp = [Application new];
    id theWindow;

    // create buffered window at default
    // location with minituarize button
    // and title bar
    theWindow = [ [Window alloc]
      initContent:NULL
      style: NX_RESIZEBARSTYLE
      backing:NX_BUFFERED
      buttonMask:NX_MINIATURIZEBUTTONMASK
      defer:YES];

    // send the window to the front
    // and display it
    [theWindow makeKeyAndOrderFront:nil];
```

```
    // go into event loop to wait for events
    [NXApp run];
}
```

> Using **<appkit/appkit.h>** to import the AppKit method declarations is more efficient than individually importing each header file. Why? Because the NeXTSTEP C compiler will use the precompiled version of **appkit.h**, **appkit.p**, which results in shorter compilation time; there are equivalent precompiled version of the individual header files.
>
> Do not attempt to import the **.p** version of any header file. Import the **.h** file as normal and the C compiler will automatically use the precompiled version if one exists.

Note that this **main**() function is completely nonstandard in that it creates and initializes objects. Once we start using ProjectBuilder and InterfaceBuilder to create our application, we will see that the objects are created in the main **.nib** file instead. In other words, we are writing the **main**() function in this manner as a learning exercise.

Create a new folder, **~/AppKitDemo** and save **AppKitDemo.m** in this folder. Since this program is self-contained, we can compile and produce the executable directly without first having to produce an object file. We need to link the application to the standard NeXT library, **NeXT_s**, to produce an executable.

```
% cc -o AppKitDemo AppKitDemo.m -lNeXT_s
% AppKitDemo
```

Figure 4.7 shows the output of **AppKitDemo**, namely a small window with a blank title bar, a miniaturize button, and a resize bar.

Figure 4.7 **AppKitDemo** in execution

Although we implemented only the code needed to create the window, the window redraws itself when moved because that functionality is part of the **Window** class. However, there is a slight problem: there is no graceful way of exiting our program! The only way to terminate the application is to:

- press **Control-z** (in the Terminal shell which we started **AppKitDemo**) to suspend the application; this returns the control of the keyboard to us so we can type the next command. The system will assign a job number to the suspended application, which should be **1**.

- use the **kill** command with the job number: **kill %1**. This is **csh**'s syntax for killing the first suspended job.

We will add the menu a little later, but for now, let's explore the code:

- **#import <appkit/appkit.h>**—imports the method declarations for all of the methods in the Application Kit.

- **id NXApp = [Application new]**—instantiates the **Application** class and assigns it to **NXApp**. By convention, **NXApp** refers to the application object.

- **id theWindow**—declares an **id** variable, **theWindow**.

- **theWindow = [[Window alloc] initContent:NULL style:NX_RESIZEBARSTYLE backing:NX_BUFFERED buttonMask:NX_MINIATURIZEBUTTONMASK**

defer:YES];—instantiates the **Window** class and then initializes the instance. The designated initialization method for a window instance is **initContent:style:backing:buttonMask:defer:** method instead of the standard **init** method. This message basically initializes the window instance to:

- be initialized with a default size (the **NULL** argument).
- have a particular window decoration (a title bar, a miniaturize button, and a resize bar).
- be buffered.
- be deferred.

The method returns a window instance, which is then assigned to **theWindow** variable.

> There are basically three types of windows: nonretained, retained, and buffered. In this case, we created a buffered window because we want it to be able to redisplay itself properly, even when we move another window on top of it. We will explore window buffering more closely in Chapter 7.
>
> We can also specify whether the Window Server should immediately create a corresponding window object to associate with the window instance we have just created. A window is actually composed of two parts: the window object and the window device. The Window Server produces a window object, which is done at the Mach level. The window that is displayed on the screen is simply a high-level interface to the Mach window object; the window that is drawn on the screen is often referred to as the *window device* to differentiate it from the Mach window object. In most cases, we use the term *window* to refer to both the window device and the Mach window since there is usually a one-to-one correspondence.
>
> Thus, the **defer** flag specifies whether the Window Server should immediately create a window device to associate with the Mach window. Deferring this creation can improve resource management since the Window Server does not need to allocate memory for the window device until it is actually displayed on the screen through one of the AppKit methods such as **makeKeyAndOrderFront:**.

- **[theWindow makeKeyAndOrderFront:nil];**—under most circumstances, a window is created offscreen. To display the window, we need to tell it to arrange itself in the window list; this list controls which windows are visible. The **makeKeyAndOrderFront:** method makes the window the *key window*, the window that will receive all keystrokes. In this case, that is beside the point because we didn't allow any provision for typing. Since we do not care what the parameter to the **makeKeyAndOrderFront:** method is, we use **nil**. The **nil** keyword is used here as place holder for the parameter to the **makeKeyAndOrderFront:** method because the method is expecting a parameter (notice the colon). By passing **nil**, we are indicating that we do not care what the value of the parameter is.

> At the lowest level, **nil** is **0x0**. We can verify this later when we use **gdb** in Appendix D.

- **[NXApp run];**—initiates the main loop for the application object. At this point, the system goes into a loop and polls for events. The Window Server routes events to the application object, **NXApp**, and **NXApp** then routes the event to the appropriate window. We will explore event processing more closely in Chapter 6.

> Sending an **orderFront:** message results in a **display** message sent to the window; the **display** method is what actually draws the window (and its contents) to the screen. We will explore the **display** method more closely in Chapter 7.

4.5.3 Implementation Pass II: Adding a Quit Menu Option

We will now implement a menu with one option, **Quit**, to allow us to quit gracefully. The changes are in bold:

Listing for **AppKitDemo.m**

```
#import <appkit/appkit.h>

// a program to demonstrate how to display
// a window and a menu with a Quit option

void main(void)
{
   // create an application object
   // to establish connection to
```

Implementation Pass II: Adding a Quit Menu Option

```
    // Window Server
    id NXApp = [Application new];
    id theWindow;
    id theMenu;
    id theMenuCell;

    // create buffered window at default
    // location with minituarize button
    // and title bar
    theWindow = [ [Window alloc]
      initContent:NULL
      style: NX_RESIZEBARSTYLE
      backing:NX_BUFFERED
      buttonMask:NX_MINIATURIZEBUTTONMASK
      defer:YES];

    // create the menu
    theMenu = [ [Menu alloc]
      initTitle: "AppKitDemo"];
    // create the menu option
    theMenuCell = [theMenu addItem:"Quit"
      action:@selector(terminate:)
      keyEquivalent:'q'];
    // set NXApp as target of the menucell
    [theMenuCell setTarget:NXApp];

    // resize menu to accomodate menu option
    [theMenu sizeToFit];
    [NXApp setMainMenu:theMenu];

    // send the window to the front
    // and display it
    [theWindow makeKeyAndOrderFront:nil];

    // go into event loop to wait for events
    [NXApp run];
}
```

Compile the program again and run it:

```
% cc -o AppKitDemo AppKitDemo.m -lNeXT_s
% AppKitDemo
```

Figure 4.8 shows **AppKitDemo** during execution. This time, **AppKitDemo** should have a menu with a **Quit** option, and the menu should be located in the upper left-hand corner of the screen, the default location for an application's Main Menu. Move the window around, and quit the application (by clicking **Quit**) after verifying that it works. Figure 4.8 illustrates **AppKitDemo** with the **Quit** menu option.

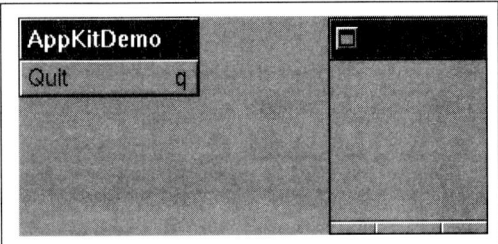

Figure 4.8 **AppKitDemo** with a **Quit** option

Let's look at the changes to the program:

- **theMenu = [[Menu alloc] initTitle:"AppKitDemo"];**—instantiates the **Menu** class and initializes its title to **AppKitDemo**.
- **theMenuCell = [theMenu addItem:"Quit" action:@selector(terminate:) keyEquivalent:'q'];**—a menu is composed of menu options (menucells), and each menu item has an action it sends to another object when the menu option is selected. This line adds a **Quit** option and specifies that it should send the **terminate:** message and to use **Command-q** as the keyboard alternative (this is standard for NeXTSTEP applications). Note that the method expects the character **q** as a parameter, not **Command-q**. This method returns a menucell, which we save in **theMenuCell** so that we can refer to it later.
- **[theMenuCell setTarget:NXApp]**—after specifying the method, we must specify the *target*, the object the menucell should send its message to. In this case, we want **NXApp** to

receive the **terminate:** message. We will explore targets more in Chapter 6 when we explore controls.

> Objective-C uses the term *selector* to refer to the method in the message expression. This term is derived from the implementation of Objective-C's message dispatch architecture, which uses the encoded method name to index a table containing the methods which a class understands. Since comparing two strings would dramatically degrade the performance, Objective-C encodes each method name into an **unsigned int** and uses the number instead. These **unsigned int**s have been typecast to **SEL** to differentiate them from other **unsigned int**s.
>
> Since a **SEL** is associated with a method name during execution, do not manually calculate the number. Instead, use the **@selector** directive to convert a method name to a **SEL** such as in the **[addItem:"Quit" action:@selector(terminate:) keyEquivalent:'q']** message expression.

- **[theMenu sizeToFit];**—adjusts the menu's size to accommodate the menu commands and automatically redisplays the menu.
- **[NXApp setMainMenu:theMenu];**—sets this menu to be the Main Menu of the application.

As before, the application polls events until it receives a **terminate:** message, which is triggered when we click on the **Quit** menu option.

> How did the menu display itself though we never requested it to? Displaying the Main Menu and "torn" submenus (submenus separated from their parent menus) is one of the many responsibilities automatically handled by **NXApp**.

Voilà! We have finished our first NeXTSTEP application. Even though this application has only one menu option, it demonstrates the framework for every NeXTSTEP application: creating an application object, creating a menu, and processing events as they come in until the **Quit** option is selected. Aside from instantiating the appropriate classes, we did not implement much other functionality since these classes already define the program framework. We purposely skipped over a few concepts such as event processing and drawing because these topics will be explored in greater detail in Chapter 6 and Chapter 7, respectively.

4.6 Suggestions

Consider extending the application in the following ways:

- adding a **Hide** option with **addItem:action:keyEquivalent:**— every NeXTSTEP application should also have a **Hide** menu option that sends a **hide:** message to **NXApp** (the keyboard alternative for **Hide** is **Command-h**).
- setting the title of the menu to the name of the application— **AppKitDemo** now currently hardcodes the title of the menu to **AppKitDemo**. A better solution is to determine the name of the application by using **[NXApp appName]** and then passing this as the parameter to **initTitle**.

4.7 Summary

In this chapter, we learned the major classes in the two main collections of classes, the Application Kit and the Common Classes. These classes provide the basic functionality that are common to all applications such as establishing a connection to the Window Server, processing events, drawing to the screen, and allocating memory. By using these classes, we can reduce the efforts required to implement an application and we can ensure user interface consistency.

We also covered some of the differences between an Objective-C application and a NeXTSTEP application: a NeXTSTEP application must have an application object to connect to the Window Server. With this connection, an application can draw to the screen and receive events from the Window Server.

Summary

We are now ready to proceed to Chapter 5 and discuss ProjectBuilder, a tool for project management, and InterfaceBuilder, a tool for implementing and testing interfaces.

Chapter 5
ProjectBuilder and InterfaceBuilder

Until now, we have been implementing applications completely in Objective-C without any regard for user interface design. In practice, however, we would go over several iterations before deciding on an acceptable interface. This iterative process can be time-consuming without the aid of a tool. InterfaceBuilder is such a tool because it allows us to graphically create and test the interface of the application without compilation. InterfaceBuilder was deferred until this point because without some understanding of Objective-C, we can never appreciate (or understand) what InterfaceBuilder is really capable of or what it is actually doing when we are using it.

So far, the user interfaces have been designed in an ad hoc manner

InterfaceBuilder provides several default windows (or, more specifically palettes) containing many of the user interface classes in the Application Kit. To add an instance to our application, we simply drag the appropriate object from the palette. To edit the object, we use an Inspector panel to edit the object's instance variables.

InterfaceBuilder allows us to graphically construct user interfaces

Initially, InterfaceBuilder may seem to be just another prototyping tool that is common in most other environments. However, it is more than just a prototyping tool since we do not discard the prototype (as with other tools) but build on it to produce our final application. However, keep in mind that while InterfaceBuilder is a powerful tool, it is ultimately used only to create interfaces. If we need to perform some calculation such as determining the area of a shape, we still need to write the appropriate code.

InterfaceBuilder is much more than a prototyping tool

As we have already seen, even the most basic NeXTSTEP application involves several files. To manage these files, we can use ProjectBuilder. Among other things, ProjectBuilder:

• writes and maintains the **Makefile**.
• writes and maintains the main program.

- creates a project file (**PB.project**) that stores all of the filenames associated with a project.
- compiles and debugs the application.

In this chapter, we will explore how InterfaceBuilder and ProjectBuilder fit into the NeXTSTEP development cycle by implementing an extended version of the **AppKitDemo** application from Chapter 4.

> ProjectBuilder does not contain the functionality for compiling and debugging the application. It is simply an interface to the Objective-C compiler (**cc**) and the GNU debugger (**gdb**). However, we will ignore this distinction in most of our discussions.

5.1 Goals

In this chapter, we will:

- explore how ProjectBuilder and InterfaceBuilder fit in the development cycle.
- demonstrate how to use ProjectBuilder for project management.
- demonstrate how to use InterfaceBuilder to create and test interfaces.
- explain how to compile applications from ProjectBuilder.

5.2 The Development Cycle

Since the interfaces for the applications we have written so far have been fairly trivial, we implemented these interfaces in an ad hoc manner. At this point, however, we need to explore how the interface fits into the NeXTSTEP development cycle, which includes the following major steps:

- creating a new project
- designing the classes
- designing the interface

- implementing the application
- debugging the application.

We have already covered the second step, designing classes. As we saw in Chapter 2, designing classes is composed of several substeps such as determining the objects from the specifications, determining the relationships of the objects, etc. We will concentrate on the third step, designing the interface, in this chapter, and we will cover the fourth and fifth steps in succeeding chapters. Figure 5.1 illustrates the steps in the development cycle.

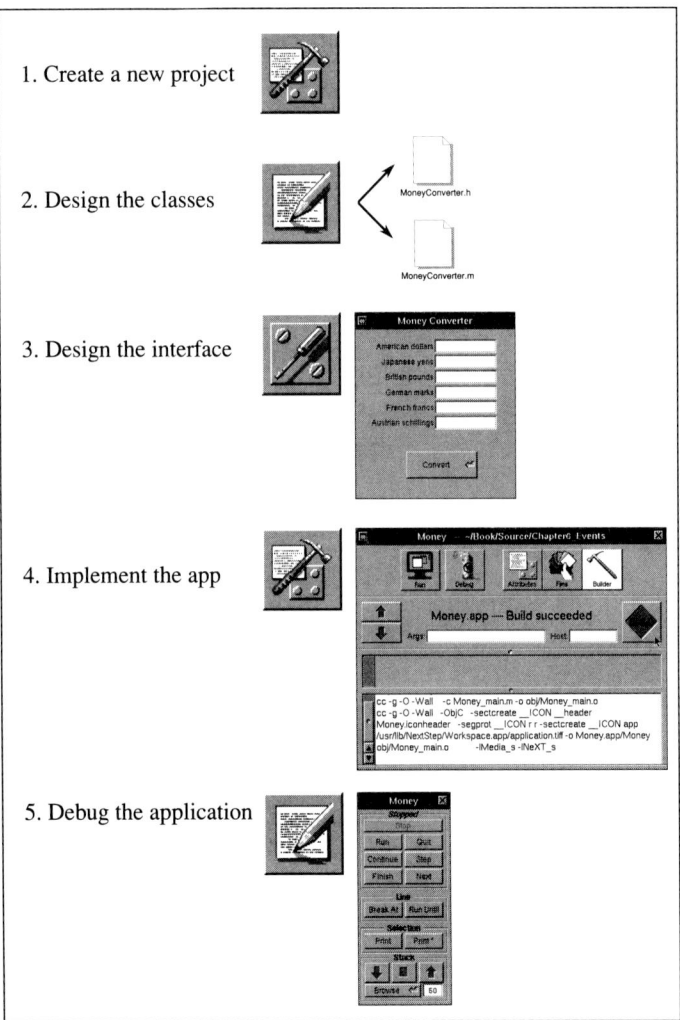

Figure 5.1 The NeXTSTEP development cycle

We will use ProjectBuilder and InterfaceBuilder to implement the **AppKitDemo** application from Chapter 4. We will add to the application a menu option to redisplay the window (we can close it through the close button) and an Info panel to preserve our name for posterity.

Since this chapter concentrates more on getting started in InterfaceBuilder and ProjectBuilder than on building an application, we will forego designing the application. Instead, we will illustrate the most common commands in the two tools.

5.2.1 Starting a Project

Always store a project in a separate folder

As previously mentioned, an application usually consists of several files (icons, classes, images, etc.), and each application is considered a project. ProjectBuilder saves this project information in a project file, **PB.project**. Since the project file is always named **PB.project**, ProjectBuilder cannot store two projects in the same folder without erasing the already existing copy. Therefore, as we recommended in Chapter 2, *always store each project in a separate folder*.

To create a new project, click on **Project ⇒ New**. This produces an openpanel to request a location where ProjectBuilder should store the project file. The exact location does not matter, as long as it is a directory since this helps localize the application. For now, save the project as **~/IBDemo/IBDemo**. Click **OK** to create the new path, as needed. Figure 5.2 illustrates this sequence.

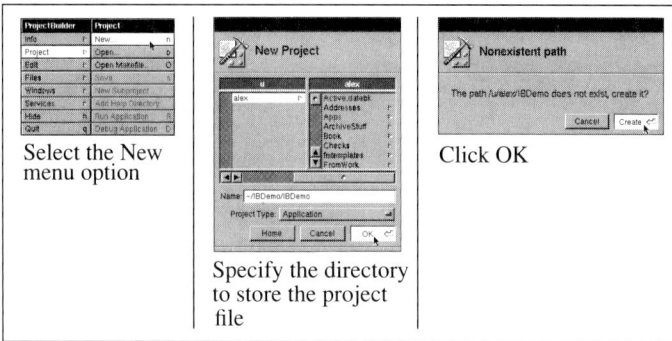

Figure 5.2 Creating a new project with ProjectBuilder

In addition to creating a project, ProjectBuilder can also create a bundle or a palette. However, we will not explore these two topics.

After saving the project file, ProjectBuilder displays the Files accessory view of the Project Window. Figure 5.3 shows the initial screen ProjectBuilder presents.

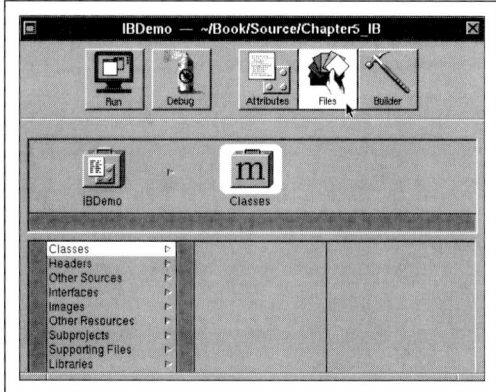

Figure 5.3 The Files accessory view of ProjectBuilder

The Files accessory view is mainly used for project management, i.e., opening and adding various files. This accessory view contains the following components:

- **Classes**—the implementation files for the classes in this project.
- **Headers**—the header files for the classes in this project.
- **Other Sources**—other source code such as the main program.
- **Interfaces**—the **.nib** (NeXT InterfaceBuilder) file(s), as created by InterfaceBuilder.
- **Images**—images file(s) in **TIFF** (Tag Image File Format) or **EPS** (Encapsulated PostScript) format.
- **Other Resources**—contains the **Help** directory, which will be covered in Chapter 10.
- **Subprojects**—a complex project can be composed of subprojects to facilitate project management. We will not be using subprojects in our examples.
- **Supporting Files**—miscellaneous files such as the **Makefile**. One of the best features of ProjectBuilder is that it automatically generates and maintains the **Makefile** (for more information about the **Makefile**, consult Appendix C).
- **Libraries**—the libraries our application needs to link with. By default, our application is linked with **NeXT_s** and **Media_s**. The former contains all the standard functions needed for all applications, and the latter contains functions the **N3DRIBImageRep** class for working with 3D graphics. We will not be using **Media_s** in our examples since we will not be working with 3D graphics.

The Attributes accessory view allows us to change the application's attributes like the default language

ProjectBuilder has other accessory views: the Attributes accessory view and the Build accessory view. The Attributes accessory view is mainly used to specify where to install the product, what the primary language should be (English, French, etc), what the application icon and document icon should look like, etc. We will learn how to change the application icon in Chapter 9. Figure 5.4 shows the Attributes accessory view.

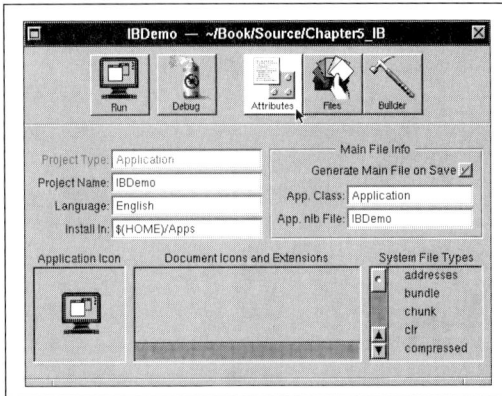

Figure 5.4 The Attributes accessory view of ProjectBuilder

The other accessory view, the Build accessory view, is mainly used for viewing the compilation process. The **Run** and **Debug** buttons are used to launch the application. Clicking the **Run** button launches the application in the same way as double-clicking on the application in the Workspace. Clicking the **Debug** button launches the application and initiates a debugging session. Figure 5.5 shows the Build accessory view.

The Build accessory view is for building the application

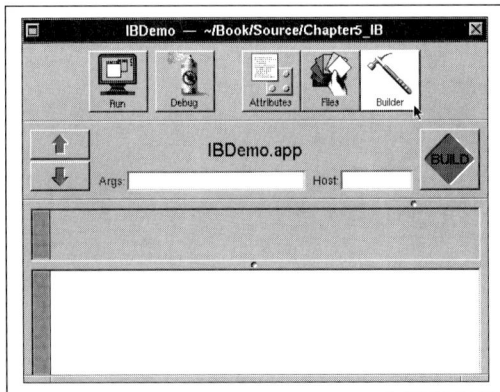

Figure 5.5 The Build accessory view

At this point, return to the Files accessory view and open the interface file by double-clicking on **IBDemo.nib** under **Interfaces**. This launches InterfaceBuilder and opens the interface file. Figure 5.6 shows the screen InterfaceBuilder presents when it opens an existing interface file.

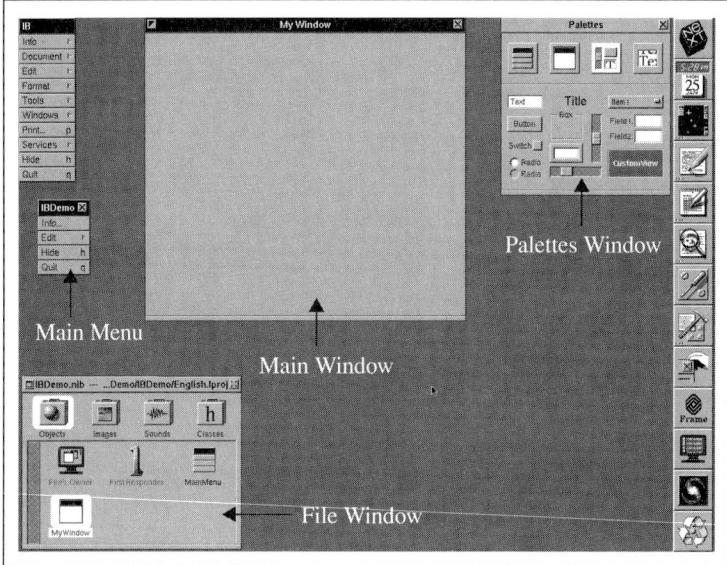

Figure 5.6 The initial screen in InterfaceBuilder

Each of these parts is further explained below.

- The *File Window* contains the resources available to each application. Each icon represents an instance in our application. The icon we are most interested in at this point is the **File's Owner** icon in the upper left-hand corner of the window. This icon typically represents an instance of the **Application** class, **NXApp**. Figure 5.7 shows the File Window.

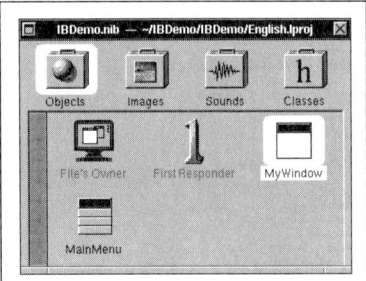

Figure 5.7 The File Window contains the resources

> If the **File's Owner** represents an instance of the application object and there can only be one such instance, why isn't the icon simply labeled **NXApp** for simplicity? As we will learn in Chapter 9, an application can have multiple interface files, and the owner of the interface file is not always **NXApp**.

- The *Palettes Window* displays the available user interface classes from the Application Kit. This window actually contains several palettes. To see the other palettes, simply click on the appropriate button. Since there are too many items in the palettes to completely list, we will gradually introduce them as we are

Starting a Project

implementing the applications. Figure 5.8 shows all the palettes in the Palettes Window.

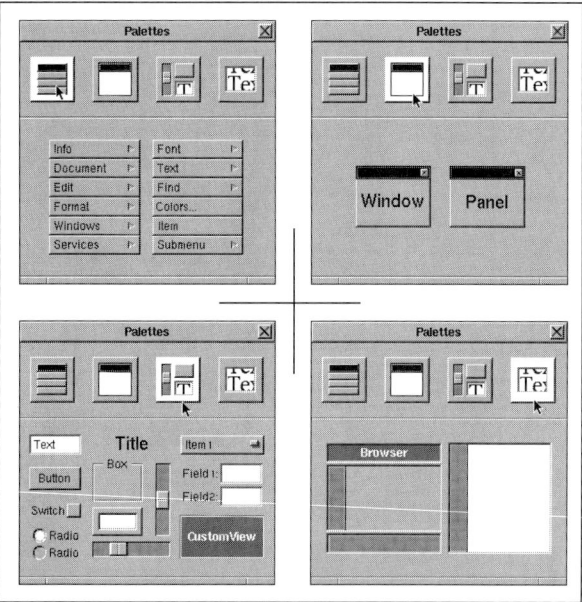

Figure 5.8 The Palettes Window contains more than one palette

- The *Main Menu* is an instance of the **Menu** class and represents the Main Menu of our application. By default, the Main Menu will be placed in the upper left-hand corner during execution. We will refer to this menu as the Main Menu to distinguish it from InterfaceBuilder's menu. Figure 5.9 shows the menu options that are automatically created when we create a new application.

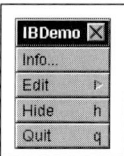

Figure 5.9 InterfaceBuilder automatically creates menu options for the Main Menu

- Since most applications include at least one window, InterfaceBuilder also instantiates the **Window** class and automatically displays this window. For lack of a better term, we will refer to this window as the *Main Window*.

5.2.2 Adding the Objects

To add an object to the application, simply drag the appropriate one from the palette. In this case, we need to add a menu option to display the window. To do so, first click on the leftmost button on the Palette Window to bring up the Menu Palette. Drag the **Item** menu option from the palette and position it above the **Info** menu option of the Main Menu: this adds the menu item to the Main Menu. Figure 5.10 illustrates this sequence.

To add an object, simply drag it from the palette

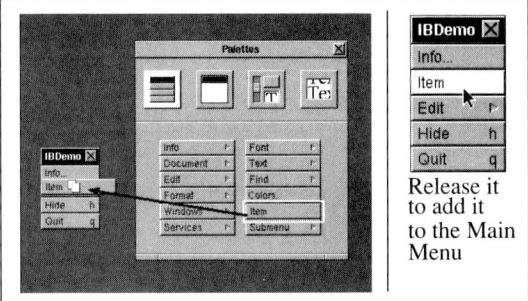

Figure 5.10 Adding a menu option to the Main Menu

Adding an Info panel to the application requires a similar procedure. First, bring up the Window Palette by clicking on the second button in the Palettes Window. Now drag the panel icon and place it somewhere near the Main Window. Releasing the mouse button allows the panel to expand to its normal size. Figure 5.11 illustrates this sequence.

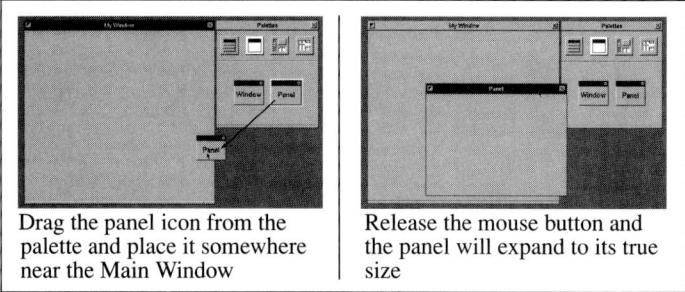

Drag the panel icon from the palette and place it somewhere near the Main Window

Release the mouse button and the panel will expand to its true size

Figure 5.11 Adding a panel to the application

> InterfaceBuilder has an option for specifically adding an Info panel to an application. However, these steps are intended to illustrate how to add objects and edit them rather than specifically explain how to add an Info panel.

Click on the third button to bring up the Miscellaneous Palette. Drag a textfield from the palette and place it in the Info panel, as shown in Figure 5.12.

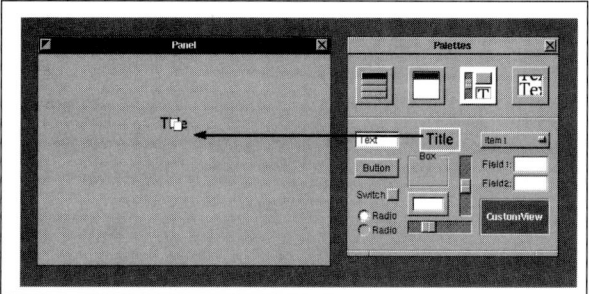

Figure 5.12 Placing a textfield in the Info panel

The Inspector shows the characteristics of the currently selected object

5.2.3 Inspecting the Objects

To edit the instance variables of an object, use the Inspector. To display the Inspector, click **Tools** ⇒ **Inspector** from InterfaceBuilder's menu. Since the Inspector shows the characteristics of the currently selected object, click on the Info panel to make it the currently selected object. To display the attributes of the currently selected object, drag the popuplist in the Inspector until **Attributes** is highlighted. Figure 5.13 illustrates this procedure.

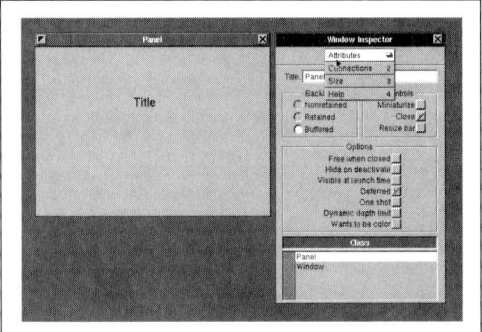

Figure 5.13 Displaying the Attributes Inspector for the Info panel

---

Each object in the palette has its own custom inspector panel. Additionally, InterfaceBuilder is extensible; that is, we can add custom palettes of objects that have their own custom inspector panels.

Be careful not to click on the textfield that is already in the Info panel. If the textfield is selected, the Inspector will display the characteristics of the textfield rather than those of the Info panel. To deselect the textfield, **Shift**-click (click while holding down the **Shift** key) the textfield or click on an area not occupied by the textfield.

To modify the title of the Info panel, type in the **Title** field and edit the text to read **My claim to fame**. Press **Return** to apply the

Inspecting the Objects

change to the window's title. Figure 5.14 shows how to modify the title of the Info panel.

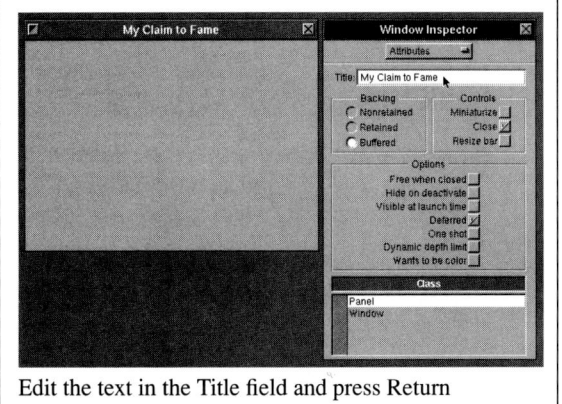

Edit the text in the Title field and press Return

Figure 5.14 Editing the title of a panel

> InterfaceBuilder only allows us to modify some of the instance variables of an object. For example, one of the instance variables for a panel is its background color. However, there is no way to edit this instance variable in InterfaceBuilder.

To modify the text of the menu option and the Info panel, select the text and edit it directly rather than use the Inspector. To edit the text in the Info panel, click on the textfield to select it: notice that there are eight little squares to indicate that the object is currently selected. Once the text is selected, double-click it to edit the text. Edit the text to read **IBDemo** and click outside the textfield's region to complete the edit. Figure 5.15 shows how to edit the text of a textfield.

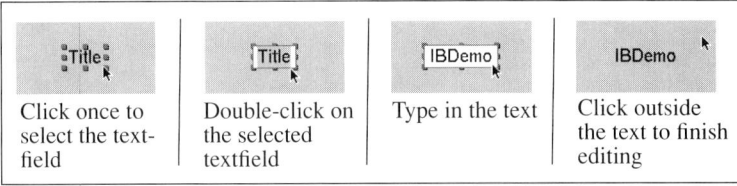

Figure 5.15 Editing the text of a textfield

> We can also alter the appearance of the text by using the Attributes Inspector. For instance, to place a border around the text, click on the third button under the **Border** label in the Attributes Inspector ( ). We can also control the alignment of the text by using the **Alignment** controls in the Attributes Inspector.

The sequence for editing an object is fairly consistent:

- click once to select the object—InterfaceBuilder responds by placing tiny squares (or highlighting) to indicate that the object is selected.
- double-click on the selected item to edit it.

Use this same sequence to edit the text in the menu option from **Item** to **Display Window**. Figure 5.16 shows how to edit the text of a menu option.

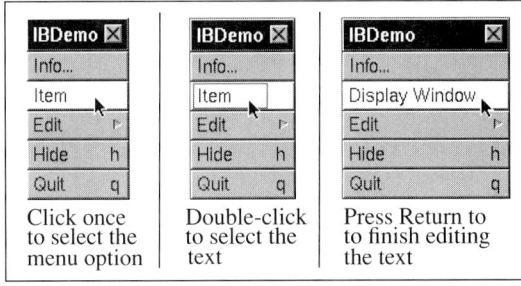

Figure 5.16 Editing the text of a menu option

At this point, the **Display Window** menu option and the Info panel are simply decoration since their responsibilities have yet to be defined. That is our next step, establishing the relationships between these objects and the others.

5.2.4 Making the Connections

Making a connection is equivalent to setting a target

As explained in Chapter 4, clicking on a menu option sends a message to another object. In this case, clicking on the **Display Window** menu option should display the Main Window. To accomplish this, we need to establish a relationship from the menu option to the Main Window. Establishing this relationship is called *setting a target* in the Application Kit terminology. In InterfaceBuilder terminology, it is called *making a connection* since InterfaceBuilder provides a graphical way of establishing this relationship.

To make a connection, drag from the control to the target

To make a connection, **Control**-drag (hold down the **Control** key and press the mouse button) *from* the source *to* the destination. In other words, we need to **Control**-drag from the **Display Window** menu option to the Main Window. To do so, position the cursor over the **Display Window** option, hold down the **Control** key and the mouse button. Now, drag toward the window. As we do so, InterfaceBuilder produces a "rubberband" that follows our movements. As we near the title bar of the window, the rubberband expands into a black rectangle box to enclose the title bar of the window.

At this point, the Inspector updates to the Connections Inspector, which displays all of the valid methods for the destination object. Since we want the window to display, select the **makeKeyAndOrderFront:** method and then click **Connect**. Once we have established the connection, InterfaceBuilder puts a dimple ( ) next to the method we selected. Figure 5.17 shows how to finish connecting the menu option to the Main Window.

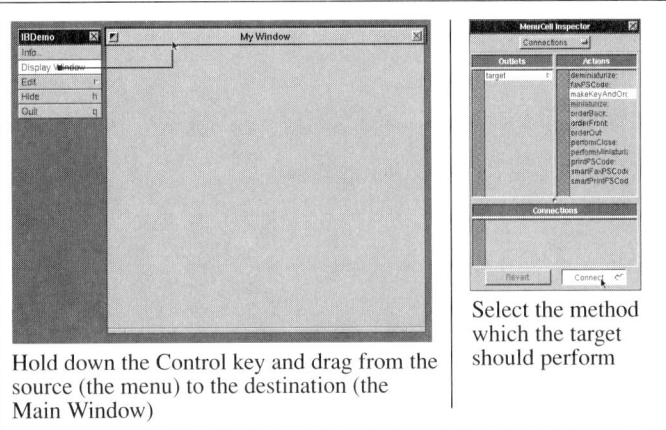

Figure 5.17 Making a connection to the Main Window

In the Connections Inspector, InterfaceBuilder does not display all the methods which the target responds to. InterfaceBuilder only displays those methods of the form, *methodName*:**sender**. We will explore this in Chapter 6.

We can also use the Connections Inspector to inspect an existing connection. For example, InterfaceBuilder provides two pre-defined connections for each application: one from the **Quit** option to the **File's Owner** icon and the other from the **Hide** option to the **File's Owner** icon, which is simply **NXApp**, the application object.

The Connections Inspector can also display existing connections

To display the connection from the **Quit** option to **NXApp**, select the **Quit** option and then bring up the Connections Inspector. Now click on the **terminate:** method in the Connections Inspector to actually display the connection. Notice that InterfaceBuilder placed a dimple ( ) next to the method to indicate that there is already a connection to this object. Use this same sequence to display the connection from the **Hide** option to **NXApp**. *Be careful not to double-click on an existing connection*

Double-clicking on an existing connection removes it

since this removes the connection. Figure 5.18 shows how to display an already existing connection.

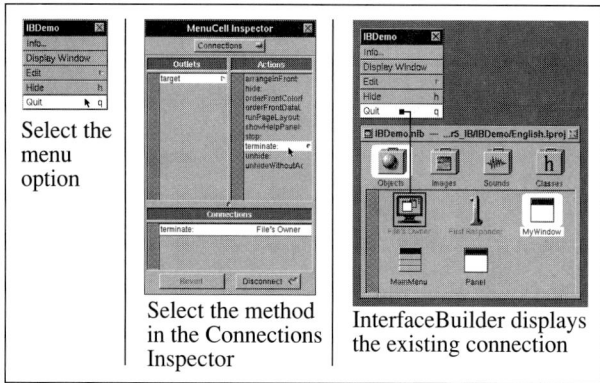

Figure 5.18 Displaying an already existing connection.

> The **Quit** menu option in our Main Menu is exactly the same as the **Quit** option we added to our **AppKitDemo** application in Chapter 4. Remember we used the statement **[theMenu addItem:"Quit" action:@selector(terminate:) keyEquivalent:'q']** to:
>
> - add a menu option named **Quit** to our menu.
> - request the destination object to perform its **terminate:** method.
> - set the keyboard equivalent for the **Quit** option to **Command-q**.
>
> Since every NeXTSTEP application must have a **Quit** option, InterfaceBuilder, as one of its initialization steps, includes a **Quit** option in the Main Menu. Likewise, InterfaceBuilder includes a **Hide** option since every application must also have a **Hide** option.

With all the connections established, we are ready to test the interface.

5.2.5 Testing the Interface

InterfaceBuilder has two modes: *Construction Mode* and *Test Mode*. The former is for constructing the interface and the latter is for testing the interface. Since we can test an interface without compilation, we can make changes fairly quickly. To enter Test Mode, click on **Document** ⇒ **Test Interface** (**Command-r**). In Test Mode, InterfaceBuilder clears the entire work area and presents the application as though it has been compiled and executing. Figure 5.19 shows how to enter the Test Mode.

The Test Mode allows us to test the interface

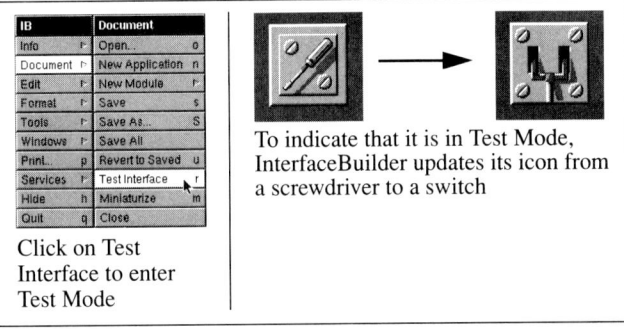

Click on Test Interface to enter Test Mode

To indicate that it is in Test Mode, InterfaceBuilder updates its icon from a screwdriver to a switch

Figure 5.19 Switching to **Test Mode** in InterfaceBuilder

In Test Mode, the application behaves identically to normal execution (i.e., as if an executable had been made) with two exceptions: the **Hide** and **Quit** options.

- **Hide** removes an application's windows and menu and condenses them into an icon. Double-clicking on the icon Oneidas the application. Since our application doesn't have an icon yet, we need to double-click on InterfaceBuilder's icon instead. However, instead of unhiding the application, double-clicking on the icon returns us to InterfaceBuilder in Construction Mode.
- **Quit** typically quits the application but in this case, selecting it also returns us to InterfaceBuilder in Construction Mode since the application is executing in InterfaceBuilder's Test Mode.

Verify that the application works by closing the window and redisplaying it with the **Display Window** option. Afterwards, move the window and click on **Quit** to return to InterfaceBuilder.

For this simple application, InterfaceBuilder basically did the following:

- instantiated five different classes: **Window**, **Panel**, **Menu**, **TextField**, and **Application**.
- displayed the window and menu.
- set the menu to be the application's Main Menu.
- specified **NXApp** as the target for the **Hide** and **Quit** menu options. Additionally, these menu options have their respective keyboard alternatives.
- sent a **run** message to **NXApp**, placing it in a loop to wait for events until we click on **Quit**.

These steps are almost identical to the control flow of **AppKitDemo** in Chapter 4. By way of its Test Mode, InterfaceBuilder allows us to continually refine the interface without compilation; this feature significantly reduces the development time, as we have seen. But, what if we wanted to execute our application outside of InterfaceBuilder? We would then have to compile the application to produce an executable.

> Make sure to save any changes to the **.nib** file before building the application since ProjectBuilder will blindly use the last *saved* version of the file. This is a gross oversight of ProjectBuilder since it should check whether the **.nib** file has been modified before building: if so, ProjectBuilder should allow us to save the file and then build the application.

5.2.6 Compiling the Application

When we created our project earlier, ProjectBuilder automatically generated a **Makefile** and wrote the application's main program. The name of the main program is the application's name appended with **_main.m**; in this case, the application's main program is **IBDemo_main.m**. We can compile this program by using the compilation facilities of ProjectBuilder. The main program is quite short:

Listing for **IBDemo_main.m**

```
/* Generated by the NeXT Project Builder
   NOTE: Do NOT change this file --
   Project Builder maintains it.
*/

#import <appkit/Application.h>

void main(int argc, char *argv[]) {

  NXApp = [Application new];
  if ([NXApp loadNibSection:"IBDemo.nib"
    owner:NXApp withNames:NO])
    [NXApp run];

  [NXApp free];
  exit(0);
}
```

The **main()** function does the following:

- instantiates the **Application** class and assigns it to **NXApp**.
- loads the main interface file, **IBDemo.nib**.
- places the application into a loop to poll for incoming events. This loop executes until **NXApp** receives a **terminate:** message.
- after the application exits from the loop, **main()** frees **NXApp** and then exits.

Click on the **Builder** button to bring up the Build accessory view. Then, click on the **Build** button to compile and link the application. ProjectBuilder uses the UNIX utility *make* to determine what files need to be compiled and linked (for more information

Click on the Build button to build the application

on **make**, see Appendix C). Figure 5.20 shows the results of clicking on the **Build** button.

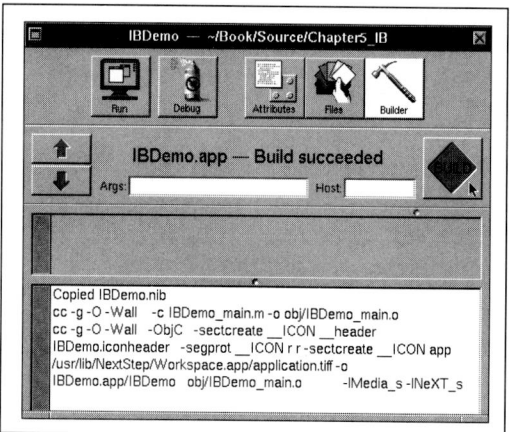

Figure 5.20 Building an application in ProjectBuilder

ProjectBuilder compiles each class (**.m** file) into an object file, then links these object files and other resources such as sounds and icons, to the appropriate libraries (**NeXT_s** and **Media_s**) to create the application. If there are any syntax errors, ProjectBuilder lists them in the output portion of the Build accessory view.

Now that the application has been compiled, we can execute it to verify that the application can work outside of InterfaceBuilder's test environment.

5.2.7 Launching the Application

We can launch the application one of five ways:

- click on the **Run** button in ProjectBuilder. If necessary, ProjectBuilder will first compile the application. To launch the application without compiling the application, **Alt**-click (hold down the **Alt** key and click) the **Run** button.
- click on the **Debug** button in ProjectBuilder to launch the application in *Debug mode*. If necessary, ProjectBuilder will first compile the application. To launch the application without first compiling it, **Alt**-click the **Debug** button.

- launch the application from the Workspace by double-clicking on the application.
- open a Terminal window and type:

    `% open ~/IBDemo/IBDemo.app`

- since the executable is actually a directory, specify the executable inside the directory itself (we will cover this in the next section):

    `% ~/IBDemo/IBDemo.app/IBDemo &`

The primary difference between these launch procedures is where the standard output and the standard error output (**stdout** and **stderr** in UNIX jargon) of the application gets redirected to. In the first four procedures, **stdout** (for example, from a **printf()** statement or runtime errors such as from the Objective-C runtime system) is redirected to the Console. To display the Console window, click on the **Tools** ⇒ **Console** in the Workspace Manager.

In the last procedure, **stdout** and **stderr** are redirected to the Terminal shell from which the application was launched. If an application is behaving differently than expected during execution, first check either the Console or the Terminal shell, as appropriate.

> In the Debug mode, **stdout** and **stderr** are actually redirected to the shell that was created when the application is launched. For more information on debugging an application, see Appendix D.

For more information on what to verify to determine whether the application works, see "Testing the Interface" on page 141.

A NeXTSTEP application is actually a directory with support files

5.2.8 Decomposing a NeXTSTEP Application

Before closing this chapter, let's take a look at what parts make up a NeXTSTEP application. A NeXTSTEP application is a directory that contains various components: the directory structure is often referred to as a *file package*. The file package is named *application*.**app**, where *application* is the name of the application (in our case, **IBDemo**). The directory contains the following components:

- **executable**—the name of the executable was specified when we first created the project in ProjectBuilder. In our case, the executable is **IBDemo**.

- *language*.**lproj**—to facilitate translating an application to different languages, NeXTSTEP localizes all language context information (such as **.nib** and help files) under one directory; this is known as *localization*. The name of the directory is dependent on what we choose as the primary language. If English is the primary language (the primary language is specified in the Preferences application in /**NextApps**), the directory would be **English.lproj** (**.lproj** is short for language project). The *language*.**lproj** directory contains the following files:

    - *file*.**nib**—one or more **.nib** files.

    - *file*.**tiff**—zero or more **TIFF** files. These are bitmap images that can be used to enhance a user interface. One common use is to add a custom **TIFF** image for the application's icon. We will explore this in Chapter 9. The suitcase labeled **Images** in the File Window contains some standard TIFF images.

    - *file*.**eps**—zero or more EPS files. These are images that can be used to enhance a user interface. When scaled or rotated, EPS files preserve their fidelity better than **TIFF** files, i.e., no "jaggies."

    - *file*.**snd**—zero or more sound files. These are prerecorded sounds that can be added to liven a user interface. The suitcase labeled **Sounds** in the File Window contains some predefined sounds.

When we create a project in a directory, ProjectBuilder creates all of the support files in the project directory. In addition, ProjectBuilder creates a *language*.**lproj** subdirectory, which it copies into the application's file package.Figure 5.21 illustrates the directory structure of an application.

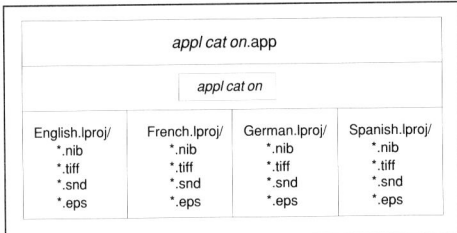

Figure 5.21 The components of an application

Although an application is actually composed of many components, it appears in the Workspace Manager as a single file named *application*.**app**. For most purposes, an application can be treated as a file. To view the components in the application (such as the files in the **Help** directory), select the *application*.**app** file and then click on **File ⇒ Open as Folder**).

For more information on localization, see **/NextLibrary/Documentation/NextDev/Concepts/Localization.rtfd.**

Since the application loads its **.nib** file(s) during runtime, we do not need to recompile or even relink an application to obtain the latest changes. When we build the application, ProjectBuilder simply copies the **.nib** file(s) into the appropriate language directory.

The **.nib** file is actually a directory. However, we do not need to consider this since it is maintained by InterfaceBuilder.

5.3 Summary

In this chapter, we learned how to use ProjectBuilder and InterfaceBuilder to create and test the interface and to manage the various files associated with each NeXTSTEP application. Also, we learned how to create an executable by using the facilities in ProjectBuilder.

In the next chapter, we will learn more commands in ProjectBuilder and InterfaceBuilder as we explore event processing.

Chapter 6
Processing Events

Like most graphical environments, NeXTSTEP is an event-driven environment and as such, the system spends most of its processing time waiting for events and then processing them. These events include keypresses, mouse movements, mouse clicks, and messages from other applications (although we won't deal with the last topic). NeXTSTEP defines two fundamental paradigms for handling these events: *target-action* and *delegation*. Target-action is involved in almost everything we do in NeXTSTEP: clicking on a button, selecting a menu item, typing, etc. Each of these activities causes another object to respond in some manner. For example, selecting the **Quit** option in the menu sends a **terminate:** message to the application object. While target-action focuses on direct manipulation, delegation allows us to extend the functionality of a class by defining another class to perform additional processing when particular events occur.

This chapter focuses on these two paradigms and the **Control** class (an abstract superclass that defines a framework for handling events) as well as its subclasses: **Button**, **Slider**, **TextField**, and **Form**. This chapter also explores how to implement target-action and delegation using InterfaceBuilder. Although InterfaceBuilder has many uses, its most powerful features are geared toward implementing target-action related methods since the relationship between a control and its target can be specified graphically.

The two paradigms in NeXTSTEP are target-action and delegation

InterfaceBuilder is mainly used for establishing target-action methods

6.1 Goals

In this chapter, we will:

- define event-driven programming.
- give an overview of the **Control** class and some of its subclasses: **Button**, **Slider**, **TextField**, and **Form**.
- explain the target-action paradigm and give some examples.
- explain the delegation paradigm is and give some examples.

- compare the differences between delegation and target-action.
- explain what an outlet is and when it is needed.

6.2 Event-Driven Programming

A command-line environment forces the user to type commands to the system

In a nongraphical environment, such as a *command-line environment*, the user types in a command at a prompt and then waits for the command to complete before proceeding. This makes it fairly easy to write the application since it only needs to read in the command, process it, and then return to wait for the next command. To a great extent, the computer, rather than the user, determines how the tasks are initiated. One extremely popular command-line environment is the ubiquitous MS-DOS operating system in the personal computer market.

A graphical environment tends to allow the user more freedom to switch between applications

In a graphical environment like NeXTSTEP, the user has much more freedom. For example, the user can select some text in a word processor, then click on another window to switch to a drawing program, draw some figures, and then click back on the word processor window to resume editing. In short, the user, rather than the computer, determines how the tasks are initiated. While this model is quite natural to use, it is quite complex to program since the application cannot wait for the command to complete before proceeding.

NeXTSTEP is an event-driven environment

Every time the user initiates an action (moves the mouse, types a key, etc.), the Window Server generates an *event* and sends it to the application. The application then forwards it to the appropriate window, which then forwards it to one of the views (we will explore this sequence in a later section). The event is a record that includes (among other things) the window where the event occurred and the type of event. Each application, therefore, must constantly wait for events (via a polling loop also known as the *event loop*), determine what type of event it is, process it accordingly, and then return to the loop. Such an environment is known as an *event-driven environment* since the impetus for the environment is the events.

> To view the entire event record, use the Digital Librarian and consult **/NextLibrary/Concepts/Events/ 04_EventRecord/EventRecord.rtfd**.

In NeXTSTEP, the event loop is initiated when the **main()** function sends a **run** message to **NXApp**. Once the application has entered into this event loop, it scans for events and then dispatches them until the user clicks on **Quit**, which sends a **terminate:** message to the application. Figure 6.1 shows the framework for a NeXTSTEP application from the event-handling viewpoint.

NeXTSTEP retrieves events until it receives a terminate: message

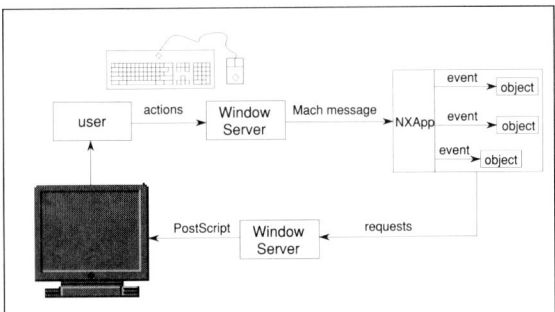

Figure 6.1 The framework for a NeXTSTEP application

This model leads to the natural blend of object-oriented programming and event-driven programming. Instead of viewing the series of events as a complex set of **if-then** statements, we can view it as a set of autonomous objects sending messages to each other. When an event is generated, the Window Server forwards it to the appropriate application in the form of a Mach message. The application object, **NXApp**, receives the Mach message and

NXApp forwards messages to the appropriate objects in the application

transforms it into an Objective-C message, which is then forwarded to the appropriate object in the application.

> Note that a Mach message is completely different from an Objective-C message. The former is generated by the Mach operating system and is used for interprocess communication; the latter is generated by the Objective-C runtime system for messaging objects. We will not cover Mach messages in our discussions.

Every application has an event queue

As mentioned earlier, an event-driven application constantly scans for events and then processes them. However, in many cases, the application may not be able to finish processing an event before another one arrives. In order to prevent the events from being lost, these events are placed in an *event queue*: each application has an application queue that is distinct from the application queue for another application. By using the Application Kit to write our application, we rarely have to deal with the event queue directly because the Application Kit classes already provide this functionality. Each application's event queue has a limit of fifty events, although an application will rarely—if ever—encounter this limit.

The Control class defines a framework for working with events

The principal class that defines a framework for handling events is the abstract superclass, **Control**, and its subclasses (**Button**, **Slider**, et al.). Since manipulating a control should provide visual feedback to the user, the **Control** class is designed to encapsulate functionality for drawing to the screen and handling events. The drawing functionality is inherited from the **View** class, and the event handling is inherited from the **Responder** class. However, the **Responder** class is so generalized that we rarely subclass from it: we tend to work with the **Responder**'s subclass, **Control**, and its subsequent subclasses (**Button**, **Slider**, et al.). Since **Control** inherits from **View**, a control is ultimately a view as well. We will explore the **View** class more closely in Chapter 7.

6.3 The Target-Action Paradigm

The **Control** class defines two key things to implement event-handling: an object to send the event to (the *target*) and a method by which it sends the message (**sendAction:to:**). The target of a control is simply the object that receives the event when the control object is manipulated. For example, when we click on the **Hide** menu option, the control object (the menu option) sends a **hide:** message to the target (**NXApp**) to request it to hide itself. Since manipulating the control often results in sending an *action* to a *target*, this paradigm is called the ***target-action*** paradigm, or target-action for short. Quite often, the control object is called the *sender* since it is the object that is sending the message, and the target object is the *receiver* since it is receiving the message (the term receiver is in accord with the definition from Chapter 2). Figure 6.2 shows the **Hide** menu option sending its action message to its target, **NXApp**.

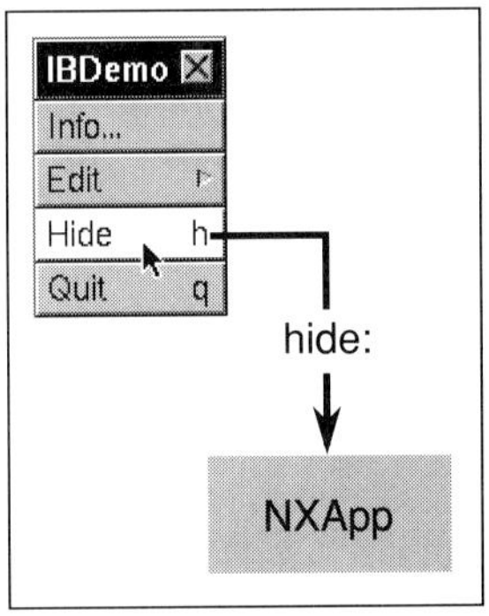

When manipulated, the control sends its message to the target

Figure 6.2 Clicking on the **Hide** menu option sends a **hide:** message to **NXApp** (the target)

There are five major subclasses of **Control**: **Button**, **Slider**, **TextField**, **Form**, and **Scroller** (we will defer the **Scroller** class until Chapter 9). By using these classes, we do not have to deal with the event queue, determine the location of the cursor, or implement a drawing mechanism. We simply have to implement the appropriate method that will be invoked when the control is manipulated. A control defines a switch; the switch determines how it can be manipulated (for instance, we can press a button but we can't press a textfield; we type in a textfield) but what the switch does in a given situation is determined by us. The controls

All controls provide visual feedback when they are manipulated

share one common trait: they provide visual feedback when they are manipulated. For instance, a button will highlight when it is pressed, a slider will move when it is dragged, etc.

Since each control can be manipulated in a slightly different way, let us digress for a moment and discuss each of the controls individually. Keep in mind that each control has a number of parameters that can greatly alter its appearance. Therefore, each control is accompanied by a diagram illustrating its common representations.

> Each of the **Control** classes works with a corresponding **Cell** subclass to implement the entire functionality. For example, a button depends on a buttoncell to implement most of the internal event-handling capability. Likewise, a slider depends on a slidercell and a textfield depends on a textfield cell. For our purposes, we will concentrate on the controls instead of the cells.

6.3.1 The Button Class

Buttons should be used when there is a limited number of choices

The button is probably the most common of all the controls because it is by far the most versatile. Buttons are most useful when there is a small set of limited choices such as setting the state of an application or for initiating/terminating an application. If there are more than four or five choices, the interface tends to be quite cluttered. Figure 6.3 shows some sample buttons.

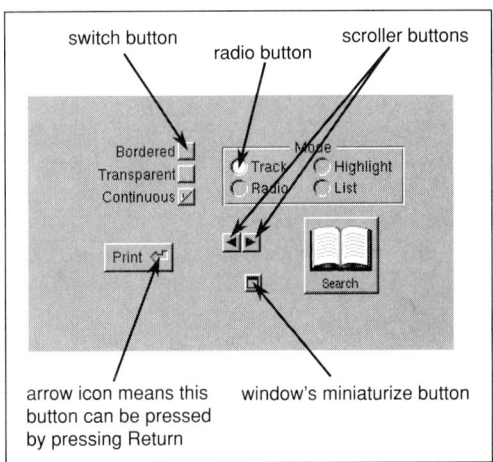

Figure 6.3 Some sample buttons

Some buttons send an action message as soon as we click on the mouse button and release it (assuming the cursor is still in the button's boundary). Other buttons like those buttons found in a scrollview, repeatedly send messages as long as we hold down the mouse button. Table 6.1 shows the most commonly used methods for working with buttons.

Button:Control:View:Responder:Object		
	Name	**Description**
Instance Variables	N/A	N/A
Methods	initFrame:(const NXRect*) frameRect	initializes a button to the size specified by *frameRect*. The default title is Button
	setTitle:(const char*)aString	sets the button's title to the text specified by *aString*

Table 6.1 Class summary table for the **Button** class

| Button:Control:View:Responder:Object ||
Name	Description
performClick:sender	highlights the button and sends the action message. This is used to programmatically press the button

Table 6.1 Class summary table for the **Button** class

The following program, **ControlDemo**, demonstrates how to display a button in a window: it is almost identical to **AppKitDemo.m** from Chapter 4 (the changes are in bold).

Listing for ControlDemo.m

```
#import <appkit/appkit.h>

// a minimal program to demonstrate how
// to add controls to a window

main()
{
  // create an application object
  // to establish connection to
  // Window Server
  id NXApp = [Application new];
  id theWindow;
  id theMenu;
  id theButton;
  NXRect theRect;

  // create a window that's at 125, 125
  // and is 200 by 300 pixels
  NXSetRect(&theRect, 125, 125, 200, 300);
  theWindow = [ [Window alloc]
    initContent:&theRect
    style: NX_TITLEDSTYLE
    backing:NX_BUFFERED
    buttonMask:NX_MINIATURIZEBUTTONMASK
    defer:YES];

  // create the menu
  theMenu = [ [Menu alloc]
```

```
    initTitle: [NXApp appName] ];
// create the menu option
[theMenu addItem:"Quit"
  action:@selector(terminate:)
  keyEquivalent:'q'];

// resize menu to accomodate menu option
[theMenu sizeToFit];
[NXApp setMainMenu:theMenu];

// create a button that's 80 by 20
NXSetRect(&theRect, 0, 0, 80, 20);
theButton = [ [Button alloc]
  initFrame:&theRect];
// set the title for the button
[theButton setTitle:"Press Here"];
// since the button is a view, we need
// to install it as the subview of the
// window's contentview or else it
// won't draw
[ [theWindow contentView]
  addSubview: theButton];

// send the window to the front
// and display it
[theWindow makeKeyAndOrderFront:nil];

// go into event loop to wait for events
  [NXApp run];
}
```

Compile the application with:

```
% cc -o ControlDemo ControlDemo.m -lNeXT_s
```

Figure 6.4 shows what **ControlDemo** looks like during execution.

Figure 6.4 **ControlDemo** during execution

The NXSetRect() function is a quick way of initializing an NXRect struct

Rather than creating a window at the default location (as in **AppKitDemo**), the main program now creates a window that is 200 by 300 pixels located at (125, 125) of the screen coordinates. In order to do this, **main()** first uses **NXSetRect()** to initialize an **NXRect struct** to the appropriate values and then passes the address of the **struct** to the **initFrame:** method. **NXRect** is simply a **struct** that contains four fields: the first two fields collectively specify the (**x, y**) location and the second two fields collectively specify the size (**width, height**) (for more information on an **NXRect struct**, see Chapter 7). Note that the **NXSetRect()** function does not create the window: it is merely a function for quickly initializing an **NXRect struct**.

After creating the window, **main()** creates a button that is 80 by 20 pixels at (0,0) by first initializing a **NXRect struct** and then passing the **struct** to [[Button alloc] initFrame:]. Note that (0,0) specifies the location of the button in its *superview*'s coordinate system instead of the screen coordinate system. The superview of the button is the content view of the window, and (0,0) is the lower left hand corner of the window (for more information on views and their coordinate systems, see Chapter 7).

This last step is the trickiest: every window has a *content view*, the rectangular region which we manipulate to display to the screen. To display the button (or any other subview, for that matter), **main()** installs it as a *subview* of the content view. When the window receives a **display** message later, it will recursively send a **display** message to the content view and all of its subviews. The **makeKeyAndOrderFront:** method ultimately sends a **display** message to the window.

Every window has a content view

To display a control inside a window:

- use **NXSetRect()** to set the values of a **NXRect struct.**
- use **alloc** to instantiate the class.
- use the designated initializer method (usually **initFrame:**, which accepts the address of an **NXRect struct**) to initialize the instance.
- add the control as a subview of the window's content view.
- send a **display** message to display the window, which displays the window and its subviews.

Figure 6.5 illustrates the various components of the window in **ControlDemo**. We will add more controls to this window as we proceed.

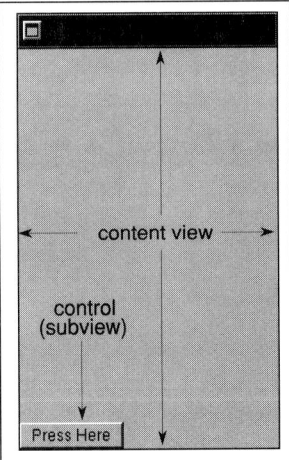

Figure 6.5 The components of **ControlDemo**

Now, let's create another window and specify it as the target of the button. When the button is pressed, it will send a message to the window requesting the window to display. Modify **ControlDemo.m** as follows:

Adding a button to **ControlDemo.m**

```
id targetWindow;
.
.
.
// create the target window for the button
targetWindow = [ [Window alloc]
  initContent:NULL
  style: NX_RESIZEBARSTYLE
  backing:NX_BUFFERED
  buttonMask:NX_MINIATURIZEBUTTONMASK
  defer:YES];
// make this window the target of the button
[theButton setTarget:targetWindow];
// when pressed, button sends
// makeKeyAndOrderFront: message to the window
[theButton setAction:@selector
  (makeKeyAndOrderFront:)];
.
.
.
// code to display window
```

Compile the application and verify that pressing the button displays the window.

6.3.2 The Slider Class

A slider provides a knob that can be dragged to continually send messages to the slider's target; sliders can be vertical or horizontal. Internally, a slider defines an upper value, a lower value, and a current value, which is reflected by the current position of the knob. Figure 6.6 shows some sample sliders.

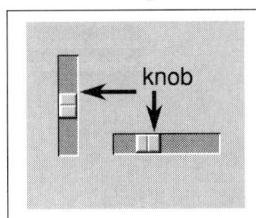

Figure 6.6 Some sample sliders

The slider is appropriate when a control needs to send continuous values to its target and the target must continually update. One example is setting the color in a color panel. As we drag a color slider, the panel provides immediate feedback by continually changing the color in the colorwell. A slider should not be used if the range between the minimum value and the maximum value is great because the slider's granularity is dependent on the number of discrete units in the range.

For example, assume there are two sliders of equal length. The first slider can range from 1 to 4, and the second can range from 1 to 10. It is easier to select a desired value on the first slider since the granularity is not as fine as the second slider. If possible, label the minimum and maximum values of the slider to inform the

Use a slider to continually send messages to a target

Label the slider with the minimum and maximum values

user of the approximate range of the values. Figure 6.7 compares these two sliders.

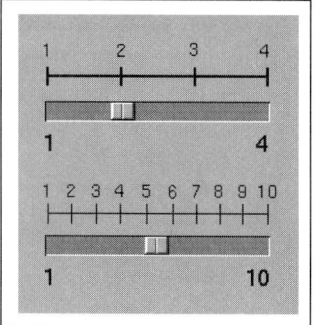

Figure 6.7 The granularity of a slider

Table 6.2 shows the most commonly used methods for working with sliders.

Slider:Control:View:Responder:Object		
	Name	**Description**
Instance Variables	N/A	N/A
Methods	initFrame:(const NXRect *) frameRect	initializes a slider to the size specified in *frameRect*
	setMinValue: (double)aDouble	sets the minimum value of the slider to *aDouble*
	setMaxValue: (double)aDouble	sets the maximum value of the slider to *aDouble*

Table 6.2 Class summary table for the **Slider** class

The following program adds a slider to the previously discussed program, **ControlDemo.m** (the changes are in bold).

Adding a slider to **ControlDemo.m**

```
id theSlider;
    .
    .
    .
```

```
// add this after installing the button
// as a subview of the content view

// create a horizontal slider 100 x 15
NXSetRect(&theRect, 0, 100, 100, 15);
theSlider = [ [Slider alloc]
  initFrame:&theRect];
// set the min value to 0.0
[theSlider setMinValue:0.0];
// set the max value to 10.0
[theSlider setMaxValue:10.0];
[ [theWindow contentView]
  addSubview:theSlider];
 .
 .
 .
// code to display window
```

As before, **main()** uses **NXSetRect()** to initialize an **NXRect struct** with the appropriate values: in this case, the slider is at (0, 100) and is 100 by 15 units. Since the width is greater than the height, NeXTSTEP creates a horizontal slider to the specified width and height. With the slider created, **main()** sets the slider's minimum to **0.0** and its maximum value to **10.0**. As the last step, **main()** installs the slider as a subview of the content view so that it will draw when the window receives a **display** message. Compile the application and verify that it works. Figure 6.8 shows **ControlDemo** with a slider and a button.

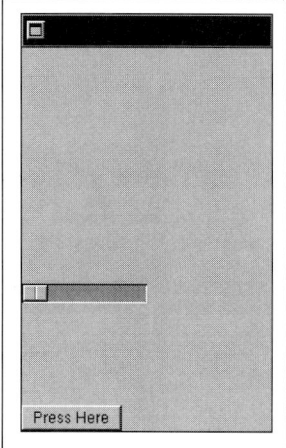

Figure 6.8 ControlDemo with a slider and a button

As mentioned previously, the slider is useful when the range of values can be predetermined. However, its primary weakness is that it cannot display its current value. This limitation leads to the textfield, which is our next topic (we will set the target of the slider to be the textfield. This means we first must learn how to use the textfield).

How do we create a vertical slider? Simply make the height to be greater than the width. For example, instead of using **NXSetRect(&theRect, 0, 100, 100, 15)**, use **NXSetRect(&theRect, 0, 100, 15, 100)**.

6.3.3 The TextField Class

A textfield is commonly used to retrieve or display a single value. Figure 6.9 shows some two sample textfields, one with a simple border and one with a bezeled border.

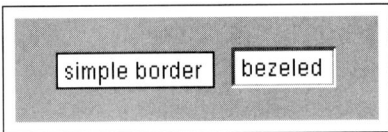

Figure 6.9 Some sample textfields

To manipulate a textfield, first select it by clicking on the field. Then type in a value and finish by typing **Return**. This causes the textfield to send the action message to its target. The target typically sends a message back to the textfield to inquire what its value is so that it can proceed.

To demonstrate the two-way communication between a control and its target, assume that we are implementing a converter application that converts from kilograms to pounds. One possible interface is to have two textfields, one for input and one for output. In the input field, we would type in a value (in kilograms), which is passed to a converter object. This converter object then converts the value to a corresponding pounds value and then sends this to the output field. Figure 6.10 shows this sample application.

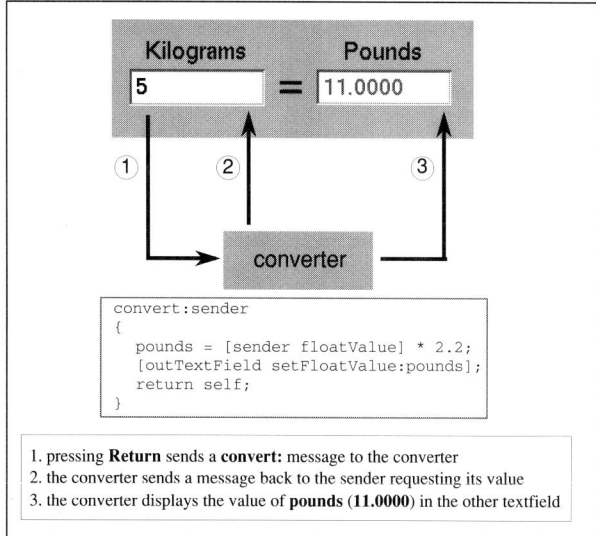

Figure 6.10 A converter application with two textfields

Table 6.3 shows the most commonly used textfield methods.

TextField:Control:View:Responder:Object		
	Name	**Description**
Instance Variables	N/A	N/A
Methods	initFrame:(const NXRect *) frameRect	initializes a textfield to the size specified in *frameRect*
	setEditable:(BOOL)flag	sets whether the text is editable or not

Table 6.3 Class summary table for the **TextField** class

The following code fragment adds a textfield to the existing **ControlDemo.m** file.

Adding a textfield to **ControlDemo.m**

```
id theTextField;
```

```
    .
    .
    .
// add this after installing the button
// as a subview of the content view
// create a textfield that's 75 by 20
NXSetRect(&theRect, 0, 150, 75, 20);
theTextField = [ [TextField alloc]
  initFrame:&theRect];
// make the text editable
[theTextField setEditable:YES];
[ [theWindow contentView]
  addSubview:theTextField];
    .
    .
    .
// code to display window
```

At this point, the code should be fairly straightforward. The only difference in this fragment is that **main()** sets the text inside the textfield to be editable. Compile the application and verify that it works. Figure 6.11 shows **ControlDemo** during execution.

Figure 6.11 **ControlDemo** with a button, a slider, and a textfield

Now, set the slider as the target of the textfield and vice versa.

Setting the target for the slider and the textfield

```
// make the textfield the target of
// the slider and vice versa
[theSlider setMinValue:0.0];
[theSlider setMaxValue:10.0];
[theSlider setTarget:theTextField];
[theSlider setAction:
  @selector(takeFloatValueFrom:)];
[theTextField setTarget:theSlider];
[theTextField setAction:
  @selector(takeFloatValueFrom:)];
.
.
.
// code to display window
```

Each time we move the slider, it sends a **takeFloatValue:** message to the textfield. This sets the value of the textfield to the internal value of the slider. Likewise, each time we enter a value in the textfield and press **Return**, the textfield sends its action message (**takeFloatValueFrom:**) to its target, the slider.

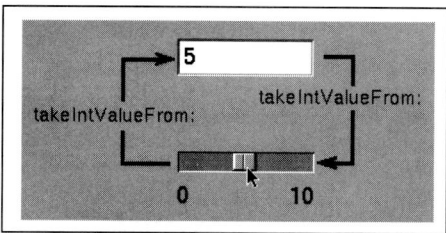

Figure 6.12 The slider is the textfield's target and the textfield is the slider's target

The textfield is useful for a single value, but what if we need to type in and display multiple values? We would then use a form.

A form is useful for retrieving or displaying data that can be logically grouped together

6.3.4 The Form Class

A form is a rectangular collection of cells and controls, although each component must be of similar size. A form is nothing more than a collection (more specifically, a matrix) of formcells that are indexed from **0** to **n**. This control is most useful for retrieving or displaying data that can be grouped logically. A classic example is personal information, such as names, addresses, and phone numbers. Figure 6.13 shows a sample form.

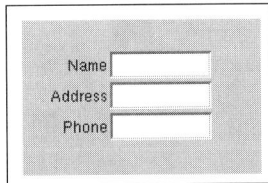

Figure 6.13 A sample form

To enter data in a form, we use the same sequence as we would with a textfield except now we need to input values in any of the fields. However, it would be quite clumsy if we needed to click at each textfield before we could edit it. Fortunately, a form defines a more elegant sequence. We simply click on each one of the fields to select the form, and we can then press **Tab** and **Shift-Tab** to skip forward and backward, respectively.

Use Tab and Shift-Tab to traverse the fields of the form

Table 6.4 shows the most commonly used methods for working with forms.

Form:Control:Responder:Object		
	Name	**Description**
Instance variables	N/A	N/A

Table 6.4 Class summary table for the **Form** class

The Form Class

Form:Control:Responder:Object		
	Name	**Description**
Methods	initFrame:(const NXRect *) frameRect	initializes a textfield to the size specified in *frameRect*
	addEntry:(const char*)title	adds an entry at the end of the form with the title specified by *title*
	sizeToFit	adjusts the form to an appropriate size to accommodate newly added fields
	(float)floatValueAt:(int)index	returns the entry at position *index* as a float
	(int)selectedIndex	returns the index of the currently selected entry

Table 6.4 Class summary table for the **Form** class

The following programs adds a form to the **ControlDemo** application.

Adding a form to **ControlDemo.m**

```
id theForm;
.
.
.
// create a form that's 150 by 100
NXSetRect(&theRect, 0, 200, 150, 100);
theForm = [ [Form alloc]
  initFrame:&theRect];
// add three entries to the form
[theForm addEntry: "Name"];
[theForm addEntry: "Address"];
[theForm addEntry: "Phone"];
// set the size of the form
[theForm sizeToFit];
[ [theWindow contentView]
  addSubview:theForm];
.
.
.
```

```
// code to display window
```

The **main()** function first creates a form that is 150 by 100 units. Then **main()** adds three fields (**Name**, **Address**, and **Phone**), and adjusts the size of the form to accommodate these entries. As before, **main()** installs the form as a subview of the window. Compile the application and verify that it works. Figure 6.14 shows **ControlDemo** with a button, a slider, a textfield, and a form.

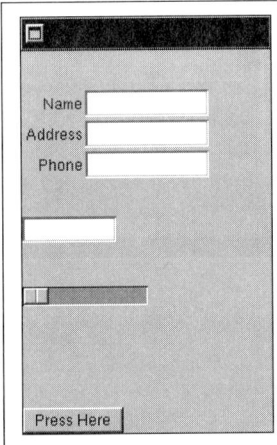

Figure 6.14 **ControlDemo** with all the controls

With the form created, set its target as follows:

Setting the target and action for the form and the button

```
[theForm setTarget:theButton];
// button should act as though
// it had been cliked
[theForm setAction:
  @selector(performClick:)];
```

Pressing **Return** in the form will send its action message (**performClick:**) to its target, the button. Thus the button will act as though it had been clicked each time we press **Return** in the form. Notice that since the button sends its action message to the other window, pressing **Return** in the form effectively brings up the other window. Figure 6.15 illustrates this sequence.

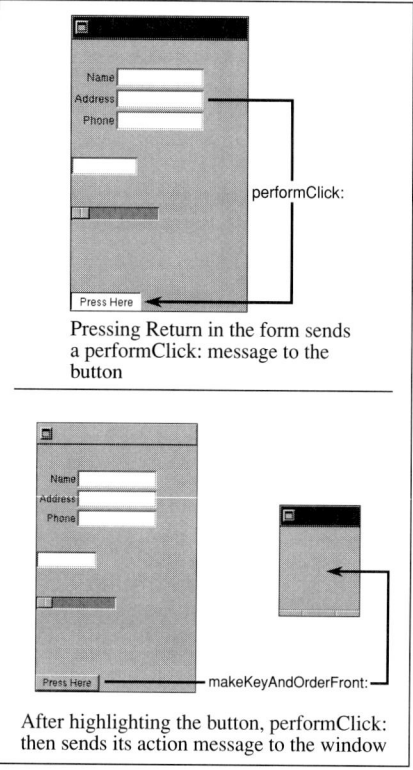

Figure 6.15 **ControlDemo** with the button as the form's target

In addition to the target-action paradigm, NeXTSTEP defines another paradigm for handling events: delegation.

6.4 The Delegation Paradigm

Use delegation to extend the functionality of a class without subclassing

Delegation allows us to extend the functionality of a class without subclassing. Consider a word processor that allows us to modify the contents of the window, the text. If we close the window and the text has not been saved, the application should display an alert panel to warn us that we will lose our changes. Initially, it may seem like we should subclass **Window** and add the functionality to display the alert panel. However, this is not a good solution since the **Window** class has a lot of overhead. Instead, we can define another object that will display the alert panel when the window is about to close: this other object is the ***delegate***.

Think of delegation as a form of message forwarding; the designers of NeXTSTEP anticipated that we will need to perform additional processing when certain events *will* happen or *after* these events have occurred. They left the possibility for us to add our own customized behavior, and all we have to do is define a delegate. The delegate should implement only those methods which correspond to the appropriate event(s).

Delegation is basically a form of message forwarding

By default, an object does not have a delegate: the delegate is a custom object that we must create and assign to one or more client objects. For example, the same delegate can control how *all* the windows (in the application) should behave when it is about to close (which is to display an alert panel). Additionally, the delegate can also accommodate other objects such as a text object, if there is one present (we will explore further in Chapter 9). By localizing functionality into a single delegate, we simplify the application by removing the need to create additional subclasses. There are several classes which can be extended with a delegate including the **Window**, **Text**, **Application**, **SavePanel**, and **OpenPanel**. For now, we will concentrate on how to add a delegate to the **Window** and **Application** classes.

An objects's delegate must be explicitly set

To intercept a delegate method, we must:

- verify that the class defines delegate methods by consulting the documentation for the class. If the class can be extended with a delegate, there will be a section at the end ("Methods Implemented by the Delegate") which lists methods the delegate can implement.
- create a custom class and instantiate it.
- assign this custom object as the delegate of the appropriate client object.
- implement the appropriate method. For example, if we wish to perform further processing when a window is about to close, we need to implement a **windowWillClose:** method in the delegate.

Table 6.5 shows some of the delegate methods for the **Window** class.

Window:Responder:Object		
	Name	Description
Instance variables	N/A	N/A
Methods	windowWillClose:sender	sent to the delegate before the window closes. The delegate can prevent the window from closing by returning nil

Table 6.5 Delegate methods for the **Window** class

Table 6.6 shows one of the delegate methods for the **Application** class.

Application:Responder:Object		
	Name	Description
Instance variables	N/A	N/A
Methods	appDidInit:sender	sent to the delegate after the application has been launched but before it has received its first event: the delegate can perform further initialization in this method

Table 6.6 Delegate methods for the **Application** class

All of the delegate methods are invoked before or after something has happened. Thus, the delegate method names have the following format: *class*{**Did**, **Will**}*method*. Some examples include:

- **windowWillClose:**
- **windowWillResize:toSize:**
- **appDidInit:**.

If delegation is available, use it instead of subclassing

How can we determine when to create a subclass and when to implement a delegate? If we can solve the problem using a delegate, then we should use it because it is a more straightforward solution. However, this may not always be possible since delegate methods have the following restrictions:

- they are defined only for certain classes in the Application Kit: some examples include **Application**, **Window**, **Text**, **SavePanel**, and **OpenPanel**. These classes were designed to be extended through delegation.
- we cannot (easily) add new delegate methods to these classes. For example, the **Window** class defines a **windowWillClose:** delegate method but not a **windowDidClose:** method. If we find we need such a method, we cannot simply add it to the **Window**'s collection of delegate methods. The problem is insurmountable.
- the delegate can extend the functionality of a class but it cannot add instance variables to the class.

Since a delegate can serve many clients, the delegate tends to be the central object in an application. A NeXTSTEP application is usually composed of the following objects at minimum:

- an application object to connect to the Window Server so that the application can draw and receive events
- one or more windows to display to the screen
- one or more subviews of the content view
- one or more controls to send action messages
- a central object responsible for initializing and creating the other objects in the application. This object tends to be the delegate of either **NXApp** or of a window in the application. The delegate is typically called a *controller object* since it is the core of the application.

Now let's explore the **windowWillClose:** method a little closer. By intercepting this message, we can perform additional processing *before* the window closes. In fact, we can prevent the window from closing by returning **nil**. Why would we want to do this? The most common case would be to verify if the user wishes to save the changes (if any) to the window's contents since closing the window would discard these changes.

By returning nil, windowWillClose: can prevent the window from closing

The Delegation Paradigm

To illustrate this method in action, first subclass **Object** and create the **WindowDelegate** class with **WindowDelegate.h** and **WindowDelegate.m**.

Listing for **WindowDelegate.h**

```
#import <objc/Object.h>

@interface WindowDelegate:Object

{
}

- windowWillClose:sender;

@end
```

Listing for **WindowDelegate.m**

```
#import <appkit/appkit.h>
#import "WindowDelegate.h"

#define SAVE NX_ALERTDEFAULT
#define CLOSE NX_ALERTALTERNATE
#define CANCEL NX_ALERTOTHER

@implementation WindowDelegate

- windowWillClose:sender
{
  int result;
  result = NXRunAlertPanel
    ([NXApp appName],
    "Unsaved changes. Close Anyway?\n",
    "Save",
    "Close anyway",
    "Cancel");

  switch(result)
    {
    case SAVE:
      printf("Save button selected\n");
```

```
      printf("Saving...\n");
      printf("Closing window\n\n");
      break;
    case CLOSE:
      printf("Close button selected\n");
      printf("Closing window\n\n");
      break;
    case CANCEL:
      printf("Cancel button selected\n");
      printf("Window won't close\n\n");
      return nil;
    }
  return self;
}

@end
```

Compile the **WindowDelegate** class with:

```
% cc -c -o WindowDelegate.o WindowDelegate.m
```

Now modify the main program so it creates a windowdelegate object and set it as the delegate of the window. This program is similar to **AppKitDemo.m** from Chapter 4 except for the changes in bold:

Listing for **Delegate_main.m**

```
#import <appkit/appkit.h>
#import "WindowDelegate.h"

// minimal program to demonstrate the
// windowWillClose: method

main()
{
  // create an application object
  // to establish connection to
  // Window Server
  id NXApp = [Application new];
  id theWindow;
  id theMenu;
  id theWindowDelegate;
  NXRect theRect;
```

The Delegation Paradigm

```
    NXSize theSize;

    // create a window that's at 125, 125
    // and is 200 by 300 pixels
    NXSetRect(&theRect, 125, 125, 200, 300);
    theWindow = [ [Window alloc]
      initContent:&theRect
      style:NX_RESIZEBARSTYLE
      backing:NX_BUFFERED
      buttonMask:NX_CLOSEBUTTONMASK
      defer:YES];

    // set the minimum size of window
    theSize.width = 100;
    theSize.height = 100;
    [theWindow setMinSize:&theSize];

    // create the menu
    theMenu = [ [Menu alloc]
      initTitle: [NXApp appName]];
    // create the menu option
    [theMenu addItem:"Quit"
      action:@selector(terminate:)
      keyEquivalent:'q'];

    // resize menu to accommodate menu option
    [theMenu sizeToFit];
    [NXApp setMainMenu:theMenu];

    theWindowDelegate =
      [ [WindowDelegate alloc] init];
    [theWindow setDelegate:theWindowDelegate];

    // send the window to the front
    // and display it
    [theWindow makeKeyAndOrderFront:nil];

    // go into event loop to wait for events
    [NXApp run];
}
```

Compile the main program with:

```
% cc -c -o Delegate_main.o Delegate_main.m
```

Link the **WindowDelegate** class to the main program with:

```
% cc -o DelegateDemo Delegate_main.o
WindowDelegate.o -lNeXT_s
```

Normally, when we click on a window's close button, the window just closes. In this case, we added some logic to create *an alert panel* with **NXRunAlertPanel()**. An alert panel, as its name suggests, is a panel that warns the user that something potentially disastrous will happen (in this case, the changes to the window may be lost). An alert panel runs in a *modal loop*, an inner loop that short-circuits the event loop to prevent the user from interacting with the rest of the application until the user presses one of the three buttons in the alert panel: **Cancel**, **Close**, or **Save** (the default). While the alert panel is displayed, the user cannot bring any other windows on top of it, not even to quit the application! **NXRunAlertPanel()** accepts from three to five arguments (this implies that alert panel can have from one to three buttons):

Before closing a window, display an alert panel for verification

- the first parameter is the title of the panel.
- the second is the message the alert panel should display.
- the third is the title for **button1**—this button automatically displays an arrow icon since it is the default action
- the fourth, if present, is the title for **button2**, the alternate button.
- the fifth, if present, is the title for **button3**, the other button.

By checking the return code, we can determine which button was pressed. The three buttons, **button1**, **button2**, and **button3** (counting from the right) return **NX_ALERTDEFAULT**, **NX_ALERTALTERNATE**, and **NX_ALERTOTHER** respectively: however since these values are not inherently obvious, we associate them with **Save**, **Close**, and **Cancel** respectively. Pressing the **Cancel** button returns **nil**, which effectively prevents the window from closing. Pressing **Save** normally should save the document. However since we did not want to complicate this example, we simply added a **printf()** statement to indicate which statement was executed in the **windowWillClose:** method.

Use the return code to determine which button in the alert panel was pressed

Figure 6.16 illustrates this entire sequence. We will encounter modal windows more in Chapter 9 when we explore the **OpenPanel** and **SavePanel** classes.

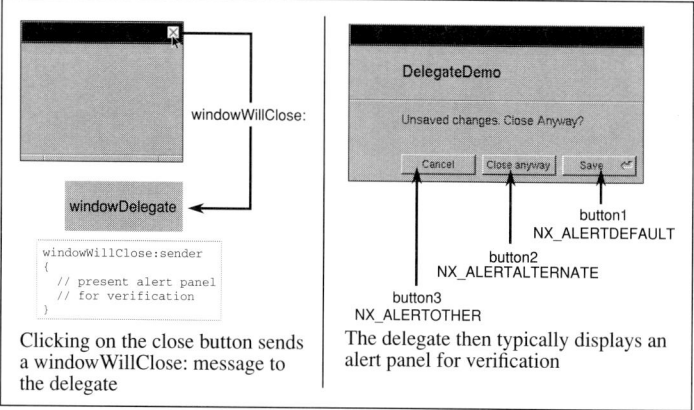

Figure 6.16 The **windowWillClose:** method in action

6.5 Designing Money

Now that we have discussed the control-action and delegation paradigms, we are ready to explore our application, a money converter. The specifications for this application are as follows:

> Money converts a given currency amount to various denominations, including American dollars, Japanese yen, British pounds, German marks, French francs and Austrian schillings. Typing in a currency amount and pressing Return converts the amount to the appropriate values for the other 5 denominations. If the user types in more than one amount, the last amount entered is used as the amount to convert.

Highlight the nouns and actions in the specifications as follows (the nouns are in bold and the actions are in bold italics):

> **Money** *converts* a given **currency amount** to various **denominations**, including **American dollars**, **Japanese yen**, **British pounds**, **German marks**, **French francs** and **Austrian schillings**. *Typing* in a currency amount and *pressing* the **Return key** converts the amount to the

appropriate **values** for the other 5 denominations. If the **user** types in more than one amount, the last amount entered is used as the amount to convert.

We now list the nouns and try to pair them with their respective actions to produce the objects:

- Money—this is not an object since it is simply the name of the application.
- currency amount—this is not an object because it does not have an action. It is input that needs to be retrieved, but that action is performed by another object. Since amount does not have any action on its own, it is simply an attribute of another object. We will return to this later.
- denominations, American dollars, Japanese yen, British pounds, German marks, French francs, and Austrian schillings—these are the output of the program, and again they do not have actions of their own. We can debate this point since it looks like these amounts need to display themselves (the same argument can be made for amount). However, these are simply floating point numbers and they cannot be objects (Objective-C treats a **float** as a type instead of an object).
- **Return** key—a hardware object that does not belong in the software model.
- user—an entity that does not need to be modelled.
- values—a synonym for denomination.

The list of actions is as follows:

- typing—since this action is performed by the user, it doesn't need to belong to an object.
- pressing—since this action is performed by the user, it doesn't need to belong to an object.
- convert—this is the central action in the application, yet no object exists to perform it. The implication is that we need to create a custom object. The most obvious name for this would be moneyconverter.

The moneyconverter is not the only object missing from the specification. We also need to consider that there is an application object, a menu, and at least one window. We must also consider what objects we will use to retrieve and display the data: these are the functions of the controls we have been discussing. However, we need to decide which controls we will be using. To interact with this application:

- we input a value.
- the application converts the value to five other values.
- the application displays all six values.

Using six separate textfields makes it awkward to enter data

As mentioned earlier, the most appropriate control for requesting a value and displaying it is a textfield. Since there are six values, we need six separate textfields. To inform the application we are ready to convert the value, we can add a button that converts the value in the last edited textfield to the appropriate values for the other five textfields. This design has a serious flaw, however. To edit a textfield, we first click on it to select it and then type in a value. However, if we decide to change another field, we need to click on it to select it. Thus, we have to switch between using the mouse and the keyboard repeatedly. Figure 6.17 illustrates this situation.

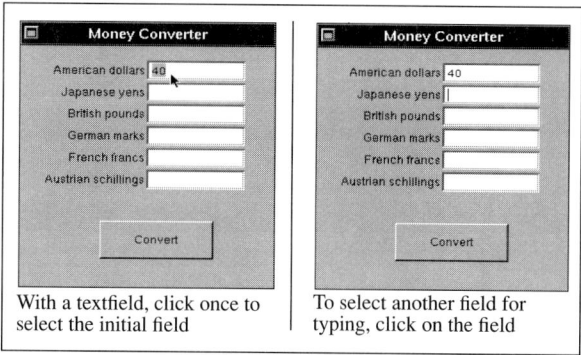

Figure 6.17 Money with six textfields and a button

Using a form requires fewer keystrokes to enter the data

To reduce the amount of keystrokes, we should use a form instead. With a form, we can click on one of its fields to select it. To skip ahead or backwards by one field, we press **Tab** and **Shift-Tab** respectively. As a final improvement, we can establish a relationship between the form and the button such that when we press **Return**, the form presses the button (by the **performClick:**

method). Pressing the button sends a message to the moneyconverter to convert the currency amount.

The list of objects includes the following:

- window
- application
- menu
- form
- button
- moneyconverter.

We now need to model the flow of the application. First, **Money** displays the window that contains the form and button. To input a value, we click on one of the fields. To start the conversion, we press **Return**, which signals the moneyconverter object to retrieve the value in the last edited field and then convert that value to the appropriate values for the other five fields.

As mentioned in Chapter 4, **Window**, **Menu**, and **Application** are core classes that appear in every application. Therefore, we will not be devoting CRC cards to these classes unless absolutely necessary (for example, one of the objects explicitly sends a message to **NXApp**). The only class that needs a CRC card is the **MoneyConverter** class. Why don't we produce CRC cards for the **Button** and the **Form** classes? Because these are internal to the **MoneyConverter** class; how they interact with the **MoneyConverter** class should be hidden from the client object

The button and the form are completely internal to the moneyconverter and do not require CRC cards

that uses the **MoneyConverter** class. Figure 6.18 shows the CRC card for the **MoneyConverter** class.

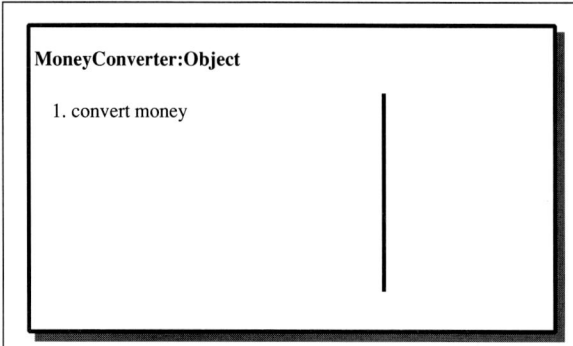

Figure 6.18 The CRC card for the **MoneyConverter** class

Table 6.7 shows the class summary table for the **MoneyConverter** class.

	MoneyConverter:Object	
	Name	**Description**
Instance variables	moneyForm	outlet for the form: this form is used for input and for displaying the conversions
Methods	convert:	converts the last edited entry and displays the appropriate value in the remaining fields of the form

Table 6.7 Class summary table for the **MoneyConverter** class

The form is internal to the moneyconverter

Since the form is internal to the moneyconverter, we group both objects and treat them as a *subsystem*, a collection of objects that works as one; an instance of a subsystem is referred to as a *composite object*. The Application Kit is full of composite objects. For example, a window contains, among other things, two buttons, a close button, and a miniaturize button. In the case of the moneyconverter, another object should not be able to access the form directly since this other object should not even be aware that the form exists.

The button is not included in the subsystem since it is not critical to the operation of the moneyconverter. We can easily substitute the button with another control (say, a slider), and the application would still work. Figure 6.19 illustrates the message diagram for the **Money** application.

The button is not part of the MoneyConverter subsystem

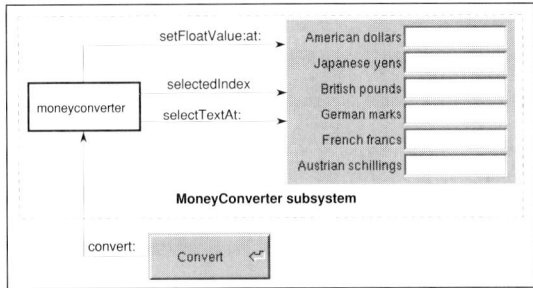

Figure 6.19 The message diagram for **Money**

There are several other tasks including installing the form and button as subviews of the content view and displaying them, which we are glossing over. Since we perform these actions in InterfaceBuilder (placing an object in a window automatically installs that object as a subview of the window's content view), we need not document them in our CRC cards.

The message diagram does not list every single message

Finally, why aren't we freeing the objects in this application? Because these objects are used for the entire application and we cannot safely free them until the application terminates. At that point, the statement **exit(0)** in the **main**() function will free all of the memory associated with our application, including our objects. From this point on, unless otherwise mentioned, we will assume that the application does not need to free the objects unless needed (as we will see, the only application that will do so is the one discussed in Chapter 9).

Money does not need to free the objects

Figure 6.20 shows the hierarchy graph for the **Money** application.

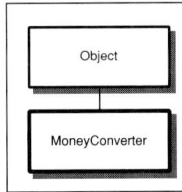

Figure 6.20 The hierarchy graph for **Money**

Now that the design is in place, we can proceed to the implementation stage.

6.6 Implementing Money

Start ProjectBuilder, create a project file, and save the application as **~/Money/Money**. Double-click on **Money.nib** under **Interfaces** in the Attributes accessory view to start InterfaceBuilder. In InterfaceBuilder, use the Window Inspector to remove the resize bar. Drag a button from the palette and place it in the Main Window. Then drag a form from the palette and place it in the Main Window.

Use Alt-drag to add extra fields to the form

Resize the form so that it has six fields instead of the standard two fields. First, click on the form to select it. With the form selected, **Alt**-drag (hold down the **Alt** key and drag) the form downward to create extra fields. Stop when the form has six fields. Figure 6.21 shows how this sequence works.

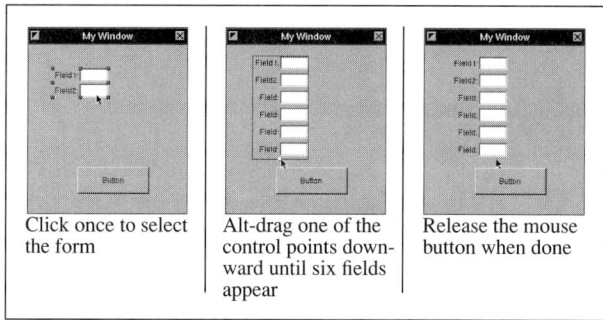

Click once to select the form | Alt-drag one of the control points downward until six fields appear | Release the mouse button when done

Figure 6.21 Adding fields to a form

Double-click to select the formcell and double-click again to edit the formcell's title

To edit the title of the field, double-click on the first field to select the formcell (like other controls, a form cooperates with a corresponding cell, in this case a formcell). With the formcell selected, double-click on it to select its text. Edit the first one to read **American** dollars. To edit the label in the second field, press the **Tab** key to skip forward. Repeat this sequence for the entire form and label the fields in the following order: **American dollars**, **Japanese yen**, **British pounds**, **German marks**, **French francs**, and **Austrian schillings** (the order is important, as we will see later). Resize the form so the textfields match the size of the

labels by dragging the right edge of the form. Figure 6.22 shows
the form labeled with the appropriate fields.

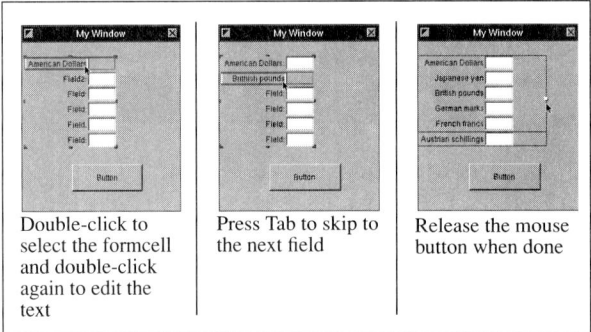

Figure 6.22 Labeling the form with the appropriate fields

Now create the **MoneyConverter** subclass:

- bring up the Class Browser by clicking on the **Classes** suitcase in the File Window. The Class Browser basically displays the classes in the Application Kit and the custom class(es) in the current application.
- select the appropriate superclass from which to subclass. Since **MoneyConverter** needs to be subclassed from **Object**, use the scrollbar to move to the left and click on the **Object** class to select it.
- select the **Subclass** option in the **Operations** pulldownlist. This creates a subclass called **MyObject**. In the Class Inspector, edit the textfield (labeled with **Class**) from **MyObject** to **MoneyConverter** and click **Rename Class**.

At this point, we have only created an entry in the class hierarchy: we have not yet defined the actions and instance variables. Figure

6.23 summarizes the entire sequence of creating the **MoneyConverter** subclass.

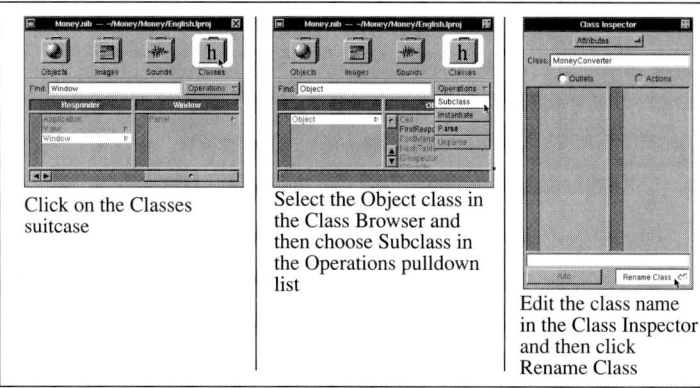

Figure 6.23 Subclassing **Object** to create **MoneyConverter**

An outlet is simply InterfaceBuilder's term for a collaborator

Since the **MoneyConverter** class needs to communicate with the form to determine the input value, it needs to define an *outlet*. An outlet is simply InterfaceBuilder's term for a collaborator, a placeholder for another object the current object will message later. With the **Outlets** button selected, type in **moneyForm** (notice the titles of the buttons change values as soon as we click on the lower text field) and press **Return** to add the outlet. Figure

6.24 shows how to add the **moneyForm** outlet to the
MoneyConverter class.

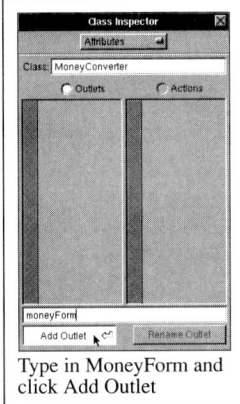
Type in MoneyForm and click Add Outlet

Figure 6.24 Adding the **moneyForm** outlet to the **Converter** class

Why does the **MoneyConverter** class need an outlet for the form but not for the button? Because a class only needs an outlet if it will be messaging the object. The moneyconverter needs to message the form later to determine the input and also to display the corresponding values in the other currencies, but it does not need to message the button for any purpose.

How, then, does the form communicate with the button if the form doesn't define an outlet? It turns out that every control has a predefined outlet, and the name of this outlet is **target**.

Click on the **Actions** button (notice the buttons change titles again) and type **convert** in the lower textfield. Click on the **Add Action** button to add the action to the class. We do not need to type the colon in the method name since InterfaceBuilder appends

InterfaceBuilder automatically adds a colon to the method name

this automatically to each method name. Figure 6.25 shows how to add the **convert:** method.

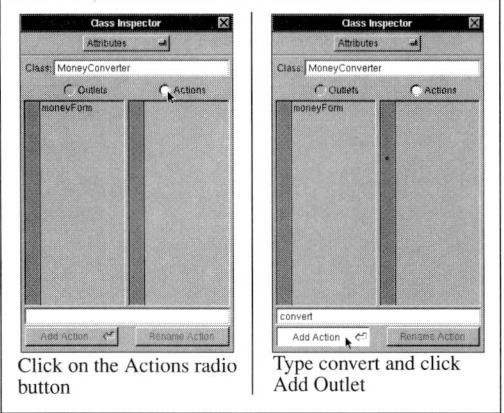

Figure 6.25 Adding the **convert:** method

InterfaceBuilder can only deal with methods that are oriented towards the control-action paradigm. As such, InterfaceBuilder only understands methods that have one parameter, **sender**. Some example includes:

- **convert:sender**
- **terminate:sender**
- **orderFront:sender**.

We cannot make a connection to a method such as **window:WillResize:to:** because InterfaceBuilder does not support a method of this type and never displays it in the Connections Inspector. Since the parameter for the methods in the Connections Inspector is always **sender**, InterfaceBuilder does not display this value.

Use the Instantiate option to instantiate the currently selected class

With all of the methods and outlets for the **MoneyConverter** class defined, we can now instantiate the class. Click on the **Classes** suitcase to bring up the Class Browser and select the **Instantiate** option in the **Operations** pulldownlist: selecting this option produces an icon in the File Window that represents an instance of the class. Figure 6.26 shows how to instantiate the **MoneyConverter** class.

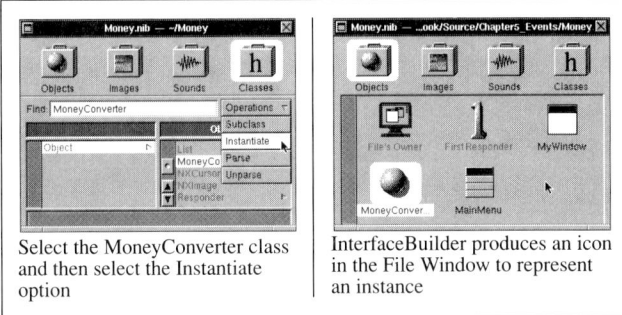

Figure 6.26 Instantiating the **MoneyConverter** class

With the instance defined, we can establish the connections in the interface. Figure 6.27 illustrates the connections we need to make.

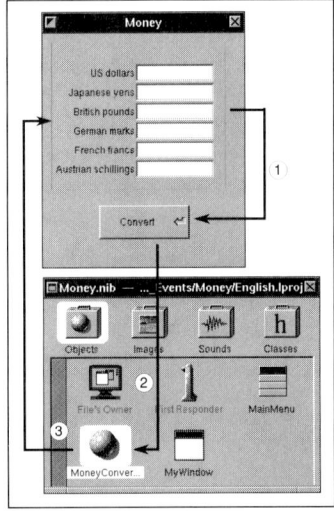

Figure 6.27 Connecting the objects in **Money.nib**

The three connections are as follows:

1. Connect the button as the target for the form and select the **performClick:** method.
2. Connect the moneyconverter as the target for the button and select the **convert:** method.

Pressing Return should send a performClick: message to the button

Connect to the entire form instead of to an individual formcell

3. Connect the form as the **moneyForm** outlet of the moneyconverter.

The button should initiate the conversion process, so connect the button to the moneyconverter. **Control**-drag from the button to the moneyconverter, select **convert:** in the Connections Inspector, and click **OK**. Pressing **Return** in the form should also initiate the process. Therefore, connect the form to the button, select **performClick:**, and click **OK**. Pressing **Return** in the form will programmatically press the button by sending it a **performClick:** message. This in turn sends a **convert:** message to the moneyconverter.

As the final step, establish the form as an outlet for the moneyconverter by **Control**-dragging from the moneyconverter to the form. In the Class Inspector, select the **moneyForm** outlet and click **OK**. Be very careful at this point, and verify that the moneyconverter is connected to the form instead of a formcell inside the form. Figure 6.28 shows the difference.

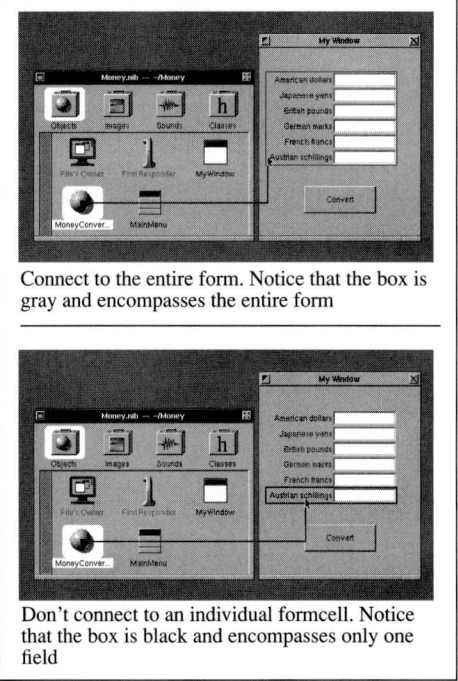

Connect to the entire form. Notice that the box is gray and encompasses the entire form

Don't connect to an individual formcell. Notice that the box is black and encompasses only one field

Figure 6.28 Connecting to the form instead of to the formcell

Why is this important? Because in the **convert:** method, the moneyconverter will be sending methods defined for the **Form** class: a formcell will not be able to respond to these methods, and the application will crash with a runtime error. Remember, the receiver is not bound to the method until runtime (for more information on the error message, consult Appendix C).

With all the connections defined, enter Test Mode (**Command-r**) and test the interface. Type in values in the form and press **Return** to cause the button to depress. However, the conversion will not occur because the **convert:** method does not contain any code. Remember, the Test Mode only allows us to test the interface, not the entire application.

> Typically, we create one or more custom classes for a given application; as part of the class definition, we add methods and outlets to the class. Once we have defined the class, we instantiate it. This produces an icon which we can inspect with the Class Inspector. Afterwards, we add controls to the interface to send messages to the instance.
>
> A control always initiates a control message. When we connect a control to a custom object (that is, we drag *from* the control *to* the custom object, which in this case is the moneyconverter), the Class Inspector displays the methods the moneyconverter understands. We then need to select the appropriate method to be invoked. On the other hand, when we connect *from* the custom object *to* the control, it means we wish to initialize an outlet of the custom object; the Class Inspector will display the appropriate outlets (in this case, there is only one, the **moneyForm** outlet) that are defined for the custom object (the moneyconverter).

Before continuing, add an arrow icon to the button to indicate that it can be activated by pressing **Return**. To do this, click on the **Images** suitcases and drag the arrow icon to the button. Release

The convert: method will send messages to a form

We can't test the convert: method from InterfaceBuilder's Test Mode

the mouse button, and the button will automatically accept the icon. Figure 6.29 illustrates this sequence.

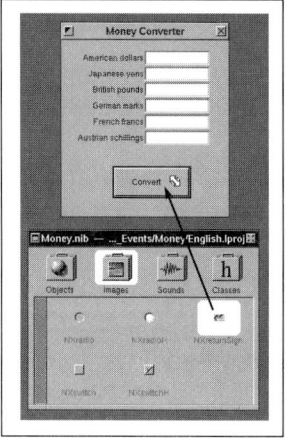

Figure 6.29 Adding an arrow icon to the button

Unparse generates the template files for the currently selected class

Now that we have the methods and outlets defined, generate the template files by selecting the **MoneyConverter** class and selecting the **Unparse** option in the **Operations** pulldown list. Click **OK** in the prompt window to indicate that we wish to add the template files (**MoneyConverter.h** and **MoneyConverter.m**, which are abbreviated with **MoneyConverter.[hm]**) to the project file. Figure 6.30 shows the effects of the **Unparse** command.

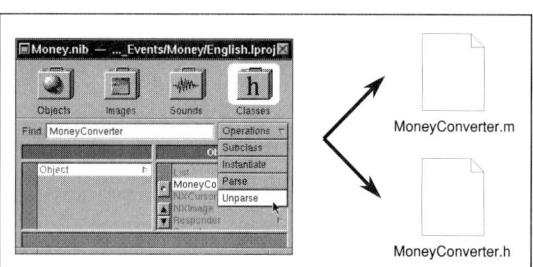

Figure 6.30 Generating the template files with the **Unparse** command

Open the interface file and the implementation file by **Command**-double-clicking on **MoneyConverter.m** in ProjectBuilder. Edit the implementation file with the changes in bold:

Listing for **MoneyConverter.m**

```
/* Generated by Project Builder */

#import <appkit/appkit.h>
#import "MoneyConverter.h"

#define MAXIMUM 6

@implementation MoneyConverter

- convert:sender
{
  int index, loop;
  float entry, value, dollar_equiv;

  // Array contains the conversion of rates
  // of other currencies to dollars
  static float rate[MAXIMUM] =
    {1.00, 135.0, 0.50, 1.67, 6.00, 14.5};

  // Determine which field of the form
  // was the last to be edited
  index = [moneyForm selectedIndex];

  // Calculate equivalent of foreign currency
  // at edited field to dollar equivalent
  entry = [moneyForm floatValueAt:index];
  dollar_equiv = entry / rate[index];
  for (loop = 0; loop < MAXIMUM; loop++)
    {
    // Calculate other currencies
    // using look-up table
    value = dollar_equiv * rate[loop];
    // display value at appropriate field
    [moneyForm setFloatValue:value at:loop];
    }
  // leave the last edited field as the
  // selected text
  [moneyForm selectTextAt:index];
  return self;
}
```

```
@end
```

> Be careful with the **Unparse** command since it can overwrite existing files. For example, assume we accidentally typed in **convest:** instead of **convert:** for the method name. Using **Unparse,** we generate the template files and add the rest of the code for the **convest:** method. At this point, we realize we mistyped the method name. We modify the method (from **convest:** to **convert:**) in **MoneyConverter.h** and **MoneyConverter.m**. However, we realize that our application will not work because the button is connected to the **convest:** method in InterfaceBuilder. We save our class files and return to InterfaceBuilder to rename the method in the Class Inspector and then unparse the class again. At this point, InterfaceBuilder will prompt us if we wish to overwrite the existing class files. InterfaceBuilder does not know the changes we have already made to the class template files; it only knows to generate blank template files from the characteristics we specified in the Class Inspector.
>
> In Chapter 7, we will learn how to use the **Parse** command, which allows us to modify a class definition without accidentally overwriting an existing definition.

6.7 Walking Through the Code

The **convert:** method first sets up an array that contains the conversion rates expressed in terms of dollars. The first entry is **1.00**, the second entry is **135.0** (which means one dollar is equivalent to 135 yen), etc. Then, **convert:** determines the input by determining which field was the *last entry edited* using the **selectedIndex** method of the **Form** class. Once **convert:** has the index of the last edited field, it retrieves the input using the **floatValueAt:** method; this returns the floating point number at the field specified by the **index** parameter.

Afterwards, **convert:** converts the input to an equivalent amount of dollars since the entire conversion array is expressed in terms of dollars. The method then calculates the entry at the current field by multiplying the dollar equivalent against the current rate in the array; **convert:** repeats this sequence for every field in the array. Finally, the method leaves the last edited field as the selected text so we don't have to click on the form to start editing it.

6.8 Suggestions

This program serves its intended purpose but has some deficiencies. This section lists them and also offers suggestions for adding new features.

6.8.1 Adding Another Menu Option

Since there is no option for reopening the window, we have to quit and then restart the application if we accidentally close the window. This can be fixed one of several ways:

- create the window without a close button.
- add an option to bring back the window.
- use the **NXRunAlertPanel**() panel function to add an alert panel for verification before closing the window.

It is not necessary to implement all three solutions. To remove the close button, make the window the currently selected object. In the Attributes Inspector, deselect the **Close** switch button. However, InterfaceBuilder will not remove the close button until the application is executing in either Test Mode or as an executable. If InterfaceBuilder removed the close button in Construction Mode, we would have no way of closing the window.

To add an option to bring back the window:

- add another menu item to the Main Menu and name it **Open Window**.
- connect the menu option to the window icon in the File Window.
- choose **makeKeyAndOrderFront:** in the Connection Inspector.

To add the alert panel, set the moneyconverter as the delegate of the window by connecting from the Main Window to the moneyconverter and then selecting **delegate** in the Connections Inspector. Then, in **MoneyConverter.[hm]**, implement the **windowWillClose:** method and use the **NXRunAlertPanel**() function to present the panel. Figure 6.31 shows how to make the moneyconverter the delegate of the Main Window.

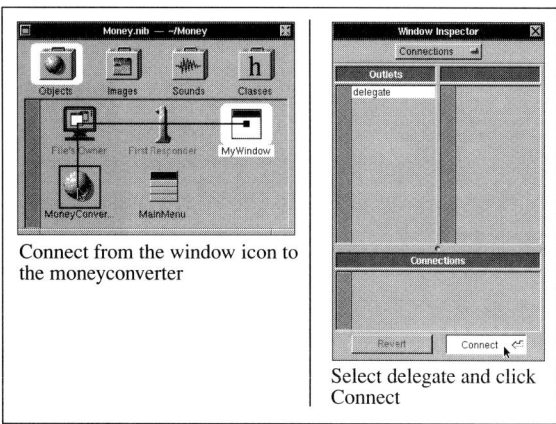

Figure 6.31 Setting the moneyconverter as the delegate of the Main Window

6.8.2 Setting a Window's Minimum Size

In the current application, we can resize the window to be so small we won't be able to see the **Convert** button. To rectify this, we can limit how small the window can be resized:

- use the Size Inspector to determine the current size of the window. Resize the window to its minimum size, but make sure the form and the button are still visible. Note the values for **width** and **height** in the **Frame** box. Since we are not interested in saving these changes, click **Document** ⇒ **Revert to Saved**

(**Command-u**) to discard these changes. Figure 6.32 illustrates how to display the Size Inspector.

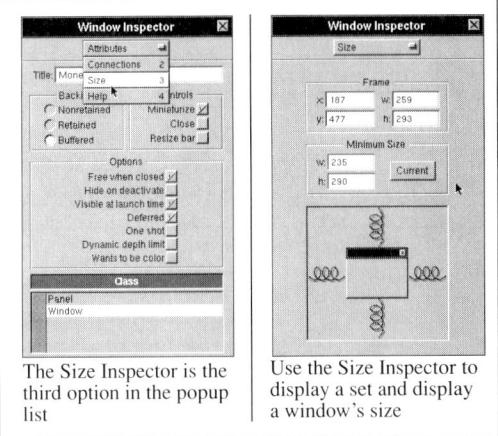

Figure 6.32 Determining the size of a window with the Size Inspector

- since the moneyconverter needs to message the window in **appDidInit:** later, add an outlet for the window to **MoneyConverter.h** and declare the **appDidInit:** method (the changes are in bold):

Adding a new outlet and method

```
/* Generated by Project Builder */

#import <objc/Object.h>

@interface MoneyConverter:Object
{
  id moneyForm;
  id theWindow;
}

- convert:sender;
- appDidInit:sender;

@end
```

- do not combine the two instance variables on the same line because InterfaceBuilder will not be able to parse the class properly: **each outlet needs to be declared as an id variable on a separate line**.

- return to InterfaceBuilder, select the **MoneyConverter** class, and select the **Parse** option in the **Operations** pulldown list. At the openpanel, select the **MoneyConverter.h** file and click **OK**. This signals InterfaceBuilder to update the **MoneyConverter** class definition with the new changes (add the **theWindow** outlet). Figure 6.33 shows the effects of the **Parse** command.

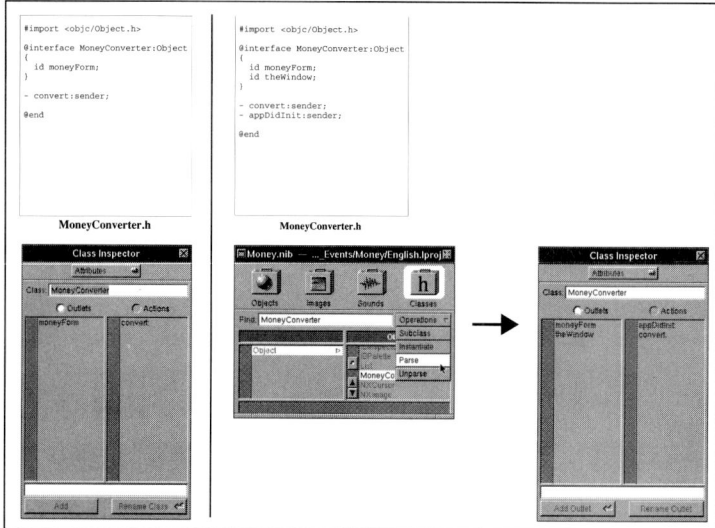

Figure 6.33 Parsing in a class updates the outlets and actions for the class in InterfaceBuilder

- connect from the moneyconverter to the Main Window. In the Connections Inspector, select the **theWindow** outlet (recently added with the **Parse** sequence from the previous step) and click **Connect**.

> InterfaceBuilder treats each instance variable of type **id** on a separate line as an outlet. It sees this declaration as two outlets, **moneyForm** and **theWindow**.
>
> ```
> @interface Moneyconverter:Object
> {
>   id moneyForm;
>   id theWindow;
> }
> ```
>
> Additionally, InterfaceBuilder treats each instance method with one parameter, **sender**, as a control-action connection and displays this in the Connections Inspector. Unfortunately, this is not always the case, as with **appDidInit:**
>
> ```
> - appDidInit:sender;
> ```
>
> This method shows up in the Connections Inspector for the **MoneyConverter** class, even though it is not a control-action oriented method.

- make the moneyconverter a delegate of **NXApp** (the **File's Owner** icon) and implement the application delegate method, **appDidInit:**. Figure 6.34 illustrates how to set the delegate for **NXApp**.

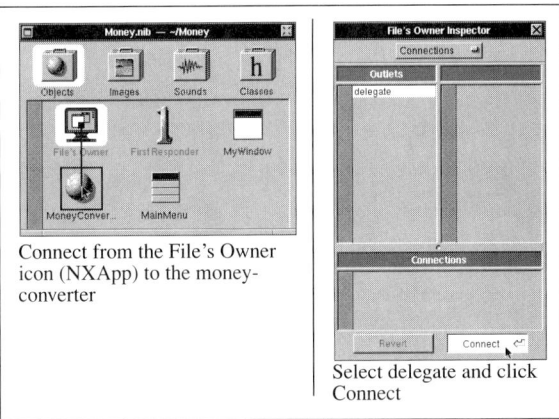

Figure 6.34 Setting the moneyconverter as the delegate of the application object

- in **appDidInit:**, initialize an **NXSize struct** with these values and send a **setMinSize:** message to the window. The **appDidInit:** method should look like (this sample fragment assumes the minimum size for the window should be 235 by 290):

Setting a window's minimum size

```
@implementation MoneyConverter

- appDidInit:sender
{
  NXSize theSize;
  theSize.width = 235;
  theSize.height = 290;
  [theWindow setMinSize:&theSize];
  return self;
}
```

As part of the initialization routine, **NXApp** sends an **appDidInit:** message to its delegate before processing the first event. This is a good place for an application to perform final initialization before the application enters the event loop.

> Note that this example is used to illustrate how the **appDidInit:** method works, not how to set the minimum size of a window. We can do this by simply using the Size Inspector and typing in the appropriate values at the **Minimum Size** fields.
>
> If there is only one window, couldn't we have simplified the solution by not adding an outlet and declare a local variable in the **appDidInit:** method as in the following example?
>
> ```
> - appDidInit:sender
> {
>   id theWindow = [NXApp mainWindow];
>
>   NXSize theSize;
>   theSize.width = 235;
>   theSize.height = 290;
>   [theWindow setMinSize:&theSize];
>   return self;
> }
> ```
>
> This will not work because the application receives an **appDidInit:** message *before* it displays its window. In this example, **theWindow** will still be a **nil** object. The application will not crash (sending a message to a **nil** object simply returns **nil**), but it will not work the way we wish either (namely, set the minimum size of the window). In Chapter 7, we will learn how to use the **awakeFromNib** method to perform further initialization for scenarios like the one we just described.

6.8.3 Autosizing

Now that we have limited the size the window can shrink to, we need to consider another related problem, enlarging the window. Ideally, when we are enlarging or shrinking the window, its contents (the button and the form) should enlarge or shrink as well: this is known as **autosizing**. In the current implementation, the

Autosizing allows the window's contents to change with the window's size

button and the form do not change size, and their placement in the window changes as the window is modified (assuming we have added a resize bar to the window). In fact, the button and the form can even overlap, which produces an unsightly user interface. To prevent this, we can use the Size Inspector to set the autosizing features of the controls in the window.

The springs in the Size Inspector indicate autosizing

The Size Inspector uses two rectangles (one inside another) to represent the window and the object inside the window: the inside rectangle is the object in the window (such as our button) and the outside represents the window. The Size Inspector then uses springs (the twisted lines) to indicate autosizing and straight lines to indicate a constant size. The direction indicates whether the size should change or remain constant, i.e., a horizontal spring indicates horizontal autosizing.

The outer spring indicates that the distance between the object and the window is variable

A spring in the inner rectangle indicates the object should autosize, and a spring in the outer rectangle indicates the distance between the object and the window should change as the window is enlarged or shrunk. A line in the inner box indicates the distance between the object and the edge of the window should remain constant, if possible. Figure 6.35 shows an object (in this case, the form from the **Money** application) with the horizontal and vertical autosize to be variable and the distance from the bottom edge of the window to be variable.

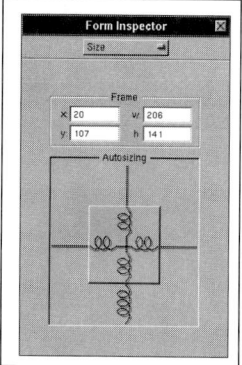

Figure 6.35 Using the autosizing features in the Size Inspector

Use the following settings to prevent the button and form from overlapping and to autosize with the window.

- set the button to autosize vertically and horizontally. Set the distance between the button and the top edge of the window to be variable.
- set the form to autosize vertically and horizontally. Set the distance between the form and the bottom edge of the window to be variable.

Figure 6.36 illustrates these settings for the button and the form (note the window now has a resize bar).

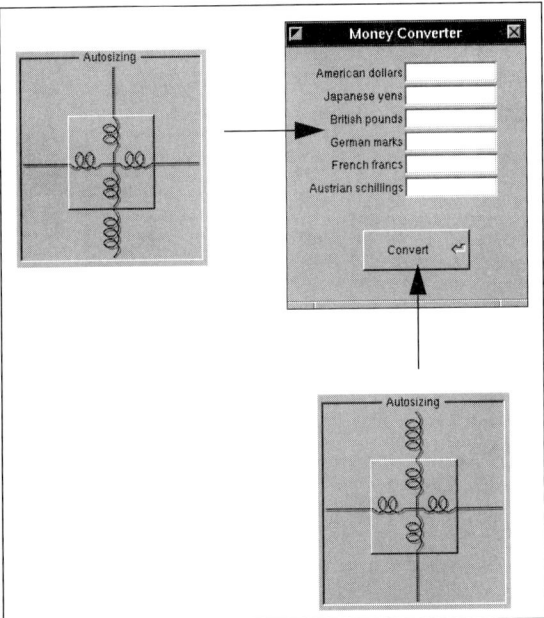

Figure 6.36 Setting the autosizing characteristics of the button and the form

By using autosizing and setting the window's minimum size, the application can control how the contents of the window resize when the window is resized.

6.9 Troubleshooting

Here are some potential problems:

- The application crashes with the following error message:

error: FormCell does not recognize selector selectedIndex

IOT trap: core dumped
- **Cause**: The **moneyForm** outlet was connected to the formcell instead of the form itself. Therefore, the message **selectedIndex** is sent to a formcell, which does not understand the message; this results in a runtime error.
- **Solution**: Connect the **moneyForm** outlet to the form instead of to the formcell (see Figure 6.28) and recompile the application.

- Clicking on the button does not do anything.
  - **Cause**: The button is probably not connected to the moneyconverter.
  - **Solution**: Connect the button to the moneyconverter and select the **convert:** method in the Connections Inspector. Recompile the application and retest it.

- Pressing **Return** does not highlight the button or convert the amount.
  - **Cause**: The form is not connected to the button.
  - **Solution**: Connect the form to the button and select the **performClick:** method in the Connections Inspector. Compile the application and test it again.

- The window can be resized to be smaller than the form, even though we have already set its minimum size in the **appDidInit:** method.
  - **Cause**: The moneyconverter has not been assigned as the delegate of the window.
  - **Solution**: Connect the window to the moneyconverter, select **delegate** in the Connections Inspector, and click **Connect**.

- The Connections Inspector does not display the **theWindow** outlet.
  - **Cause**: The **theWindow** instance variable was not declared on a separate line, it was not declared as type **id**, the **MoneyConverter.h** file was not saved, or the updated class definition was not parsed in InterfaceBuilder.
  - **Solution**: Declare the **theWindow** instance variable to be type **id** on a separate line, save the **MoneyConverter.h** file,

and then use **Parse** to update the class definition for **MoneyConverter**.

- Changes made in the **.nib** file or class template files are not incorporated into the application.
    - **Cause**: The changes were probably not saved. ProjectBuilder only uses the latest saved version of the **.nib** file.
    - **Solution**: Save all files associated with a project before building the project.

6.10 Summary

Processing events is the heart of programming in an event-driven environment like NeXTSTEP. NeXTSTEP defines two paradigms for processing events: target-action and delegation. In the target-action paradigm, manipulating one object sends a message to another object, the target. For example, clicking on the **Quit** menu option sends a **terminate:** message to **NXApp**.

Delegation is used to extend the functionality of a class without subclassing. For example, to display an alert panel when a window is about to close, we can create an object with this functionality and assign it as the delegate of the window.

In the next chapter, we will explore how to examine the event record and how to perform another fundamental task in a graphical environment: drawing.

Summary

Chapter 7
Drawing With PostScript

Most environments perform drawing in two different languages: the environment uses one language to create the images on the screen (the exact language is system-dependent). It then converts the images to PostScript, a powerful device-independent 2D imaging language that is the de facto standard in the printing industry, to produce the output on the printer. This conversion introduces some inconveniences:

- the system has to spend time converting images.
- there are discrepancies between what is displayed on the screen and what is displayed on paper.

NeXTSTEP is unusual because it uses PostScript to perform imaging on the screen and on the printer. This ***unified imaging model*** results in a more ***WYSIWYG*** (what-you-see-is-what-you-get or *wizzywig*) printed output. This chapter explores how to perform rudimentary drawing on the NeXT through the PostScript language and the **View** class, an abstract superclass that provides a framework for drawing to the screen and to the printer.

Most environments use two languages to produce output on the screen and on the printer

NeXTSTEP uses PostScript to image to the screen and to the printer

7.1 Goals

In this chapter, we will:

- describe the **View** class and how it is most commonly used.
- illustrate how to process mouse events.
- introduce the PostScript language.
- demonstrate how to interface PostScript with Objective-C using single operator C functions and **pswraps**.

7.2 The View Class

The **View** class is an abstract superclass that provides a framework for drawing and handling events. Most of the objects displayed on the screen (and printer) are instances of **View** and its

A view always exists inside a window

subclasses. These include the buttons, sliders, text, etc. A view never exists in isolation: it is always part of a window.

Coordinates are specified as floating point numbers

All drawing performed in NeXTSTEP is based on the first quadrant of a Cartesian coordinate system with the origin in the lower left corner of the screen: the x axis extends to the right and the y axis extends upwards. In NeXTSTEP, coordinates can be specified as floating-point numbers, although we will not do so in our examples.

Each window maintains its own coordinate system

The screen coordinate system is used to specify where to draw a window, but each window itself maintains its own coordinate system (known as the *base coordinate system*) with the origin at the lower left corner of the window instead of the screen. Figure 7.1 shows the relationship between the screen and the base coordinate system.

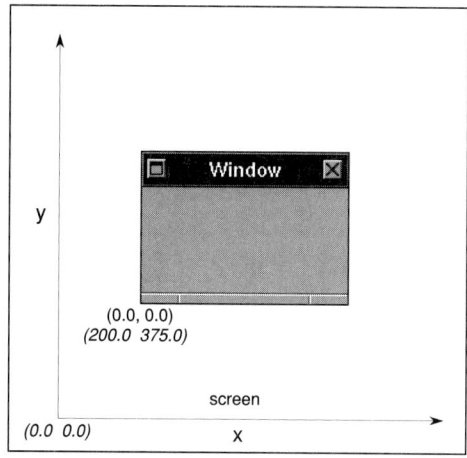

Figure 7.1. Coordinates in the base system and screen system

Views in a window draw relative to the window's base coordinate system

The views in a given window draw relative to the window's base coordinate system instead of the screen coordinate system. We shall see why this is important when we display the views.

7.2.1 Creating a View

All drawing in NeXTSTEP is based on rectangular areas

NeXTSTEP draws everything—this includes the windows and the views inside the windows—in rectangular areas. NeXTSTEP defines some C **structs** to facilitate specifying these rectangles. A rectangle is specified by two pairs of floating point numbers, one pair for the origin and one for the size. **NXRect** is simply a **struct** with two fields, and each field is a pair of floating point numbers:

The **NXRect** struct

```
typedef struct _NXRect
    {
    NXPoint     origin;
    NXSize      size;
    } NXRect;
```

NXPoint is a **struct** with two floating point numbers to specify the **x** and **y** coordinates of a given point:

The **NXPoint** struct

```
typedef struct _NXPoint
    {
    NXCoord     x;
    NXCoord     y;
    } NXPoint;
```

NXSize is also a **struct** with two floating point numbers to specify the **width** and the **height** of the rectangle:

The **NXSize** struct

```
typedef struct _NXSize
    {
    NXCoord     width;
    NXCoord     height;
    } NXSize;
```

NXCoord itself is a **typedef** for a floating point number:

The **NXCoord** typedef

```
typedef float NXCoord;
```

Since **View** is an abstract superclass, we never instantiate it. Instead, we subclass **View** and then instantiate its subclasses. Creating a view is much like creating a window:

- use the **NXSetRect()** function to initialize an **NXRect struct** with the origin and size of the view.
- use the **alloc** method to instantiate the class.
- use the designated initializer method, **initFrame:**, to initialize the instance.

The following code fragment creates a view that is 200 by 200 at 325 and 300 pixels from the origin of the base coordinate system of the window that contains the view. The values contained in the **theRect struct** is the view's *frame rectangle*, which specifies the size and position of the view inside the superview's coordinate system.

Creating a view

```
#import <appkit/appkit.h>
#import "SquareView.h"

id theSquareView;
id theWindow;
NXRect theRect;

theWindow = [ [Window alloc]
    initContent:NULL
    style: NX_TITLEDSTYLE
    backing:NX_BUFFERED
    buttonMask:NX_MINIATURIZEBUTTONMASK
    defer:YES];
NXSetRect(&theRect, 325, 300, 200, 200);
theSquareView = [[SquareView alloc]
    initFrame:&theRect];
```

Figure 7.2 shows where the view is located in the window's base coordinate system.

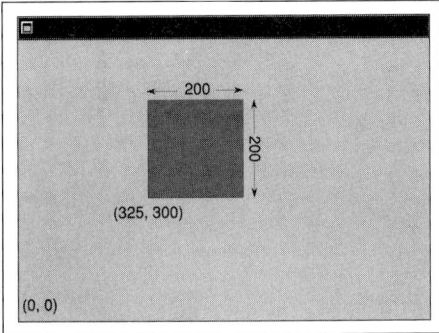

Figure 7.2. A view's location inside its window

Note that the previous code fragment only creates the view. To display it, we must perform some more steps:

- install it as part of a window.
- tell the view to display itself.

7.2.2 Adding Subviews

A view always has a *superview*, the view that contains it, and 0 or more *subviews*. The coordinate system of a given view is always specified relative to its superview. By default, when a window is created, it contains a *content view* (the gray area inside the window). To draw inside a window, add the view as a subview of the content view. To add a view as a subview of the content view:

A view always has a superview and 0 or more subviews

- get the **id** of the content view using the **contentView** method.
- add the view as a subview of the window's content view using the **addSubview:** method.

This is illustrated in the following code fragment (this code assumes a window already exists):

Installing a view

```
[[theWindow contentView]
    addSubview:theSquareView];
```

Note that any view—not just the content view—can be the superview of a given view. Now that our view is part of a window, we need to display it to make it visible.

> To determine which window contains the given view, send a **window** message to the view. Likewise, to determine the view's superview, send a **superview** message to the view. This is illustrated below:
> ```
> whichWindow = [theView window];
> whichSuperview = [theView superview];
> ```

7.2.3 Displaying the Views

The content view draws before any other view in the window

Views are arranged in a hierarchy that determines their drawing order. A view always draws before its subviews. Since the content view is the superview of all the views in a window, it draws before any other view. Figure 7.3 shows the drawing order of the views in a window.

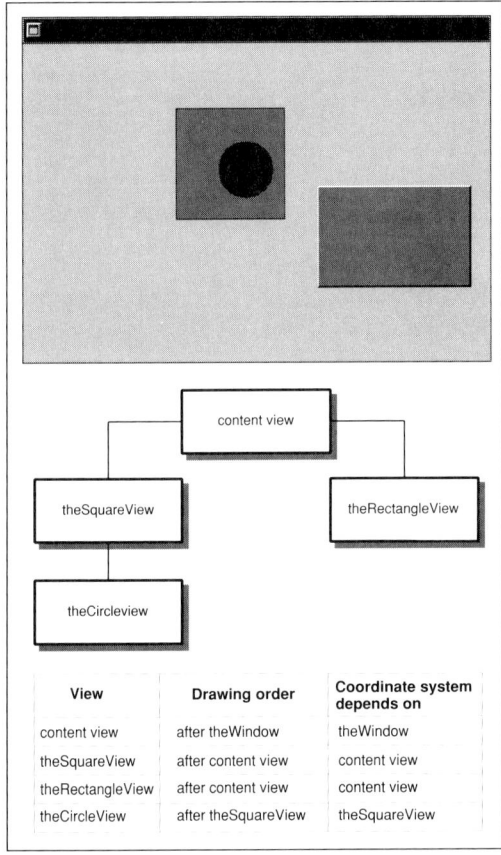

Figure 7.3. Drawing order of views in a window

Each view defines its own coordinate system (the *local coordinate system*), which can be inherited from its superview or be set by the view. For example, the coordinate system can be rotated so that all drawing is rotated when displayed (this will be explored a little later). In most cases, the frame rectangle of a view is completely enclosed by its superview's frame rectangle. However, there are times when part of a subview lies outside its superview. An application can draw anywhere in the view's coordinate system but only the region that is within the superview's frame

Each view defines its own coordinate system

rectangle will be visible; the rest of the drawing is said to be *clipped*. Figure 7.4 illustrates these concepts.

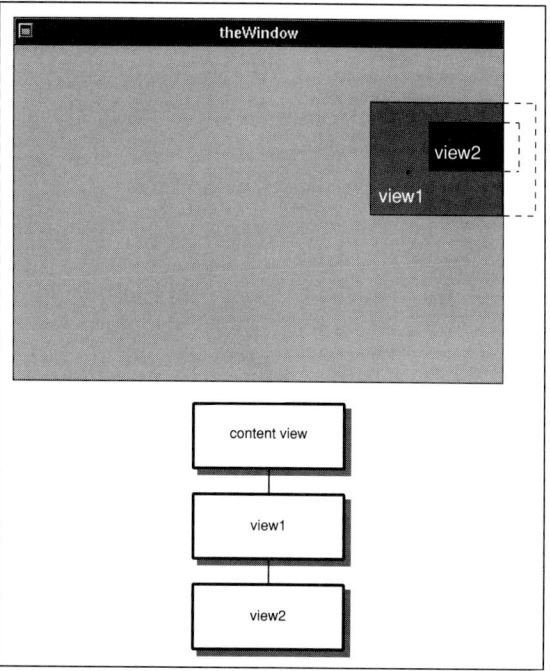

Figure 7.4. A view's frame rectangle can be outside of its superview's

A graphics state maintains all the information associated with a view

Since NeXTSTEP is a multi-window environment, it must be able to save and restore the parameters associated with each window: the view needs to be drawn, the current drawing color, the current coordinate system, etc. These parameters are referred to as the *graphics state*; each window and each view has an associated graphics state. Fortunately, the Application Kit maintains most of this information for us. We simply need to write code to draw the objects and the Application Kit handles how and when the objects will be drawn.

The display message automatically sends a drawSelf:: message

To display a view, send it a **display** message, which will in turn send a **drawSelf::** message. The **View** subclass in question inherits the **display** method from the **View** class, but it needs to override the **drawSelf::** method. The **display** method simply performs some initialization to the drawing environment, but the

drawSelf:: method itself contains code to perform the actual drawing. The **display** method:

- saves the current graphics state using **PSgsave()**.
- sets the *clip path*, i.e., establishes where the view's boundaries are so that any drawing that takes place outside these boundaries will be clipped.
- sends a **drawSelf::** message to the view. The **drawSelf::** method is where the actual drawing code is implemented.
- recursively notifies the subviews to display themselves.
- restores the graphics state using **PSrestore()**.

This entire process is called *focusing*, and NeXTSTEP handles it each time a views uses the **display** method to draw. As we will see later, if a view draws without using the **display** method, it must explicitly perform the aforementioned steps.

The display method performs focusing before drawing

The following code fragment shows a sample implementation of the **display** and **drawSelf::** methods. Assume we have a simple application that draws a line from (0, 0) to (50, 25) each time we click a button. The button sends a **draw:** message to the view, and the **draw:** method in turn sends a **display** message. The **display** method performs the aforementioned initialization and then sends a **drawSelf::** message to the view. This is illustrated in the following code fragment.

An example of **display** and **drawSelf::**

```
-draw:sender
{
   [self display]; // sends a drawSelf:: message
   [return self];
}

-drawSelf :(NXRect *)r :(int)rectCount
{
   // draw a line in black
   PSsetgray(0.0);
   PSmoveto(0.0);
   PSlineto(50.0, 25.0);
   PSstroke();
```

```
    }
```

> The **drawSelf::** receives different arguments from **display** depending on the circumstances. These parameters can be used to optimize drawing when scrolling a view. Since we are not scrolling, we need not concern ourselves with these parameters.

An application should never send a drawSelf:: message to a view

Note that an application should never send a view a **drawSelf::** message directly. The application should send the **display** message to the view, which in turn sends a **drawSelf::** message to itself. In some cases, the Window Server sends a **display** message to the view automatically. For example, sending a **makeKeyAndOrderFront:** message to a window will result in a **display** message. This message in turn draws the window, the content view and all of its subviews, which includes the view in question. This insures that the view is always drawn properly without any extra effort on our part.

> A view receives a **display** message under the following circumstances:
> - the application explicitly sends it.
> - its window is told to display itself (such as when the window receives a **makeKeyAndOrderFront:** message).
> - its superview is told to display itself.

7.3 Mouse Events

As we discussed in Chapter 6, NeXTSTEP is an event-driven environment. **NXApp**, the application object, basically retrieves events from an event queue and then forwards them to the active window. If the event is a mouse event or keyboard event, the window passes them to the appropriate view in the view hierarchy. Each event is of the type:

```
eventType:(NXEvent *)theEvent
```

The fields of an **NXEvent struct** are as follows:

```
typedef struct _NXEvent {
   int type              /* event type */
   NXPoint location;     /* mouse location */
   long time;            /* time since startup */
   int flags;            /* key state flags */
   unsigned int window;  /* window number */
   NXEventData data;     /* type-specific info */
   DPSContext ctxt;      /* context number */
} NXEvent;
```

The first field, **type**, defines the type of event the event (keyboard event, kit-defined event, mouse event, etc.). We will concern ourselves only with the mouse events:

- **mouseDown:**
- **mouseUp:**
- **mouseDragged:**
- **mouseMoved:**
- **mouseEntered:**
- **mouseExited:**.

To respond to a particular type of event, we can implement a method with the same name as the event message. We will explore only two messages, **mouseUp:** and **mouseDown:**.

> What if the cursor is in an area occupied by two views when an event is generated? The last view to draw is the first to receive events. In Figure 7.4, if we click in **view2**, **NXApp** would send a **mouseDown:** message to **view2** even though it is in **view1**'s boundary. The key is that **view2** draws after **view1** and therefore is the first to receive the event.

The event record is fairly complex, but the only field of the record we are interested in is the **location** field. This specifies the cursor's location: **location** is of type **NXPoint**, which, as explained

The application receives the mouse event in the form of a C struct

in Chapter 6, contains two other fields, **x** and **y**. Since **eventRecord** is a pointer to the event record, **eventRecord->location.x** and **eventRecord->location.y** specify the x and y coordinates of the cursor respectively (**->** is a C notation for a pointer to a field in a **struct**). The following code fragment illustrates how to override the **mouseDown:** method to print the location of the cursor inside a view.

Displaying a view's coordinates in its window's coordinate system

```
-mouseDown:(NXEvent *)theEvent
{
   // location field contains the cursor's
   // location in the window's base system
   printf("Window coordinates at %1.f, %1.f",
      theEvent->location.x,
      theEvent->location.y);
   return self;
}
```

The **location** field specifies the coordinates in the window's base coordinate system, which is not always as useful as if it was expressed in the view's coordinate system.

> For more information on the various types of events and the meaning of other fields, see **/NextLibrary/Documentation/ NextDev/Concepts/Pre3.0_Concepts/05_Events.rtfd**.

7.4 Converting Coordinates

The **View** class defines many methods for converting coordinates from one system to another (from the window's coordinate system to the view's, for example). Table 7.1 is the class summary table for the **View** class.

View:Responder:Object		
	Name	**Description**
Instance variables	N/A	N/A
Methods	convertPoint:(NXPoint *) aPoint fromView:aView	converts a point from *aView*'s coordinate system to the coordinate system of the receiving view. If *aView* is nil, then this method converts from window coordinates
	convertPoint:(NXPoint *) aPoint toView:aView	converts a point from the view's coordinate system to the coordinate system of *aView*. If *aView* is nil, then this method converts to window base coordinates
	convertPointFromSuperView: (NXPoint *)aPoint	converts a point from the coordinate system of the view's superview to the view's coordinate system
	convertPointToSuperView: (NXPoint *)aPoint	converts a point from the view's coordinate system to that of its superview

Table 7.1 Class summary table for the **View** class

The following code fragment demonstrates a view that overrides the **mouseDown:** method to print the coordinates of the cursor in the view's coordinate system and the window's base system:

Printing a view's coordinates in its coordinate system

```
-mouseDown:(NXEvent *)theEvent
{
    // location field contains the cursor's
```

```
        // location in the window's base system
        printf("Window coordinates at %.1f, %.1f",
            theEvent->location.x,
            theEvent->location.y);
        // convert to view's system
        [aView convertPoint:theEvent->location
            fromView:nil];
        // print location field, which now
        // contains the coordinates in view's system
        printf("Window coordinates at %.1f, %.1f",
            theEvent->location.x,
            theEvent->location.y);
        return self;
    }
```

7.5 PostScript

All drawing in NeXTSTEP is in PostScript

NeXTSTEP uses PostScript to perform all drawing to the screen (and to any other output device). In fact, the Window Server, the system program an application needs to communicate with in order to function, has an embedded PostScript interpreter.

PostScript offers the following features:

- device independence—PostScript can render to any device that understands the language. PostScript is supported on various hardware including typesetters and laser printers.
- resolution independence—PostScript can display at whatever resolution the medium is capable of supporting. For example, the screen resolution is typically between 75 and 92 dots per inch (*dpi*) whereas a laser printer's resolution tends to be around 300 to 600 dpi; however, we don't need to write code to support the different resolution because PostScript handles the necessary conversion to produce the image at the higher resolution.
- numerous functions for text and graphic support—PostScript has extensive commands to manipulate text and graphics including scaling (magnifying and shrinking the image), rotation, etc.

PostScript is an interpreted language

Whereas Objective-C is a compiled language, PostScript is an interpreted one. We don't compile a PostScript program to produce an executable. During runtime, the PostScript interpreter interprets each statement in the source code. There are two consequences of this implementation:

- the PostScript program can have syntax errors and can still execute as long as the interpreter does not encounter the offending commands. For a compiled language like Objective-C, the compiler flags all syntax errors before the program can be compiled and linked.
- an interpreted language is always slower than a compiled one since the system must translate each command to machine code during runtime. For a compiled language, the translation is done once during compilation. This results in better performance since the system doesn't have to continually translate each command during runtime.

Write the majority of the application in Objective-C since it is a more efficient and more generalized language than PostScript: PostScript is more suitable for imaging than for processing. We add PostScript code only if we need to draw an object not already supported by the AppKit. For example, we don't need to write code to display a button since the **Button** class contains code to draw its instances: **Button** inherits this code from **View**. However, if we have a class that needs to draw a circle, we would need to add PostScript code to the class' **drawSelf::** method.

At this point, we will provide a brief introduction to the syntax of PostScript. Afterwards, we will explore how to interface PostScript with Objective-C since they are two completely different languages.

Write PostScript code only to draw something not already supported by the AppKit

> NeXTSTEP actually uses *Display PostScript*, a superset of PostScript which includes a lot of extensions for interactive display. Additionally, NeXTSTEP includes other extensions such as compositing, transparency (also known as the *alpha channel*) etc. However, for our purposes, we will limit our discussions primarily to standard PostScript.

7.5.1 PostScript Primer

To draw something, send PostScript code to the Window Server

In one sense, PostScript is a programming language and in another, it is a *page description language* because PostScript was pioneered to describe what a printed page would look like for the laser printer. To program in PostScript, simply issue English-like commands to describe what the page should look like. In NeXTSTEP, we issue the PostScript commands to the Window Server, since it—or, more specifically, the interpreter inside the server—controls what is displayed on the screen.

To produce a drawing, construct a path and then paint it

PostScript uses a coordinate system similar to the one found in the **View** class (actually, it's the other way around since the **View** class was invented with PostScript as the model); that is, the x axis increases to the right and the y axis increases upward. To draw something in PostScript, create a path and then "paint" it. To create a path, issue commands to move the cursor. As the cursor moves, it creates an invisible path. To make the path visible, we either stroke it or fill it. Figure 7.5 shows this process.

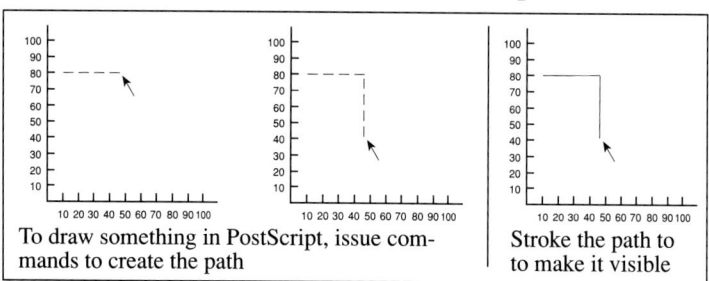

Figure 7.5. Drawing a shape with PostScript

PostScript is a stack based language

Note that the syntax for PostScript is a little unusual in that the arguments to a command are specified before the command. For instance, PostScript uses **0 15 moveto** instead of **moveto 0 15**. PostScript is a *stack based language;* the arguments (also known as *operands*) are placed on the stack, and the commands (also known as *operators*) remove the operand(s) from the stack before executing. Placing an operand on a stack is known as *pushing* and removing an operand from a stack is known as *popping*. Figure

7.6 shows how a typical PostScript command works with the stack.

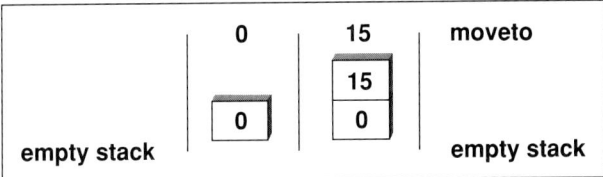

Figure 7.6. Execution of a typical PostScript command

A stack is known as a *last-in-first-out* (**LIFO**) structure because the last item placed on the stack is the first one to be removed. PostScript uses this scheme to process each command immediately without having to devote large buffers to store the entire program. This results in a more efficient environment.

To experiment with PostScript, use Yap in /**NextApps**. Yap is a PostScript application which can execute PostScript commands and display the output in a window. To start Yap, double-click on /**NextDeveloper/Apps/Yap.app**. Then, click **Document ⇒ New** to create a new document. Type in the following PostScript code (which produces a square that is 50 by 50 units) and save it as **~/PostScript/square_outline.ps**.

Yap is useful for tinkering with PostScript

Listing for **square_outline.ps**

```
50  50 moveto
100 50 lineto
100 100 lineto
50  100 lineto
50  50 lineto
```

```
        stroke
```

> Yap is an acronym for Yet Another Previewer, an allusion to the more powerful Preview application in **/NextApps**, which can display PostScript files in a window. Preview is more oriented towards previewing page-oriented PostScript files whereas Yap is more oriented to interactive tinkering. For more information on Yap, see **/NextLibrary/ Documentation/NextDev/DevTools/10_Yap/Yap.rtfd**.

To execute the code and display the output in the window, click **File ⇒ Execute** (**Command-E**) to execute it. Resize the output window if the square does not display. Figure 7.7 shows the execution of **square_outline.ps**.

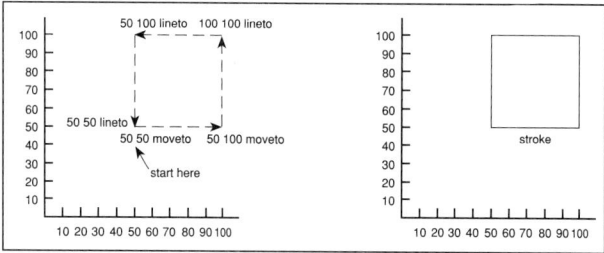

Figure 7.7. Execution of **square_outline.ps**

> When an image is printed, one unit in PostScript is equal to 1/72 of an inch (this figure has its origin in the typesetting industry). However, one screen unit (that is, one pixel) is about 1/92 of an inch. This is totally transparent to our program since PostScript performs the conversion.

Now, modify the program to fill the square to black, and name this program **black_square.ps**. This program introduces some new commands: **rlineto** (for relative lineto), **setgray** (for setting the gray level), and **fill** (for filling an area).

Listing for **black_square.ps**

```
50 50 moveto
50 0 rlineto
0 50 rlineto
-50 0 rlineto
closepath
0 setgray
fill
```

Instead of using absolute coordinates, **rlineto** allows us to specify a relative offset from our current position. Thus, **50 0 rlineto** means to move 50 units to the right and **-50 0 rlineto** means to move 50 units to the left. The new operator, **closepath**, closes the path from the current point to the starting point. In this case, it is used to close the square. The **0 setgray** command is used to set the color to 0. In PostScript, 0 is black. Figure 7.8 shows the execution of **black_square.ps**.

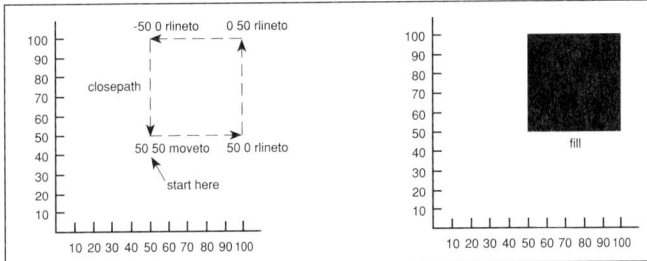

Figure 7.8. Execution of **black_square.ps**

PostScript does allow us to specify colors, although that is a much more complicated model. For our discussion, we will limit ourself to the various gray levels. In PostScript, **0** is black, **.333** is dark gray, **.667** is light gray, and **1** is white. Any other value produces a varying level of gray.

To draw a circle in PostScript, use the **arc** operator, which adds a circular path to the current one. This operator expects five parameters on the stack:

• the x coordinate of the arc's center

- the y coordinate of the arc's center
- the radius
- the arc's starting angle
- the arc's ending angle.

The **arc** operator traces the path from the starting angle to the ending angle counterclockwise. The code below shows how to draw three-quarters of a circle 30 units wide at (50, 50).

Listing for **circle.ps**

```
50 50 30 0 270 arc
fill
```

Figure 7.9 shows the execution of **circle.ps**. To draw a complete circle, we can specify 360 (degrees) as the ending angle.

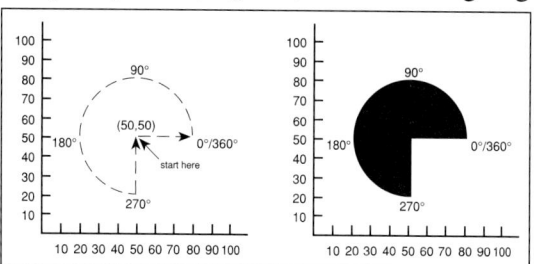

Figure 7.9. Execution of **circle.ps**

PostScript uses a percent sign (%) to denote comments. The listing below illustrates this.

Some sample PostScript comments

```
% this is a comment line
% PostScript program to draw a filled square
% the origin is at (50, 50)
50 50 moveto
50 0 rlineto
0 50 rlineto
-50 0 rlineto
closepath
```

```
fill
```

7.5.2 PostScript Special Effects

Because of its extensive collection of operators, we can easily create special effects in PostScript. In this section, we will illustrate how to:

- rotate the axes—this rotates the image.
- scale the axes—this enlarges or reduces the image.
- create shadows—this produces a pseudo 3D look.

To rotate the axes, use the **rotate** operator. This operator pops an operand from the stack and rotates the axes counterclockwise by that many degrees. The following code fragment illustrates how to use the **rotate** operator:

Rotating the axes

```
45 rotate
```

Any drawing performed in this graphics state will be rotated. Remember that NeXTSTEP maintains a separate graphics state for each view and window. Thus, rotating the axes of a view doesn't affect another window or view (although it does affect the view's subviews). Figure 7.10 illustrates the effects of rotating the axes.

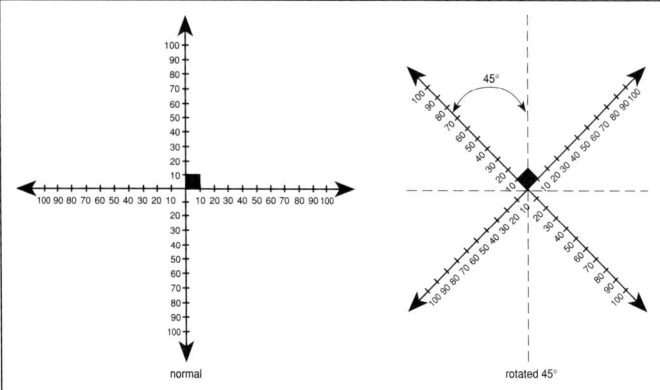

Figure 7.10. Rotating the axes

To illustrate this, add the line in bold to **square_outline.ps** and execute the following program in Yap.

Modifying **square_outline.ps** to rotate the square

```
45 rotate
50 50 moveto
100 50 lineto
100 100 lineto
50 100 lineto
50 50 lineto
stroke
```

To scale the axes, use the **scale** command. This changes the size of the coordinate's system units by the amount specified by the operands. The following code fragment shows how to magnify the x axis by 3 and the y axis by 3 (this increases the area by 9).

Scaling the axes by 3

```
3 3 scale
```

We can use this feature to produce a rectangle from the code that produces a square. However, instead of modifying the size of the square itself, use the **scale** operator to scale the x axis to be greater than 1. The following code fragment produces a rectangle with the width twice that of the height:

Modifying **square_outline.ps** to scale the square

```
% scale the x axis by 2
% and leave the y axis alone
% thus, a square will be drawn as a rectangle
% with the width twice as much as the height
2 1 scale
50 50 moveto
100 50 lineto
100 100 lineto
50 100 lineto
50 50 lineto
stroke
```

To create a shadow effect, draw the shadow in one color, change the color to a lighter color, and then draw the same image slightly shifted from the original location. Figure 7.11 shows the two stages of this technique.

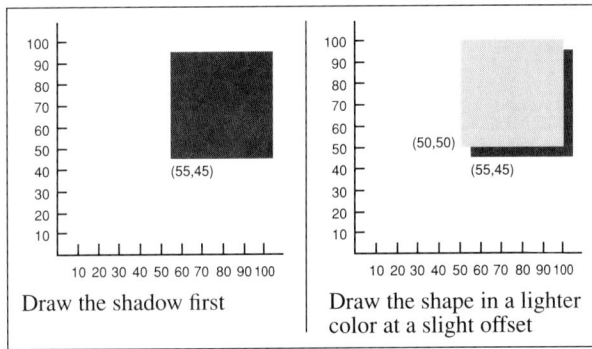

Figure 7.11. Producing a shadow effect in PostScript

Modify **black_square.ps** with the changes in bold to produce a square with a shadow. Notice that the square is now light gray (it used to be black), and the shadow is black:

Listing for **shadow_square.ps**

```
% this draws the shadow in black
55 45 moveto
50 0 rlineto
0 50 rlineto
-50 0 rlineto
closepath
0 setgray
fill
% this draws the square in light gray
50 50 moveto
50 0 rlineto
0 50 rlineto
-50 0 rlineto
closepath
.667 setgray
fill
```

So far, we have learned how to draw in pure PostScript, but these examples have been noninteractive. What if we wish to place an interface on the program? We then need to interface our PostScript program with Objective-C in one of two ways: single operators and **pswraps**.

7.5.3 Interfacing to Objective-C Using Single Operators

Single operators are C interfaces to the PostScript operators

Single operator C functions are C interfaces to the PostScript operators. These functions names start with **PS** followed by the PostScript operator name, as in **PSmoveto**, **PSlineto**, etc. Table 7.2 lists some single operators and their PostScript operator equivalents.

Single operator C functions	PostScript equivalent operators
PSmoveto(50, 50);	50 50 moveto
PSlineto(10, 10);	10 10 lineto

Table 7.2 Single operator C functions and Postscript operators

Single operator C functions	PostScript equivalent operators
PSstroke();	stroke

Table 7.2 Single operator C functions and Postscript operators

The following fragments compare **square_outline.ps** in pure PostScript against another version in Objective-C with single operator C functions:

Listing for **square_outline.ps**

```
50 50 moveto
100 50 lineto
100 100 lineto
50 100 lineto
50 50 lineto
stroke
```

Equivalent code using single operator C functions

```
- drawSelf:(NXRect *)r :(int)rectCount
{
   PSmoveto(50, 50)
   PSlineto(100, 50)
   PSlineto(100, 100)
   PSlineto(50, 100)
   PSlineto(50, 50)
   PSstroke()
   return self;
}
```

Since NeXTSTEP is based on a client-server architecture—the client is our Objective-C application and the server is the Window Server, which contains an embedded PostScript interpreter—performing any PostScript operation requires *interprocess communication* between the Window Server and our application. Interprocess communication is one application (process, in UNIX terminology) communicating with another completely separate

Performing any PostScript operation requires interprocess communication between the application and the Window Server

application. This interprocess communication is quite time-consuming and can easily degrade the performance of the application. In the upcoming section, we explore how to minimize the interprocess communication.

7.5.4 Interfacing to Objective-C Using pswraps

pswraps is more efficient than single C operators because it requires fewer interprocess messages

If we need to send a lot of PostScript code to the server, we should place it in a separate file for *pswraps*, a preprocessor that converts a PostScript file into C functions that can communicate with the Window Server. Using **pswraps** is more efficient than using single operators because the application can send all the PostScript code in one interprocess message to the Window Server. For example, assume the application needs to send five PostScript operators to the Window Server to draw a rudimentary shape. If the application use single operators, it would have to generate five interprocess messages to the Window Server. Using **pswraps** allows the application to send all five operators in one interprocess message, resulting in less interprocess communication between the application and the Window Server. This improves the performance of the application because, as we pointed out earlier, interprocess communication can be time-consuming.

> The single operators are actually one line wraps for the PostScript operators. To see all the single operators, consult the file **/NextLibrary/Documentation/NextDev/NextStep/Reference/03_CFunctions/SingleOpFuncts.rtf.**

pswraps generates a .c and a .h file from the .psw file

A file that contains PostScript code to be included in an Objective-C program is called a *wraps* file. A wraps file usually has a **.psw** (for PostScript wraps) extension. Basically **pswraps** reads the wraps file and then generates a C file (**.c**) with an associated header file (**.h**). In our source code, we then include the **.h** file. NeXTSTEP (specifically ProjectBuilder) automatically uses **pswraps** to convert all **.psw** file(s) and then compiles the generated files (**.h** and **.c**) to form the object files. ProjectBuilder then links these object files to form the executable. Figure 7.12 shows how **pswraps** is used in the development process.

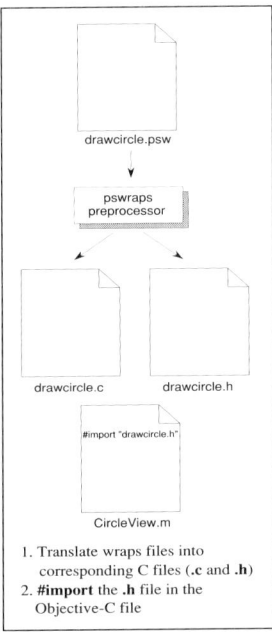

Figure 7.12. How **pswraps** fits in the program structure

To modify the application, modify the **.psw** file and then rebuild the application. Don't modify the C code generated by **pswraps** because this technique is highly error-prone.

Like any standard source code file, a wraps file can contain as many functions as necessary. A wraps function has four parts:

- the **defineps** keyword
- the name of the function followed by the parameter(s), if any
- the body of the function
- the **endps** keyword.

Figure 7.13 shows a sample wraps function. Note that the definition looks like a C function, but the body contains only PostScript code.

```
// wraps routine to draw a circle
defineps drawcircle(float xOffset, yOffset,
                angle, xScale, yScale)
   % tranlate axes
   xOffset yOffset translate
   % rotate
   angle rotate
   % scale
   xScale yScale scale
   % move to new origin
   0 0 moveto
   % draw circle
   0 0 5 0 angle arc
   % fill to white
   1 setgray
   fill
endps
```

declaration

wraps body

Figure 7.13. A sample wraps function

The following code fragment shows how an Objective-C program would invoke a wraps function. This example assumes the earlier example where a button is connected to the **draw:** method. Each time the button is pressed, a line is drawn from (0, 0) to (50, 25).

Calling a pswraps function

```
- draw:sender
{
   [self display]; // this calls drawSelf::
   [return self];
}

- drawSelf:(NXRect *)r :(int)rectCount
{
   // draw a line in black
   float gray, linewidth;
   gray = 0.0;
   linewidth = 2.0;
   drawline(gray, linewidth);
   return self;
}
```

Listing for **drawline.psw**

```
// wraps to draw a line
// from (0,0) to (50,25)
defineps drawline (float gray, linewidth)
    % set the gray level
    gray setgray
    linewidth setlinewidth
    % draw the line
    0 0 moveto
    50 25 lineto
    stroke
endps
```

Note that **drawline** is a C function (that will be generated by the **pswraps** preprocessor) and can thus be accessed from C (through a function call). However, **drawline** is completely inaccessible from PostScript.

> Note that the body of the pswraps can only contain PostScript code so we must use **%** for comments. Be extremely careful when using **pswraps** since it doesn't verify if the PostScript syntax is correct. Remember, PostScript is an interpreted language, and the interpreter will not catch syntax errors until it encounters the offending line during execution.

7.6 Instance Drawing

One of the many extensions NeXTSTEP adds to PostScript is *instance drawing*, which is useful for drawing a temporary image over a fixed image. A common example of instance drawing is

Instance drawing is used to draw a temporary image over a fixed image

when an application draws a rectangle around objects to indicate which objects we are selecting. Figure 7.14 shows this sequence.

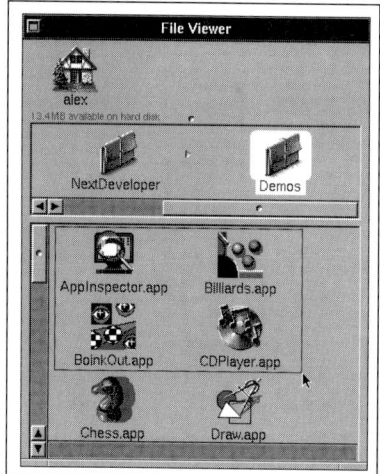

Figure 7.14. An example of instance drawing

Instance drawing draws directly to the screen

When an application draws to a window, NeXTSTEP first updates the offscreen buffer and then updates the window on the screen accordingly. When an application uses instance drawing, it draws directly to the on-screen window instead of the offscreen buffer. To use instance drawing, perform the following steps:

- erase any previous instance by using **PSnewinstance()**, which restores the image from the offscreen buffer.
- turn on instance drawing with **PSsetinstance(YES)**.
- perform the necessary drawing, which will draw directly to the screen instead of the offscreen buffer.
- turn off instance drawing with **PSsetinstance(NO)**.

For example, assume we have a view that draws a square, and we wish to print coordinates of the cursor in the view when the user clicks in the view's boundary. The easiest way to do this is to override the **mouseDown:** method. The following code illustrates this:

Printing a view's coordinates

```
- mouseDown:(NXEvent *)theEvent
```

```
{
   char buffer[30];

   // convert from window co-ordinates to
   // view co-ordinates
   [self convertPoint:&theEvent->location
      fromView:nil];

   // lock focus so graphics commands
   // are applied to this view
   [self lockFocus];
   // erase old instance drawing
   PSnewinstance();
   // start new instance drawing to draw directly
   // to the window
   PSsetinstance(YES);
      // select font otherwise output
      // will be upside down
      PSselectfont("Times-Roman", 16.0);
      // print co-ordinates on view
      PSmoveto(theEvent->location.x,
         theEvent->location.y);
      sprintf(buffer, "%.1f, %.1f",
         theEvent->location.x,
         theEvent->location.y);
      // set color to light gray
      PSsetgray(NX_LTGRAY);
      // show the string
      PSshow(buffer);
   PSsetinstance(NO);

   // balance lockFocus with unlockFocus
   [self unlockFocus];
   return self;
}
```

This method can be broken down into the following steps:

- convert the coordinates in the event from the window's base coordinate system to the view's coordinate system by using the **convertFromPoint:** method.
- focus on the view to force all subsequent commands to go to this view with the **lockFocus** method. As mentioned earlier, this is one of the tasks the **display** method automatically performs.

However, since this view is drawing outside of the **display** method, it needs to explicitly perform the focusing.

- erase any remaining instance drawing from the previous **mouseDown:** event.
- turn on instance drawing.
- print the coordinates of the cursor in the view's local coordinate system. There are two things to note in this step:
  - before using **PSshow()**, the method uses **PSselectfont()** to select a font.
  - the method displays the string using **PSshow()**.
  - since the **PSshow** operator expects a string as a parameter, the **mouseDown:** method needs to convert the coordinates from **float** to a string by using the **sprintf()** function.

> If a view does not select a font before using **PSshow()**, then the output will be upside down. Why? The default font will be used, and this font expects the view to be already flipped. For more information on flipped views, see Chapter 9.

- turn off instance drawing.
- remove the focus from this view (with **unlockFocus**), since the application may draw to another view. Each **lockFocus** message should be balanced with an **unlockFocus** message.

What would happen if the application didn't use **PSnewinstance()** to erase the previous instance drawing? The view would print each set of coordinates over the previous image and would soon be filled with strings, resulting in a mess. Figure

7.15 shows the results of correct and incorrect uses of instance drawing.

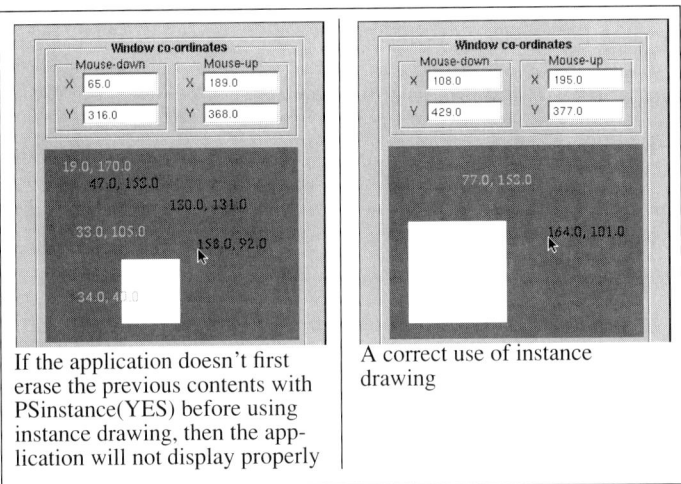

Figure 7.15. Correct and incorrect use of instance drawing

We are now ready to design an application, **Shapes**, which illustrates instance drawing and the other concepts covered so far.

> An alternative to using instance drawing is to use multiple buffered windows and compositing. However, these are fairly advanced techniques beyond the scope of this book.

7.7 Designing Shapes

The specifications for our application are as follows:

> Shapes has two rectangular regions in a window, the first region displaying a square and the second displaying a circle. The user can rotate, scale, and translate each shape by manipulating a series of controls. Clicking and releasing the mouse button in either of the rectangular regions prints two sets of coordinates, one where the mouse button was clicked and one where the mouse button was released. Each set of coordinates is expressed in terms of the win-

dow's base coordinate system and the local coordinate system.

Highlighting the nouns and verbs produces the following results:

Shapes has two **rectangular regions** in a **window**, the first region *displaying* a **square** and the second displaying a **circle**. The **user** can *rotate*, *scale*, and *translate* each **shape** by *manipulating* a **series of controls**. *Clicking* and *releasing* the **mouse button** in either of the rectangular regions *prints* two sets of **coordinates**, one where the mouse button was clicked and one where the mouse button was released. Each set of coordinates is expressed in terms of the **window's base coordinate system** and the **local coordinate system**.

Let's first explore the nouns:

- Shapes—the name of the application.
- rectangular regions—a synonym for the frame rectangle for each of the view. It is not an object.
- window—InterfaceBuilder automatically provides a window.
- square, circle—these describe the type of drawings we will be performing. As we learned earlier, the only way to draw an object that is not supported by the AppKit is to subclass the **View** class and add our own drawing code. These two nouns represent the names of the subclasses we have to create. We will return to these two nouns later in the design stage.
- user—the user is beyond the scope of the software model.
- shape—a term used interchangeably with square and circle.
- series of controls—the controls that send the action messages to the views. We will determine exactly which controls (sliders, buttons, etc) will be used later in the design stage.
- boundary—a synonym for the frame rectangle for each of the view. It is not an object.
- coordinate—an attribute of the views listed above.
- cursor—this is an object, but it is controlled by the AppKit. We do not need to consider it as part of the design, just as we do not

need to consider the application object; they are both implicit in every NeXTSTEP application.
- mouse button—a hardware object that does not need to be modeled.
- window's base coordinate system, local coordinate system—the base coordinate system is internal to the window, and the local coordinate system is internal to each view.

Now consider the verbs:

- display—as we learned earlier, each view draws after it receives a **display** message. However, the actual drawing is performed in the **drawSelf::** method instead of the **display** method. Each view needs to implement the **drawSelf::** method instead of the **display** method.
- clicking—pressing down on the mouse button to generate a **mouseDown:** event. The actual method the view uses is **mouseDown:**. This method prints the coordinates of the cursor where the **mouseDown:** event occurred.
- releasing—letting up the mouse button to generate a **mouseDown:** event. The actual method the view uses is **mouseUp:**. This method prints the coordinates of the cursor where the **mouseUp:** event occurred.
- manipulating—this is inherent in the definition of the controls, i.e., manipulating the controls sends messages to their targets, the shapes.

Let's consider the shapes at this point. Since there are two types of shapes, we need to create two subclasses of the **View** class; two natural names for these subclasses would be **SquareView** and **CircleView**. Consider what each shape needs to do:

- draw itself to the screen
- rotate
- scale
- translate.

As each shape, which is actually a view, is manipulated (rotated, scaled, or translated), we want it to update to correctly display its new state. This means each shape must maintain at least three

To update a shape, erase it and then redraw it at the new location

instance variables: **rotation**, **scale**, and **translation**. To draw itself properly, each shape must first erase itself and draw itself again with the updated values. If the shape didn't erase itself, it would leave a messy trail. By continually erasing and drawing itself as we manipulate the controls, the shape will seem to animate. Figure 7.16 illustrates this concept.

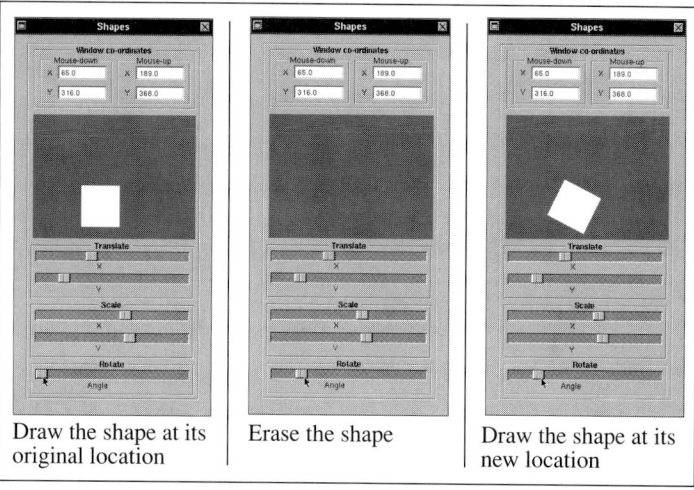

| Draw the shape at its original location | Erase the shape | Draw the shape at its new location |

Figure 7.16. Updating a view in response to the user's actions

> Most drawing in NeXTSTEP is performed in two steps: the object first draws to an offscreen buffer, and the buffer is then copied to the screen; a buffered window works in this fashion. Double-buffering provides a smooth update but requires more memory (the buffer is the size of the window) and results in a performance delay, although this is rarely noticeable.

ShapeView is an abstract superclass that encapsulates most of the functionality

Each shape must be able to erase itself as well as perform the aforementioned actions. However, since both shapes need to perform all of these actions, it would be more efficient if the actions were defined once in an abstract superclass rather than in both the **SquareView** and the **CircleView** classes. For lack of a better name, let us call this class **ShapeView**.

We have mentioned the controls on several occasions but we need to explore the user interface a little more closely. As we manipulate each control, it needs to update the shape continually. This requires a series of sliders, which are ideal for continually sending values to their targets.

As we click down in each view (in its frame rectangle), we want the view to print the coordinates of the cursor in the view's coordinate system as well as in the window's base coordinate system. To conserve screen real estate, we can print the former in the view itself and the latter in a textfield outside the view's frame rectangle. We can arrange for the view to perform a similar sequence when we release the mouse button. However, since the **mouseUp:** event can easily occur at the same location as the **mouseDown:** event, we should differentiate between the two sets of coordinates: the easiest way to do this is to print one set in one color and the other in a different color. Figure 7.17 shows a preliminary interface for the **Shapes** incorporating the requirements of the user interface so far.

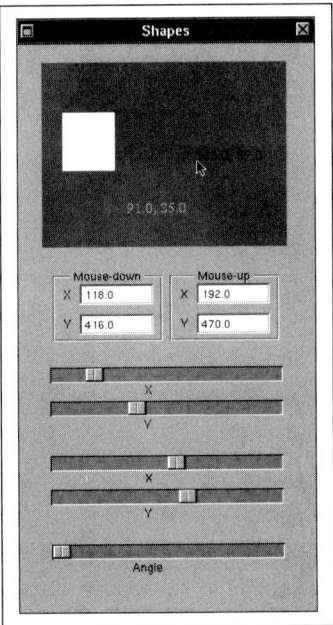

Figure 7.17. A preliminary interface for **Shapes**

However, notice that the interface is somewhat confusing because:

- it does not group related objects. One way to alleviate this confusion is to group the controls.
- the textfields containing the coordinates should be moved above the view to remove the possibility of mistaking the textfields for the targets of the sliders.
- the sliders are not labeled: thus, there is no way of knowing what the minimum and maximum values of the sliders are.

Figure 7.18 shows an interface incorporating these changes.

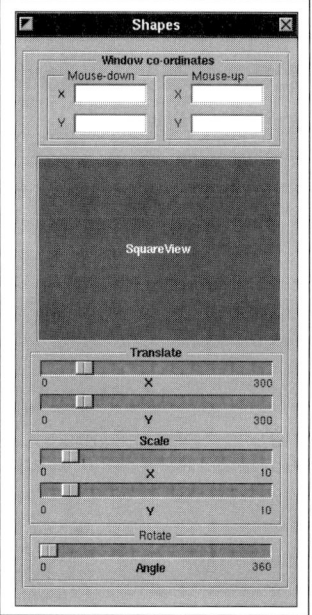

Figure 7.18. A more refined interface for **Shapes**

Now consider what happens when we move a slider (assume the slider which controls the rotation):

- the slider sends a **rotate:** message to the view.
- the view sends a message back to the slider inquiring what its value is and rotates the axes with this value.
- the view erases itself by sending itself an **erase** message.
- the view rotates its axes and then draws itself.

Although the exact messages sent are different, the model for all three sliders is the same. With this design, we can easily add another class to draw another shape. The class should be a subclass of **ShapeView**, and it needs to implement a **drawSelf::** method to draw the actual shape. For example, to add a class to draw a triangle, we can add a **TriangleView** class, and this class would have a **drawSelf::** method containing the PostScript code to draw the triangle.

This design has three classes: **ShapeView**, **SquareView**, and **CircleView**. Figure 7.19 shows the CRC card for the **ShapeView** class.

```
ShapeView:View:Control:Responder:Object

    1. translate the axes
    2. scale the axes
    3. rotate the axes
    4. display
    5. erase
    6. process mouseDown: events
    7. process mouseUp: events
```

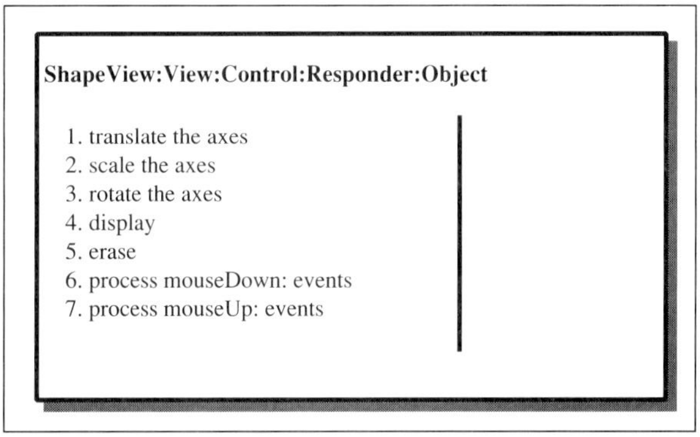

Figure 7.19. The CRC card for the **ShapeView** class

Figure 7.20 shows the CRC card for the **SquareView** class.

```
SquareView:ShapeView:View:Control:Responder:Object

    1. draw the square
```

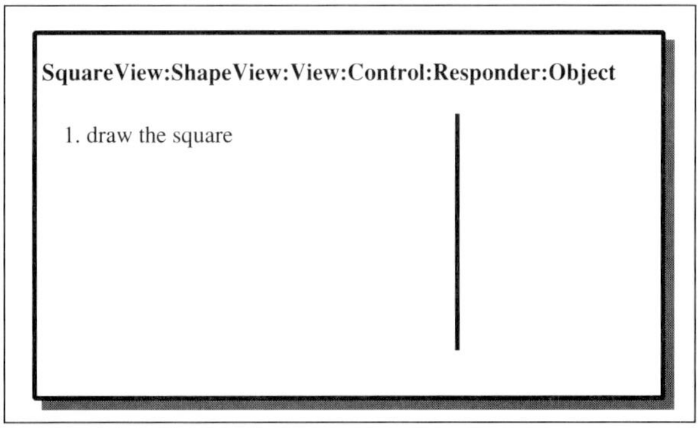

Figure 7.20. The CRC card for the **SquareView** class

248   Designing Shapes

Figure 7.21 shows the CRC cards for the **CircleView** class.

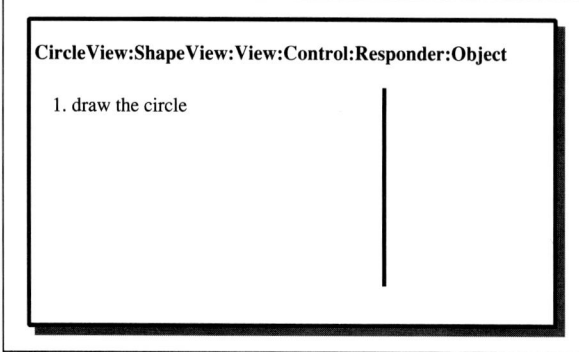

Figure 7.21. The CRC card for the **CircleView** class

Table 7.3 is the class summary table for the **ShapeView** class.

ShapeView:View:Responder:Object		
	Name	Description
Instance variables	angle	the angle of the axes
	xScale	the x value for the scale factor
	yScale	the y value for the scale factor
	x	the x offset for the axes
	upWindowMatrix	outlet for the textfield matrix: this displays the coordinates of the mouseUp: event in the window's coordinate system
	downWindowMatrix	outlet for the textfield matrix: this displays the coordinates of the mouseDown: event in the window's coordinate system
Methods	translate:sender	translates the x and y axes and redraws the shape
	scale:sender	scales the x and y axes and redraws the shape
	rotate:sender	changes the angle and redraws the shape
	erase	erases the shape
	mouseDown:(NXEvent *) theEvent	processes the mouseDown: event
	mouseUp:(NXEvent *) theEvent	processes the mouseUp: event

Table 7.3 Class summary table for the **ShapeView** class

Table 7.4 is the class summary table for the **SquareView** class.

SquareView:ShapeView:Responder:Object		
	Name	Description
Instance variables	N/A	N/A
Methods	drawSelf:(NXRect*)rects :(int)rectCount	draws the square

Table 7.4 Class summary table for the **SquareView** class

Table 7.5 is the class summary table for the **CircleView** class.

CircleView:ShapeView:Responder:Object		
	Name	Description
Instance variables	N/A	N/A
Methods	drawSelf:(NXRect*)rects :(int)rectCount	draws the circle

Table 7.5 Class summary table for the **CircleView** class

Figure 7.22 shows the message diagram for **Shapes**, although it only includes the squareview. The message diagram for the circle-view would be identical.

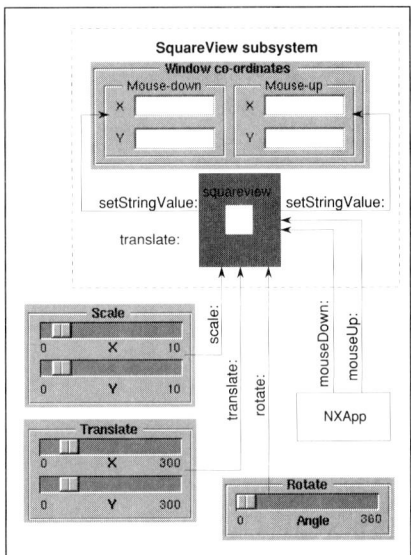

Figure 7.22. The message diagram for **Shapes**

Note the following:

- the textfield matrices are internal to the squareview. Together, they form the **SquareView** subsystem. We include the matrices as a matter of completeness.
- the **mouseDown:** and **mouseUp:** messages are sent from **NXApp** in response to us clicking in the view's boundary.

Figure 7.23 shows the hierarchy graph for **Shapes**.

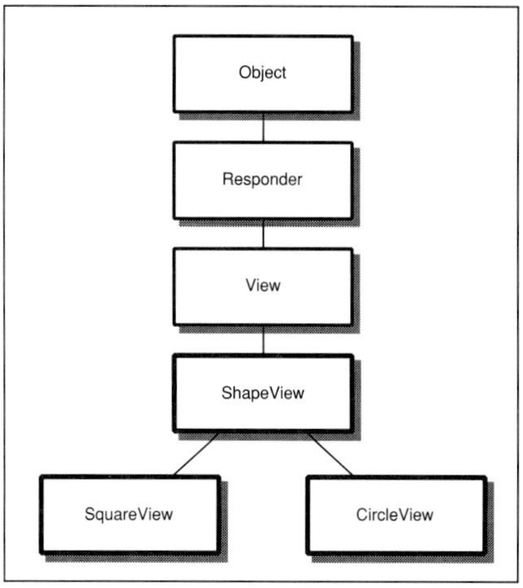

Figure 7.23. The hierarchy graph for **Shapes**

7.8 Implementing Shapes

SquareView will use single operators and CircleView will use pswraps

We will implement this application in two passes: we will first implement the **ShapeView** and **SquareView** classes and then add the **CircleView** class. To demonstrate the differences between the single operator and the **pswraps** generated functions, we will implement **SquareView** using the former and **CircleView** using the latter. Start ProjectBuilder and save the projects as **~/Shapes/Shapes**. Double-click on **Shapes.nib** to start InterfaceBuilder.

First, subclass the **View** class to create the **ShapeView** class. Rather than let InterfaceBuilder unparse the class to generate template files, write the template files first and then parse them into InterfaceBuilder. Type in the following code:

Listing for ShapeView.h

```
/* Generated by Project Builder */

#import <appkit/View.h>

@interface ShapeView:View
```

```
{
   float angle;
   float xScale;
   float yScale;
   float x;
   float y;
   id downWindowMatrix;  // outlet w/ coord of
                         // mouse down event
   id upWindowMatrix;    // outlet w/ coord of
                         // mouse-up event
}

- initFrame:(NXRect *)frameRect;
- scale:sender;
- translate:sender;
- rotate:sender;
- erase;
- mouseDown:(NXEvent *)theEvent;
- mouseUp:(NXEvent *)theEvent;
- (BOOL)acceptsFirstMouse;

@end
```

Save the file as **ShapeView.h** and then return to InterfaceBuilder. Select the **ShapeView** class and then select the **Parse** command in the **Operations** pulldownlist in the Files Window. Select **ShapeView.h** in the openpanel. As mentioned in Chapter 6, parsing the class tells InterfaceBuilder to read the class header file and build the class definition accordingly. This definition allows InterfaceBuilder to display the appropriate methods and outlets in the Class Inspector.

Parse the ShapeView class

With the **ShapeView** class created, create the **SquareView** class. Subclass the **ShapeView** class and call this new subclass **SquareView**. Notice that in the Class Inspector, the instance variables and methods are noneditable, since they are inherited from the **ShapeView** class. Unparse the **SquareView** class to generate the template files, and click **OK** to add these to the project when prompted.

InterfaceBuilder does not allow us to edit inherited instance variables and methods

Instantiate the **SquareView** class by selecting the **Instantiate** option in the **Operations** pulldown list. Instantiating a subclass of the **View** class is different from instantiating the other classes. For

Instantiating the View class is different than instantiating other classes

254   Implementing Shapes

example, to instantiate the **MoneyConverter** class in the previous chapter, we used the **Instantiate** option in the **Operations** pull-downlist.

Add a CustomView instance and then use the Inspector to set the class of the view

To instantiate a subclass of the **View** class, we need to drag a **CustomView** instance from the palette and place it in the window. With the **CustomView** instance selected, bring up the Attributes Inspector and select **SquareView** in the scrolling list. After clicking **OK**, the **CustomView** instance will change to a **SquareView** instance. This is InterfaceBuilder's way of telling us the view is now an instance of the **SquareView** class. Figure 7.24 shows the steps in instantiating the **SquareView** class (this sequence applies to other subclasses of **View** as well).

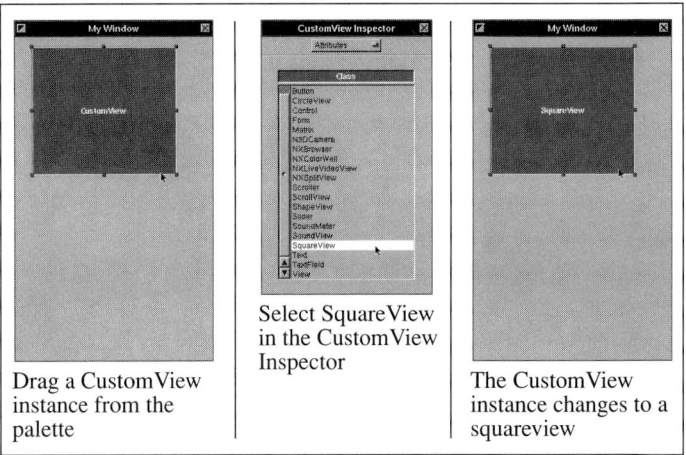

Drag a CustomView instance from the palette

Select SquareView in the CustomView Inspector

The CustomView instance changes to a squareview

Figure 7.24. Instantiating the **SquareView** class

Add the sliders to the Main Window

Now, add the controls that will be used to manipulate the view. Drag a slider from the palette and position it under the view. Since both of the sliders are related, it is easier (and more efficient) to create a matrix of two sliders instead of creating two individual sliders. Figure 7.25 shows how to create a matrix of two sliders and how to control the distance between them.

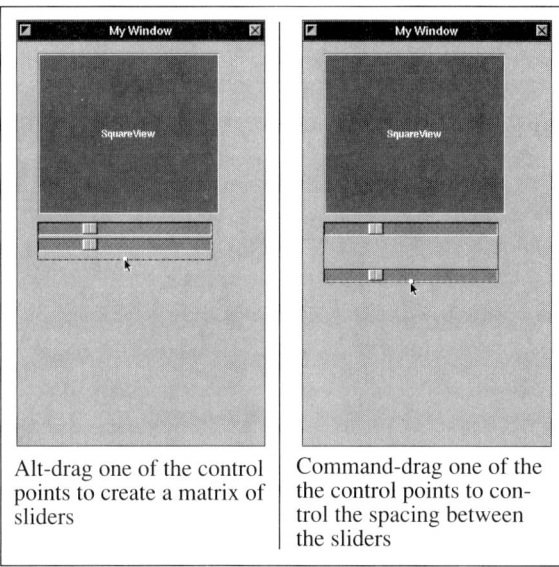

| Alt-drag one of the control points to create a matrix of sliders | Command-drag one of the the control points to control the spacing between the sliders |

Figure 7.25. Creating a matrix of two sliders

At this point, this object is no longer a slider, but a matrix of two slidercells. To verify this, select one of the sliders and notice that the Inspector displays information about a matrix. Double-click the slider to select the slidercell. When we are using only one control, we can ignore the distinction between the view (slider) and the cell (slidercell). However, when we are working with a matrix, this distinction is quite important. Using a matrix of two slidercells is more efficient than using two separate sliders because the former involves creating two separate views (a view requires a lot of overhead) and two cells, while the latter involves creating one view with two cells.

Now, select the first slidercell by clicking on the matrix and then double-clicking on the slidercell. Set the minimum, current, and maximum values to **0**, **50**, and **300** respectively. Repeat this for the **Translate Y** slider.

> We choose a value other than **0** for the current value because we want the figure to draw initially (when it first appears) at a location other than (0,0). We choose **300** for the maximum values because that allows the shape to draw off the screen, which illustrates clipping.

Use textfields to label the ranges of the sliders

Label the sliders by first dragging a textfield (the one that reads **Title**) from the palette. Position it below the first slider and edit the text to read **X**. Again, since we will be labeling a matrix of sliders, it is natural to create a matrix of textfields. Select the text and then **Alt**-drag one of the control points downward to create a matrix of two textfields. Select the second textfieldcell and edit it to read **Y**. Copy this matrix of textfields twice. Position the first matrix at the left end of the slider to label the minimum values of the two sliders. Edit both values to read **0**. Position the second matrix of textfields at the right edge of the slider matrix and edit its value to be **300**. Figure 7.26 shows the user interface so far.

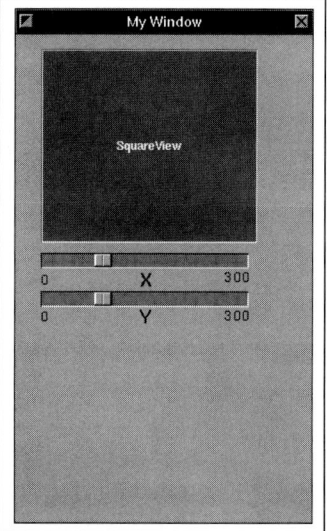

Figure 7.26. The user interface with the sliders labeled

Since both sliders will be controlling the translation values of the axes, and the textfields are labels for the sliders, select all matrices and select **Format ⇒ Layout ⇒ Group** (**Command-g**) to group them. This basically establishes the selected objects as the content view of a box: a box is simply a view that collects related controls for aesthetic reasons. Figure 7.27 illustrates this sequence.

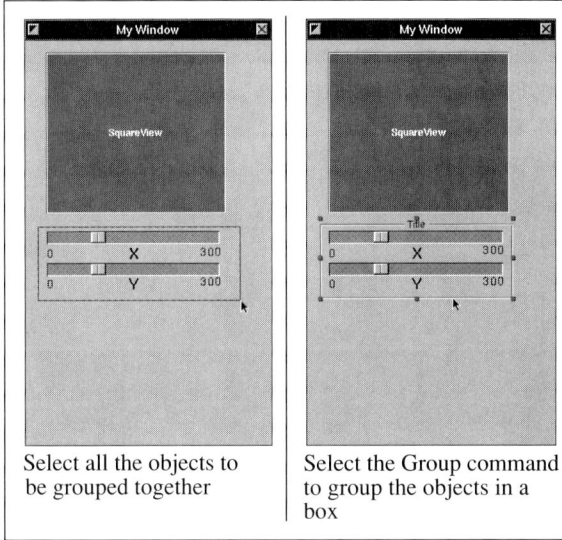

Select all the objects to be grouped together

Select the Group command to group the objects in a box

Figure 7.27. Grouping objects with a box

Why didn't we simply create one matrix with two slidercells, six textfieldcells, and a box? Because the **Matrix** class demands that each element be of the same size and class.

To select an object that has been grouped in a box, select the box first and double-click on the desired object. Use the Inspector to verify that the desired object is the one that is selected.

Now that all the objects are grouped, we can move them around as one object. We can also copy them as one object. Select the group, copy it, then paste it back. Select both groups then select the **Format ⇒ Layout ⇒ Make Column** option (**Command-C**) to align them in a column (vertically). Now edit the title of the

A group of objects can be moved as a single object

Set the values for the sliders

box. Double-click on the title to select it. Then, edit the title of the first box to read **Translate** and the title of the second box to read **Scale**. To emphasize the title, set the font to bold.

Select the **Scale X** slider and set the minimum, current and maximum values to **1**, **1**, and **10** respectively. Note that the maximum values for these two sliders are completely arbitrary: we can set them to anything we want, as long as they are greater than the minimum values (**1** in both cases). Since the minimum values for the sliders are now **1**, edit the both values of left textfield matrix (the labels) to be **1**. Edit both values of the right textfield matrix to be **10**.

> Since we cannot scale to 0 in PostScript, specifying **1** for the minimum and current values relieves us of the extra burden for checking if the value of **scale** is valid.

The last control is a single slider rather than a matrix of slider-cells

The last control is a single slider. Drag a slider from the palette and position it below the two boxes. Use the Inspector to set the minimum, current and maximum values to **0**, **0**, and **360** respectively. To label the slider, drag a textfield from the palette and position it below the last slider. Edit the text to read **Angle**. Drag two more textfields and edit their values to be **0** and **360**. Position the **0** textfield at the left edge of the slider, and **360** at the right edge of the slider. Group the slider and textfields together and label the title of the box to read **Rotate**. Again, set the font to bold. Select all three groups of sliders and then press **Command-C** to align them in a column.

> Since this slider contains the angle (in degrees) to which the view's axes should rotate, **360** is a logical maximum. Again, by controlling the input to the **ShapeView** class, we can reduce our coding efforts later.

Add two matrices of sliders

Now add the two matrices of textfields that will display the x and y coordinates of the **mouseDown:** and **mouseUp:** events. Drag a textfield (the one with the word **Text** in the middle) from the palette and position it above the view. Double-click on the textfield and remove the text. Convert the textfield into a matrix, and then group the matrix in a box. Edit the title of the box to be **Mouse-down**. Copy this box, select both boxes, and press **Command-R** to align them horizontally. Edit the title of the second box to read **Mouse-up**.

Now select both textfield matrices, group them, and then change the title of the box to **Window coordinates**. Copy this box and then paste it. Place the second box above the circleview and then align it horizontally with the first box. Group both boxes and remove the title of the box. Finally, select all of the objects on the left, and group them. Remove the title of this box. Select all of the objects on the right, group them, and remove the title of this box also. As a final step, edit the title of the window to be the name of the application, **Shapes**. Figure 7.28 shows how the user interface should look at this point.

Group both matrices of textfields

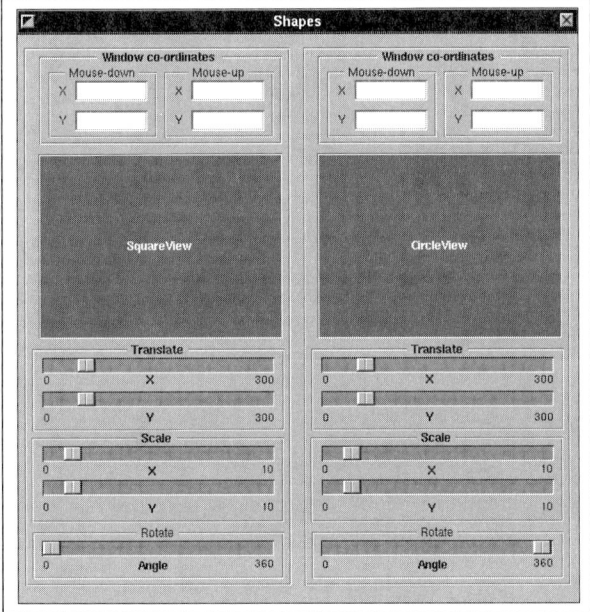

Figure 7.28. The user interface with the controls defined

Make the connections to establish the actions in the application. Figure 7.29 shows the connections we need to make.

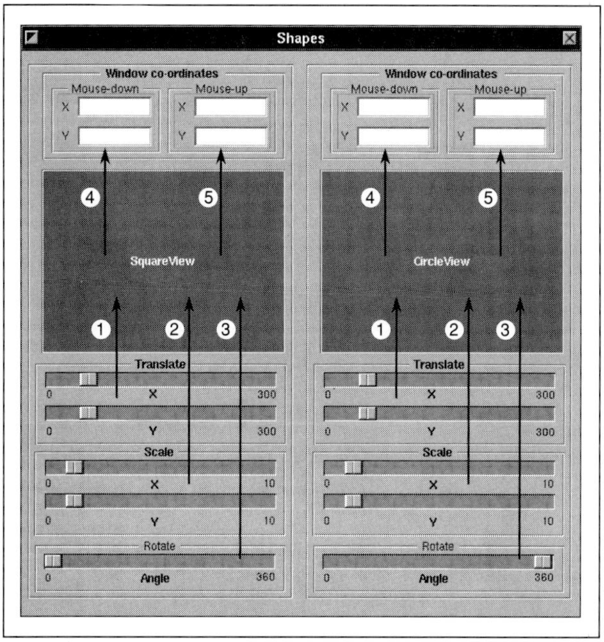

Figure 7.29. Making the connections in **Shapes.nib**

The five connections are as follows (these also apply to the circle-view):

1. Connect the squareview as the target for the **Translate** matrix and select the **translate:** method.
2. Connect the squareview as the target for the **Scale** matrix and select the **scale:** method.
3. Connect the squareview as the target for the **Rotate** slider and select the **rotate:** method.
4. Connect the **mouseDown:** matrix as the **downWindowMatrix** outlet of the squareview.
5. Connect the **mouseUp:** matrix as the **upWindowMatrix** outlet of the squareview.

Select the first box and double-click to select the matrix. Connect it to the **SquareView**. Select the **translate:** action in the Connections Inspector and then click **Connect**.

> In the Class Inspector, InterfaceBuilder dims **SquareView**'s instance variables and actions to remind us that they are non-editable because they are all inherited from **ShapeView**. The actions could be overridden (if we defined them in **SquareView.h** and then parse them in) but we still would not be able to edit the inherited instance variables.

Select the second box and double-click to select the matrix. Connect to the **SquareView** and select the **rotate:** method in the Connections Inspector.

Select the last box and double-click to select the slider and connect it to the **SquareView**. Select the **rotate:** method in the Connections Inspector. Note that this last connection is from the slidercell itself since this slider is not part of a matrix, as is the case with the first two sets of controls.

Now, make the connections from the **SquareView** to its outlets. Connect from the squareview to the first matrix. Verify that the connection box is light gray and encloses the entire matrix instead of an individual textfield inside the matrix; to insure that the squareview is connected to the matrix, check the Connections Inspector. In the Connections Inspector, select **downWindowMatrix**. Connect from the squareview to the other matrix of textfields and select **UpWindowMatrix** in the Connections Inspector. At this point, save the interface file.

Create **ShapeView.m** and add the file to ProjectBuilder.

Listing for ShapeView.m

```
/* Generated by Project Builder */

#import <appkit/appkit.h>
#import "ShapeView.h"
```

Implementing Shapes

```
@implementation ShapeView

- initFrame:(NXRect *)frameRect
{
   [super initFrame:frameRect];
   angle = 360;
   xScale = 1;
   yScale = 1;
   x = 50;
   y = 50;
   return self;
}

- translate:sender
{
   // sender is a matrix: thus, obtain
   // cell by asking the matrix
   // for the selected cell
   id cell = [sender selectedCell];
   int tag = [cell tag];

   switch(tag)
       {
       case 0:
           x = [cell floatValue];
           break;
       case 1:
           y = [cell floatValue];
           break;
       }
   // display view with updated values
   [self display];
   return self;
}

- scale:sender
{
   // sender is a matrix: thus, obtain
   // cell by asking the matrix
   // for the selected cell
   id cell = [sender selectedCell];
   int tag = [cell tag];

   switch(tag)
```

```
      {
      case 0:
         xScale = [cell floatValue];
         break;
      case 1:
         yScale = [cell floatValue];
         break;
      }
   // display view with updated values
   [self display];
   return self;
}

- rotate:sender
{
   angle = [sender floatValue];
   [self display];
   return self;
}

- erase
{
   // &bounds contains the view's location
   // and size expressed in its own coordinate
   // system: by drawing in bounds, the view
   // avoids unnecessary drawing
   PSsetgray(NX_DKGRAY);
   NXRectFill(&bounds);
   return self;
}

- mouseDown:(NXEvent *)theEvent
{
   char buffer[30];

   // round co-ordinates to 1 digit
   // after decimal point
   // print co-ordinates in window co-ordinates
   sprintf(buffer, "%.1f", theEvent->location.x);
   [[downWindowMatrix cellAt:0 :0]
      setStringValue:buffer];
   sprintf(buffer, "%.1f", theEvent->location.y);
   [[downWindowMatrix cellAt:1 :0]
      setStringValue:buffer];
```

Implementing Shapes

```objc
        // convert from window co-ordinates to
        // view co-ordinates
        [self convertPoint:&theEvent->location
           fromView:nil];

        // lock focus so graphics commands
        // are applied to this view
        [self lockFocus];
        // erase old instance drawing
        PSnewinstance();
        // start new instance drawing to draw directly
        // to the window
        PSsetinstance(YES);
            // select font otherwise output
            // will be upside down
            PSselectfont("Times-Roman", 16.0);
            // print co-ordinates on view
            PSmoveto(theEvent->location.x,
                theEvent->location.y);
            sprintf(buffer, "%.1f, %.1f",
                theEvent->location.x,
                theEvent->location.y);
            // set color to light gray
            PSsetgray(NX_LTGRAY);
            // show the string
            PSshow(buffer);
        PSsetinstance(NO);

        // balance lockFocus with unlockFocus
        [self unlockFocus];
        return self;
}

- mouseUp:(NXEvent *)theEvent
{
    char buffer[40];
    sprintf(buffer, "%.1f", theEvent->location.x);
    [[upWindowMatrix cellAt:0 :0]
        setStringValue:buffer];
    sprintf(buffer, "%.1f", theEvent->location.y);
    [[upWindowMatrix cellAt:1 :0]
        setStringValue:buffer];

    // convert from window co-ordinates to
    // view co-ordinates
```

```
   [self lockFocus];
   [self convertPoint:&theEvent->location
      fromView:nil];

   // don't use PSnewinstance(), since we don't
   // want to erase the drawing from mouseDown:
   // start new instance drawing to draw directly
   // to the window
   PSsetinstance(YES);
      // select font otherwise output
      // will be upside down
      PSselectfont("Times-Roman", 16.0);
      // print co-ordinates on view
      PSmoveto(theEvent->location.x,
         theEvent->location.y);
      sprintf(buffer, "%.1f, %.1f",
         theEvent->location.x,
         theEvent->location.y);
      // set color to black
      PSsetgray(NX_BLACK);
      // show the string
      PSshow(buffer);
   PSsetinstance(NO);

   // balance lockFocus with unlockFocus
   [self unlockFocus];

   return self;
}

-(BOOL)acceptsFirstMouse
{
   // allows the view to use the first
   // mouse click that activates the window
   return YES;
}

@end
```

Edit **SquareView.h** and **SquareView.m** with the changes in bold, and add the two files to the project.

Listing for **SquareView.h**

```
/* Generated by Project Builder */

#import "ShapeView.h"

@interface SquareView:ShapeView
{
}

-drawSelf: (NXRect *)rects :(int)rectCount;

@end
```

Listing for **SquareView.m**

```
/* Generated by Project Builder */

#import <appkit/appkit.h>
#import "SquareView.h"

@implementation SquareView

-drawSelf: (NXRect *)rects :(int)rectCount
{
   // erase current drawing
   [super erase];
   // translate axes to current offsets
   PStranslate(x, y);
   // rotate axes to current angle
   PSrotate(angle);
   // scale axes to current values
   PSscale(xScale, yScale);
   // draw a square that's 5 by 5 units
   PSmoveto(-5, -5);
   PSrlineto(10, 0);
   PSrlineto(0, 10);
   PSrlineto(-10, 0);
   PSclosepath();
   // set color to white
   PSsetgray(1.0);
   PSfill();
   return self;
```

```
}
@end
```

Now that the classes implemented, build the application. Execute it and verify that the controls work correctly. Click in the squareview and, while holding the mouse button down, drag somewhere in the boundaries of the view and release the mouse button. The squareview should print two sets of coordinates of the view: the ones in gray indicate where the **mouseDown:** event occurred, and the ones in black indicate where the **mouseUp:** event took place. These coordinates are in the view's coordinate system, whereas the values in the textfields are in the window's base coordinate system. After verifying that the application behaves as expected, quit it and return to ProjectBuilder.

As mentioned earlier, we will implement the drawing code for the **CircleView** class in a separate wraps file instead of using single C operator functions. Since InterfaceBuilder cannot generate the wraps file, we must write it ourselves. Enter the following code and save it as **~/Shapes/drawcircle.psw**.

Listing for drawcircle.psw

```
// wraps routine to draw a circle
defineps drawcircle(float x, y,
        angle, xScale, yScale)
   % translate axes
   x y translate
   % rotate
   angle rotate
   % scale
   xScale yScale scale
   % move to new origin
   0 0 moveto
   % draw circle
   0 0 5 0 angle arc
   % fill to white
   1 setgray
   fill
endps
```

Add the wraps file to the project

Save this file and add it to the project file under **Other Sources**. Return to InterfaceBuilder to finish the interface. Create a new subclass of **ShapeView** and call it **CircleView**. Select the entire left box (which includes the matrices and the view), copy it, then paste it back. Align the two boxes using **Command-R**. Select the second squareview and use the Inspector to change it to **CircleView**. Since both views have the same connections, we do not need to remake them.

Unparse the class and add these template files to the project. Modify **CircleView.h** and **CircleView.m** as follows (the changes are in bold):

Listing for CircleView.h

```
/* Generated by Project Builder */

#import "ShapeView.h"

@interface CircleView:ShapeView
{
}

- drawSelf:(NXRect *)rects :(int)rectCount;

@end
```

Listing for CircleView.m

```
/* Generated by Project Builder */

#import <appkit/appkit.h>
#import "CircleView.h"
// for drawcircle function
#import "drawcircle.h"

@implementation CircleView

- drawSelf:(NXRect *)rects :(int)rectCount
{
   // erase current drawing
   [super erase];
```

```
        // use wraps file to draw circle
        drawcircle(x, y, angle, xScale, yScale);
        return self;
    }

    @end
```

Save the **.nib** file and return to ProjectBuilder. Make the application and test it again to verify that the circleview has been added.

7.9 Walking Through the Code

Now that the entire application is done, we can examine the code a little more closely. As usual, the main program loads in the **.nib** file, which contains the main window along with both of our custom views, the squareview and the circleview. **NXApp** first instantiates each of these views and then initializes them through an **initFrame:** message.

The designated initializer method for **ShapeView**

```
    - initFrame:(NXRect *)frameRect
    {
        [super initFrame:frameRect];
        angle = 360;
        xScale = 1;
        yScale = 1;
        x = 50;
        y = 50;
        return self;
    }
```

The **initFrame** method first use **super**'s (**View**'s) **initFrame:** method to initialize the shapeview's (squareview and circleview) **frameRect** variable, the **struct** that contains the values for the frame rectangle. **NXApp** obtains these values from the **.nib** file.

Once **frameRect** is initialized, **initFrame:** proceeds to initialize the variables defined in **ShapeView**, namely **angle**, **xScale**, **yScale**, **x**, and **y**. Now, every shapeview will have **angle** set to

360, **xScale** set to **1**, **yScale** set to **1**, **x** set to **50**, and **y** set to **50**. Since the **CircleView** and the **SquareView** classes inherit from the **ShapeView** class, their instances are similarly initialized.

> At this point, the values of the instance variables are independent of the values of the corresponding sliders since the sliders have yet to send any message to their targets. Thus, **Shapes** will initially draw the views based on the values of the instance variables instead of the values of the sliders. To test this, return to InterfaceBuilder and change the initial value of the circleview's **Angle** slider to **0** and recompile the application. When the application launches, the circleview will still draw a complete circle (the ending angle is **360**) instead of a line (the ending angle is **0**), because it first uses the value of the **angle** instance variable instead of the value of the slider.
>
> Once the application is executing, moving a slider will update the appropriate instance variable, which in turn redraws the shape accordingly.

NXApp then orders the window to the front, which automatically sends it a **display** message. The window then sends a **display** message to its content view and all of its subviews. Every view is then asked to draw itself via the **drawSelf::** method.

> A window created in InterfaceBuilder automatically displays itself. To disable this, select the window and then click on the **Visible at Launch Time** option in the Attributes Inspector.

As we move each control, it updates the appropriate instance variable and sends a **display** message to the view. For this discussion, let's assume we are moving the **X Scale** slider of the circleview, which sends a **scale:** message to the shapeview.

The **scale:** method of **ShapeView**

```
- scale:sender
```

```
{
   // sender is a matrix: thus, obtain
   // cell by asking the matrix
   // for the selected cell
   id cell = [sender selectedCell];
   int tag = [cell tag];

   switch(tag)
      {
      case 0:
         xScale = [cell floatValue];
         break;
      case 1:
         yScale = [cell floatValue];
         break;
      }
   // display view with updated values
   [self display];
   return self;
}
```

Since **sender** is the matrix itself, **scale:** must first determine which cell initiated the message. To determine this, **scale:** determines the selected cell with the **selectedCell** method and then determines the tag of the selected cell with the **tag** method. InterfaceBuilder automatically sets the tag of the first cell to **0**, the second to **1**, etc. The **scale:** method then uses a **switch** statement to update the appropriate instance variable. Then, the method sends a **display** message, which, after performing some initialization (such as focusing on the view), sends a **drawSelf::** message to the view.

Use the selectedCell method to determine which cell in the matrix is selected

Displaying the view and calling **drawcircle()**

```
- drawSelf: (NXRect *)rects :(int)rectCount
{
   // erase current drawing
   [super erase];
   // use wraps file to draw circle
   drawcircle(x, y, angle, xScale, yScale);
   return self;
}
```

Before redrawing itself, the circleview erases itself by using **super**'s (**ShapeView**'s) **erase** method.

Erasing the view's contents

```
- erase
{
    // &bounds contains the view's location
    // and size expressed in its own coordinate
    // system: by drawing in bounds, the view
    // avoids unnecessary drawing
    PSsetgray(NX_DKGRAY);
    NXRectFill(&bounds);
    return self;
}
```

The bounds rectangle defines the view's location and size in its own coordinate system

The **erase** method erases the view by filling the entire area of the view's boundary with dark gray, the color of the content view. The frame rectangle defines the size and location of the view in its superview's coordinates, and the *bounds rectangle* defines the view's location and size in its own coordinate system. Like the frame rectangle, the bounds rectangle is defined as a **struct** in the **View** class. By only drawing in the bounds rectangle, the application avoids any unnecessary drawing.

> A view's bounds rectangle will change if its coordinate system is modified (through scaling, for example). However, the frame rectangle will remain unchanged since it is expressed in the superview's coordinate system.

Once the view's boundary is filled to dark gray, **drawSelf::** draws the circle by calling the **drawcircle** function in the wraps file. The **drawcircle()** function draws a circle using five parameters (**x**, **y**, **angle**, **xScale**, and **yScale**) and then returns to **drawSelf::**. Note that instead of importing the wraps file itself (**drawcircle.psw**), the **CircleView** class imports the header file (**drawcircle.h**) generated by **pswraps** preprocessor.

Drawing a circle in **drawcircle.psw**

```
// wraps routine to draw a circle
defineps drawcircle(float x, y,
         angle, xScale, yScale)
   % translate axes
   x y translate
   % rotate
   angle rotate
   % scale
   xScale yScale scale
   % move to new origin
   0 0 moveto
   % draw circle
   0 0 5 0 angle arc
   % fill to white
   1 setgray
   fill
endps
```

As a final note, the **rotate:** method is slightly different from the **scale:** and the **translate:** methods.

The **rotate:** method of **ShapeView**

```
- rotate:sender
{
   angle = [sender floatValue];
   [self display];
   return self;
}
```

Since **sender** is actually the slider itself, the method does not need to determine which cell sent the message because there is only one. The method can ask **sender** (instead of having to first ask what the selected cell is) for its value directly and then display the view.

7.10 Suggestions

The application is fully functional and demonstrates how to interface Objective-C and PostScript. However, the following suggestions can demonstrate even more capabilities of the PostScript language.

7.10.1 Adding Support for Printing

Since NeXTSTEP is built on PostScript, objects that can draw themselves to the screen can automatically image themselves to the printer. For example, **Window** and **View** already define methods for imaging to the printer. To add support for printing, it is only a matter of sending the appropriate method to the window (which then sends **display** messages to its views).

First, add a **Print** menu option to the Main Menu. Drag the menu item labeled **Item** and edit the menu option's text to read **Print...**. Then add a keyboard alternative of **p** for the **Print** menu option.

Now, connect the **Print** menu option to the window and select the **smartPrintPSCode:** in the Connections Inspector. The **smartPrintPSCode:** method automatically displays the standard printpanel to ask us for miscellaneous information like what page(s) to print, what printer to select, etc. Once we have entered all the information, **smartPrintPSCode:** prints the window on a single sheet of paper. There is a counterpart method, **printPSCode:**, which does everything **smartPrintPSCode:** does, and it prints on multiple pages, if necessary.

To print only the contents of the window (that is, without the window decorations such as the title bar, close button, etc), connect the **Print** menu option to the window's content view and select the **printPSCode:** method in the Connections Inspector.

7.10.2 Drawing Shadows

Modify **CircleView**'s and **SquareView**'s **drawSelf::** methods to draw shadows below the shapes.

7.10.3 Adding a Triangle Class

To keep things simple, make the triangle a square with three sides; that is, in the new **Triangle** class, modify the **drawSelf::** method so that it only draws three sides.

7.10.4 Detecting Mouse Clicks

Modify the **mouseDown:** method to detect how many mouse clicks are generated. The **data** field in the **NXEvent struct** is a **union** that contains different information depending on the type of event. For a mouse event, the **data** field is composed of the following fields:

Excerpted listing of the **NXEventData** struct

```
typedef union
    {
    struct
        {
        short reserved;
        short eventNum;    /* event number */
        int click;         /* single, double, etc */
        int unused;        /* unused */
        } mouse;

    // rest of the union is deleted
    } NXEventData;
```

> A **union** is a data structure that allows us to interpret its data in different ways. For example, if the event is keyboard-related, the number of clicks would be meaningless. Instead, the event should contain, among other things, what key was pressed. The **data** field, defined as a **union**, allows the event to be interpreted in different ways, depending on the type of the event.

To detect the number of mouse-clicks, add code like the following:

Detecting the number of mouse clicks in a view's boundary

```
- mouseDown:(NXEvent *)theEvent
{
   int clickCount = theEvent->data.mouse.click;
   if (clickCount == 1)
      printf("One mouse click\n")
   else if (clickCount == 2)
      printf("Two mouse clicks\n");
   else if (clickCount == 3)
      printf("Three mouse clicks\n");
   return self;
}
```

Note that NeXTSTEP treats each *n* clicks as (*n*-1) clicks first. If we double-click, then NeXTSTEP will send two **mouseDown:** messages to the view. In the first message, **clickCount** will be set to one, and in the second message **clickCount** will be set to two. Assuming we click and then double-click, the output would be:

Output from a single and double-click

```
One mouse click  (From the single click)
One mouse click  (From the double-click)
Two mouse click  (From the double-click)
```

7.11 Troubleshooting

Here are some potential problems:

- The text is displayed upside-down in a view.
  - **Cause**: The view did not select a font before attempting to draw. Hence, it uses a default font, which expects a flipped view. For more information on flipped views, see Chapter 9.
  - **Solution**: Selecting a font overcomes this problem. To select a font, use **PSselectfont()** and pass it two parameters: a font, such as Times-Roman; and a point size, such as 16.

- The first time a slider is moved, the shape "skips" to another location. However, the shape then proceeds to update itself smoothly.
    - **Cause**: The initial value of a slider does not match the initial value of the corresponding instance variable (for example, the value of the **Rotate** slider should match the value of the **angle** instance variable). When the slider is moved, the view sends a message back to the control asking it for its value. The view then redraws the shape at the new location. Since the difference between the two values can be great, the shape will seem to skip to the new location rather than update smoothly.
    - **Solution**: Make sure the initial values of the sliders match those of the corresponding instance variables.
- The coordinates in the view print on top of each other without erasing the previous iteration.
    - **Cause**: The application is not resetting instance drawing to clear the drawing from the previous iteration.
    - **Solution**: Clear the previous drawing using **PSnewinstance(YES)** before issuing a new instance drawing.
- The application launches, but its icon stays highlighted.
    - **Cause**: The application probably contains PostScript syntax errors. Since PostScript is interpreted, the interpreter cannot find syntax errors until runtime.
    - **Solution**: Look at the Console in the Workspace (**Tools** ⇒ **Console**) or the Terminal shell from which the application was launched to locate the syntax error(s). Fix these and recompile.
- Dragging some of the controls (such as the **Rotate** slider for the circle) feels sluggish.
    - **Cause**: The application probably contains PostScript syntax errors, and it is too busy sending out error messages to the Console to execute properly.
    - **Solution**: Look at the Console (**Tools** ⇒ **Console**) or the Terminal shell from which the application was launched to locate the syntax error(s). Fix these and recompile.

- The application produces an error about a view not in focus.
    - **Cause**: An application must first lock the focus on a view to specify the destination for the PostScript code.
    - **Solution**: Use **[self lockFocus]** to lock the view before sending PostScript code to perform drawing. Note that this is not necessary if the application draws the view through **display** because this method automatically locks the focus on a view. Use **[self lockFocus]** when done.

7.12 Summary

The **View** class is an abstract superclass that provides a framework for receiving events and drawing. To draw something that is not inherently supported in the Application Kit like the circleview and the squareview, we must add PostScript code in the **drawSelf::** method. The PostScript code can be added by using single C operator functions or **pswraps**. The single operators are more convenient because they can be mixed with Objective-C code. Using **pswraps** is more complex since we need to produce a separate wraps file. However, **pswraps** is more efficient because the entire PostScript code in the wraps file can be downloaded to the Window Server, resulting in less interprocess communication between the application and the Window Server.

The **View** class also provides a framework for handling mouse and key events: in this chapter, we explored the **mouseUp:** and **mouseDown:** events. To process an event in a view's boundary, the view can override the method with the same name as the event. For example, to intercept **mouseDown:** events, the view simply overrides the **mouseDown:** method.

In our next chapter, we explore how to customize NeXTSTEP applications by using the defaults database and how to manage a complex interface by using multiple **.nib** files.

Chapter 8
Customizing NeXTSTEP Applications

Most NeXTSTEP applications support some form of customization by allowing us to specify values for different defaults in the application. For example, a word processor typically allows us to specify the font when we create a new document. If we do not specify a font, the application uses an internal default to determine the font to use. If we specify a different initial font, we expect the application to save this setting and use it the next time we start our application. Each NeXTSTEP user has a separate defaults database, which stores all the defaults for that given user.

Most NeXTSTEP applications support some form of customization

To explore how customization works, we will add a Preferences panel to control whether the **Money** application (from Chapter 6) should truncate its output. Since the Preferences panel is not needed for the application's core functionality, we will place it in a separate **.nib** file and only load it in as needed. Hence, we will also learn how to use multiple **.nib** files to manage an application's user interface.

We will explore how to use multiple .nib files to manage a complex user interface

8.1 Goals

In this chapter, we will:

- explain what the defaults database is and how it used to customize applications.
- show how to add defaults support to an existing application.
- show how to use the **dread** and **dwrite** commands to customize our environment.
- illustrate how to use multiple **.nib** files to manage an application.

8.2 The Defaults Database

NeXTSTEP creates a **~/.NeXT** directory that contains custom information for a particular user's environment, including:

- the files in the Recycler waiting to be recycled
- the names of docked applications
- the defaults' values for the various applications.

These customization values are stored in the **.NeXTDefaults.L** and **.NeXTDefaults.D** files, which are referred to collectively as the *defaults database*. Since this database is encoded, don't access it directly. Use the **dread** command instead.

> When we recycle files or folders, the Workspace moves the files to the **~/.NeXT/.NextTrash** directory. The Workspace only deletes these files when we click **File** ⇒ **Empty Recycler**. To see what's in the recycler, we can either double-click on the recycler icon or issue the following shell command:
>
> ```
> % ls -ald $HOME/.NeXT/.NextTrash/*
> ```
> The **-a** parameter specifies that **ls** should list even the hidden files (files and folders that start with a .); the **-l** parameter specifies a long (verbose) listing; and the **-d** parameter specifies that **ls** should list only the filename of a folder, rather than than the files inside a folder.

8.2.1 Reading Defaults with dread

The **dread** command reads the defaults database and returns the current values associated with the defaults of a given application. Each entry in the database is as follows:

```
owner name value
```

dread reads the defaults database and prints out the defaults' value

where **owner** is the name of the application, **name** is a default of the application to be customized (such as the font), and **value** is the value of the default (such as the font name). The **dread** command supports various parameters but the most commonly used ones are:

- **dread -l**—reads our entire defaults database and lists the defaults with their associated values. This is usually not desirable since the output can be quite lengthy. A sample output may be (the output has been edited for space considerations):

Listing the defaults for all the applications

```
% dread -l
NeXT1 Keymap /NextLibrary/Keyboards/USA
Terminal NXFixedPitchFont Ohlfs
Terminal NXFixedPitchFontSize 12
Terminal Rows 24
Webster ShowPictures YES
```

This shows that the current keymap is the **USA** keyboard, the default font and font size for the Terminal application is **Ohlfs** at **12** points, the default window size for Terminal is **24** rows, and Webster (the on-line dictionary) should display pictures.

- **dread -o owner**—displays all the current names and values for the application specified by *owner*. For example, to determine what the current values for the defaults of the Edit application are, use:

Listing the defaults for a given application

```
% dread -o Edit
Edit NXFont Ohlfs
Edit NXFontPanelPreviewFrame "0 0 281 47"
Edit NXFontSize 12
```

Before using the defaults database to save the application's defaults, the application should first register what defaults it is willing to support.

8.2.2 Registering Defaults

When an application starts, it should not require us to perform any special setup before being usable. If we do not specify any additional options, the application should start with the defaults set to reasonable values. To register defaults with their initial values for the application, the application needs to implement a class method, **initialize**, in the class responsible for managing the defaults. We will call this new class **PrefsController**.

An application needs to register what defaults it is willing to support

Initializing the class object in **PrefsController.m**

```
+ initialize
{
  // make sure that self is a PrefsController
  // class before setting class initialization:
  // this prevents subclasses from performing
  // reinitialization
  if (self == [PrefsController class])
    {
    const char *appName = [NXApp appName];

    static NXDefaultsVector theDefaults =
      {
        {"Truncate", "NO"},
        {"Prompt", "NO"},
        {NULL, NULL}
      };

    NXRegisterDefaults(appName, theDefaults);
    }
  return self;
}
```

The class receives the initialize message before any other message

Before we can understand registering the defaults, let us digress and explore how a class is initialized. As mentioned in Chapter 2, each class has an associated class object. Before even sending **alloc** and **init** to the class object, **NXApp** automatically messages it with an **initialize** message (notice the + before the method name to indicate that it's a class method) to perform some class initialization: the exact initialization varies for each class.

Sending an initialize message also sends an initialize message to its superclasses

Sending an **initialize** method to a class also sends an **initialize** method to each of its superclasses (this is needed to ensure that all the inherited information is initialized properly). That is, sending an **initialize** method to **PrefsController** results in an **initialize** method sent to **Object** (**PrefsController**'s superclass) and **PrefsController**. Thus, it is possible for the same message to be sent to the class many times, once for the class that defines it and once for each inheriting class.

To prevent code from being repeated each time the method is invoked, the application can do two things:

- the **initialize** method can check if the class object is of the appropriate class before performing initialization. For the **PrefsController** class, this checking is performed with the **if ([self == [PrefsController class])** statement. For example, assume that **PrefsController** has a subclass called **MyPrefsController**. **PrefsController**'s **initialize** method would be executed twice, once for **PrefsController** and once for **MyPrefsController**. However, the first time the method is executed, the initialization would be performed since **self** would be the **PrefsController** class object. However, in the second occurrence, **self** would be the **MyPrefsController** class object and the method would simply return. If the method did not perform this check, the subclass would perform the initialization again, which could have undesirable side-effects.

The initialize method should check if the class object is of the appropriate class

> Technically speaking, **PrefsController**'s **initialize** method does not need to perform the conditional check, since **PrefsController** does not have any subclasses. However, an **initialize** method can set up a version number for the class for object management purposes. Without the conditional check, the subclass can potentially reset the version number of its superclass, which would totally defeat the concept of object management with version numbers.
>
> Additionally, an **initialize** method can potentially create arrays, hash tables, and other data structures. If these are repeatedly created, they would produce a memory leak.

- never explicitly send an **initialize** method to a class since **NXApp** will automatically send this message to the class. If the application explicitly sends an **initialize** method, the conditional check would fail since in both cases, **self** would be the **PrefsController** class object. For more information on how to deal with this dilemma, see **Object**'s **initialize** method.

Never explictily send an initialize method

The **initialize** method is a good place to register the initial values for the application's defaults since these values should only be set

The initialize method is a good place to register defaults

once. To register the defaults, use **NXRegisterDefaults()**, which expects two parameters:

- the name of the application, also referred to as the *owner* of the default.
- an **NXDefaultsVector**, a **struct** that contains a list of defaults and value pairs terminated by a **{NULL, NULL}** entry.

NXRegister-Defaults() creates a registration table

The **NXRegisterDefaults()** function creates a *registration table* and then initializes each default with the appropriate value. It searches for the value of a given default in a predetermined order. As soon as a value for a default is found, **NXRegisterDefaults()** proceeds to the next one. The search order is as follows:

- command-line parameters—assuming we added two defaults, **Truncate** and **Prompt**, to the **Money** application, we can start the **Money** application with the **Truncate** default set to **YES** and the **Prompt** default set to **NO** with:
  ```
  % Money.app/Money -Truncate YES -Prompt NO &
  ```

  The dash (-) indicates that the word is a default and the following word is the value for the default. Note that command-line options:

  - do not update the values in the defaults database.
  - cannot be used if we launch applications using the Workspace.

- application-specific defaults—the application proceeds to search the database for the default that it owns (in this case, **Money**). If it cannot find the default that it needs, it proceeds to the next step.

- global defaults—if the application cannot find a value for a default it owns, it then searches for the same default owned by **GLOBAL**.

- values passed to the **NXRegisterDefaults()**—as a last resort, **NXRegisterDefaults()** initializes the default to the value passed in the **NXDefaultsVector**, specified in the **initialize** method.

Figure 8.1 shows the precedence rules the application uses when it builds its registration table.

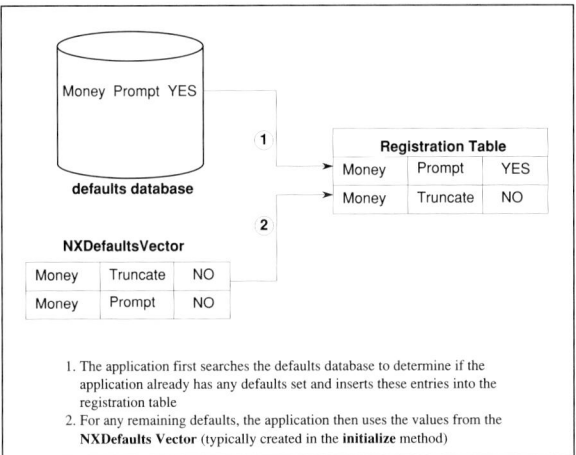

Figure 8.1 The precedence order for building the registration table

The **NXDefaultsVector struct** basically specifies initial values for the defaults in case we do not specify them when we start the application. By creating a registration table to cache the values of the defaults, **NXRegisterDefaults()** improves the performance: the application then does not need to open the database each time it wants to determine the value of a default. However, if the application requests a default that does not exist in the registration table, **NXRegisterDefaults()** has no choice but to read from the defaults database and search for the default in the order listed above.

A registration table improves performance by caching the values of the defaults

Note the values for the defaults are not automatically saved to the defaults database when the application registers its defaults: the application must explicitly save them to the database to preserve their values. This is practical because defaults that do not already have corresponding values in the defaults database can always

An application only saves defaults which have changed

obtain the initial values from the **NXDefaultsVector struct** in the **initialize** method upon start-up.

> The primary weakness with the aforementioned scheme is that we can be caught in a no-win situation because **dread** only reads the defaults which are *already* in the defaults database. However, an application doesn't write a default to the defaults database until the default has changed from its initial value. Thus, there is no easy way to determinine *all* the defaults which an application is willing to support short of using a debugger or consulting the source code (we can find out the supported defaults by using the application's Preferences panel). These two luxuries may not always be available because an application must already contain debug information before we can effectively debug it, and the source code is rarely accessible.

NXGetDefault-Value() returns the value of a default in the registration table

Once we have created the registration table to contain the defaults, we can use the table to determine the values of the defaults to customize the application's behavior. To determine the value of a default, use the **NXGetDefaultValue**() function, which returns a **char** pointer to the value or **0** if the database can't be opened. This code fragment queries the registration table for the value of the **Truncate** default and then sets the state of a button (**truncateSwitch**) to reflect whether the **Truncate** default is set or not (the **awakeFromNib** method will be explained shortly).

Determining whether a default is set or not

```
- awakeFromNib
{
  const char *appName = [NXApp appName];
  const char *truncateFlag;

  truncateFlag =
    NXGetDefaultValue(appName, "Truncate");
  // make sure truncateFlag is not NULL before
  // comparing it
  if (truncateFlag)
```

```
    {
    if (strcasecmp(truncateFlag, "YES") == 0)
      truncateSwitch setState:ON];
    else
      [truncateSwitch setState:OFF];
    }
  return self;
}
```

> The capitalization convention for the default names is the same as that for the Objective-C classes, i.e., the first word of every phrase is capitalized. The convention for the values is less standardized: some applications use **YES** rather than **Yes** to indicate that a given default is set. An application should not depend on the capitalization and use **strcasecmp()** to ignore the case when comparing strings.

Since we can write the value of a default in the database directly (using **dwrite**, which will be introduced shortly), it is possible for the value of a default in the database to differ from the value of the corresponding default in the registration table. In the example above, assume that we start the application, and the database contains the value of **Yes** for the **Truncate** default. Upon start-up, the registration table will also contain **Yes** for the **Truncate** default. However, we then update the value of **Truncate** in the database. At this point, the values in the registration table and the database will no longer match. Ideally, the application should use the value in the database since it is newer.

The default's value in the registration table may not match the default's value in the database

The application can ensure that it is obtaining the latest copy of the value by first using **NXUpdateDefault()** and then using **NXGetDefaultValue()**. **NXUpdateDefault()** updates the value of the default in the registration table if its value does not match the corresponding value in the database. If the two values match, the function simply returns. After updating the value in the registration table (if needed), the application can use **NXGetDefaultValue()** to obtain the default's value from the reg-

NXUpdateDefault() updates the value of a default

istration table, as before. Figure 8.2 shows the effects of using the **NXUpdateDefault**() function.

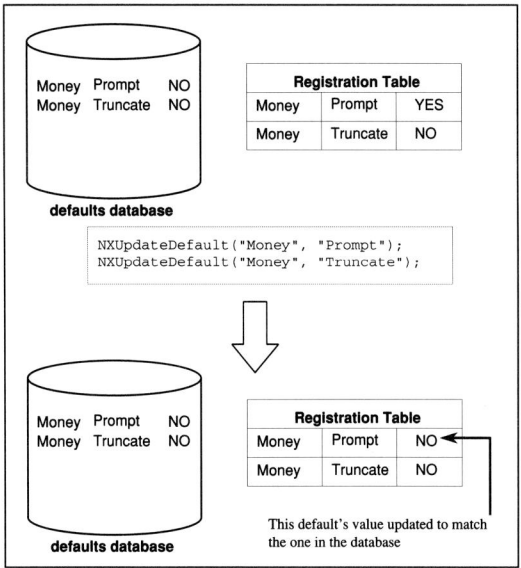

Figure 8.2 Using **NXUpdateDefault**() to update a default's value in the registration table

8.2.3 Writing Defaults with dwrite

While **dread** prints out the values of the defaults database, **dwrite** writes the values of the defaults to the database. The format of the **dwrite** command is:

```
% dwrite owner value
```

Provide an interface to dread and dwrite

Do not force the user to learn **dread** and **dwrite** to customize an application; provide an interface to these commands instead. The most common way to hide the details of these commands is to provide a Preferences panel. A Preferences panel tends to have multiple accessory views. We switch between the views by making a selection in a popup list. Figure 8.3 illustrates a typical Preferences panel.

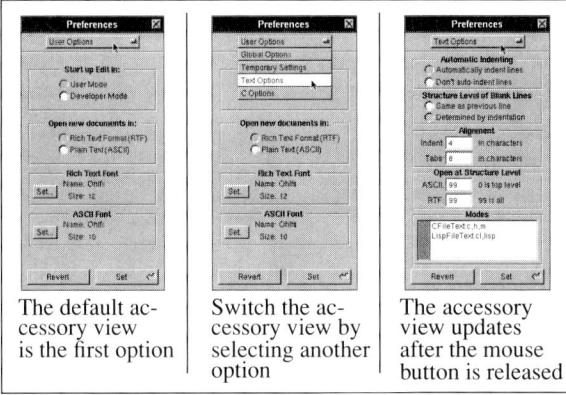

Figure 8.3 The views in a Preferences panel is controlled by a popuplist

Although every application should contain a Preferences panel and an Info panel, the main interface file should not include these objects because they may never be accessed. Ideally, we want to place rarely used features in a separate **.nib** file and load them only as needed.

The Preferences panel and the Info panel should not be placed in the main .nib file

8.3 Using Multiple .nib Files

For non-trivial applications, the interface can easily become complex and unmanageable due to the number of outlets and actions. One way to manage this complexity is to apply the same technique to interfaces that we used to manage complex applications: encapsulation. We accomplish this by using one main **.nib** file to insure that an application has the required minimum interface to function and load in modules as needed. Using this scheme produces the following benefits:

Use multiple .nib files to manage complex interfaces

- reusability—we can reuse the modules as easily as we can reuse classes.
- manageability—instead of having a single monolithic **.nib** file, we separate the various components of the interface into several smaller **.nib** files.

- improved launch time—by initially loading the main **.nib** file and loading a module when it is needed (for example, load in the Info panel's **.nib** file only when the **Info** menu option is selected), the application launches quicker than it would if it loads every **.nib** file upon start-up.

> We would not reuse a class in the *same* application, but we reuse a module. We explore this further in Chapter 9 when we implement a word processor that can manage an indeterminate number of windows.

8.3.1 Setting the File's Owner

The File's Owner of the main .nib file defaults to NXApp

Every **.nib** file has a *File's Owner*, an object that is always created before the other objects in the **.nib** file. Through the **File's Owner**, other objects external to the **.nib** file can access the objects defined in the **.nib** file. For the main interface file, the **File's Owner** defaults to **NXApp**, the application object (the icon labeled **Files' Owner** in the Files Window). For a module, however, the **File's Owner** owner tends to be an instance of a custom subclass. A module is similar to the main interface file except:

- it does not contain a menu since an application should only have one Main Menu.
- the class of the **File's Owner** does not default to any class—we must explicitly set it when we create the module.

InterfaceBuilder doesn't allow connections between .nib files

For example, assume we are trying to add a Preferences panel to the **Money** application to control whether to truncate the output or not. Since we are trying to modularize the design, we place the Preferences panel in a separate **.nib** file (a module). To manage the **.nib** module, we create a **PrefsController** class, instantiate it, and make it the **File's Owner**. All the controls in the Preferences module send messages back to the prefscontroller. The prefscontroller then needs to communicate with the moneyconverter but InterfaceBuilder doesn't allow connections between **.nib** files becasue that would violate encapsulation. Figure 8.4 illustrates the dilemma.

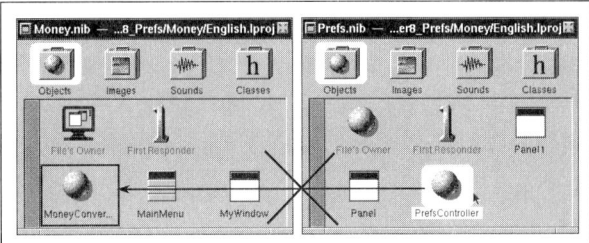

Figure 8.4 InterfaceBuilder doesn't allow connections between **.nib** files since this would violate encapsulation

How do we solve this problem? It turns out that an object can be an instance in the main **.nib** file and the **File's Owner** of a module. With this knowledge, we can create an outlet in the **MoneyConverter** class (in the main **.nib** file) for the prefscontroller and also make the prefscontroller the **File's Owner** of the Preferences module; remember, the **File's Owner** must *already* exist before it can own a file or module. Figure 8.5 shows how the same object (the prefscontroller) can appear in two **.nib** files and how the **MoneyConverter** class defines an outlet for the prefscontroller.

An object that is an outlet in one .nib file can be the File's Owner of another .nib file

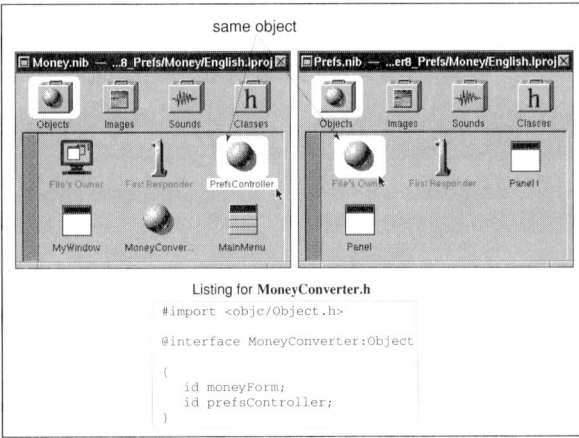

Figure 8.5 An object can appear as an instance in one **.nib** file and as the **File's Owner** in another **.nib** file

In summary, the **File's Owner** serves as a link through which objects in different **.nib** files can communicate. We will explore

The File's Owner serves as a link to external objects

the **File's Owner** more when we add a Preferences panel to the **Money** application later in the chapter. At this point, we need to explore a topic that we have glossed over: when and how are outlets initialized?

8.3.2 Initializing Outlets

Once we have used InterfaceBuilder to create the **.nib** file, we can load the **.nib** file using the **loadNibSection:owner:withNames:** method of the **Application** class as follows:

Loading a **.nib** file

```
[NXApp loadNibSection:"Prefs.nib"
    owner:prefsController withNames:NO];
```

This statement does the following:

- loads the **.nib** file and creates its objects in the interface file, except for the **File's Owner**, which needs to exist before the interface can be loaded. For example, in the listing above, the prefscontroller must already exist.
- sets the ownership to the object passed to the **owner** parameter, in this case, **prefsController**.
- prevents the names generated by InterfaceBuilder from being loaded. InterfaceBuilder names the objects in the **.nib** file, which we can access by using **NXGetNamedObject()**. In our case, we don't need these names and not loading them reduces the amount of memory our application requires.

Loading the .nib file initializes all the outlets which were connected

Loading in the **.nib** file initializes the outlets referenced by the objects in the interface. For example, in the **Money** application from Chapter 6, the **MoneyConverter** class defines and initializes an outlet, **moneyForm** so it can reference the moneyform later. To initialize an outlet, do one of the following:

- implement **appDidInit:** with the appropriate initialization code. However, this may not always work since **appDidInit:** is a delegate method for the **Application** class. Thus, the object that owns the outlet must be the delegate of the application object.

- create a method, **set*OutletName*:anObject** (where ***OutletName*** is the outlet's name) to initialize *each* outlet immediately after it is created. Add whatever further initialization code is required in this method. The following code fragment illustrates how **setMoneyForm:** selects the text in the form's first slot immediately after the form is initialized.

Initializing an outlet

```
- setMoneyForm:anObject
{
  moneyForm = anObject;
  [moneyForm selectTextAt:0];
  return self;
}
```

Note that we need to create such a method only if we need to perform *further* initialization: **NXApp** will automatically create the outlet even if the method is not implemented. For example, in the original **Money** application, although the **MoneyConverter** class did not implement the **setMoneyForm:** method, **NXApp** still created and initialized the **moneyForm** outlet for us. **NXapp** created the outlet when we parsed the class (in InterfaceBuilder), and initialized the outlet when we established the connection.

- implement the **awakeFromNib** method, which is sent after the outlets are initialized. For example, to dynamically arrange the button below and to the right of the form, try the following code fragment (assume the **MoneyConverter** class already has a **convertButton** outlet):

Messaging outlets before they are defined

```
- setMoneyForm:anObject
{
  NXRect theFrame;
  moneyForm = anObject;
  [moneyForm getFrame:&theFrame];
```

```
        [convertButton moveTo:theFrame.origin.x + 50,
            theFrame.origin.y - 25];
}
```

This may not work reliably, however, because **convertButton** may not be defined yet; that is, it may be **nil**, and sending a message to it would not do anything except return **nil**. An application cannot reliably determine the order in which the outlets are initialized. Fortunately, the Application Kit defines an **awakeFromNib** method, which is sent by **NXApp** after all the outlets in the **.nib** file are initialized. Thus, we can solve the problem of dynamically arranging the form and the button as follows:

Messaging two outlets during initialization

```
- awakeFromNib
{
  NXRect theFrame;
  [moneyForm getFrame:&theFrame];
  [convertButton moveTo:theFrame.origin.x + 50,
      theFrame.origin.y - 25];
}
```

An outlet that has been defined but not yet initialized is set to **nil**. An application can use this phenomenon to test whether a **.nib** file has already been loaded. For example, assume we have the following header file for the **PrefsController** class:

Listing for **PrefsController.h**

```
#import <objc/Object.h>

@interface PrefsController:Object

{
  id prefsPanel;
  id switchView;
  id promptSwitch;// switchbutton outlet
              // to control quit prompt
  id truncateSwitch;// switchbutton outlet
```

```
                        // to control truncation
    id popUpButton;// trigger button for popuplist
}

+ initialize;
- awakeFromNib;
- displayPrefsPanel:sender;
- setTruncate:sender;
- (BOOL)shouldTruncate;
- displayPrefsPanel:sender;
- showAccessoryView:sender;

@end
```

In the implementation file, the application can determine whether the **.nib** has been loaded with:

Determining whether a **.nib** file has been loaded

```
- displayPrefsPanel:sender
{
  if (!switchView)
    [NXApp loadNibSection:"Prefs.nib"
      owner:self withNames:NO];
  // rest of code deleted
}
```

The object first checks if an outlet—any outlet will do—if it is **nil** (this will be true if the **.nib** file has not been loaded). If so, the method proceeds to load in the **.nib** file, which would then initialize the outlets to the **id**'s of the objects the outlets are connected to.

> This assumes that the outlets have been connected; if they haven't been, they will still be **nil**. Of course, the only way the outlets would not be properly connected would be because of an oversight. Not loading of an interface file until it is needed is often referred to as ***lazy loading***.

Loading the same .nib file continually produces a memory leak

What would happen if the method loaded the **.nib** without first checking if it has already been loaded? This would produce a memory leak since the application would constantly load in a new **.nib** file without freeing the objects from the previous method invocation. The application would still function, but it would grow in size each time it loads in the **.nib** file.

8.4 Redesigning Money: Adding a Preferences Panel

The original specifications for **Money** (from Chapter 6) are as follows:

> **Money** *converts* a given **currency amount** to various **denominations**, including **American dollars, Japanese yen, British pounds, German marks, French francs**, and **Austrian schillings**. *Typing* in a currency amount and *pressing* the **Return key** converts the amount to the appropriate **values** for the other 5 denominations. If the **user** types in more than one amount, the last amount entered is used as the amount to convert.

We now extend the specification to include a preferences panel (the nouns and verbs have been highlighted):

> **Money** *converts* a given **currency amount** to various **denominations**, including **American dollars, Japanese yen, British pounds, German marks, French francs**, and **Austrian schillings**. *Typing* in a currency amount and *pressing* the **Return key** converts the amount to the appropriate **values** for the other 5 denominations. If the **user** types in more than one amount, the last amount entered is used as the amount to convert. Additionally, *clicking* on the **Preferences option** *displays* a **Preferences panel**, which can be *used* to *customize* whether Money should *truncate* the output or not.

The new nouns include:

- Preferences option—a new menu item that will be added via InterfaceBuilder.
- Preferences panel—the panel that contains the controls needed to set the values for the various defaults.
- output—a synonym for values.

The new verbs include:

- used—a helping verb.
- customize—represents reading from and writing to the defaults database. The reading and writing functionality will be implemented in a new class, **PrefsController**.
- truncate—represents truncating the output. Since we are already using a form to output the values, we can truncate the data by using one of the existing form methods (explored later in "Implementing Money" on page 309).

Since the user may never use the Preferences panel, place the interface for the Preferences panel in a separate **.nib** module and load it only as needed. To manage this **.nib** file, create a **PrefsController** class to encapsulate the preferences functionality. As mentioned earlier, a Preferences panel tends to have a popuplist that can be used to switch between views to display the various defaults. Before continuing, let us digress and discuss the user interface a little more closely.

Create a PrefsController class to manage the defaults

The application only has one new feature in the user interface: the Preferences panel with a popuplist. We need to decide what control to use to display the current value of the **Truncate** default. Initially, a textfield may seem like the logical choice since it can accept and display a single value. However, we would have no way of knowing what string to type in (**yes**, **no**, **Yes**, **No**, **on**, **off**, **On**, or **Off**) to set the attribute. A better solution would be to use a switchbutton for displaying and setting a value for which there are only two possible combinations such as the **Truncate** default.

A switchbutton is ideal for defaults that can only have two possible states

Redesigning Money: Adding a Preferences Panel

Figure 8.6 illustrates the drawbacks of using a textfield and the benefits of using a switchbutton.

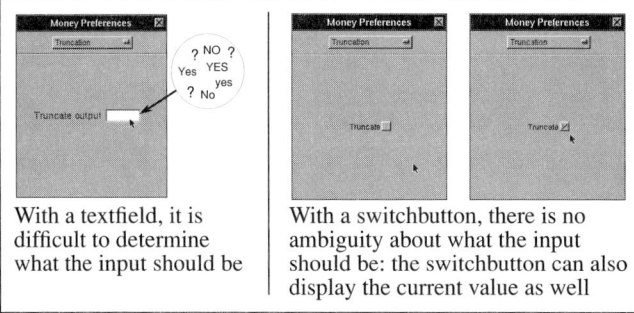

With a textfield, it is difficult to determine what the input should be

With a switchbutton, there is no ambiguity about what the input should be: the switchbutton can also display the current value as well

Figure 8.6 A switchbutton is more appropriate than a textfield for options that only have two possible values

A popuplist is a matrix of menucells

A popuplist is basically a matrix of menucells with a button as the trigger. A popuplist is used in cases where screen space is at a premium as in a Preferences panel. To make a selection in a popuplist, click on the trigger button, select a choice, and then release the mouse button. At this point, the title of the selected menucell replaces the button's title, and the matrix sends its action message to its target.

Once the popuplist is created, attach it to the cover button

The following program illustrates how to create a popuplist with three entries. Once the popuplist and button are created, we need to attach the button to the popuplist so it can display itself when we click (and hold down) on the mouse button. The target of the popuplist is the targetobject, an instance of the newly created **TargetObject** class. This program is similar to the first iteration of **ControlDemo.m** from Chapter 6 except for the changes in bold. Note that we have commented out the line that sets the title of the button, although the application would work just as well if the line were uncommented.

Listing for PopUp_main.m

```
#import <appkit/appkit.h>
#import "TargetObject.h"

// a minimal program to demonstrate how
// to use a popuplist
```

```
main()
{
  // create an application object
  // to establish connection to
  // Window Server
  id NXApp = [Application new];
  id theWindow;
  id theMenu;
  id theButton;
  NXRect theRect;
  id thePopUpList;
  id theTargetObject;
  id menuCell;

  // create a window that's at 125, 125
  // and is 200 by 300 pixels
  NXSetRect(&theRect, 125, 125, 200, 300);
  theWindow = [ [Window alloc]
    initContent:&theRect
    style: NX_TITLEDSTYLE
    backing:NX_BUFFERED
    buttonMask:NX_MINIATURIZEBUTTONMASK
    defer:YES];

  // create the menu
  theMenu = [ [Menu alloc]
    initTitle: [NXApp appName]];
  // create the menu option
  [theMenu addItem:"Quit"
    action:@selector(terminate:)
    keyEquivalent:'q'];

  // resize menu to accomodate menu option
  [theMenu sizeToFit];
  [NXApp setMainMenu:theMenu];

  // create a button that's 80 x 20
  NXSetRect(&theRect, 0, 0, 80, 20);
  theButton = [ [Button alloc]
    initFrame:&theRect];
  // set the title for the button
  // [theButton setTitle:"Press Here"];
  // since the button is a view, we need
  // to install it as the subview of the
```

```
    // window's contentview or else it
    // won't draw
    [ [theWindow contentView]
      addSubview: theButton];

    // create the target of the popuplist
    theTargetObject =
      [[TargetObject alloc] init];

    // create the popuplist
    thePopUpList = [[PopUpList alloc] init];
    // add items to the popuplist
    // and set each tag
    // addItem: returns the added menucell
    menuCell = [thePopUpList addItem:"Item 1"];
    [menuCell setTag:1];
    menuCell = [thePopUpList addItem:"Item 2"];
    [menuCell setTag:2];
    menuCell = [thePopUpList addItem:"Item 3"];
    [menuCell setTag:3];

    // set the target and action for
    // the popuplist
    [thePopUpList setTarget:theTargetObject];
    [thePopUpList
      setAction:@selector(printSelection:)];

    // attach button to popuplist
    NXAttachPopUpList(theButton, thePopUpList);

    // send the window to the front
    // and display it
    [theWindow makeKeyAndOrderFront:nil];

    // go into event loop to wait for events
    [NXApp run];
}
```

Now create the class files for the **TargetObject**, the class that actually implements the **printSelection:** method.

Listing for TargetObject.h

```
#import <objc/Object.h>
```

```
@interface TargetObject:Object

{
}

- printSelection:sender;

@end
```

Listing for **TargetObject.m**

```
#import <appkit/appkit.h>
#import "TargetObject.h"

@implementation TargetObject

- printSelection:sender
{
  int index;
  // print the class of the sender
  // which should be Matrix
  printf("The class of sender is %s\n",
    [sender name]);
  // get the selected cell and its tag
  index = [[sender selectedCell] tag];
  switch(index)
    {
    case 1:
      printf("Item 1\n");
      break;
    case 2:
      printf("Item 2\n");
      break;
    case 3:
      printf("Item 3\n");
      break;
    }

  return self;
}

@end
```

In addition to performing the functionality in the **ControlDemo** application, this **main()** function:

- creates a popuplist and adds three entries to it. As **main()** is creating each entry, it sets the **tag** of the corresponding menucell so that the popuplist's target can later determine which menucell is selected (in the **printSelection:** method).
- sets the targetobject to be the target of the popuplist.
- sets the action of the popuplist to be the **printSelection:** method.
- attaches the popuplist to the button using the **NXAttachPopUpList()** function. This allows the popuplist to popup when we click on the button. When we release the mouse, the popuplist sends its message to its target.

Compile the application as follows:

```
$ cc -c -g -o TargetObject.o TargetObject.m
$ cc -c -g -o PopUp_main.o PopUp_main.m
$ cc -g -o PopUp PopUp_main.o TargetObject.o
-lNeXT_s
```

The sender of the message is the matrix

Note that although we set the target to be the popuplist, because of the way the **PopUpList** class is implemented, the **sender** of the message is the matrix instead. Thus, the **printSelection:** method must first ask the sender (the matrix) for the currently selected cell (using **selectedCell**) and then query the cell for its **tag** to determine which menucell sent the message. The method then proceeds to print which menucell was selected.

> One drawback of the aforementioned scheme is that we have to manually set the **tag** of each newly added menucell since we are using the cell's **tag** as an index. This can be error-prone, if we forget to update the tags of the menucells as we create them (by default, the tags of the menucells in a popuplist default to **0**). Additionally, if we find that we need to insert a new menucell between two existing ones, we would have then have to renumber the tags or number them nonconsecutively.
>
> In our upcoming application, we will introduce a better way of determining the currently selected option by using the title of the selected item and then searching for it in the popuplist.

Now that we have covered the user interface more extensively, let's return to the **PrefsController** class. Its four main responsibilities are the following:

- determining whether the output should be truncated or not. It does this by reading the defaults database.
- updating the status of the **Truncate** default in the defaults database.
- displaying the Preferences panel.
- determining which accessory view to display: the **PrefsController** class actually depends on another class, **SwitchView**, to display the accessory view.

Figure 8.7 shows the CRC card for the **PrefsController** class.

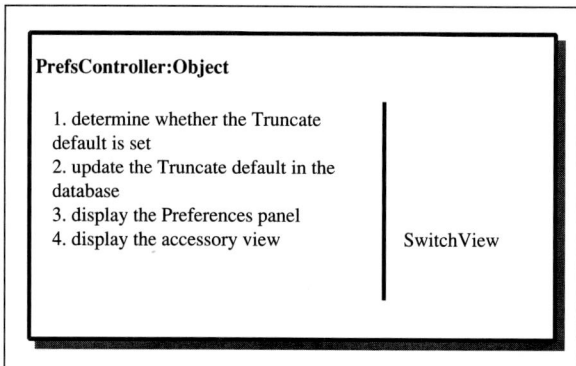

Figure 8.7 The CRC card for the **PrefsController** class

The **SwitchView** class displays the appropriate accessory view in response to the request from the **PrefsController** class. Although this application contains only one default (whether to truncate the output or not), implementing a class to switch between multiple views allows us to add more views (for the new defaults), should the need arise. Figure 8.8 shows the CRC card for the **SwitchView** class.

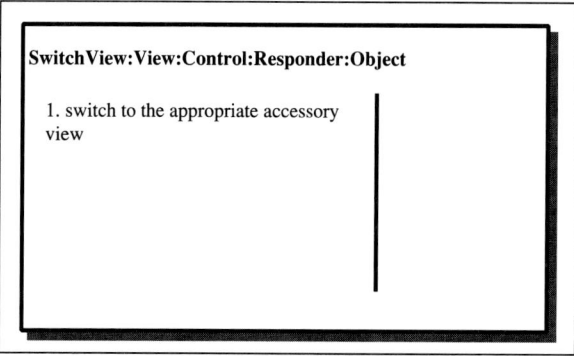

Figure 8.8 The CRC card for the **SwitchView** class

Modify the convert: method to truncate the output

Of course, we need to modify the **convert:** method so that it truncates the output when appropriate. In order to determine whether or not to truncate the output, the moneyconverter needs to query the prefscontroller for the status of the **Truncate** default. Therefore, the **PrefsController** class is listed as a collaborator of the

MoneyConverter class. Figure 8.9 shows the updated CRC card for the **MoneyConverter** class.

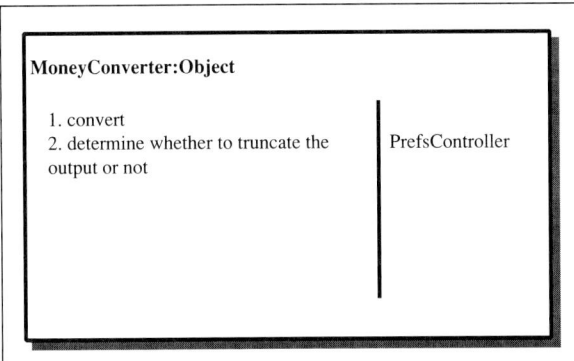

Figure 8.9 The updated CRC card for the **MoneyConverter** class

Table 8.1 shows the class summary table for the **PrefsController** class.

PrefsController:Object		
	Name	**Description**
Instance variables	truncateSwitch	switchbutton outlet that controls the Truncate default
	promptSwitch	switchbutton outlet that controls the Prompt default
Methods	initialize	initializes the class object and registers the defaults
	awakeFromNib	performs further initialization after the .nib file is loaded
	setTruncate:sender	sets or unsets the Truncate default
	(BOOL)shouldTruncate	determines the status of the Truncate default
	displayPrefsPanel:sender	displays the Preferences panel
	showAccessoryView:sender	determines which accessory view to pass to the switchview for display

Table 8.1 Class summary table for the **PrefsController** class

Table 8.2 shows the class summary table for the **SwitchView** class.

SwitchView:View:Control:Responder:Object		
	Name	**Description**
Instance variables	accessoryView	accessory view of the Preferences panel
Methods	drawSelf:(NXRect*)rects :(int)rectCount	draws the accessory view

Table 8.2 Class summary table for the **SwitchView** class

Although the **MoneyConverter** class does not have any new methods, it does have one new instance variable, the **prefsController** outlet. Table 8.3 shows the updated summary class table for the **MoneyConverter** class.

MoneyConverter:Object		
	Name	**Description**
Instance variables	moneyForm	outlet for the form; this form is used for input and for displaying the conversions
	prefsController	outlet for the prefscontroller
Methods	convert:	converts the last edited entry and displays the appropriate value in the remaining fields of the form: truncate the output if the Truncate default is set

Table 8.3   Class summary table for the **MoneyConverter** class

Figure 8.10 shows the updated message diagram with the new classes.

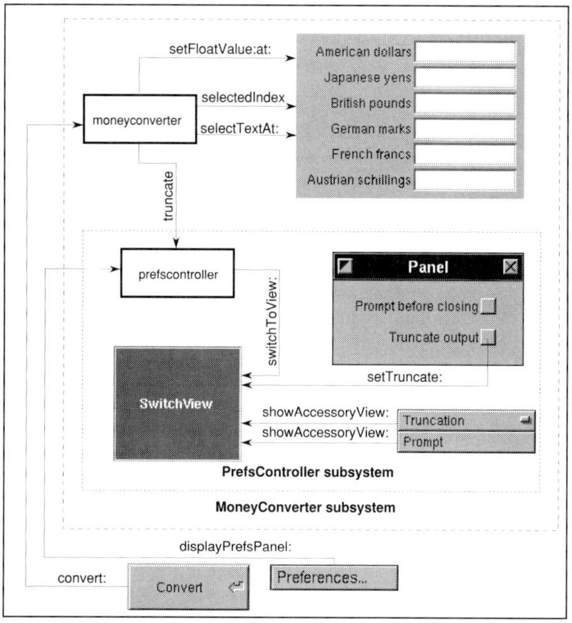

Figure 8.10 The message diagram for **Money**

Note the following:

- the switchview, Preferences panel, switchbutton (labeled **Truncate**), and button (which activates the popuplist) are internal to the prefscontroller. Together they form the **PrefsController** subsystem.
- since the **Convert** button and the **Preferences** menu option are controls which are external to both the **MoneyConverter** and the **PrefsController** subsystems, they are not integral to the operation of the application: that is, they can be replaced with other controls and the application would still work.

Figure 8.11 shows the updated hierarchy graph that incorporates the new classes.

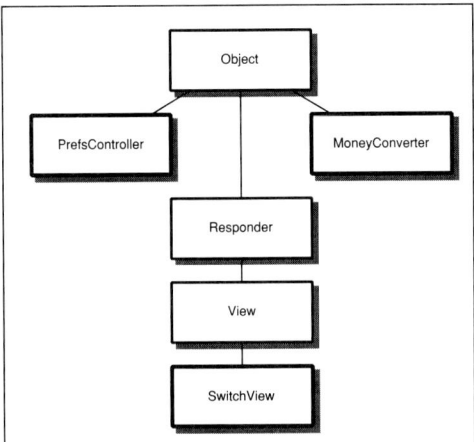

Figure 8.11 The updated class hierarchy graph for **Money**

8.5 Implementing Money

Copy the directory that contains the **Money** application from Chapter 6 and rename the directory something like **Money_Prefs**. Type in the header file for the **PrefsController** class and the **SwitchView** class.

Listing for PrefsController.h

```
#import <objc/Object.h>

@interface PrefsController:Object

{
   id prefsPanel;
   id switchView;
   id promptSwitch;// switchbutton outlet
                  // to control quit prompt
   id truncateSwitch;// switchbutton outlet
                    // to control truncation
   id popUpButton;// trigger button for popuplist
}

+ initialize;
```

```
- awakeFromNib;
- displayPrefsPanel:sender;
- setTruncate:sender;
- (BOOL)shouldTruncate;
- displayPrefsPanel:sender;
- showAccessoryView:sender;

@end
```

Listing for **SwitchView.h**

```
#import <appkit/View.h>

@interface SwitchView:View

{
  id accessoryView;
}

- switchToView:newView;
- drawSelf:(NXRect *)rects :(int)rectCount;

@end
```

Drag these files from the Workspace to the suitcase under the **Headers** entry to add them to the project. Figure 8.12 illustrates how to add files to the project by dragging.

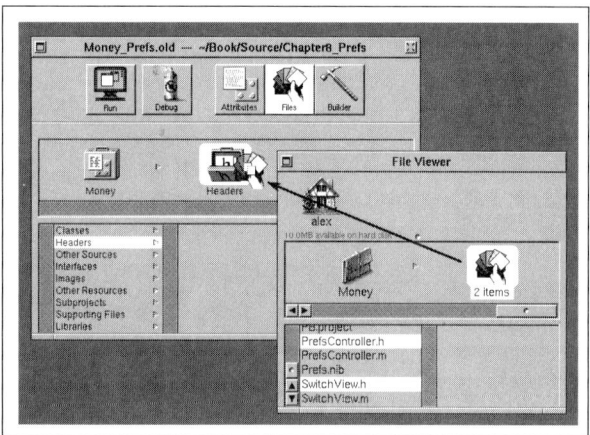

Figure 8.12 Adding header files to a project by dragging them from the Workspace

Select the **Interfaces** entry and double-click on the **Money.nib** file to start InterfaceBuilder. In InterfaceBuilder, create a new module by selecting **Document** ⇒ **New Module** ⇒ **New Empty**. Subclass **Object** to create **PrefsController**. Select the **File's Owner** icon and, using the Inspector, set the class to **PrefsController**. Figure 8.12 illustrates this sequence.

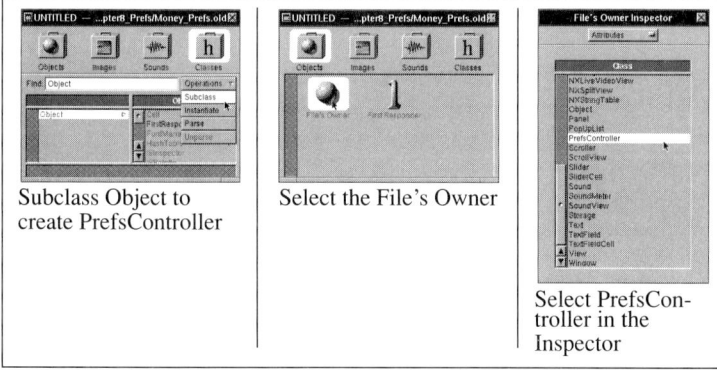

Figure 8.13 Setting the class of the **File's Owner**

Drag a panel from the palette and place it near the middle of the screen. Resize the panel so it is rectangular (taller than wide).

Drag a popuplist from the palette and place it in the panel. Double-click on the popuplist to select a menucell in the popuplist. Double-click on the first menucell and edit its title to read **Truncation**. Double-click on the second menucell then double-click on it again to change its title to **Prompt**. Figure 8.14 illustrates how to edit the entries in a popuplist.

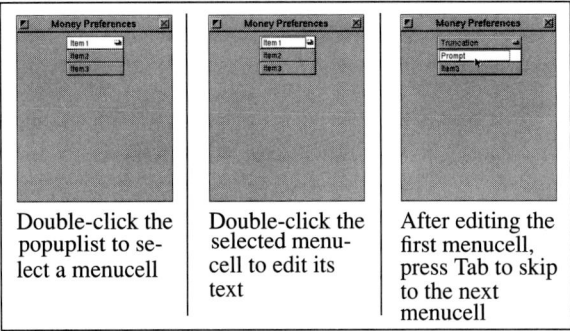

| Double-click the popuplist to select a menucell | Double-click the selected menucell to edit its text | After editing the first menucell, press Tab to skip to the next menucell |

Figure 8.14 Editing the entries in a popuplist

Select the third menucell and cut it to remove it from the popuplist. Click on the first button again to make it the default selection when the popuplist is first displayed.

Now create the panel to contain the controls the switchview will be using. Drag a panel from the palette and then add two switchbuttons to the panel. Edit the title of the first switchbutton to read **Truncate output**, and the title of the second to read **Prompt before closing**.

Drag a **CustomView** object from the palette and resize it so its width is equal to that of the Preference Panel. Be careful not to obscure the popuplist already in the Preferences panel. Use the Class Inspector to set the class of the **CustomView** instance to

SwitchView and click OK. Figure 8.15 illustrates how the Preferences panel will look at this point.

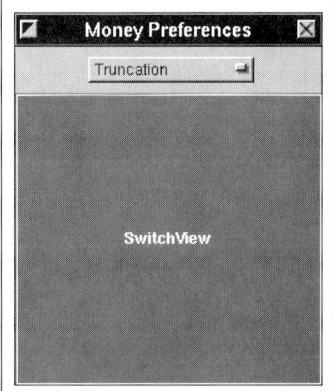

Figure 8.15 The Preferences panel with the switchview

At this point, connect all the objects together as follows. Figure 8.16 illustrates all the connections which we need to perform.

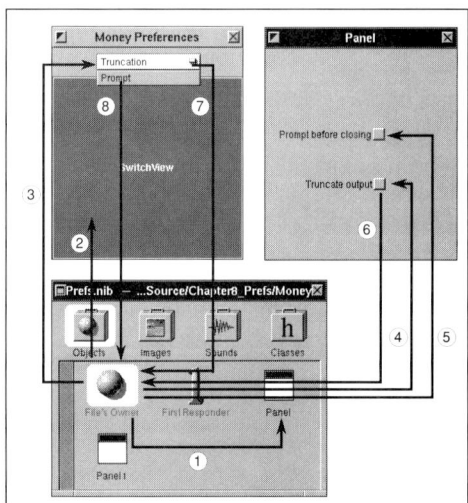

Figure 8.16 Connecting all the objects in **Prefs.nib**

The eight connections are as follows:

1. Connect the panel (labelled **Panel**) as the **prefsPanel** outlet of the **File's Owner**.
2. Connect the switchview as the **switchView** outlet of the **File's Owner**.

3. Connect the button as the **popUpButton** outlet of the **File's Owner**.
4. Connect the **Truncate output** switchbutton as the **truncateSwitch** outlet for the **File's Owner**.
5. Connect the **Prompt before closing** switchbutton as the **promptSwitch** outlet for the **File's Owner**.
6. Connect the **File's Owner** as the target for the **Truncate output** switchbutton and select the **setTruncate:** method.
7. Connect the **File's Owner** as the target for the **Truncation** menucell and select the **showAccessoryView:** method.
8. Connect the **File's Owner** as the target for the **Prompt** menucell and select the **showAccessoryView:** method.

Save this interface as **Prefs.nib** and then open the **Money.nib** file. Subclass **Object** to create **PrefsController**. Now parse in the class files then instantiate the class. Since the moneyconverter needs to message the prefscontroller, create an outlet for the prefscontroller in the **MoneyConverter** class. Add a new outlet, **prefsController**, and a new class method, **initialize**, to the header file of the **MoneyConverter** class (the changes are in bold):

Listing for MoneyConverter.h

```
/* Generated by Project Builder */

#import <objc/Object.h>

@interface MoneyConverter:Object
{
  id moneyForm;
  id prefsController;
}

- convert:sender;

@end
```

Return to InterfaceBuilder and parse in the header file for the **MoneyConverter** class. Clicking on the Connections Inspector for the moneyconverter instance should now produce a new outlet, **prefsController**.

Before making all the connections, add a **Preferences** option to the Main Menu of the application. Bring up the menu palette and drag an **Info** submenu from the palette to the Main Menu. This submenu contains three submenu items: **Info**, **Preferences**, and **Help**. By default, only the **Help** option is enabled. Since we will not yet be implementing the **Help** menu option but the **Preferences** option instead, disable the **Help** option and enable the **Preferences** option using the Inspector. Figure 8.17 illustrates how to enable the **Preferences** menu option; use a similar sequence to disable the **Help** menu option.

By default, the Preferences menu option is disabled

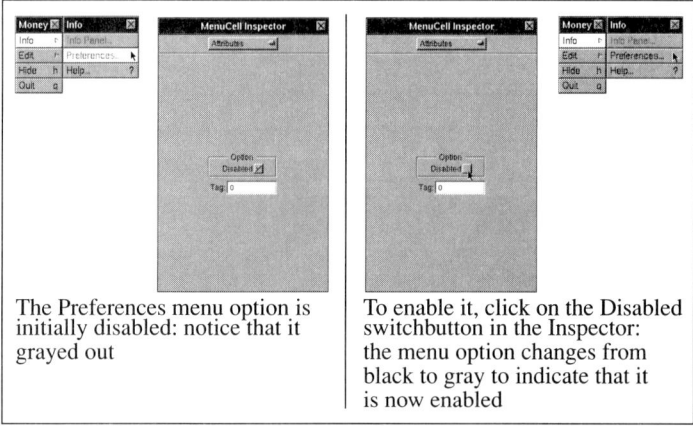

The Preferences menu option is initially disabled: notice that it grayed out

To enable it, click on the Disabled switchbutton in the Inspector: the menu option changes from black to gray to indicate that it is now enabled

Figure 8.17 Enabling the **Preferences** menu option

Since the **Info** submenu contains a menu option for an Info panel, remove the original **Info** menu option.

Figure 8.18 shows the connections that need to be made in the main **.nib** file, **Money.nib**.

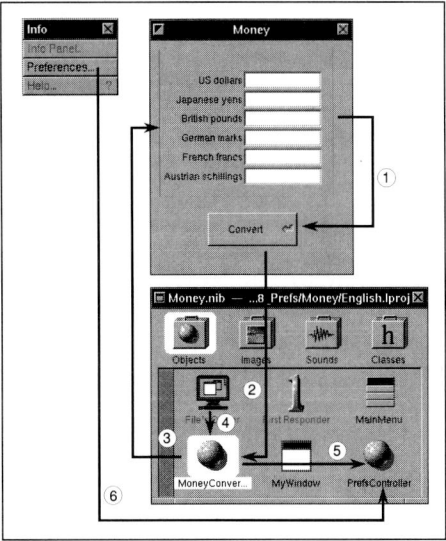

Figure 8.18 Connecting the objects in **Money.nib**

There is actually one instance of the **PrefsController** class, even though it appears in both the **Money.nib** and **Prefs.nib** files. Recall that the **File's Owner** must already exist before the objects in the interface file. Thus, the prefscontroller is instantiated once and is referred to in both the **Prefs.nib** and **Money.nib** file.

The six connections are as follows (note that connections 1 through 3 should already be made because we copied them from the **Money** application from Chapter 6):

1. Connect the button as the target for the form and select the **performClick:** method.
2. Connect the moneyconverter as the target for the button and select the **convert:** method.
3. Connect the form as the **moneyForm** outlet of the moneyconverter.

4. Connect the moneyconverter as the delegate of the **File's Owner**.
5. Connect the prefscontroller as the **prefsController** outlet for the moneyconverter.
6. Connect the prefscontroller as the target for the **Preferences** menu option and select the **displayPrefsPanel:** method.

Save the **.nib** file and modify the code for the **MoneyConverter** class. Modify the **convert:** method so that it queries the prefscontroller for the **Truncate** default (the changes are in bold):

Listing for MoneyConverter.m

```
/* Generated by Project Builder */

#import <appkit/appkit.h>
#import "MoneyConverter.h"
#import "PrefsController.h"

#define MAXIMUM 6

@implementation MoneyConverter

- convert:sender
{
  int index, loop;
  unsigned int right,left = 10;
  float entry, value, dollar_equiv;
  id cell;

  // Array contains the conversion of rates
  // of other currencies to dollars
  static float rate[MAXIMUM] =
    {1.00, 135.0, 0.50, 1.67, 6.00, 14.5};

  // Determine which field of the form
  // was the last to be edited
  index = [moneyForm selectedIndex];

  // Calculate equivalent of foreign currency
  // at edited field to dollar equivalent
  entry = [moneyForm floatValueAt:index];
  dollar_equiv = entry / rate[index];
```

Implementing Money

```
        // check if the Truncate default is set
        // and then set the number of figures
        // to the right of the decimal point
        if ([prefsController shouldTruncate] == YES)
          right = 2;
        else
          right = 6;
        // set floating point format for each
        // formcell in the form
        for (loop=0; loop < MAXIMUM; loop++)
          {
          // get each cell
          cell = [moneyForm cellAt:loop :0];
          [cell setFloatingPointFormat:NO
            left:left right:right];
          }

        for (loop = 0; loop < MAXIMUM; loop++)
          {
          // Calculate other currencies
          // using look-up table
          value = dollar_equiv * rate[loop];
          // display value at appropriate field
          [moneyForm setFloatValue:value at:loop];
          }
        // leave the last edited field as the
        // selected text
        [moneyForm selectTextAt:index];
           return self;
    }

    @end
```

Type in the implementation file for the **SwitchView** class:

Listing for SwitchView.m

```
    #import <appkit/appkit.h>
    #import "SwitchView.h"

    @implementation SwitchView

    - drawSelf:(const NXRect *)rects :(int)rectCount
```

```
{
  // erase the entire area
  PSsetlinewidth(1.0);
  PSsetgray(NX_LTGRAY);
  NXRectFill(&bounds);

  // draw upper line at view's boundary
  PSsetgray(NX_DKGRAY);
  PSmoveto(bounds.origin.x,
    bounds.size.height);
  PSrlineto(bounds.size.width, 0);
  PSstroke();

  // draw lower line for bezel effect
  PSsetgray(NX_WHITE);
  PSmoveto(bounds.origin.x,
    bounds.size.height - 1.0);
  PSrlineto(bounds.size.width, 0);
  PSstroke();

  return self;
}

- switchToView:newView
{
  NXRect rect;

  // remove the old view
  [accessoryView removeFromSuperview];

  // add the new subview
  accessoryView = newView;
  [self addSubview:accessoryView];

  // center the view
  [accessoryView getFrame:&rect];
  rect.origin.y = bounds.origin.y +
    (bounds.size.height -
    rect.size.height) / 2.0;
  rect.origin.x = bounds.origin.x +
    (bounds.size.width -
    rect.size.width) / 2.0;
  [accessoryView moveTo:rect.origin.x
    :rect.origin.y];
```

```
                // display ourselves -- display
                // sends drawSelf:: to first erase the
                // switchview and then ask the subview
                // (the accessoryView) to display itself
                [self display];
                return self;
            }

            @end
```

Type in the implementation file for the **PrefsController** class:

Listing for **PrefsController.m**

```
            #import <appkit/appkit.h>
            #import "PrefsController.h"
            #import "SwitchView.h"

            @implementation PrefsController

            #define TRUNCATE 0
            #define PROMPT 1
            #define OFF 0
            #define ON 1

            + initialize
            {
              // make sure that self is a PrefsController
              // class before setting class initialization:
              // this prevents subclasses from performing
              // reinitialization
              if (self == [PrefsController class])
                {
                const char *appName = [NXApp appName];

                static NXDefaultsVector theDefaults =
                  {
                    {"Truncate", "NO"},
                    {"Prompt", "NO"},
                    {NULL, NULL}
                  };

                NXRegisterDefaults(appName, theDefaults);
                }
```

```
  return self;
}

- awakeFromNib
{
  const char *appName = [NXApp appName];
  const char *truncateFlag;

  truncateFlag =
    NXGetDefaultValue(appName, "Truncate");
  // make sure truncateFlag is not NULL before
  // comparing it
  if (truncateFlag)
    {
    if (strcasecmp(truncateFlag, "YES") == 0)
      [truncateSwitch setState:ON];
    else
      [truncateSwitch setState:OFF];
    }
  return self;
}

- setTruncate:sender
{
  const char *appName = [NXApp appName];
  int state = [truncateSwitch state];
  if (state == OFF)
    NXWriteDefault(appName, "Truncate", "NO");
  else
    NXWriteDefault(appName, "Truncate", "YES");
  return self;
}

- (BOOL)shouldTruncate
{
  const char *truncateFlag;
  const char *appName = [NXApp appName];

  // value in database may be newer than value
  // in registration table because of Prefs
  // panel; thus, update value in table to
  // match value in database
  NXUpdateDefault(appName, "Truncate");
  // get value from registration table
  // now that it's been updated
```

Implementing Money

```
          truncateFlag =
            NXGetDefaultValue(appName, "Truncate");
          // make sure truncateFlag is not NULL before
          // comparing it
          if (truncateFlag)
            {
            if (strcasecmp(truncateFlag, "YES") == 0)
              return YES;
            }
          return NO;
        }

        - displayPrefsPanel:sender
        {
          if (!prefsPanel)
            {
            [NXApp loadNibSection:"Prefs.nib"
              owner:self withNames:NO];
            [switchView switchToView:truncateSwitch];
            }
          [prefsPanel makeKeyAndOrderFront:nil];
          return self;
        }

        - showAccessoryView:sender
        {
          int index;
          id popUpList;

          // the popuplist is the button's target
          popUpList = [popUpButton target];
          // get title of selected item and
          // then get index of title in
          // popuplist
          index = [popUpList indexOfItem:
             [popUpList selectedItem]];
          switch(index)
            {
            case TRUNCATE:
              [switchView switchToView:truncateSwitch];
              break;
            case PROMPT:
              [switchView switchToView:promptSwitch];
              break;
            }
```

```
    return self;
}

@end;
```

Save the files and click on **Build** in the ProjectBuilder to build the application. Run the application and verify the following:

- type in a value and click on the **Convert** button: the output should be displayed up to six decimal places since that is the default behavior.
- click on the Preferences panel and verify whether the switchbutton for the **Truncate** default is set. Click on the switchbutton to turn off truncation and convert another set of values; the output should now be truncated to two decimal places.
- use the popuplist to display the other view in the Preferences panel, the one containing the **Prompt** switchbutton. Notice that this switchbutton does not do anything since it was not connected to a target (this is left as a suggestion at the end of the chapter).
- close the Preferences panel and reopen it. Verify that the Preferences panel is still displaying the same view as when it was closed.
- use the command-line to start the application and set the **Truncate** default. For example, to start **Money** with **Truncate** set to **YES** use:
    ```
    % Money.app/Money -Truncate YES &
    ```

Recall that NeXTSTEP creates an entire directory to store the application (in this case, **Money.app**). Thus, to start an application, specify the executable inside the directory. To verify that the command-line parameters do not update the values already registered in the database, first read the defaults database to determine the value for the **Truncate** default.

```
% dread -o Money
Truncate NO
```

Start the application with the **Truncate** default set to another value and then read the database again to verify that the default is unchanged. This verifies that the command-line parameters do not overwrite the values in the defaults database.

```
% Money.app/Money -Truncate YES &
% dread -o Money
Truncate NO
```

8.6 Examining the Code

When the application first starts, it registers its attributes through the **initialize** method of the **PrefsController** class:

Initializing a class object

```
+ initialize
{
  // make sure that self is a PrefsController
  // class before setting class initialization:
  // this prevents subclasses from performing
  // reinitialization
  if (self == [PrefsController class])
    {
    const char *appName = [NXApp appName];

    static NXDefaultsVector theDefaults =
      {
        {"Truncate", "NO"},
        {"Prompt", "NO"},
        {NULL, NULL}
      };

    NXRegisterDefaults(appName, theDefaults);
    }
  return self;
}
```

The moneyconverter first instantiates the **PrefsController** class then sets one of its outlets to point to the prefscontroller. As part of the instantiation process, **NXApp** automatically sends an **initialize** message to the **PrefsController** class object to initialize it; this method registers the defaults for the application, as explained in "Registering Defaults" on page 281.

Immediately after loading the **.nib** file, **NXApp** sends an **awakeFromNib** message to the prefscontroller. By overriding this method, the prefscontroller can perform further initialization:

Performing initialization in the **awakeFromNib** method

```
- awakeFromNib
{
  const char *appName = [NXApp appName];
  const char *truncateFlag;

  truncateFlag =
    NXGetDefaultValue(appName, "Truncate");
  // make sure truncateFlag is not NULL before
  // comparing it
  if (truncateFlag)
    {
    if (strcasecmp(truncateFlag, "YES") == 0)
      [truncateSwitch setState:ON];
    else
      [truncateSwitch setState:OFF];
    }
  return self;
}
```

The method determines if the **Truncate** default is set by obtaining the value from the registration table and then setting the state of the switchbutton accordingly: the switchbutton is set (with a check value) if the value of **Truncate** value is **YES** (note that the method use **strcasecmp()**, which ignores the case of the string to be compared). This check is needed since the switchbutton is the default accessory view, and we want it to display with the appropriate state when the application first displays the Preferences panel (see below).

Afterwards, **Money** displays the main window. Clicking on the Preferences menu option sends a **displayPrefsPanel:** message to the prefscontroller.

Loading the .nib file of the Preference panel

```
- displayPrefsPanel:sender
{
  if (!prefsPanel)
    {
    [NXApp loadNibSection:"Prefs.nib"
      owner:self withNames:NO];
    [switchView switchToView:truncateSwitch];
    }
  [prefsPanel makeKeyAndOrderFront:nil];
  return self;
}
```

The method determines whether the **.nib** file has already been loaded by checking if the **switchView** outlet is not **nil**. If **switchView** is **nil**, the method loads in the interface file, which initializes all the outlets to non-**nil** values. Afterwards, **displayPrefsPanel:** orders the Preferences panel to the front and makes it the key window.

Each time we make a selection in the popuplist, it sends a **showAccessoryView:** message to the prefscontroller to determine which option in the popuplist was selected.

Displaying the appropriate accessory view

```
- showAccessoryView:sender
{
  int index;
  id popUpList;

  // the popuplist is the button's target
  popUpList = [popUpButton target];
  // get title of selected item and
  // then get index of title in
  // popuplist
  index = [popUpList indexOfItem:
    [popUpList selectedItem]];
  switch(index)
    {
    case TRUNCATE:
      [switchView switchToView:truncateSwitch];
```

```
      break;
    case PROMPT:
      [switchView switchToView:promptSwitch];
      break;
    }
  return self;
}
```

As mentioned earlier, a popuplist is basically a matrix of menucells. To determine which menucell is selected, the method takes advantage of the fact that the popuplist is the button's target. Thus, **showAccessoryView:** obtains the **id** of the popuplist by sending the trigger button a **target** message. With the **id** of the popuplist, **showAccessoryView:** determines the index of the selected item by:

- obtaining the title of the selected item.
- determining the index of this title in the popuplist.

Note that by using these two steps, we avoid having to set the tags of the menucells as we did earlier in our **PopUp** application. Using this technique, we can add more menucells to the popuplist without having to worry about whether the tags are properly set for the newly added menucells: the only thing we have to insure is that the titles of the menucells are different. Unlike a matrix, a popuplist does not automatically increment the tags of its elements.

Using the title to determine the selected cell in a popuplist is more robust than using the tag of the cells

The **showAccessoryView:** method then uses the index in a **switch** statement to determine which accessory view to pass to **switchToView:** for displaying.

Switching between accessory views

```
- switchToView:newView
{
  NXRect rect;

  // remove the old view
  [accessoryView removeFromSuperview];

  // add the new subview
```

```
        accessoryView = newView;
        [self addSubview:accessoryView];

        // center the view
        [accessoryView getFrame:&rect];
          rect.origin.y = bounds.origin.y +
          (bounds.size.height -
        rect.size.height) / 2.0;
        rect.origin.x = bounds.origin.x +
          (bounds.size.width -
          rect.size.width) / 2.0;
        [accessoryView moveTo:rect.origin.x
          :rect.origin.y];

        // display ourselves -- display
        // sends drawSelf:: to first erase the
        // switchview and then ask the subview
        // (the accessoryView) to display itself
        [self display];
          return self;
      }
```

The **switchToView:** method does the following:

- removes the old accessory view from the view hierarchy.
- sets the accessory view to the view passed to the method (**newView**).
- centers the accessory view by calculating the difference between the accessory view's width and the switchview's width and then dividing this difference by two; the method does the same for the height.
- moves the accessory view to this new center.

Figure 8.19 illustrates how to center a view in its superview.

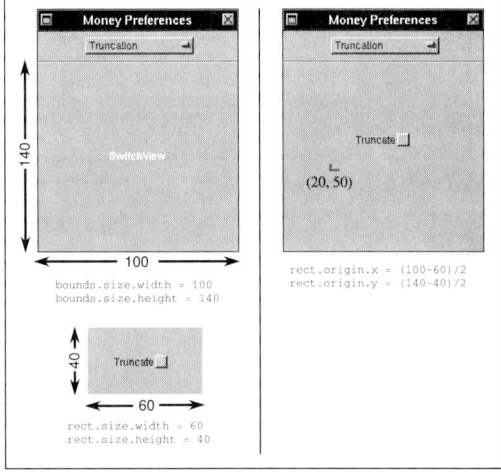

Figure 8.19 Centering a view in its superview's coordinate system

The accessory view sends itself a **display** message, which ultimately sends itself a **drawSelf::** method:

Erasing the view and drawing the bezel line

```
- drawSelf:(const NXRect *)rects :(int)rectCount
{
  // erase the entire area
  PSsetlinewidth(1.0);
  PSsetgray(NX_LTGRAY);
  NXRectFill(&bounds);

  // draw upper line at view's boundary
  PSsetgray(NX_DKGRAY);
  PSmoveto(bounds.origin.x,
    bounds.size.height);
  PSrlineto(bounds.size.width, 0);
  PSstroke();

  // draw lower line for bezel effect
  PSsetgray(NX_WHITE);
  PSmoveto(bounds.origin.x,
    bounds.size.height - 1.0);
  PSrlineto(bounds.size.width, 0);
  PSstroke();
```

330   **Examining the Code**

```
    return self;
}
```

The **drawSelf::** method first erases the entire area of the switchview and then draws a dark gray line from the left edge to the right edge of the view's top boundary. By drawing a white line immediately below the dark gray line, the method produces a bezeled line. Figure 8.20 illustrates this technique.

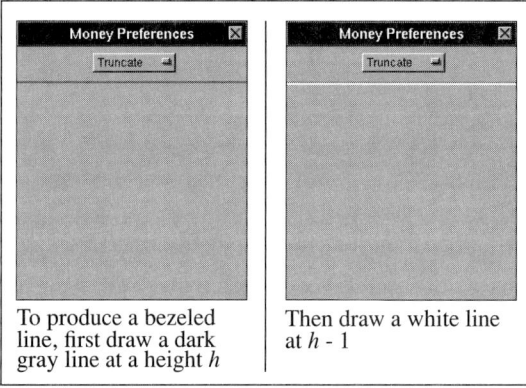

Figure 8.20 Drawing a bezeled line

Recall that a superview always draws before requesting its subview to display itself. Thus, when the switchview is done displaying itself, it requests its subview (the accessory view, which is one of the two switchbuttons) to display.

Clicking on the switchbutton sends a **setTruncate:** message to the prefscontroller as follows:

Setting the **Truncate** default

```
- setTruncate:sender
{
  const char *appName = [NXApp appName];
  int state = [truncateSwitch state];
  if (state == OFF)
    NXWriteDefault(appName, "Truncate", "NO");
  else
    NXWriteDefault(appName, "Truncate", "YES");
```

```
    return self;
}
```

This method checks the state of the button then writes out the value of the **Truncate** default accordingly. The only remaining method is the **convert:** method, which was modified slightly to take advantage of the **Truncate** default (only the modified code is shown):

Excerpted listing of convert:

```
// check if the Truncate default is set
// and then set the number of figures
// to the right of the decimal point
if ([prefsController shouldTruncate] == YES)
  right = 2;
else
  right = 6;
// set floating point format for each
// formcell in the form
for (loop=0; loop < MAXIMUM; loop++)
  {
  // get each cell
  cell = [moneyForm cellAt:loop :0];
  [cell setFloatingPointFormat:NO
    left:left
    right:right];
  }
```

The moneyconverter first asks the prefscontroller whether the **Truncate** attribute is set by sending it a **shouldTruncate** message, which returns a **Boolean** value:

Determining the state of the Truncate default

```
- (BOOL)shouldTruncate
{
  const char *truncateFlag;
  const char *appName = [NXApp appName];

  // value in database may be newer than value
  // in registration table because of Prefs
```

```
                    // panel; thus, update value in table to
                    // match value in database
                    NXUpdateDefault(appName, "Truncate");
                    // get value from registration table
                    // now that it's been updated
                    truncateFlag =
                      NXGetDefaultValue(appName, "Truncate");
                    // make sure truncateFlag is not NULL before
                    // comparing it
                    if (truncateFlag)
                      {
                      if (strcasecmp(truncateFlag, "YES") == 0)
                        return YES;
                      }
                    return NO;
                  }
```

Notice that the **shouldTruncate** method first uses **NXUpdateDefault()** before obtaining the default's value with **NXGetDefaultValue()**. **NXUpdateDefault()** updates the value of the **Truncate** default in the registration table to match the corresponding value in the registration table, if necessary. This insures that any change we make to the **Truncate** default (either through the Preferences panel or the **dwrite** command) is immediately propagated to the **shouldTruncate** method. For more information on the differences between using **NXGetDefaultValue()** and **NXUpdateDefaultValue()**, see "Registering Defaults" on page 281.

After determining the value of the **Truncate** default, **convert:** sets the floating point format of the each cell in the form using the **setFloatingPointFormat:left:right** method. This method expects three parameters:

- **YES** or **NO**—this specifies whether the output should be autoranged: if **YES**, the values passed to the **right** and **left** parameters are added together to form a maximum field width. The numbers to the right of the decimal point are padded with zeros, if necessary, to fill this width. Since we don't want padding, we specify **NO**.
- **left**—this specifies the maximum number of digits that can be specified to the left of the decimal point. Since we don't expect

too many values beyond the billion range, we hard-code our program to specify **10**.

- **right**—this specifies the maximum number of digits that can be specified to the right of the decimal point (the mantissa). The value of this parameter depends on whether the **Truncate** default is set: if so, **right** is set to **2** decimal points (in converting money, few users care for values beyond the second decimal point). If not, **right** is arbitrarily set to **6**.

Setting the floating point format affects all subsequent invocations of the **setFloatValue:** method. Therefore, we don't need to change the rest of the **convert:** method.

8.7 Suggestions

Our application now supports a limited form of customization but it still lacks some features. The following sections offer some suggestions for extending the application.

8.7.1 Implementing the Quit Prompt

The **Prompt before closing** switchbutton was added so that the user can specify whether the application should display an alert panel before quitting. To implement this, add a delegate to the window and override the **windowWillClose:** method, as shown in Chapter 6.

8.7.2 Adding Support for Significant Figures

Instead of hard-coding the number of significant figures (to the right of the decimal point), add another accessory view with a slider to allow the user to specify how many digits should be in the output and pass this value as the **right** parameter to **setFloatingPointFormat:left:right**. Remember to add this default (call it **RightSigFigures** or something similar) to the **NXDefaultsVector** struct along with an initial value.

8.7.3 Implementing Dynamic Conversion Rates

Instead of hard-coding the conversion rates, add another accessory view which would allow the user to dynamically adjust the conversion rates. Use a form to capture the input.

8.7.4 Adding an Info Panel

Add an Info panel to the application. Since the functionality for this is fairly minimal, don't add another class to manage it. Set the moneyconverter as the owner of the **.nib** module:

Loading in the .nib file lazily

```
- displayInfoPanel:sender
{
  if (!infoPanel)
    [NXApp loadNibSection:"Info.nib"
      owner:self withNames:NO];
}
```

In order for this to work, add an **infoPanel** outlet to the **MoneyConverter** class. Since the **Info Panel** menu option under the **Info** submenu is normally disabled, enable it using the Inspector. In the Info panel, include the name of the application, the name of the authors, and the version number of the application.

8.8 Troubleshooting

Here are some problems that can arise:

- The accessory view of the Preferences panel does not match the choice in the popuplist.
    - **Cause**: Since the **displayPrefsPanel:** method assumes the default accessory view is the **Truncate output** switchbutton, make sure the trigger button for the popuplist is the **Truncation** menucell.

- **Solution**: Use InterfaceBuilder to set the trigger button for the popuplist to be the first menucell and set the title to be **Truncation**.
- One or both of the accessory views are empty.
  - **Cause**: One or both of the accessory views have not been connected as outlets to the prefscontroller. An outlet not connected is **nil**, and sending a message to a **nil** object does nothing. Thus, sending a message to the accessory view to display itself results in nothing being displayed.
  - **Solution**: Connect the prefscontroller to both accessory views (the switchbuttons) to initialize them.
- The form does not display all six figures, even when the **Truncate** default is not set.
  - **Cause**: The form may be too small.
  - **Solution**: Enlarge the form.
- The **Preferences** menu option cannot be connected to the prefscontroller.
  - **Cause**: The **PrefsController** class was never instantiated in the main **.nib** file. The prefscontroller is the **File's Owner** for the **Prefs.nib** module; thus, the prefscontroller must already exist in the main **.nib** file before it can own the module. Recall that an object that appears in two interface files is the same object. For more information, see "Setting the File's Owner" on page 290.
  - **Solution**: Subclass **Object** to create **PrefsController** and instantiate it in the **Money.nib** interface file. Then, connect the prefscontroller as the **prefsController** outlet of the moneyconverter.
- The **Preferences** menu option is grayed out, and clicking on it does not display the Preferences panel.
  - **Cause**: The menu option is disabled.
  - **Solution**: Click on the **Preferences** menu option in InterfaceBuilder and use the Inspector to enable the menu option.
- The **Prompt before closing** switchbutton does not stay set between sessions.

- **Cause**: The switchbutton for the **Prompt** default does not have any functionality and cannot save its state between sessions.
- **Solution**: Implement a method to write out the value of the **Prompt** default each time the switchbutton is selected.

8.9 Summary

A NeXTSTEP application should provide support for defaults, customizable attributes that allow the user to tailor the application. To preserve the values of these defaults between sessions, the application saves these values in the defaults database, located in **~/.NeXT**. The defaults can be set through a Preferences panel or the **dwrite** command. The **dwrite** command has a counterpart, **dread**, which can display the values of all the defaults already in the user's defaults database.

Upon start-up, an application registers the defaults it is willing to support in a registration table. If the application later needs the value of a default, it first checks the defaults database to determine if the default has been set, i.e., did the user set this default from a previous session. If the application cannot find the desired default, it then uses the corresponding default's value in the registration table. By using this precedence order, a NeXTSTEP application can start with the set defaults from a previous session and still provide initial values for the other defaults that have not yet been set by the user.

Since the Preferences panel is not necessary for the core functionality, place its user interface in a separate **.nib** file and only load it as needed. By using multiple **.nib** files, we can manage complex user interfaces as well as maximize system resources.

In the next chapter, we explore multiple **.nib** files further and another fundamental task: manipulating text.

Chapter 9
Processing Text

Although NeXTSTEP provides a graphical user interface, we still spend a fair amount of our time working with text. This chapter focuses on the **Text** class, one of the most complex classes in the Application Kit. The **Text** class defines an object which manages text: almost everything that is displayed as text is an instance of this class. The **Text** class includes support for multiple fonts and colors, formatting with the ruler, spelling check, and a host of other features. Unlike most of the other Application Kit classes, the **Text** class is designed to be complete and should not be subclassed. A text object typically depends on a delegate for added functionality.

A text object depends on a text delegate for added functionality

In this chapter, we will implement a word processor which supports multiple windows. This application will incorporate many of the ideas which we have covered so far including multiple **.nib** files, defaults support, delegation, event processing, freeing objects, and other topics which we will soon learn.

The application in this chapter will incorporate all the topics covered so far

9.1 Goals

In this chapter, we will:

- describe what functionality the **Text** class offers and how it is used.
- explain how to manipulate text, i.e., determine the currently selected text, support cut and paste, etc.
- define the first responder and the responder chain.
- explain how a scrollview works.
- explore how to use the openpanel and the savepanel.
- illustrate how to save the text to a file then read the text back from the file.
- explain how to use the text delegate method to determine if a document has been edited.

The Text class has a flipped coordinate system

9.2 Creating the Text

As a subclass of the **View** class, the **Text** class inherits methods to draw to the screen. Unlike the other **View** subclasses, the **Text** class has a flipped coordinate system, which produces the following results:

- the origin is translated to the upper left.
- the x axis increases to the right.
- the y axis increases downward instead of upward; this allows the text to start from the top and grow downward.

Figure 9.1 compares two views, one with a regular coordinate system and one with a flipped coordinate system.

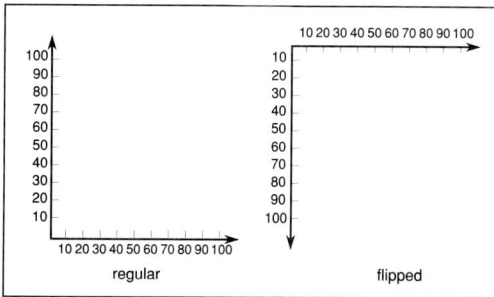

Figure 9.1 A regular coordinate system vs. a flipped coordinate system

Use initFrame: text:alignment: to initialize the text object

Instantiating the **Text** class is similar to instantiating any other subclass of the **View** class: first initialize an **NXRect** struct with the values of the frame rectangle then send a message to the designated initializer method, **initFrame:text:alignment:**. The following code fragment shows how to create a text object that is 200 by 300 units that initially contains the text, **This is the initial text**:

Instantiating the **Text** class

```
NXSetRect(&theRect, 0.0, 0.0, 200.0, 300.0);
theText = [ [Text alloc] initFrame:&theRect
  text:"This is the initial text"
  alignment:NX_LEFTALIGNED];
```

The **initFrame:text:alignment:** method expects three parameters:

- a pointer to the **NXRect struct** that contains the size of the frame rectangle of the text object.
- a pointer to a null-terminated array of characters, the text that will be shown when the text object is displayed.
- the text alignment, which can be one of four things:
    - **NX_LEFTALIGNED**—aligns the text along the left edge like these paragraphs.
    - **NX_RIGHTALIGNED**—aligns the text along the right edge. It is rarely used except in headings and poetry.
    - **NX_CENTERED**—centers the text.
    - **NX_JUSTIFIED**—aligns the text along the left and right edges; the **Text** class currently ignores this parameter and defaults to **NX_LEFTALIGNED**.

9.3 Selecting the Text

Unlike the instances of other **View** subclasses, we do not manipulate a text object using coordinates. Instead, we specify the text in the text object using character position; that is, we treat the text instance as though it were a regular array of characters. Following the array indexing scheme in C, the first position is 0, the second is 1, etc. For example, to set the selection programmatically, we can use the **setSel::** method, which expects a starting position and ending position. By setting the start position to equal the end position, we can set an empty selection; this removes the need to first click on the text before typing. The following code fragment illustrates how to use the **setSel::** method.

A text object can be treated as an array of characters

Setting the selection in a text object

```
// set selection at start of the text
[theText setSel:0 :0];
```

To determine the currently selected text, use the **getSel::** method, which returns the starting position and the length of the selection.

Use getSel:: to determine the currently selected text

The method expects the addresses of two **NXSelPt structs**. An **NXSelPt struct** contains many fields, but the only field we need is **cp**, the character position. By subtracting the ending position from the starting position, we can determine how many characters are selected. The following code fragment illustrates how to use the **getSel::** method.

Determining how many characters are selected

```
NXSelPt start, end;
[theText getSel:&start :&end];
printf("Start position is %d\n", start.cp);
printf("End position is %d\n", end.cp);
printf("Number of chars selected is %d\n",
  end.cp - start.cp);
```

Use getSubstring: start:length: to actually get a copy of the text

The **getSel::** method allows us to determine the starting and ending position of the selection. To get a copy of the text, however, we need to use the **getSubstring:start:length:** method. This method takes three arguments: a pointer to a character array, the starting position, and the total numbers of characters to copy into the array. If we copy only part of the text, we must allocate an extra character for the null terminator (**\0**) and append this to the string. The following example shows how to copy the first fifty characters into a buffer.

Copying fifty characters into a buffer

```
char buffer[51];
[theText getSubstring:buffer start:0 length:50];
buffer[50] = '\0';
```

Notice that:

- the buffer is fifty-one characters because we are not copying the entire text and therefore we must account for the null terminator.
- we have to manually append the null terminator.

We may want to process only part of the selected text

By using these three methods, we can determine the currently selected text; this is useful if we wish to process only the currently selected text. For example, instead of saving the entire text, we may want to save only the currently selected text. The following code fragment demonstrates how to determine the currently selected text and how to allocate a buffer large enough for the selected text.

Copying the selected text into a buffer

```
char *textBuffer;
int count;
[theText getSel:&start :&end];
count = end.cp - start.cp;
// allocate room for null terminator
textBuffer = malloc(count+1);
[theText getSubstring:textBuffer
  start:start.cp length:count];
// append null terminator
textBuffer[count] = '\0';
```

We don't need to append the null terminator if we are copying the entire text object. However, this is rarely done: in most cases, we would copy only part of the text, as shown in the code fragments.

9.4 Cutting and Pasting the Text

Now that we know how to select the text, we need to discuss how to modify it. The most direct way of working with a text object is to simply type the text. However, the **Text** class defines four other methods that allow us to modify the text further: **copy:**, **cut:**, **delete:**, and **paste:**. Before we can understand how these methods work, we must digress a little and talk about the *pasteboard server* (abbreviated *pbs*) and its *pasteboard*.

The most direct way of working with a text object is to type the text

The pasteboard server is a program that is continually executing in the background, like the Window Server. The main function of the pasteboard server is to provide a repository for applications to share data: this repository is the *pasteboard*.

The pasteboard server gives us access to the pasteboard

For our purposes, we can view the pasteboard as containing one set of data at a time. The three commands interact with the pasteboard as follows:

- **Copy** copies the highlighted text into the pasteboard and replaces the text previously stored there.
- **Cut** copies the text into the pasteboard then deletes the highlighted text.
- **Paste** copies the text from the pasteboard and inserts it at the current selection of the text object. Note that pasting the text from the pasteboard does not destroy its contents: we can paste the text as many times as we wish.

Delete removes the highlighted text and does not interact with the pasteboard. This is not a menu command: to delete text, we usually highlight it then press the **Backspace** key.

> Technically speaking, **pbs** manages several pasteboards to coordinate all the information the applications share with each other. We will deal only with the primary pasteboard, which controls the **Copy**, **Cut**, and **Paste** menu options. Similarly, a pasteboard can hold multiple representations of its data; for example, it may store the text in PostScript as well as ASCII format. However, for simplicity, we will assume two things:
>
> - there is only pasteboard, the one that manages the information for the cut and paste related commands.
> - the pasteboard holds only the ASCII representation of the text.

The cut and paste commands apply to the currently selected object

We rarely have to deal with the pasteboard directly if we are only working with ASCII text. For our purposes, we only have to know that the four menu commands send the respective messages (**cut:**, **copy:**, **delete:**, and **paste:**) to the text object or more specifically, the currently selected object. The currently selected object often is the text object, although it can be something else. For example, many applications allow us to cut the currently selected by first selecting the object (which can be a graphic object) then selecting **Cut**. How does the application know what the currently selected object is? In short, what is the first responder?

9.5 Setting the First Responder

Before we can define what the first responder is, we need to define the following two terms: *key window* and *main window*. The main window is where we usually focus our attention on, and the key window is the window which receives events. The key window and the main window are usually the same window, although there are cases when they are not.

The key window and the main window are usually the same one

For example, assume we are typing in a window in Edit. At this point, the key window and the main window are the same window. We then bring up the Find Panel. At this point, the Find Panel becomes the key window, and our document window remains the main window. To distinguish the key window from the main window, NeXTSTEP highlights the key window's title bar to black and the main window's title bar to dark grey. The key window is simply a window through which we can work with the main window. Figure 9.2 shows how this process works.

The main window's title bar is dark grey, and the key window's title bar is black

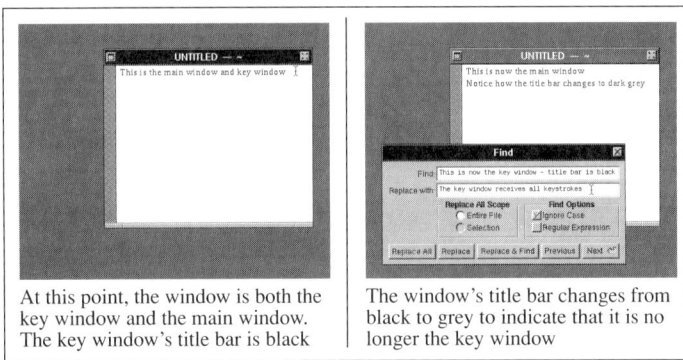

At this point, the window is both the key window and the main window. The key window's title bar is black

The window's title bar changes from black to grey to indicate that it is no longer the key window

Figure 9.2 The key window and the main window may or may not be the same window

The *first responder* is the object in the key window which is first to receive mouse events and key events; every window can have its own first responder but only the first responder in the key window can receive keyboard events *and* mouse events. Unless explicitly set, the first responder for a window is the window itself, although the first responder is usually an instance of the **Control** class (or one its subclasses) or the **View** class (or one its

The first responder is the first object to receive events

subclasses such as **Text**). By clicking on the text or using any of the selection methods (such as **setSel::**), we set the first responder to be the text object.

The first responder forwards events it does not understand to its next responder

Thus, in our previous discussion, the four messages (**cut:**, **copy:**, **delete:**, and **paste:**) are not necessarily sent to the text object directly but to the first responder, which just happens to be the text object. What happens if the first responder receives a message it cannot process such as when a text object receives a **close:** message, which is also be sent to the first responder? The first responder then forwards the event to another object, its *next responder*. NeXTSTEP defines a *responder chain*, a series of responders which are given the chance to respond to events that cannot be processed by the first responder. The next responders in the responder chain are as follows:

- the view's superview—for example, the superview for the text object (which is a view) is the content view.
- the content view's window.
- the window's delegate, if there is one.
- if the main window is different than the key window, the search then restarts at its first responder and repeats as explained in the previous three steps.
- the application object (**NXApp**).
- **NXApp**'s delegate.

This cycle stops as soon as a method returns a value other than **nil** (remember that most methods return **self** upon completion). If nothing in the responder chain can process the event, the event is then discarded. In this case, the **close:** message will be processed by the key window because it is the first object that implements the method. Figure 9.3 shows how this search works.

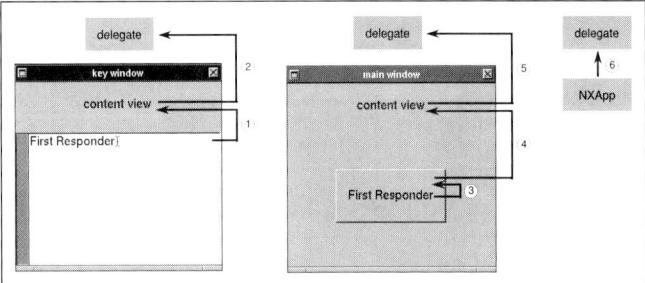

Figure 9.3 The search order when a target is not explicitly set

The following menu options message the first responder:

- the **Cut**, **Copy**, and **Paste** menu commands for reasons already covered.
- the **Miniaturize** and **Close** menu options since they can either be sent to either the key window or the main window.

To demonstrate the search sequence for a target, modify the **AppKitDemo.m** file from Chapter 4 so that it does *not* explicitly set a target for the **Quit** menu option. That is, remove this line:

```
[theMenuCell setTarget:NXApp];
```

At this point, the menu option does not have an explicit target (that is, its target is **nil**). Thus, the menu option will send the **terminate:** message to the first responder. Ultimately, **NXApp** will still receive the action message of the menu option (**terminate:**) because of the aforementioned responder chain.

9.6 Scrolling the Text

Unlike the objects from other **View** subclasses, which tend to maintain their sizes—that is, their frame rectangles are constant once the objects are created—a text object's frame rectangle tends to grow since the text object accumulates text as we are typing. It

A text's frame rectangle grows as we type in text

346   Scrolling the Text

is conceivable (and quite likely) that the text can grow beyond the boundaries of any superview, even if the superview is the size of the entire screen. Figure 9.4 shows what happens when the text object grows beyond the boundaries of its superview: the additional text is present, but it is clipped. Recall that only the portion of a view which falls in the boundaries of its superview is displayed.

Figure 9.4 A text object can grow beyond the boundaries of its superview

To manage the text, we can install the text as part of a scrollview

How, then, do we accommodate a text object that will naturally grow? We accomplish this with the help of another class, **ScrollView**. A scrollview is an object that facilitates the various tasks involved in scrolling such as displaying the correct portion of the view being scrolled, providing scrollers, etc. The scrollview manages these activities with the help of its content view, which contains a *clipview*. The clipview is responsible for determining what portion of the view is going to be displayed. The view to be scrolled (in this case, the text object) is actually installed as the subview of the clipview, and is referred to as the *document view.* Figure 9.5 illustrates the relationships between the views in a scrollview.

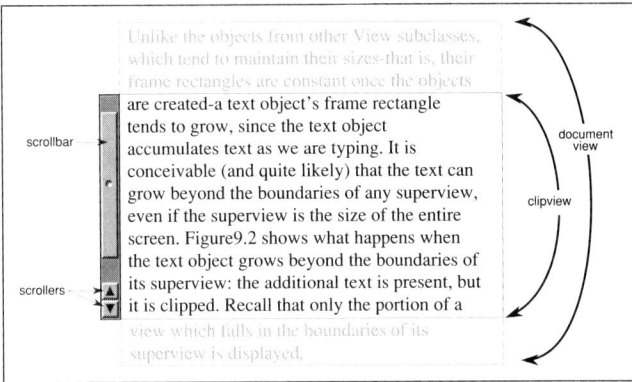

Figure 9.5 The components of a scrollview

To allow the text to be scrolled:

- create a scrollview, which in turn creates the necessary subviews, including the clipview and the scrollers.
- create a text object and set its frame rectangle to the size of the content view of the scrollview.
- set the minimum and maximum size of the text.
- set the document view of the scrollview by sending it the **setDocView:** message along with the view to be scrolled (in this case, the text object); this message is actually forwarded to the clipview, which then sets the text object as the document view.
- enable the scrollers in the scrollview.
- configure the text object to notify its superview (the scrollview) each time the text object's frame changes, which happens whenever we type or delete a character. This notification allows the scrollview to determine when to display the scrollers. For example, the scrollview should not display scrollers until the text is larger than the content view of the clipview.

As we will see later, InterfaceBuilder provides all of the functionality listed above (and more) when we drag one of the scrollviews from the palette. The following short program illustrates scrolling by creating two windows; one window contains a text object inside a scrollview, and the other window contains a text object

InterfaceBuilder provides a scrollview with all the aforementioned functionality

348 Scrolling the Text

by itself. The code is similar to **AppKitDemo.m** from Chapter 4 except for the changes in bold.

Listing for Scroll.m

```
#import <appkit/appkit.h>

// minimal program to demonstrate
// a text object and scrolling

main()
{
  id NXApp = [Application new];
  id theWindow;
  id theMenu;
  id theText;
  id theScrollView;
  NXRect theRect;
  NXSize theSize;
  id otherWindow, otherText;
  NXSize otherSize;

  // create the window
  NXSetRect(&theRect, 200.0, 300.0, 350.0, 150.0);
  theWindow = [ [Window alloc]
    initContent:&theRect
    style: NX_TITLEDSTYLE
    backing:NX_BUFFERED
    buttonMask:NX_MINIATURIZEBUTTONMASK
    defer:YES];
  [theWindow setBackgroundGray:NX_WHITE];

  // create a scrollview
  NXSetRect(&theRect, 0.0, 0.0, 350.0, 150.0);
  theScrollView = [ [ScrollView alloc]
    initFrame:&theRect];
  [theScrollView
    setVertScrollerRequired:YES];
  [theScrollView
    setHorizScrollerRequired:NO];
  [ [theWindow contentView]
    addSubview :theScrollView];

  // get the size of the content view
```

```
[theScrollView getContentSize:&theSize];

// create another text object
NXSetRect(&theRect, 0.0, 0.0,
  theSize.width, theSize.height);
theText = [ [Text alloc] initFrame:&theRect
  text:"Text in scrollview"
  alignment:NX_LEFTALIGNED];
[theText setOpaque:YES];
// notify superview when frame
// rectangle changes -- allows scrollview
// to update the scrollers
[theText notifyAncestorWhenFrameChanged:YES];
[theText setVertResizable:YES];
[theText setHorizResizable:NO];
// select all the text

// create min and max size of text
theSize.width = 0.0;
[theText setMinSize:&theSize];
theSize.height = 1000000;
[theText setMaxSize:&theSize];

// set the text as docview of scrollview
[theScrollView setDocView:theText];

// create other window
NXSetRect(&theRect, 100.0, 100.0, 350.0, 150.0);
otherWindow = [ [Window alloc]
  initContent:&theRect
  style: NX_TITLEDSTYLE
  backing:NX_BUFFERED
  buttonMask:NX_MINIATURIZEBUTTONMASK
  defer:YES];
[theWindow setBackgroundGray:NX_WHITE];

// create other text
NXSetRect(&theRect, 0.0, 0.0, 350.0, 150.0);
otherText = [ [Text alloc]
  initFrame:&theRect
  text:"Text without scrollview"
  alignment:NX_LEFTALIGNED];
[otherText setOpaque:YES];
[ [otherWindow contentView]
  addSubview:otherText];
```

```
    // create min and max size of text
    otherSize.width = 0.0;
    [otherText setMinSize:&otherSize];
    otherSize.height = 1000000;
    [theText setMaxSize:&otherSize];

    // create the menu
    theMenu = [ [Menu alloc]
      initTitle: [NXApp appName] ];
    [theMenu addItem:"Quit"
      action:@selector(terminate:)
      keyEquivalent:'q'];
    [theMenu sizeToFit];
    [NXApp setMainMenu:theMenu];

    // display both windows
    [theWindow makeKeyAndOrderFront:nil];
    // set the selection in the text
    [theText setSel:0 :0];
    [otherWindow orderFront:nil];

    // Enter event loop
    [NXApp run];
}
```

The scrollview should only display scrollers if the text's boundary is larger than the clipview

Each time we type a character, we are changing the text's frame rectangle. By using **notifyAncestorWhenFrameChanged:**, the text can provide constant feedback to its ancestor, the scrollview; the scrollview can then determine whether it needs to produce the scrollers. The scrollview displays these if the text has grown beyond the boundaries of the clipview. In order for this notification to work, we must also set the minimum and maximum size of the text with **setMinSize:** and **setMaxSize:**, respectively.

9.7 Saving the Text

Save the text instead of the text object itself

Once we have a text object, we typically save its text to a file. Under most circumstances, we want to save the text instead of the text object itself. For simplicity, we will use the term "the text" to refer to "the text of the text object" from this point on. First, we will explore saving the text, then we will proceed to loading the text.

To save the text:

• obtain the filename using a savepanel.

• write the text to disk under the filename obtained from the previous step.

Now let's consider the **SavePanel** class and how to use it.

9.7.1 Using the SavePanel

To conform to the NeXTSTEP guidelines, our examples will use a savepanel to obtain the filename the document should be saved to. Figure 9.6 shows a typical savepanel.

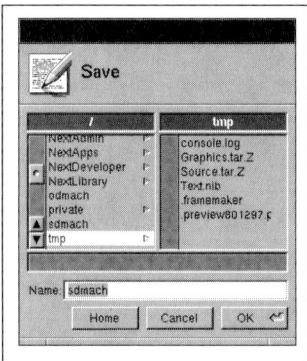

Figure 9.6 A typical savepanel

Since each application should have only one instance of the **SavePanel** class, use **new** instead of **alloc** and **init** to instantiate the class, as shown in the following code fragment:

Use new to instantiate the SavePanel class

Instantiating the **SavePanel** class

```
id savePanel;
savePanel = [SavePanel new];
```

We do not need to initialize the instance as we would with instances of classes that have multiple instances per application.

NeXTSTEP automatically initializes the savepanel

Display the savepanel modally using runModal

The main functionality of the savepanel is to return a filename; our application still needs to provide code to actually write the document to a file. This will be presented in the next section.

To display the savepanel, use the **runModal** method. The savepanel is *modal*; that is, once it is displayed on the screen, it does not allow us to interact with the rest of the *current* application until we click either **OK** to indicate we are done typing in the filename, or **Cancel** to remove the savepanel. The **runModal** method:

- returns **1** if a valid filename was entered (it can either be typed in the textfield or selected in the browser) and the **OK** button was pressed.
- **0** if the **Cancel** button was pressed.

> The **SavePanel** class defines its own event processing loop, which disrupts the main event loop of **NXApp**. Therefore, we cannot interact with the rest of the application until we press the **OK** button or the **Cancel** button to terminate the inner event loop.
>
> Note that this applies only to the current application. We can still switch to another application and interact with it normally. However, the savepanel (or another panel that is displaying modally, such an alert panel) will still be above all other windows.
>
> The **NXRunAlertPanel**() function from Chapter 6 creates a panel and places it in a modal loop for us. Since a modal panel effectively prevents the user from interacting with the application, it should only be used when it is impossible for the application to proceed until it receives further information from the user. The four most common occurrences of modal panels are alert panels, openpanels, savepanels, and printpanels.

To obtain the filename (the path is included) last used, use the **filename** method. The following code fragment illustrates how to display the savepanel to obtain the filename.

Obtaining the filename from the savepanel

```
if ([savePanel runModal])
  {
  fullPathName = [savePanel filename];
  [document saveDocumentToFile:fullPathName];
  }
```

> There is a similar method, **runModalForDirectory: file:**, that allows us to specify which directory should be selected initially and which filename should be displayed in the textfield when the savepanel is displayed.

Notice that the savepanel does not have any functionality to actually save the text to a file: the savepanel can only return the filename the text should be saved to. We can specify an extension to be automatically appended to the filename by using the **setRequiredFileType:** method. This provides two advantages:

- we can specify different extensions for different filetypes. For example, NeXTSTEP uses different extensions to differentiate between file formats: **.nib** is for an interface file, **.project** is for a project file, **.m** is for an Objective-C implementation file, etc.
- we can associate different icons with different filetypes. This allows the Workspace to display different icons for different data files. We will learn how to use InterfaceBuilder to associate icons with various file extensions later.

The following code fragment illustrates how to use **setRequiredFileType:** to append an extension to a filename. In order for this to work, set the file extension *before* displaying the savepanel.

The savepanel only returns the filename which the document should be saved to

Appending a file extension using **setRequiredFileType:**

```
- showSavePanel:sender
{
static const char
  *const wordTypes[] = {"word", NULL};
```

Writing the Text to a File

```
[savePanel setRequiredFileType:wordType];
if ([savePanel runModal])
  {
  fullPathName = [savePanel filename];
  [document saveDocumentToFile:fullPathName];
  }
// rest of method deleted
```

setRequiredFile Type: automatically prepends a period to the extension

This fragment first declares an array that contains two entries specifying the extensions: **word** and **NULL**. **NULL** is not an extension, but actually a terminating value. The **setRequiredFileType:** method does not require a period because it is automatically prepended to the extension. If we type **/tmp/hello** in the savepanel, the file will be saved as **/tmp/hello.word**. Now that we have the filename, we need to save the text to a file, which is the topic of the next section.

> Why do we need the **static** and **const** keywords in front of the array declaration?
>
> - **static** allows us to initialize the array as it is being declared.
> - **const** specifies that the contents of the array should not be changed during the execution of the current function or method (**showSavePanel:**).

9.7.2 Writing the Text to a File

A stream can be associated with memory, files, or ports

Before we can effectively discuss how to write the text to a file, we must discuss the concept of a *stream*. A stream can best be thought of as a mechanism through which data can be written or read using a common set of functions to a variety of data sources including memory, files, etc. The application does not care what the stream is connected to: it only needs to write to or read from the stream.

Most of the text methods expect a stream as a parameter

Unlike most of the standard C functions which expect a *FILE* data type as a parameter, most of the text methods expect a stream as a parameter. Since NeXTSTEP does not provide a complete object-oriented system for manipulating streams, we have to use a combination of C functions and text methods.

In writing the text to a file, we have to determine whether the file already exists. We must do this for two reasons:

- if we save a new document, the application should present us with a savepanel to prompt us for the filename.
- if we save an existing document, the application should just update the already existing file without presenting a savepanel since the application already has the filename.

There are a number of ways to determine if a file already exists, but we will use the following conventions:

- when the application creates a new document, it will name the document **UNTITLED** and set this as the window's title.
- once the application has successfully saved the document to a file, it updates the window's title to the filename with the entire path. By storing the entire path, the application can still differentiate between a new document and a document intentionally saved as **UNTITLED**.
- when the application needs to determine whether the document has already been saved to a file, the application can simply compare the window's title against the string **UNTITLED**.
- the application then needs to open a new memory stream for writing by using the **NXOpenMemory**() function.

The application can then proceed to save the text by:

- writing the text to the stream using **writeText:**.
- saving the stream to a file using **NXSaveToFile**(). This function creates the file if necessary.
- closing and freeing the stream using **NXCloseMemory**() with the **NX_FREEBUFFER** constant.

The following code fragment shows a **saveDocumentToFile:** method that writes the text to a file. This method expects a filename.

Writing the text to a file

```
#define SAVE_ERROR "Can't save file"
.
.
.
- saveDocumentToFile:(const char *)fullPathName
{
  NXStream *stream = NULL;
  const char* title = [window title];

  // get a stream first
  if (stream =
    (NXOpenMemory(NULL, 0, NX_WRITEONLY)))
    {
    // write text into stream
    [theText writeText:stream];
    // write the stream to the file
    // and check for error code
    if (NXSaveToFile(stream, fullPathName) != 0)
      {
      [self showError:SAVE_ERROR];
      // free stream
      NXCloseMemory(stream, NX_FREEBUFFER);
      return nil;
      }
    else
      // save succeeded: update misc info
      {
      // update the title of the window
      [window setTitle:fullPathName];
      // update window to clean state
      [window setDocEdited:NO];
      // free stream
      NXCloseMemory(stream, NX_FREEBUFFER);
      }
    }
  else
    // Couldn't get stream
    {
    [self showError:SAVE_ERROR];
    return nil;
    }
  return self;
```

```
      }
```

For now, ignore the **setDocEdited:** message since we will cover it shortly. Once we have saved the text to a file, we need to be able to load the file to verify that it was saved correctly: this is the topic of the next two sections.

9.8 Loading the Text

To load a file:

- use an openpanel to obtain the filename(s) to be loaded.
- load the file(s) specified by the filename(s) obtained in the previous step.

The **OpenPanel** class, which is the complement of the **SavePanel** class, is explored further in the next section.

9.8.1 Using the OpenPanel

The standard interface for determining which file(s) to open is an instance of the **OpenPanel** class. An openpanel allows an application to specify multiple files, a savepanel does not. This is practical because we may want to open multiple files at once for displaying, but we would never save more than one file at a time. Figure 9.7 shows a typical openpanel.

An openpanel allows us to open multiple files

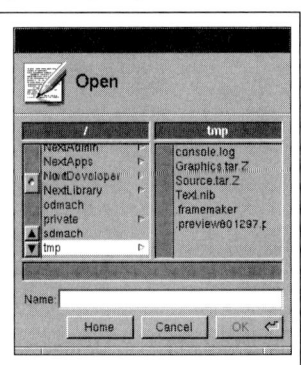

Figure 9.7 A typical openpanel

OpenPanel inherits most of its functionality from SavePanel

OpenPanel is a subclass of the **SavePanel** and is similar in functionality. The **OpenPanel** class adds some methods to allow multiple files to be opened. To instantiate the **OpenPanel** class, use the **new** method, as shown in the following code fragment. Like the **SavePanel** class, each application should have only one instance of the **OpenPanel** class.

Instantiating the **OpenPanel** class

```
openPanel = [OpenPanel new];
```

> Since the **new** method insures that we cannot have more than one instance per application, we can avoid assigning the savepanel or openpanel to a variable and simply call the **new** method to return the **id** of the object each time we need to access the object:
>
> ```
> [[OpenPanel new] allowMultipleFiles:YES];
> ```

To display an openpanel with all files, use the **runModal** method, inherited from the **SavePanel** class. To process the text returned from the savepanel:

- use the **allowMultipleFiles:** method with a **YES** parameter to allow multiple file selection. By default, an openpanel only allows one file to be selected.
- use the **filenames** method, which returns a **NULL** terminated list of filenames *without* the path, to determine which files were selected.
- use the **directory** method to obtain the current directory and append a slash (/) before each filename in the filenames list to construct the entire pathname of each file.

These steps are demonstrated in the following code fragment.

Obtaining multiple filenames from the openpanel

```
- showOpenPanel:sender
```

```
{
const char *file, *directory;
const char *const *filenames;
  .
  .
  .
char fullPathName[MAXPATHLEN];
id openPanel = [OpenPanel new];

// ensure that the openpanel allows multiple
// files to be selected
[openPanel allowMultipleFiles:YES];
  .
  .
  {
  // get list of filename(s) selected
  // the filenames method returns a
  // a pointer to all the strings
  filenames = [openPanel filenames];
  // get directory first
  directory = [openPanel directory];
  do
    {
    // get filename
    file = *(filenames++);
    // construct entire pathname
    strcpy(fullPathName, directory);
    // append directory to filename
    strcat(fullPathName, "/");
    strcat(fullPathName, file);
    [[Document alloc]
      initDocumentFromFile:fullPathName];
    }
  while (*(filenames) != NULL);
    }
return self;}
```

MAXPATHLEN is predefined to be **1024** and is the longest permissible path length.

Figure 9.8 illustrates this sequence.

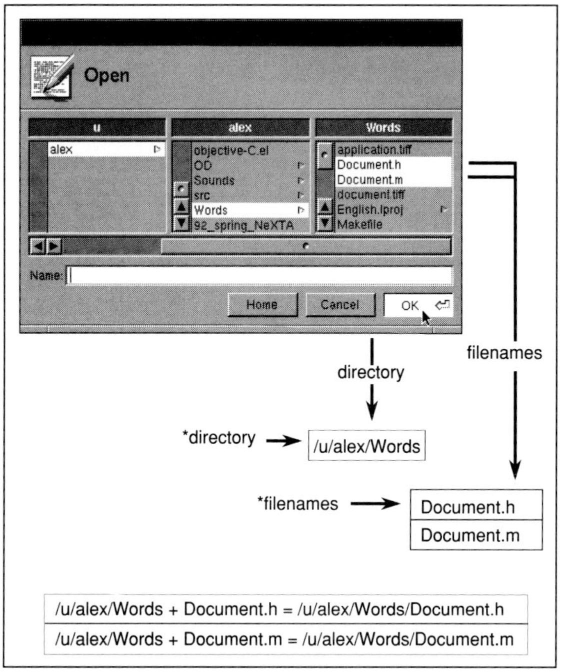

Figure 9.8 Retrieving the selected filename(s)

The openpanel can selectively display files

To restrict certain files from displaying, use the **runModalForDirectory:file:types:** method. Specify a null-terminated list of suffixes (not including the '.') to be used to filter out other files. That is, only files with extensions that match the ones listed will display. The following code fragment shows how to display an openpanel that allows multiple file selection and how to allow only files with a **.word** extension to appear in the openpanel.

Displaying only files with a specified extension

```
# define FILE_EXTENSION "word"
.
static const char
  *const wordTypes[] = {FILE_EXTENSION, NULL};
.
.
if ([openPanel runModalForTypes:wordTypes])
```

```
{
// see code fragment above for obtaining
// multiple filenames from the openpanel
}
```

Once we have determined which file(s) have been selected, we can load the text, which is the topic of the next section.

> To list all files, specify **NULL** as the first entry.

9.8.2 Loading the Text From a File

As mentioned earlier, NeXTSTEP does not provide an object-oriented interface for manipulating files. Therefore, we need to use a combination of C functions and text methods to load the text from a file:

- use the **NXMapFile()** function to map an existing file into a memory stream.
- read the stream into the text object using **readText:**.
- free all the memory associated with the stream using the **NXCloseMemory()** function with **NX_FREEBUFFER** as a parameter.

The following code fragment illustrates how to read the text from a file; **fullPathName** is the parameter specifying the full pathname of the file that is returned from the openpanel:

Loading the text from an existing file

```
#define OPEN_ERROR "Can't open file"
.
.
.
NXStream *stream;

// obtain a stream for an existing file
if (stream =
  NXMapFile(fullPathName, NX_READONLY))
  {
```

```
        [self init];
        // read text from stream
        [theText readText:stream];
        //update the window's title
        [window setTitle:fullPathName];
        // display the document
        [self showDocument];
        // free memory associated with stream
        NXCloseMemory(stream, NX_FREEBUFFER);
        return self;
        }
    else
        {
        [self showError:OPEN_ERROR];
        return nil;
        }
    .
    .
    .
```

9.9 Adding a Text Delegate

A text object often depends on a delegate

To extend its functionality, a text object usually depends on a delegate. There are several delegate methods for the **Text** class, but we will explore only one, **textDidGetKeys:isEmpty:**. Each time the text is updated, it sends its delegate this message. With this method, an application can determine whether the text has been edited since it was saved.

Use isDocEdited: to determine whether the document has been saved since it was last modified

As mentioned earlier, a view—a text object is ultimately a view since **Text** is a subclass of **View**—always exists inside a window, and a window is often associated with a document. Thus, when we say that the text has not been saved, we also mean that the document inside the window has not been saved. When a document has been modified (that is, the text has been modified) and not saved, the window updates its close button from ☒ to ☒. A document that has been modified since it was last saved is referred to as being *dirty* (☒). We can determine if a document is marked dirty or not using the **isDocEdited:** method of the **Window** class, which returns a Boolean value. **NO** means the document is not marked dirty, and **YES** means the document is marked dirty. The following code fragment demonstrates how to use the **textDidGetKeys:isEmpty:** and **setDocEdited:** methods together.

Checking if the text has been edited since it was last saved

```
- textDidGetKeys:sender isEmpty:(BOOL)flag
{
  if ([window isDocEdited] == NO)
    [window setDocEdited:YES];
  return self;
}
```

The delegate first checks if the window is marked dirty. If it is, the method simply returns. However, if the window is not marked dirty, the delegate sets the window to dirty by sending it a **setDocEdited:YES** message to update the window's close button from ☒ to ☒.

> The text delegate receives the **textDidGetKeys: isEmpty:** method only if the key is processed by the text object. Some keyboard alternatives (such as **Command-w**) do not specify an explicit target. Even though the text object is the first object to receive this message—the text, if present, is typically the first responder in a window—it does not process this event since it doesn't implement the method associated with the keyboard alternative (**close:**).
>
> As far as the text object is concerned, keyboard alternatives (such as **Command-h**, **Command-q**, etc.) that do not modify the text do not qualify as keystrokes. However, some keyboard alternatives are processed by the text object; these include **Command-x** (**cut:**), **Command-c** (**copy:**), and **Command-v** (**paste:**). These are standard methods which a text object already implements.

The text delegate receives a testDidGetKeys: isEmpty: message each time we type a key

9.10 Designing Words

We are now ready to design **Words**, a simple word processor. The specification for **Words** is as follows:

> When Words is first launched, it displays a blank document, which is a window with a scrollview and a text object. As soon as the user types a key, the window modifies its close button from ☒ to ☒ to indicate that it has been modified. In addition to typing, the user can select, copy, cut, and paste the text.
>
> To save a document, the user first selects the window then chooses the Save menu option to display a savepanel; each document is saved with a .word extension. To close a document, the user clicks on the close button of the window.
>
> To open one or more existing document(s), the user issues the Open command from the menu, which displays an openpanel; only files with a .word extension are displayed. To create a new document, the user issues the New command from the menu, which produces a blank window with a scrollview containing a text object, as above.

Highlighting the nouns and verbs produces:

> When **Words** is first *launched*, it *displays* a blank **document**, which is a **window** with a **scrollview** and a **text object**. As soon as the user *types* a **key**, the window *modifies* its **close button** from ☒ to ☒ to indicate that it has been modified. In addition to typing, the user can *select*, *copy*, *cut*, and *paste* the text.
>
> To *save* a document, the user first *selects* the window then chooses the **Save command** in the **menu** to *display* a **savepanel**; each document is saved with a **.word extension**. To *close* a document, the user *clicks* on the close button of the window.
>
> To open one or more existing document(s), the user issues the **Open command** from the menu, which *displays* an **openpanel**; only **files** with a .word extension are displayed. To *create* a new document, the user issues the **New command** from

the menu, which produces a blank window with a scrollview containing a text object, as above.

The candidate nouns are as follows:

- Words—the name of the application.
- document—an object we need to model; we will return to this later.
- window—provided by the Application Kit.
- scrollview—provided the Application Kit.
- text object—provided by the Application Kit.
- key—a hardware entity that does not belong in our software model
- close button—this object is internal to the window, which is already provided by the Application Kit.
- Save command—an option in the Main Menu.
- menu—provided by the Application Kit.
- savepanel—an object that can retrieve the filename.
- .word extension—not an object but a parameter that is passed to the savepanel to append to each document's filename.
- Open command—an option in the Main Menu.
- files—from a design perspective, these should be objects. However, since NeXTSTEP does not provide an object-oriented interface to files, we will not treat this noun as an object.
- openpanel—an object used to retrieve the filenames of the documents to be opened.
- New command—an option in the Main Menu.

Thus, we have narrowed our list of nouns to the following:

- document
- window
- scrollview
- text object
- **Save** command
- savepanel
- menu

- **Open** command
- openpanel
- **New** Command

At this point, we have a rough idea what the objects need to do. Since **Words** supports multiple documents, the documents should be designed so that they do not need to know about each other. Each document needs to be able to perform the following actions:

- create
- open
- save
- close
- display.

Create another object to manage the documents

Since the user can easily create multiple documents, managing the documents should be the responsibility of another object: let's call this the textcontroller object. Thus, when the user creates a new document, saves a modified document, or open existing ones, the textcontroller object should perform some processing then forward the action to the current document. For example, in opening a document, the textcontroller object should obtain the filename(s) then request each document to open itself.

Now, let us consider the verbs:

- launch—this action does not need to be simulated since it is simply the user double-clicking on the application.
- displays—displays the document.
- create—the textcontroller receives this message then instantiates the **Document** class.
- open—the textcontroller receives this then requests the document to open itself.
- save—the textcontroller receives this then requests the document to save itself.
- type—performed by the user and does not need to be modeled.
- select—performed by the user and does not need to be modeled.
- copy—copies the currently selected text into the pasteboard.

- cut—copies the currently selected text into the pasteboard then deletes the highlighted text.
- paste—pastes the text from the pasteboard to the current position of the text object.
- update—each time the user presses a key, the document needs to update its status to dirty.
- click—performed by the user and does not need to be modeled.
- close—closes the current document.

To explore other data and actions we may have missed, let's design a preliminary interface. So far, we have identified eight major actions:

- create
- close
- open
- save
- display
- copy
- cut
- paste.

In the applications we have implemented so far, we did not have to consider freeing the objects during execution since they allocated a fixed number of objects: an application object, a menu, a Main Window (and its contents, such as the content view, textfields, et al.) and at most a Preferences panel (and its contents). However, **Words** can allocate an indeterminate number of objects because we cannot know in advance how many documents will be created. We should free the document each time its associated window is closed; otherwise, the memory occupied by our application will continue to grow as it opens more files. In short, the application will have a memory leak. Thus, another action which the document is responsible for is freeing itself.

Since each document is dynamically allocated, free them after closing the window

To conform to the NeXTSTEP user-interface guidelines, include the document-related actions in a menu structure. These are menu options common to every application that deals with documents,

Include the document-related actions in a menu

including **Open**, **Create**, **Save**, and **Close**. The display action is something that is performed by the document instead of something initiated by the user directly. Therefore, the action should not be included in the menu. Additionally, the cut and paste related menu options (**Copy**, **Cut**, and **Paste**) should also be included in the menu since these actions are standard menu options in many applications. Figure 9.9 shows a preliminary design for the interface to **Words** with the new submenus.

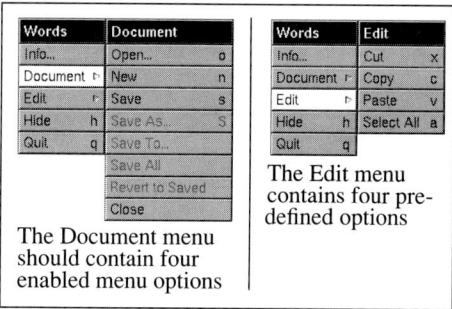

Figure 9.9 A preliminary interface for **Words**

Some of the menu options are automatically added when we add a **Document** menu using InterfaceBuilder. The text manipulation commands (**Select All**, **Copy**, **Cut**, and **Paste**) are included with the **Edit** menu. Note that:

- to select part of the object, we can simply use the mouse. The **Select All** menu option is intended to select all of the text.
- the menu does not contain a **Delete** option since it is more straightforward to highlight the text then press the **Backspace** key.

Most of the functionality is provided by our two custom classes (**TextController** and **Document**) and the following four AppKit classes: **Text**, **OpenPanel**, **SavePanel**, and **ScrollView**. Since most of the functionality provided by the **ScrollView** is transparent to us when we use InterfaceBuilder, we will not prepare a CRC card for it.

The document has to be set as the delegate of the window

The **Document** class can perform most of its actions without collaborators, but it relies on the **Window** class for displaying and updating the close button to indicate that the document has been edited. Additionally, in order to free itself and its contents, it has to rely on the **Window** class since each document is associated with a window. Notice that the document has to be set as the delegate for the text object in order to receive the text delegate message, **textDidGetKeys:isEmpty:**. This method determines if the document has been edited since it was saved. Figure 9.10 shows the CRC card for the **Document** class.

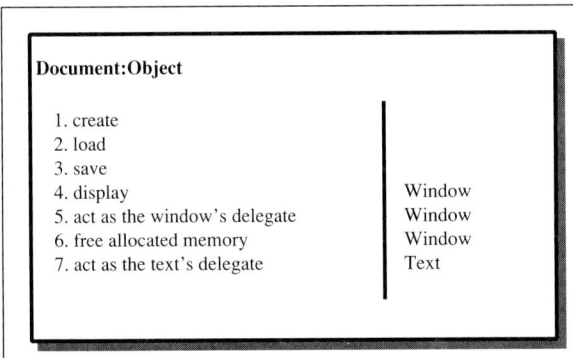

Figure 9.10 The CRC card for the **Document** class

Figure 9.11 shows the CRC card for the **TextController** class. The textcontroller object is the receiver of most of the menu commands; it does some preprocessing then passes the command to the document object. To determine which is the active document, the textcontroller can query **NXApp** for the main window, which also represents the current document. Notice that when the textcontroller object needs to close a document, it accomplishes this without having to message a document. To close a document, we simply click on the close button, which is forwarded to the window by **NXApp**. One other responsibility which the textcon-

Query NXApp to determine the current window and document

troller should perform is displaying an alert panel if we try to close a dirty document.

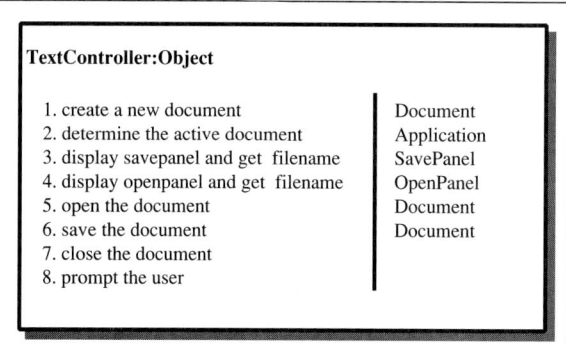

Figure 9.11 The CRC card for the **TextController** class

Figure 9.12 shows the CRC card for the savepanel object. The only actions the savepanel needs to perform are displaying itself and retrieving the filename.

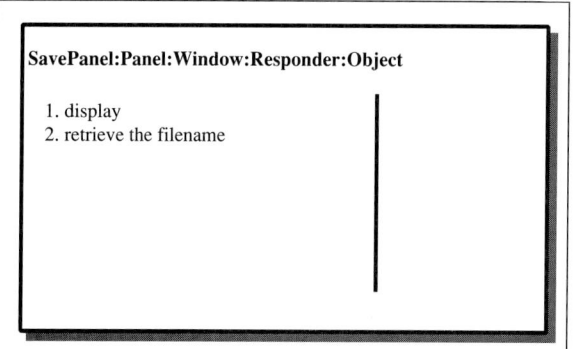

Figure 9.12 The CRC card for the **SavePanel** class

Figure 9.13 shows the CRC card for the openpanel object. Again, the only actions the openpanel object needs to perform are displaying itself and retrieving the filename(s).

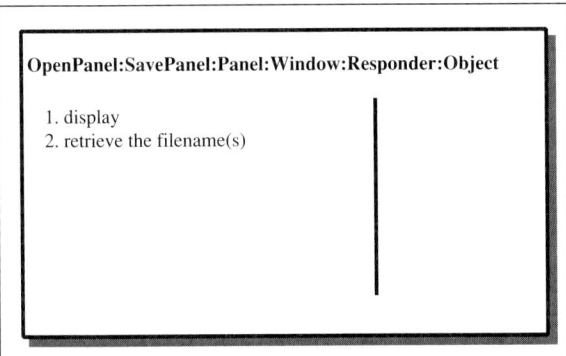

Figure 9.13 The CRC card for the **OpenPanel** class

Figure 9.14 shows the CRC card for the window object. Notice that the window, not the document itself, is the object that indicates whether the document has been edited since it was last saved. The window does this by changing the state of its close button.

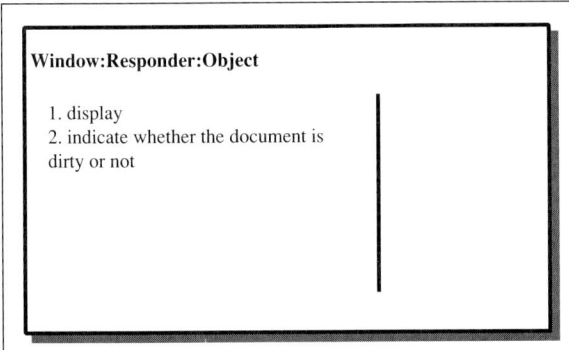

Figure 9.14 The CRC card for the **Window** class

With the CRC cards prepared, we can now produce the class summary tables for the **TextController** and **Document** classes in order to prepare the message diagram. Table 9.1 is the class summary table for the **TextController** class.

TextController:Object		
	Name	**Description**
Instance variables	N/A	N/A
Methods	newDocument:sender	creates a document object
	showSavePanel:sender	displays the savepanel, retrieves the filename then requests each document to save itself
	showOpenPanel:sender	displays the openpanel, retrieves the filename(s) then requests each document to open itself

Table 9.1 Class summary table for the **TextController** class

Table 9.2 shows the class summary table for the **Document** class.

	Document:Object	
	Name	**Description**
Instance Variables	window	outlet for the window
Methods	theText	outlet for the text
	textController	outlet for the textcontroller
	init	initializes a newly created document
	initDocumentFromFile: (const char *)fullPathname	opens a document specified by *fullPathName*
	saveDocumentToFile: (const char *)fullPathName	saves the document to the file specified by *fullPathName*
	textDidGetKeys:isEmpty: sender	checks whether the document has been saved since it was last edited
	showError:(const char *) errorMessage	displays the error specified by *errorMessage* in an alert panel
	windowWillClose:sender	closes and frees the window as needed

Table 9.2 Class summary table for the **Document** class

Figure 9.15 shows the message diagram for **Words**.

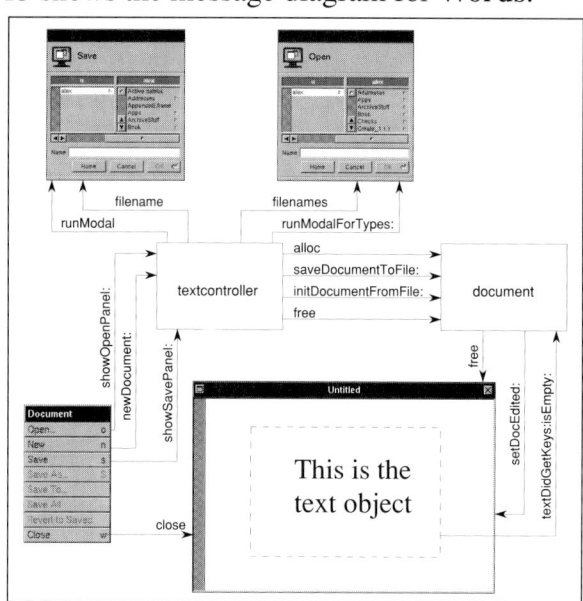

Figure 9.15 The message diagram for **Words**

Figure 9.16 shows the hierarchy graph for the custom classes in **Words**.

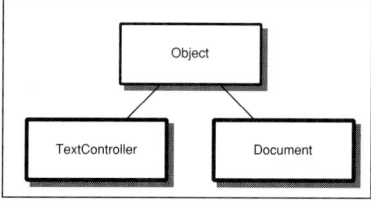

Figure 9.16 The hierarchy graph for the custom classes in **Words**

9.11 Implementing Words

Start a new project in ProjectBuilder and name it **~/Words/Words**. Double-click on **Words.nib** to start InterfaceBuilder. Select the Main Window and use **Command-x** to cut it. Since most applications usually contain a Main Window, InterfaceBuilder will present a panel for verification. Click **OK** to cut the Main Window.

Drag the **Document** menu item from the Menu palette and place it under the **Edit** menu option. Notice that the following menu options are disabled since they are not supported by default: **Save To**, **Save All**, **Revert to Saved**, and **Close**. Enable the **Close** menu option using the Inspector. Additionally, add a **Command-w** keyboard alternative to this menu option by double-clicking on the right area of the menu option then typing a letter, in this case **w**. Figure 9.17 illustrates this entire sequence.

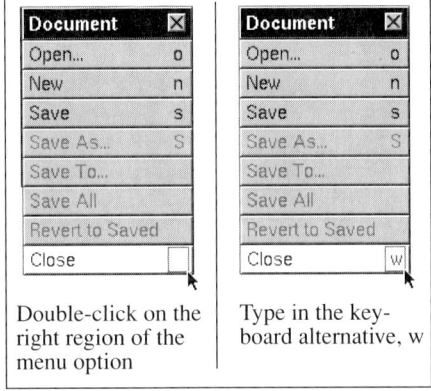

Figure 9.17 Adding a **Command-w** keyboard alternative to the **Close** menu option

Subclass **Object** to create the **TextController** class. Instantiate this class to produce an icon in the File Window. Save the interface then type in the following class files for the **TextController** class.

Listing for **TextController.h**

```
#import <objc/Object.h>

# define FILE_EXTENSION "word"
# define UNTITLED "UNTITLED"

@interface TextController:Object
{
}

- awakeFromNib;
- newDocument:sender;
```

```
- showOpenPanel:sender;
- showSavePanel:sender;

@end
```

Listing for **Textcontroller.m**

```
#import <appkit/appkit.h>
#import "Document.h"
#import "TextController.h"

// this class is responsible for managing
// the savepanel and openpanel
// it is also responsible for responding
// to remote messages from the Workspace

@implementation TextController

// automatically sent after the .nib file
// has finished loading
- awakeFromNib
{
  // using the new method first creates
  // the objects; since there is only one
  // openpanel and savepanel per application,
  // subsequent invocations return the
  // existing savepanel and openpanel,
  // as appropriate
  id savePanel = [SavePanel new];
  id openPanel = [OpenPanel new];
  // by default, an openpanel only allows
  // one file to be opened
  [openPanel allowMultipleFiles:YES];
  return self;
}

// create a new document in response
// to the New menu option
- newDocument:sender
{
  id document = [[Document alloc] init];
  [document showDocument];
  [[document window] setTitle:UNTITLED];
  return self;
```

```
}

// open the document in response to
// the Open menu option
- showOpenPanel:sender
{
  const char *file, *directory;
  const char *const *filenames;
  static const char
    *const wordTypes[] = {FILE_EXTENSION, NULL};
  char fullPathName[MAXPATHLEN];
  id openPanel = [OpenPanel new];

  // ensure that the openpanel allows multiple
  // files to be selected
  [openPanel allowMultipleFiles:YES];
  // display only files with "word" extension
  if ([openPanel runModalForTypes:wordTypes])
    {
    // get list of filename(s) selected
    // the filenames method returns a
    // a pointer to all the strings
    filenames = [openPanel filenames];
    // get directory first
    directory = [openPanel directory];
    do
      {
      // get filename
      file = *(filenames++);
      // construct entire pathname
      strcpy(fullPathName, directory);
      // append directory to filename
      strcat(fullPathName, "/");
      strcat(fullPathName, file);
      [[Document alloc]
        initDocumentFromFile:fullPathName];
      }
    while (*(filenames) != NULL);
      }
  return self;
}

// save the document in response to
// the Save menu option
- showSavePanel:sender
```

```objc
{
  const char *wordType = FILE_EXTENSION;
  const char *fullPathName, *title;
  id document = [[NXApp mainWindow] delegate];
  id savePanel = [SavePanel new];

  // make sure there is a document first
  if (document)
    {
    // if document has not been saved
    // then present savepanel to get filename
    title = [[document window] title];
    if (strcmp(title, UNTITLED) == 0)
      {
      [savePanel setRequiredFileType:wordType];
      if ([savePanel runModal])
        {
        fullPathName = [savePanel filename];
        return [document saveDocumentToFile:
          fullPathName];
        }
      else
        return nil;
      }
    // else just save the file
    else
      return [document saveDocumentToFile:title];
    }
  return self;
}

@end
```

Parse in the **TextController** class and instantiate it. Afterwards, perform the connections. Figure 9.18 shows the connections we have to make in **Words.nib**.

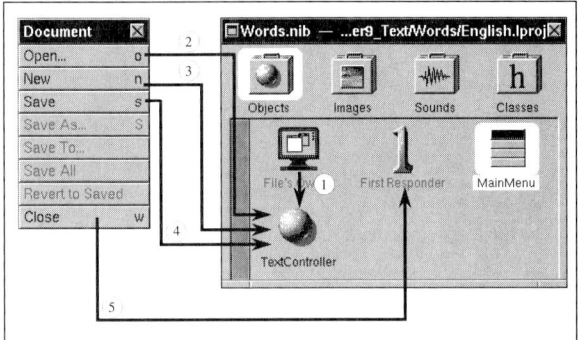

Figure 9.18 Making the connections in **Words.nib**

The five connections are as follows:

1. Connect the textcontroller as the delegate of the **File's Owner**.
2. Connect the textcontroller as the target of the **Open** menu option and select the **showOpenPanel:** method.
3. Connect the textcontroller as the target of the **New** menu option and select the **newDocument:** method.
4. Connect the textcontroller as the target of the **Save** menu option and select the **showSavePanel:** method.
5. Connect the first responder as the target of the **Close** menu option and select the **performClose:** method.

Note that there are four other connections already in the **Edit** submenu, and each of these sends a similarly named message to the first responder. The **Cut**, **Copy**, **Paste**, and **Select All** menu options send **cut:**, **copy:**, **paste:**, and **selectAll:** messages to the first responder. During runtime, the first responder will most likely be the text object in the scrollview of the key window. The text object understands the four text-related commands (**cut:**, **copy:**, **paste:**, and **selectAll:**). However, the text object will not be able to process the **performClose:** method. By definition, the first responder will forward the event up the responder chain until the event is processed by an object that implements the method. In this case, the **performClose:** event will be forwarded up the

The performClose: method is intended for the window

Implementing Words

responder chain until it reaches the window. For more information on the responder chain, see Chapter 6.

Now, type in the header file for the **Document** class as follows:

Listing for **Document.h**

```
#import <objc/Object.h>

@interface Document:Object
{
  id window;
  id theText;
  id textController;
}

- init;
- initDocumentFromFile:
  (const char *)fullPathname;
- showDocument;
- saveDocumentToFile:
  (const char*)fullPathname;
- textDidGetKeys:sender isEmpty:(BOOL)flag;
- showError:(const char*)errorMessage;
- window;

@end
```

A module does not have a Main Window

Save this file and return to InterfaceBuilder and create a module by clicking **Document ⇒ New Module ⇒ New Empty**. Since a module does not have a Main Window, we must first add one. Click on the third button in the Palettes Window to display the appropriate accessory view. Then, drag a window and place it somewhere on the screen.

Add a scrollview to the Main Window

Click on the fourth button in the Palettes Window to display the last accessory view. Drag a scrollview from the palette and place it in the Main Window. Resize the scrollview so it occupies the entire window, and save this **.nib** file as **Document.nib**. Figure 9.19 illustrates this sequence.

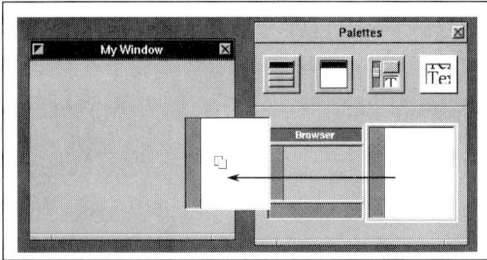

Figure 9.19 Adding a scrollview to **Document.nib**

Now we need to set the class of the **File's Owner** to **Document**. However, before we can do that, we must first create the **Document** class. Use the Class Browser to subclass **Object** to create **Document**. Then, parse the header file, **Document.h**, to create the class template file. Afterwards, select the **File's Owner** icon and set its class to be **Document**.

Set the class of the File's Owner to be Document

Since a document needs to be able to message its textcontroller, we need to create a corresponding outlet so that we can connect the document to the textcontroller. Subclass **Object** to create **TextController**. Then, parse in **TextController.h** to create the class template files. Afterwards, instantiate **TextController** to produce an icon in the File Window.

Create a textcontroller so that the document can message it

Now, connect the objects together. Figure 9.20 illustrates the connections we need to make.

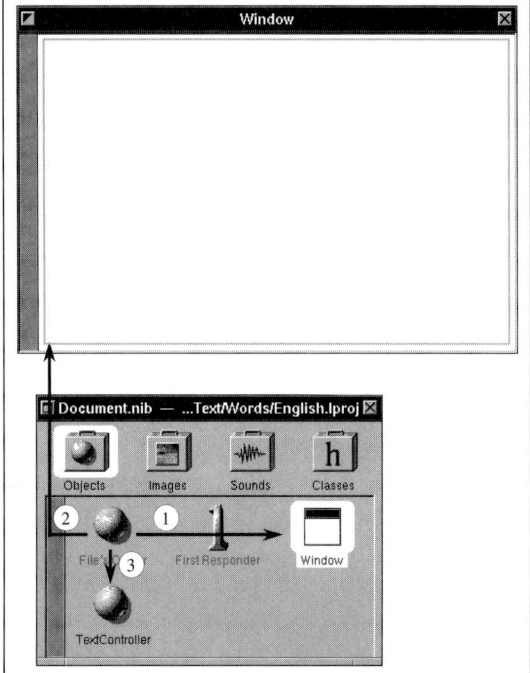

Figure 9.20 Connecting the objects in **Document.nib**

There are three connections:

1. Connect the window as the **window** outlet of the **File's Owner**.
2. Connect the text inside the scrollview as the **theText** delegate of the **File's Owner**.
3. Connect the textcontroller as the **textController** outlet of the **File's Owner**.

Save this **.nib** file as **Document.nib**. Now type in the following class files for the **Document** class.

Listing for Document.m

```
#import <appkit/appkit.h>
#import "Document.h"
#import "TextController.h"
```

```
#define SAVE NX_ALERTDEFAULT
#define CLOSE NX_ALERTALTERNATE
#define CANCEL NX_ALERTOTHER

#define SAVE_ERROR "Can't save file"
#define OPEN_ERROR "Can't open file"

@implementation Document

// initialize a new document
- init
{
  [super init];
  [NXApp loadNibSection:"Document.nib"
    owner:self withNames:NO];
  // make the document the delegate of the window
  // allows us to determine the current document
  // in showSavePanel:
  [window setDelegate:self];
  // make the document the delegate of the text
  // every time a key is pressed, the delegate
  // of the text object will receive a
  // textDidGetKeys: isEmpty: message
  // this allows us to update the window from
  // a clean state to a dirty state
  [theText setDelegate:self];
  return self;
}

// load a document from a file
- initDocumentFromFile:
  (const char *)fullPathName
{
  NXStream *stream;

  // obtain a stream for an existing file
  if (stream =
    NXMapFile(fullPathName, NX_READONLY))
    {
    [self init];
    // read text from stream
    [theText readText:stream];
    //update the window's title
    [window setTitle:fullPathName];
```

```objc
      // display the document
      [self showDocument];
      // free memory associated with stream
      NXCloseMemory(stream, NX_FREEBUFFER);
      return self;
      }
    else
      {
      [self showError:OPEN_ERROR];
      return nil;
      }
}

// display the document -- one improvement
// is to stagger the window rather than display
// each one on top of each other
- showDocument
{
  // set the text selection to 1st char
  [theText setSel:0 :0];
  [window makeKeyAndOrderFront:self];
  return self;
}

// write the document to file
- saveDocumentToFile:(const char *)fullPathName
{
  NXStream *stream = NULL;
  const char* title = [window title];

  // get a stream first
  if (stream =
    (NXOpenMemory(NULL, 0, NX_WRITEONLY)))
    {
    // write text into stream
    [theText writeText:stream];
    // write the stream to the file
    // and check for error code
    if (NXSaveToFile(stream, fullPathName) != 0)
      {
      [self showError:SAVE_ERROR];
      // free stream
      NXCloseMemory(stream, NX_FREEBUFFER);
      return nil;
      }
```

```objc
    else
      // save succeeded: update misc info
      {
      // update the title of the window
      [window setTitle:fullPathName];
      // update window to clean state
      [window setDocEdited:NO];
      // free stream
      NXCloseMemory(stream, NX_FREEBUFFER);
      }
    }
  else
    // Couldn't get stream
    {
    [self showError:SAVE_ERROR];
    return nil;
    }
  return self;
}

// use an Alert panel to display error messages
- showError:(const char *)errorMessage
{
  NXRunAlertPanel(NULL,
    errorMessage, "OK", NULL, NULL);
  return self;
}

// called every time a key is pressed
// if the window is marked dirty, we don't do
// anything -- if it's not dirty, we set
// it to dirty
- textDidGetKeys:sender isEmpty:(BOOL)flag
{
  // if window is not dirty, then set
  // it to dirty
  if ([window isDocEdited] == NO)
    [window setDocEdited:YES];
  return self;
}

- free
{
  // free the window since it's
  // dynamically allocated
```

Implementing Words

```objc
  [window free];
  // free everything allocated
  // by the superclasses
  return [super free];
}

// since the document object is the delegate of
// the window, the window will, before closing,
// send a windowWillClose: message to
// the document
- windowWillClose:sender
{
  int result;

  // display alert panel only if window
  // is dirty
  if ([window isDocEdited])
    {
    result = NXRunAlertPanel
      ([NXApp appName],
      "Unsaved changes. Close Anyway?\n",
      "Save",
      "Close anyway",
      "Cancel");

    switch(result)
      {
      case SAVE:
        // display savepanel;
        // showSavePanel: returns
        // nil if user presses Cancel
        // this prevents window from
        // closing
        return [textController
          showSavePanel:sender];
        break;
      case CLOSE:
        // delay freeing the object until
        // we are done with the current
        // event (closing the window)
        return [NXApp delayedFree:self];
      case CANCEL:
        // returning nil prevents the window
        // from closing
        return nil;
```

```
      }
    }
    return self;
}

- window
{
    return window;
}

@end
```

Make the application then execute it. Test the following scenarios to verify that the application is working correctly:

- create a new document and type a key to verify that the window's close button changes from ☒ to ☒.
- save a document and verify that **Words** can open the file.
- verify whether the openpanel displays only files with a **.word** extension.
- click the close button of a dirty document and determine whether **Words** presents an alert panel. Test all the different possibilities: **Cancel**, **Close Anyway**, and **Save**.
- open multiple files and verify whether **Words** opens the appropriate files.

9.12 Walking Through the Code

As usual, the **main()** function loads in the main **.nib** file (**TextController.nib**) after the application launches. **NXApp** then sends an **awakeFromNib** message to the textcontroller.

Instantiating **OpenPanel** and **SavePanel** in **awakeFromNib**

```
- awakeFromNib
{
    // using the new method first creates
    // the objects; since there is only one
    // openpanel and savepanel per application,
    // subsequent invocations return the
    // existing savepanel and openpanel,
```

```
    // as appropriate
    id savePanel = [SavePanel new];
    id openPanel = [OpenPanel new];
    // by default, an openpanel only allows
    // one file to be opened
    [openPanel allowMultipleFiles:YES];
    return self;
}
```

The **awakeFromNib** method:

- instantiates the **OpenPanel** and **SavePanel** classes.
- sets the openpanel to select multiple files because, by default, an openpanel allows only one file to be selected.

Afterwards, **Words** simply processes each message as it arrives. Clicking on the **New** menu option sends a **newDocument:** message to the textcontroller:

Creating a new document

```
- newDocument:sender
{
  id document = [[Document alloc] init];
  [document showDocument];
  [[document window] setTitle:UNTITLED];
  return self;
}
```

This method instantiates the **Document** class then initializes the resulting instance with the **init** method:

Initializing a new document

```
- init
{
  [super init];
  [NXApp loadNibSection:"Document.nib"
    owner:self withNames:NO];
  // make the document the delegate of the window
  // allows us to determine the current document
  // in showSavePanel:
```

```
    [window setDelegate:self];
    // make the document the delegate of the text
    // every time a key is pressed, the delegate
    // of the text object will receive a
    // textDidGetKeys: isEmpty: message
    // this allows us to update the window from
    // a clean state to a dirty state
    [theText setDelegate:self];
    return self;
}
```

The **init** method loads in the **.nib** file and sets the document as the **File's Owner**. The document then sets itself as the delegate of the window and of the text object. Doing this serves two purposes:

- each time the user types a key, **NXApp** sends a **textDidGetKeys:isEmpty:** message to the document. This method sets the window to a dirty state if it is not already dirty. If so, then the method simply returns.
- by associating the document with a window, **Words** can determine which is the active document by searching for the delegate of the current window, as demonstrated in the **saveDocumentToFile:** method.

After initializing the document, the **newDocument:** method displays the document using the **showDocument** method.

Displaying the document

```
- showDocument
{
    // set the text selection to 1st char
    [theText setSel:0 :0];
    [window makeKeyAndOrderFront:self];
    return self;
}
```

The **showDocument** method performs the following steps:

- to save the user the trouble of having to click on the scrollview to select the text, **showDocument** automatically selects the text by setting the selection to the first character.

- makes the window the key window then orders it to the front of the other windows.

As a final step, the **newDocument:** method sets the title of the newly created document to the **UNTITLED** constant, which is defined to be **UNTITLED**. Note that the textcontroller has to send a **window** message to the document requesting it to return the **id** of its window.

Clicking on the **Open** menu option sends a **showOpenPanel:** message to the textcontroller:

Displaying the openpanel

```
- showOpenPanel:sender
{
  const char *file, *directory;
  const char *const *filenames;
  static const char
    *const wordTypes[] = {FILE_EXTENSION, NULL};
  char fullPathName[MAXPATHLEN];
  id openPanel = [OpenPanel new];

  // ensure that the openpanel allows multiple
  // files to be selected
  [openPanel allowMultipleFiles:YES];
  // display only files with "word" extension
  if ([openPanel runModalForTypes:wordTypes])
    {
    // get list of filename(s) selected
    // the filenames method returns a
    // a pointer to all the strings
    filenames = [openPanel filenames];
    // get directory first
    directory = [openPanel directory];
    do
      {
      // get filename
      file = *(filenames++);
      // construct entire pathname
      strcpy(fullPathName, directory);
      // append directory to filename
      strcat(fullPathName, "/");
      strcat(fullPathName, file);
```

```
        [[Document alloc]
          initDocumentFromFile:fullPathName];
        }
    while (*(filenames) != NULL);
        }
   return self;
 }
```

The **showOpenPanel:** method first sets the extension to the **FILE_EXTENSION** constant (defined to be **word**) then initializes the openpanel so that it allows multiple files to be selected. Afterwards, the method displays the openpanel using the **runModalForTypes:** method. Recall that the method automatically prepends a period (**.**) to the file extension that is passed as a parameter. Thus, the method only displays files with a **.word** extension. In the **showOpenPanel:** method:

- the openpanel runs in a modal loop until we click **OK** or **Cancel** to dismiss it.
- if the return value is other than **0** (we typed a filename in the textfield or selected one or more files in the browser and pressed **OK**), **showOpenPanel:** then constructs the entire pathname by concatenating the directory to each relative pathname stored in the **filenames** pointer. This sequence is described in "Using the OpenPanel" on page 357.
- **showOpenPanel:** then creates a new document and initializes its contents with the file specified by **fullPathName** in the **initDocumentFromFile:** method:

Creating and initializing a new document

```
 - initDocumentFromFile:
   (const char *)fullPathName
 {
   NXStream *stream;

   // obtain a stream for an existing file
   if (stream =
     NXMapFile(fullPathName, NX_READONLY))
     {
     [self init];
```

```
        // read text from stream
        [theText readText:stream];
        //update the window's title
        [window setTitle:fullPathName];
        // display the document
        [self showDocument];
        // free memory associated with stream
        NXCloseMemory(stream, NX_FREEBUFFER);
        return self;
        }
     else
        {
        [self showError:OPEN_ERROR];
        return nil;
        }
  }
```

The **initDocumentFromFile:** method:

- maps an existing file into a stream using the **NXMapFile()** function.
- initializes the document using the **init** method. This method loads in the **Document.nib** file, sets the document to be the delegate of the window, and sets the document to be the delegate of the text.
- reads the text into the stream.
- updates the window's title to reflect the filename.
- displays the document using **showDocument**.
- closes the stream and frees the associated memory.

Clicking on the **Save** menu option sends a **showSavePanel:** message to the textcontroller:

Displaying the savepanel

```
  - showSavePanel:sender
  {
    const char *wordType = FILE_EXTENSION;
    const char *fullPathName, *title;
    id document = [[NXApp mainWindow] delegate];
    id savePanel = [SavePanel new];
```

```
  // make sure there is a document first
  if (document)
    {
    // if document has not been saved
    // then present savepanel to get filename
    title = [[document window] title];
    if (strcmp(title, UNTITLED) == 0)
      {
      [savePanel setRequiredFileType:wordType];
      if ([savePanel runModal])
        {
        fullPathName = [savePanel filename];
        return [document saveDocumentToFile:
          fullPathName];
        }
      else
        return nil;
      }
    // else just save the file
    else
      return [document saveDocumentToFile:title];
    }
  return self;
}
```

The **showSavePanel:** method does the following:

- it checks if there is a document. If the application does not have a main window, the document would be **nil** since the document is the delegate of the main window.
- if **document** is **nil**, then the method simply returns **self**.
- if **document** is not **nil**:
    - the method checks if the document is already named (it would only be named if it had previously been saved). If the document is already associated with a file, **showSavePanel:** simply requests the document to save itself by sending it a **saveDocumentToFile:** message with the existing filename. This alleviates the user from having to type in the filename again to save the document.
    - if the document is not already associated with a file, **showSavePanel:** presents a savepanel to ask which filename the document should be saved to. Notice that the

method uses the **setRequiredFileType:** method to automatically append an extension (**.word**) to the filename.

Clicking **Cancel** returns **nil**, which is used by the **windowWillClose:** method (this method will be explained shortly). Clicking **OK** sends a **saveDocumentToFile:** method to the document requesting it to save itself.

Requesting a document to save itself

```
- saveDocumentToFile:(const char *)fullPathName
{
  NXStream *stream = NULL;
  const char* title = [window title];

  // get a stream first
  if (stream =
    (NXOpenMemory(NULL, 0, NX_WRITEONLY)))
    {
    // write text into stream
    [theText writeText:stream];
    // write the stream to the file
    // and check for error code
    if (NXSaveToFile(stream, fullPathName) != 0)
      {
      [self showError:SAVE_ERROR];
      // free stream
      NXCloseMemory(stream, NX_FREEBUFFER);
      return nil;
      }
    else
      // save succeeded: update misc info
      {
      // update the title of the window
      [window setTitle:fullPathName];
      // update window to clean state
      [window setDocEdited:NO];
      // free stream
      NXCloseMemory(stream, NX_FREEBUFFER);
      }
    }
  else
    // Couldn't get stream
    {
```

```
    [self showError:SAVE_ERROR];
    return nil;
    }
  return self;
}
```

The **saveDocumentToFile:** method works exactly as described in "Writing the Text to a File" on page 354. The only difference is the method sets the document name to the filename once the document is written to the file successfully. This allows the textcontroller to later check if the document is already associated with a filename, as explained in the previous section.

Clicking on the close button sends a **windowWillClose:** message to the window's delegate, the document itself.

Presenting an alert panel before closing a window

```
- windowWillClose:sender
{
  int result;

  // display alert panel only if window
  // is dirty
  if ([window isDocEdited])
    {
    result = NXRunAlertPanel
      ([NXApp appName],
      "Unsaved changes. Close Anyway?\n",
      "Save",
      "Close anyway",
      "Cancel");

    switch(result)
      {
      case SAVE:
        // display savepanel;
        // showSavePanel: returns
        // nil if user presses Cancel
        // this prevents window from
        // closing
        return [textController
          showSavePanel:sender];
```

```
          break;
        case CLOSE:
          // delay freeing the object until
          // we are done with the current
          // event (closing the window)
          return [NXApp delayedFree:self];
        case CANCEL:
          // returning nil prevents the window
          // from closing
          return nil;
        }
    }
  return self;
}
```

If the window is not marked dirty, the method simply returns. However, if the window is marked dirty, **windowWillClose:** presents an alert panel with three choices: **Save**, **Close**, and **Cancel**.

- Clicking **Save** sends a **showSavePanel:** message to the textcontroller to display the savepanel. Clicking **OK** returns **self** (from **showSavePanel:**), which allows the window to close after the file is saved. Clicking **Cancel** at the savepanel returns **nil**, which prevents the window from closing.

- Clicking **Cancel** (at the alert panel) returns **nil**, which prevents the window from closing.

- Clicking on **Close** sends a **delayedFree:** message to **NXApp**. This message tells **NXApp** to finish processing the current event (the **close** message) then to free the current object (the document) by sending it a **free** message:

Freeing the document

```
- free
{
  // free the window since it's
  // dynamically allocated
  [window free];
  // free everything allocated
  // by the superclasses
  return [super free];
```

}

Since the window is dynamically allocated—it's an object, and all objects are dynamically allocated—the document sends a **free** message to the window to free it and all of its subviews. The document then frees itself by requesting its superclass (**Object**) to free the memory occupied by the object itself.

Note that the document has to delay freeing itself until **NXApp** finishes closing the window, or the application will crash. Why? Because if the document immediately sends itself a **free** message instead of sending a **delayedFree:** message to **NXApp**, the **free** method would not be able to return since the window would no longer exist! The **delayedFree:** message (sent from **Document**'s **windowWillClose:** method) delays **NXApp** from sending a **free** message to the document (which frees the window) until **NXApp** has finished processing the current event, which is closing the window.

> Note that the window can be freed if we select the **Free when closed** option in the Window Inspector (under the **Attributes** option of the popuplist). If we set this option for the window, we should *not* free it again in **Document**'s **free** method. Why? Because the window will have already been freed and trying to free it again would result in a runtime error (the message would be similar to **objc: FREED(id): message free sent to freed object=0xbe970**).
>
> Admittedly, it would be easier to specify that the window should free itself in InterfaceBuilder. However, the point of this example is to illustrate that an object should free all the instance variables that it dynamically allocates.

9.13 Suggestions

To make the application more "NeXTish," implement the following additions.

9.13.1 Enabling the Menu Options

Consider enabling these two menu options:

- **Save As**—this method should present the savepanel and allow the document to be saved under a different filename.
- **Revert to Saved**—this should discard the changes made to the document since the last time the document was saved. Use **NXMapFile()** and reread the text from the file. Remember to mark the document as clean since all the changes have been discarded.

9.13.2 Updating the OpenPanel and SavePanel

Instead of displaying the user's home directory, the savepanel and openpanel should remember the directory the last file was selected from then display it instead. Store the directory in a **static** variable so it retains its value each time the appropriate method (**showOpenPanel:** or **showSavePanel:**) is invoked. Then, display the savepanel and openpanel using **runModalForDirectory:file:**, which allows a file and a directory to be specified.

9.13.3 Adding Printing Support

Add a **print:** method to the **Document** class so that each document knows how to print itself. To add support for printing:

- add a **print:** method to **Document.h** as follows:

Listing for **Document.h**

```
#import <objc/Object.h>

@interface Document:Object
{
  id window;
  id theText;
  id textController;
}
```

```
- init;
- initDocumentFromFile:
  (const char *)fullPathname;
- showDocument;
- saveDocumentToFile:
  (const char*)fullPathname;
- textDidGetKeys:sender isEmpty:(BOOL)flag;
- showError:(const char*)errorMessage;
- window;
- print:sender;

@end
```

- add the following method to **Document.m** (**Text** inherits the **printPSCode:** method from **View**):

Excerpted listing for Document.m

```
- print:sender
{
  [theText printPSCode:sender];
  return self;
}
```

- add an **Item** menu option to the Main Menu.
- rename this option to **Print...** (the **...** indicates that the menu option displays a panel for additional input).
- add **p** as the keyboard alternative for the menu option.
- select the **First Responder** icon in the Class Browser. This icon is a graphical representation of the first responder. Recall that when the first responder receives a message, it will try to process it. If it can't, it then forwards it its next responder. Thus, the **print:** message will eventually reach the document since it is the delegate of the window (the delegation relationship was set in **Document**'s **init** method).
- select the **First Responder** icon and then click the **Classes** suitcase to display the Class Inspector.
- in the Class Inspector, add a **print:** method.
- connect the **Print...** menu option to the **First Responder** icon.
- select the **print:** method and click **Connect**.

- make the application and test the print features.

For more information on printing, consult the documentation for the **PrintPanel**, **Text**, and **View** classes.

> Why couldn't we simply connect from the **Print...** menu option to the **First Responder** directly? If we do, then the application will present five print panels, one after another. What is the cause of this? Recall that the first responder stops forwarding its event only when the return code is something other than **nil**. The **printPSCode:** method, unfortunately, returns **nil**. Thus, the **printPSCode:** message is first sent to the first responder (the text object), which is then forwarded all the way up to the responder chain. The objects in the responder chain include:
>
> - the text object
> - the clipview
> - the scrollview
> - the content view
> - the window.
>
> Each one of these objects understands **printPSCode:** and displays a print panel accordingly. By returning **self** in **Document**'s **print:** method, the search sequence will stop at the text object, and the application will display only one print panel.

9.13.4 Saving Part of a Document

In the **saveDocumentToFile:** method, check if there is text is highlighted. If so, save only the highlighted text; otherwise, save the entire document.

9.13.5 Adding a Preferences Panel

Consider adding support for the following defaults:

- a Preferences panel to allow the user to specify a font and font size when the text is initially created. The following statements sets the initial font to **Times-Roman** and the font size to **14** points:
  ```
  NXWriteDefault("Words", "NXFont", "Times-Roman");
  NXWriteDefautl("Words", "NXFontSize", "14");
  ```

NeXTSTEP includes four fonts:

- **Times-Roman**
- **Helvetica**
- **Ohlfs**
- **Courier**.

When a text object is initialized, it automatically searches for a **NXFont** and a **NXFontSize** default in the defaults database to determine which font and font size it should use to format itself. The search order starts with the default owned by the application, proceeds to the default owned by **GLOBAL**, and ends with the command-line parameters, as explained in Chapter 8. Note that this addition allows the *initial* font and font size to be specified. There is still no provision to change the font after the document is displayed.

> There are two types of text objects: an *ASCII text object* and a *Rich Text Format (RTF) object*. The latter is much more flexible and can support many other features such as embedded graphics and multiple fonts. While an ASCII text object reads the defaults database to determine what font it should use to format itself, a rich text object actually stores the format (including the window size) with its text.
>
> Since all of the on-line documentation includes multiple fonts and/or graphics, they are stored as Rich Text Format files: these files typically have a **.rtf** extension. The Workspace uses Edit as the default application to open RTF files since it is one of the few bundled application that supports RTF.

- a Preferences panel to specify whether **Words** should initially display a blank document upon start-up. Override the **appDidInit:** method in the **TextController** class to read the defaults database to determine whether to display a blank document upon start-up.

9.13.6 Opening Files from the Workspace

Extend **Words** so that it can open its files directly from the Workspace. Before doing this, let's explore how this sequence works. Double-clicking on a file from the Workspace results in the following sequence:

1. the Workspace sends an **openFile:ok:** message to **NXApp**.
2. **NXApp** then queries its delegate by sending it an **appAcceptsAnotherFile:** message.
3. if the delegate returns **YES**, **NXApp** sends it a **app:openFile:type:** message to request it to open the file.
4. the **app:openFile:type** method should return **YES** to indicate if it has successfully opened the file, or **NO** to indicate that it could not open the file.

Figure 9.21 illustrates this entire sequence.

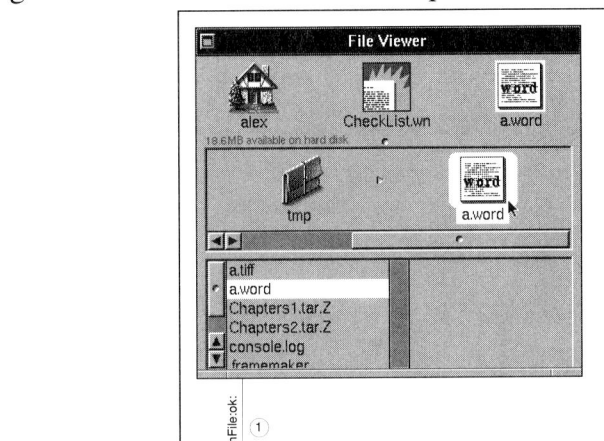

Figure 9.21 Double-clicking on a file from the Workspace sets off a complex series of events

The code to implement this functionality is simple. Add the following two methods to the implementation file of the **TextController** class:

Adding another method to the **TextController** class

```
- (BOOL)appAcceptsAnotherFile:sender
{
  // Double-clicking on a file in the WSM
  // causes the following actions:
  // * NeXTSTEP sends an openFile:ok
  //   message to NXApp
  // * openFile:ok sends a appAcceptsAnotherFile:
  //   message to check if it's OK to open
  //   a file; by returning YES, the app
  //   allows files to be opened from the WSM
  // * openFile:ok then sends a
  //   app:openFile:type message to actually
  //   open the file; the app:openFile:type
  //   should return YES if successful and
  //   NO if not
```

```
                // the printf statements illustrate the orders
                // these messages are being sent
                return YES;
            }

            // actually open the file here
            - (int)app:sender openFile:(const char*)filename
                 type:(const char *)filetype
            {
               return [[Document alloc]
                 initDocumentFromFile:filename] YES ? NO;
            }
```

The app:openFile: type method returns a Boolean value

The **?:** construct in C returns the first value if the expression is true (that is, not **nil**), and the second value otherwise. Thus, **app:openFile:type:** will either return **YES** or **NO**, depending on whether the document was created successfully or not. If a document is created successfully (through [**[Document alloc] initDocumentFromFile: filename**]), the return code will be **self**. Thus, the expression is not **nil**, which means **app:openFile:type:** will return **YES**. Since **appAcceptsAnotherFile:** and **app:openFile:type:** are both delegate methods, we need to establish the textcontroller as the delegate of **NXApp** before the textcontroller will receive these messages.

> The **app:openFile:type:** method is documented as returning a **Boolean** value, although the method is declared to return an **int**. This mismatch not pose a problem, since **YES** and **NO** are ultimately defined to be **1** and **0** respectively.

The application's icon should be 48 by 48 pixels

Words will now launch when we double-click on any **.word** document. However, for aesthetics reasons, we should create a custom document icon to differentiate it from a standard ASCII icon. First, use IconBuilder to create an icon that is 48 by 48 pixels and save this icon as **document.tiff**. Afterwards, return to ProjectBuilder.

Display the Attributes accessory view then drag the **document.tiff** icon from the Workspace into the icon well under the label **Document Icons and Extensions**. Then, double-click on the text under the icon and change it to **word**. Figure 9.22 shows how to add a document icon in ProjectBuilder.

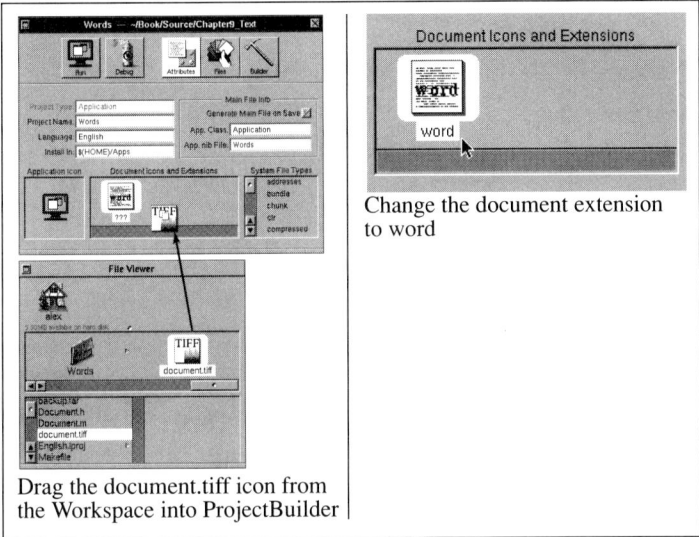

Figure 9.22 Adding an icon and changing the extension for an application's documents

For directions on how use IconBuilder, use the Digital Librarian to find all files with IconBuilder in the title. Double-click on **IconBuilder.rtfd** to open the documentation.

To change the application icon, create another icon that is 48 by 48 pixels and save the icon as **~/Words/Words/application.tiff**. Then, drag this icon into the icon well under the label

To change the application's icon, create an icon that is 48 by 48 pixels

406 Opening Files from the Workspace

Application Icon. Figure 9.23 illustrates this sequence (this figure assumes that the new application icon is a large **W**).

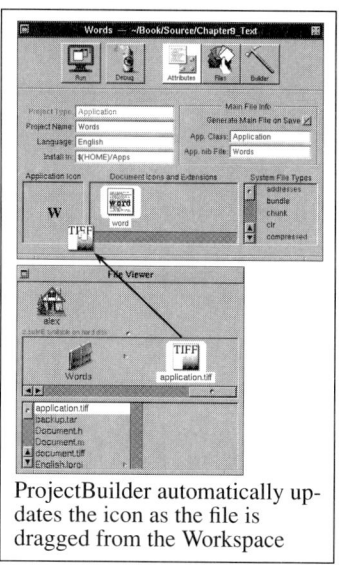

ProjectBuilder automatically updates the icon as the file is dragged from the Workspace

Figure 9.23 Changing the application's icon

To install an application, type install in the Args field in ProjectBuilder

At this point, install the application. Installing an application is stripping all the debugging information from the executable then copying it to the installation directory. To install the application, specify **install** as an argument in the **Args** field of ProjectBuilder in the Build accessory view then click **Build**. Once the application is installed, inform the Workspace that **Words** should be the default application to open **.word** documents. To do so:

- select a **.word** document in the Workspace.
- display the Inspector by clicking **Tools** ⇒ **Inspector**.
- display the **Tools** accessory view by selecting the **Tools** menu option in the popuplist (**Command-3**).
- select the **Words** icon and click **Set Default**.

Figure 9.24 illustrates this sequence.

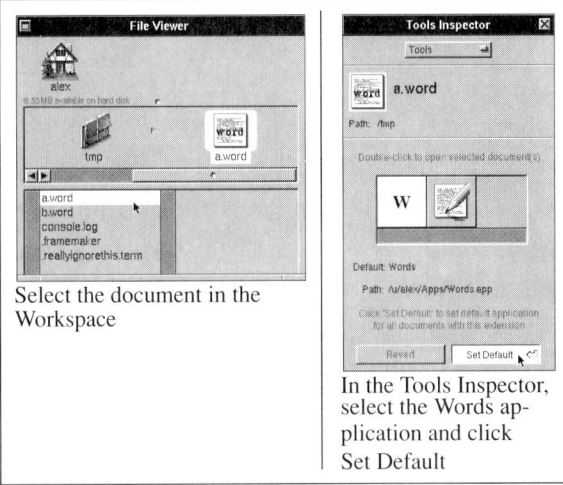

Figure 9.24 Setting **Words** as the default application for **.word** documents

In summary, to support launching **Words** through double-clicking on a **.word** document:

- set the textcontroller as the delegate of **NXApp**.
- implement these two methods, **appAcceptsAnotherFile:** and **app:openFile:type:**, in **NXApp**'s delegate, the textcontroller.
- install the application in the desired installation directory.
- create a document icon for a **.word** document (optional).
- create an application icon for the **Words** application (optional).
- drag the document icon into the icon well, and change the extension of the icon to **word** (optional).
- select a **.word** document in the Workspace.
- use the Inspector in the Workspace to specify that **Words** should be the default application to open **.word** documents.
- click **Set Default** in the Inspector.

9.14 Troubleshooting

Here are some problems that can arise:

- The openpanel still displays all files, even though the application sets the extension with the **setRequiredFileType:** method.
    - **Cause**: The application must set the extension with **setRequiredFileType:** before displaying the openpanel.
    - **Solution**: Modify the application so that it sets the file extension before displaying the openpanel.
- Closing a dirty window does not present an alert panel for verification, even though the document implements the **windowWillClose:** method.
    - **Cause**: Since **windowWillClose:** is a window delegate method, the textcontroller must be the window's delegate.
    - **Solution**: Use InterfaceBuilder to set the document as the delegate of the window.
- Trying to overwrite an existing file produces an error.
    - **Cause**: The file may be owned by another user. **Words** sets the permission on its document so that only the user who created it can overwrite the existing file.
    - **Solution**: Change the ownership of the file using **chown** or save the document under a different name.
- The Workspace still displays the default document icon for **.word** documents.
    - **Cause**: There are several possibilities:
        - The application has been compiled but has not been installed in an install directory.
        - The application does not have a document icon.
        - The extension of the document icon does not match that of the application, which is **word**.
    - **Solution**: Use the solution for the appropriate problem:
        - Install the application by specifying **install** in the **Args** file of the Build accessory view.
        - Drag a document icon from the Workspace.

- Change the extension of the document icon to **word** (not **.word**) in ProjectBuilder.
- Double-clicking on **.word** documents from the Workspace launches Edit instead of Words.
    - **Cause**: There are several possibilities:
        - **NXApp**'s delegate has not implemented **appAcceptsAnotherFile:** and **app:openFile:type:**.
        - The application has been compiled but has not been installed.
        - The extension of the document icon does not match that in the application, which is **word**.
        - **Words** has not been set as the default application to open **.word** documents.
    - **Solution**: Use the solution for the appropriate problem:
        - Implement **appAcceptsAnotherFile:** and **app:openFile:type:** in **NXApp**'s delegate.
        - Install the application by specifying **install** in the **Args** file of the Build accessory view.
        - Change the extension of the document icon to **word** (not **.word**) in ProjectBuilder.
        - Use the Inspector in the Workspace to set **Words** as the default application for **.word** documents.

9.15 Summary

The **Text** class defines an object that manages and displays text. Unlike most of the other classes, the **Text** class is designed to be extended through delegation instead of subclassing. In this chapter, we explored the most common text delegate method, **textDidGetKeys:isEmpty:**, which can be used to determine whether the text has been modified since it was last saved.

We also learned how to use the **ScrollView** class to provide scrolling since a text object's frame rectangle tends to be larger than its superview's. To complete the framework, we used the **OpenPanel**, and **SavePanel** classes to implement the standard interface for loading and saving files.

Summary

In the next chapter, we will explore the NeXTSTEP on-line help facility.

Chapter 10
Implementing On-Line Help

One of the best features of NeXTSTEP is its comprehensive help system. By choosing a control and pressing a **Help** key, we can obtain help information that is cross-referenced with other related information (this cross-reference scheme is known as *hypertext*) on the application in general or on a particular feature. The Application Kit provides a **NXHelpPanel** class that facilitates implementing this feature, and InterfaceBuilder provides a HelpBuilder that allows us to build the system graphically. This chapter concentrates on how to use the **NXHelpPanel** class and the HelpBuilder component of InterfaceBuilder to add on-line help to the **Words** application.

The on-line help system offers hypertext

10.1 Goals

In this chapter, we will:

- demonstrate how to use the on-line help system.
- explain how to add on-line help to an existing application.

10.2 The On-Line Help System

The central component of the on-line help system is the **NXHelpPanel** class. This class provides a panel that displays help information for a given application. The panel is set up like a book: there is a table of contents, an index, and text body, composed of one or more help file(s). There is usually a one-to-one correspondence between each entry in the table of contents and a help file. Since the text in the help files is in Rich Text Format, it can include multiple fonts and graphics.

The NXHelpPanel class is the central element of the help system

To illustrate the on-line help system, double-click on **/NextApps/Preferences.app** to launch the Preferences application. At the Main Window, hold down the **Control** and **Alt** keys; this changes the cursor from the standard arrowhead cursor (🭯) to the help cursor, a question mark (❓). Now click on the keyboard

To display help for a feature, hold down the Control and Alt keys and click on the feature

412   The On-Line Help System

icon to display help information for this feature of the Preferences application. Figure 10.1 shows the help panel and the help text that should be displayed for the keyboard icon.

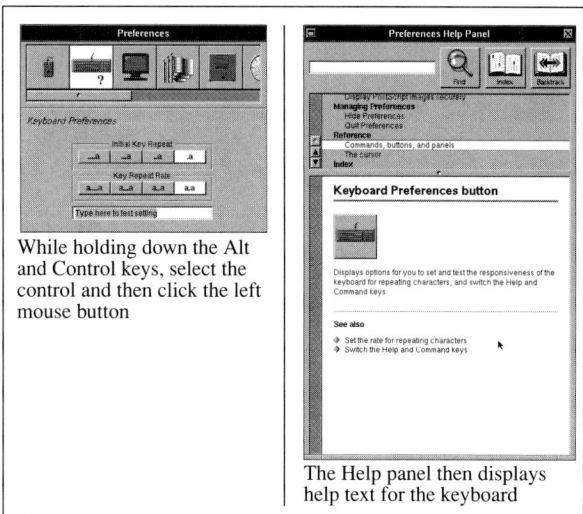

Figure 10.1 The on-line help for the keyboard in the Preferences application

The files in the help system are connected through a series of links and markers, which is the topic of our next discussion.

Our discussion assume the following:

- we are using the non*ADB* (*Apple Desktop Bus*) keyboard, which does not provide a **Help** key. On the newer **ADB** systems, we can achieve the same functionality by simply holding down the **Help** key. On NeXTSTEP/Intel systems, the **F1** function key serves as the **Help** key.
- the mouse is configured right-handed, i.e., the **Right** option is selected in the Preferences application. If the mouse is configured left-handed, reconfigure it using the Preferences application or use the right mouse button instead of the left mouse button.

10.3 Using Links

Edit provides a **Help** submenu which has tools for working with links and markers. Unlike other menu options, the **Help** submenu is only available in *Developer Mode* (as opposed to the default *User Mode*). To verify whether the **Help** submenu is already present, click on the **Format** menu option. If the **Help** submenu does not appear, then toggle Edit to **Developer Mode** as follows:

- Click **Info** ⇒ **Preferences.**
- Click the button marked **Developer Mode**.
- Click **Set**.
- Quit Edit and relaunch it to verify whether the **Help** submenu is now present.

Figure 10.2 shows how to enable Edit in **Developer Mode**.

> Edit's Help menu is only available in Developer Mode

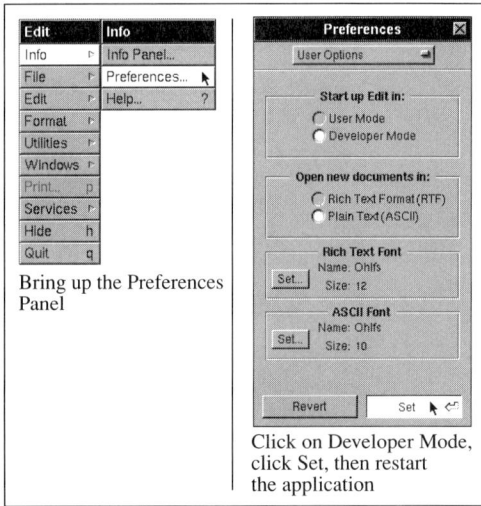

Figure 10.2 Enabling **Developer Mode** in Edit

Another menu option which only appears in **Developer Mode** is the **Gdb** menu option, although this does not appear until we are debugging an application. For more information on the **Gdb** menu option, see Appendix D.

Create a new document with **Command-n**. Since a help file requires links and links are only supported in Rich Text Format, convert the file to Rich Text Format by clicking **Format** ⇒ **Text** ⇒ **Make Rich Text** (**Command-R**). Type in the following text:

```
This help text will be displayed.
```

Save the file as **/tmp/HelpText** (Edit will append a **.rtf** extension for a **Rich Text Format** file). Create another RTF file and type in the following text:

```
Click here to display the other file.
```

Use the Link Inspector to specify which file should display when a link is clicked

Save the file as **/tmp/Click**. With the cursor at the end of the line, insert a link at the current cursor location by clicking **Format** ⇒ **Help** ⇒ **Insert Link**. In the Link Inspector, click **Set** to display an openpanel. In the openpanel, specify the file to be displayed when the link is clicked. Select **/tmp/HelpText.rtf** and click **OK**. Figure 10.3 shows how to use the Link Inspector.

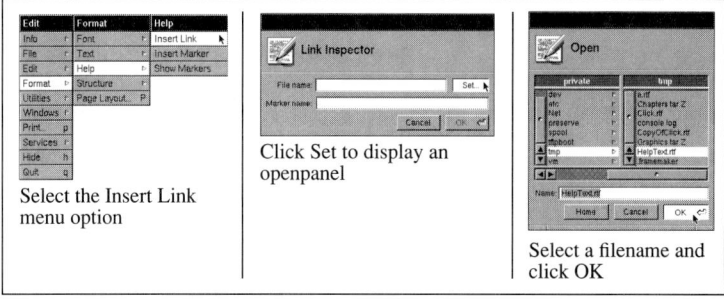

Select the Insert Link menu option

Click Set to display an openpanel

Select a filename and click OK

Figure 10.3 Inserting a link in a document

By default, Edit does not display a link

By default, Edit does not display links. To do so, click **Format** ⇒ **Help** ⇒ **Show Links**. Each link is displayed as a small solid diamond (♦). To edit an existing link, **Command**-click (hold down the **Command** key and click) on the link to display the Link Inspector as before.

Click on the link to display its associated file

To demonstrate the link, first close **/tmp/HelpText.rtf** by clicking on the close button. Then click on the link diamond beside **Click**. This should open the file the link is associated with, namely

/tmp/HelpText.rtf. Figure 10.4 shows how to inspect the link to insure that it is working.

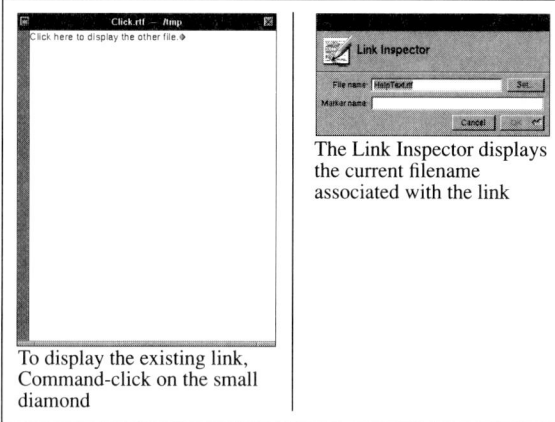

Figure 10.4 Displaying and editing a link

A link allows one file to be associated with another, but NeXTSTEP provides an even finer control through the use of markers.

> The **Insert Link** menu option will be unavailable until the file is saved because the link requires a filename.

10.4 Using Markers

After creating a link, we can specify an optional marker, a named position holder inside the help text. Clicking on the link displays the help text, and if a marker is present, the text from the marker to the end of the line is highlighted.

A marker is an optional named position holder in the help text

To demonstrate the use of a marker:

- **Command**-click on the link in **/tmp/Click.rtf**.
- in the **Marker** field, type **FirstMarker** and save the file.
- open **/tmp/HelpText.rtf** and position the cursor at the start of the word **will**.

- click **Format** ⇒ **Help** ⇒ **Insert Marker** to display the Marker Inspector.
- type in **FirstMarker** and click **OK** to insert a marker in the help text.
- save the **/tmp/HelpText.rtf** file.

At this point, we have specified that clicking on the link in **/tmp/Click.rtf** will display the **/tmp/HelpText.rtf** file. Additionally, the word **will** (along with the rest of the line where **will** appears) will be highlighted since it contains a marker (**FirstMarker**). This marker matches the one specified in **/tmp/Click.rtf**.

By default, Edit does not display markers

Since Edit does not normally display markers, click on **Format** → **Help** → **Show Markers** to display the marker. A marker appears as a diamond (◆), although it does not have a 3D look, as does a link (◆). Figure 10.5 shows how to insert a marker in a file.

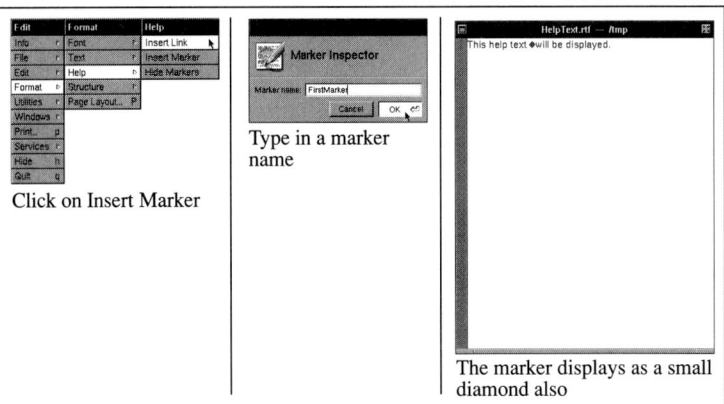

Figure 10.5 Inserting a marker in a file

To test the marker, click on the link in **/tmp/Click.rtf**. Since we have specified a marker name for the link, this displays the file associated with the link (**/tmp/HelpText.rtf**) and highlights the text from the marker until the end of the line, i.e., from the word **will** until the end of the line.

> Rather than using multiple files with links, we can use one RTF file that contains all the help text and markers for all the help entries in the table of contents. However, this would prevent us from creating a true hypertext system since it would be pointless to cross-reference a document to itself.

We are now ready to add on-line help to the **Words** application from Chapter 9. Unlike the other chapters, we will not attempt to implement this using classes; we will use InterfaceBuilder (more specifically, its HelpBuilder component) instead. Consequently, we will not need a design stage and the tools associated with this stage such as CRC cards and message diagrams.

This application will not include a design stage

10.5 Adding On-line Help to Words

To demonstrate the on-line help facility, we will add three files to provide help for three of the custom features of **Words**: opening a file, saving a file, and creating a file. We do not need to add help text for standard features (such as using the mouse, printing, etc.) since these are automatically provided for us by NeXTSTEP.

We will provide three help files for Words

When we select an entry in the table of contents or the index of the help system, the application first searches for the file containing the help text in the *language*.**lproj/Help** directory of the application's package (for more information on the *language*.**lproj** directory, see "Decomposing a NeXTSTEP Application" on page 146). If the application cannot find the associated help text in that directory, it searches for the help text in **/usr/lib/NeXTSTEP/Resources/***language*.**lproj/Help.store**. We will refer to these entries in the table of contents and index files as *standard help entries*. Since the help system automatically searches the **Help.store** file for the associated help text for the standard entries, our application only needs to provide help text for the features which are unique to our application.

> Note that Edit does not automatically search the **/usr/lib/NextStep/Resources/English.lproj/Help.store** file. Edit will complain with a **File Not Found** error message when we select any of the standard entries.

Adding a Help directory automatically provides the table of contents and index files

Open the project file of **Words** by double-clicking on **~/Words/Words/PB.project**. Create a **Help** directory in the *language*.**lproj** folder by clicking on **Project** ⇒ **Add Help Directory**. The **Help** directory contains two files, **TableOfContents.rtf** (the table of contents) and **Index.rtfd** (the index in **Rich Text Format Directory**). To add the help text, we need to add RTF files to the **Help** directory and create the necessary links. We can also create markers, although, as always, they are optional.

> An RTF file that contains graphics is stored as an ***Rich Text Format Directory***. Each graphic image is stored as a separate **TIFF** or **EPS** file, and NeXTSTEP stores all of these files in a directory to manage them. The standard index directory (**Index.rtfd**) is a Rich Text Format Directory and .contains many graphics as well as text in Rich Text Format.
>
> Since a **.rtfd** directory appears as a single file (just as an **.app** package) in the Workspace, click **File** ⇒ **Open as Folder** to see its contents.

In ProjectBuilder, double-click on the **Help** entry under the **Other Resources** selection in the Files accessory view to open the **Help** directory. Now create three RTF files for the three help files that we will display.

Help files should be in RTF

Since all help files should be RTF files and RTF files save their window sizes as part of the format, duplicating the files with the Workspace is the easiest way to preserve the window size. The quickest way to duplicate a file is to use **File ⇒ Duplicate** (**Command-d**) in the Workspace. We need to make three copies of the **TableofContents.rtf** file and then modify the text accordingly.

Press **Command-d** to make the first duplicate. Rename this file to **Open.rtf**. Press **Command-d** to duplicate the **Open.rtf** file and rename this to **New.rtf**. Finally, press **Command-d** again to duplicate **New.rtf** and rename this file **Save.rtf**. At this point, the **Help** directory should have five files:

- **Index.rtfd**
- **TableOfContents.rtf**
- **New.rtf**
- **Open.rtf**
- **Save.rtf**.

The last three RTF files in the list (the ones which are related to the commands in **Words**) will have two links to cross-reference with the other two commands. For example, the **New.rtf** file will have two links, one to **Open.rtf**, and one to **Save.rtf**. Each of the three RTF files will also have a marker to specify what text should be highlighted in that given file.

> The **Duplicate** command often does not refresh the File Viewer properly. To rectify this, click on **View ⇒ Update Viewers** (**Command-u**).

Use Command-d in the Workspace to duplicate a file

Select all three files and double-click on them to open them in Edit. Select **New.rtf**, delete the existing text, and modify the text. Figure 10.6 shows the file after it has been modified.

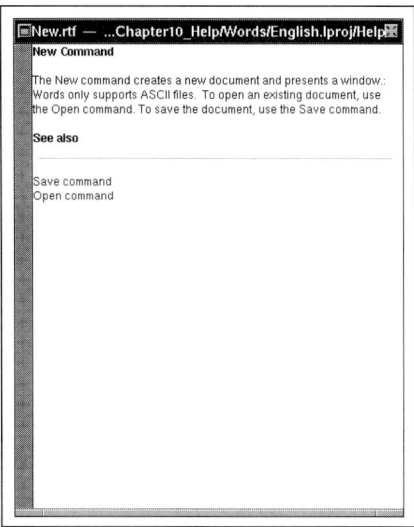

Figure 10.6 The **New.rtf** file after it has been modified

Insert the link into New.rtf

At this point, cross-reference **New.rtf** with **Save.rtf** and **Open.rtf** as follows:

- insert a link before the phrase **Save command** by clicking **Format** ⇒ **Help** ⇒ **Insert Link**.
- at the Link Inspector, click **Set** to display the openpanel.
- select **Save.rtf** as the help file and then click **OK**.
- at the Link Inspector, type **save** for the marker name to specify that the text in **Save.rtf** should be highlighted from the **save** marker until the end of the line.
- repeat this procedure for the **Open** command, except select **Open.rtf** in the openpanel and specify **open** for the marker name.

Insert the marker after inserting the links

With the links to the other two commands inserted, now insert the marker in **New.rtf** as follows:

- click after the word **The** at the start of the paragraph.
- click **Format** ⇒ **Help** ⇒ **Insert Marker** to insert a marker.

- type **new** as the marker and click **OK** to insert a marker.

Figure 10.7 shows the **New.rtf** file with the links and the marker.

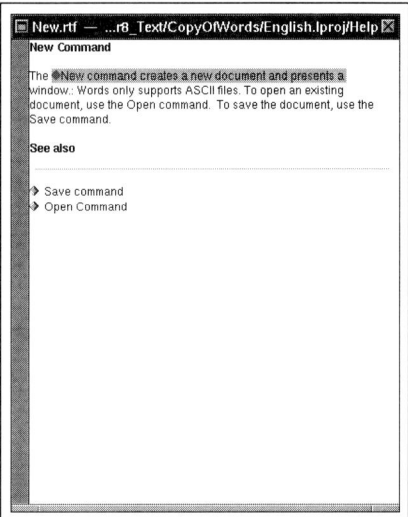

Figure 10.7 The **New.rtf** file with the links and marker

Copy the entire text using **Command-c**. Then in **Open.rtf**, highlight the entire document and use **Command-v** to replace the highlighted text with the text in the pasteboard. Follow these steps to modify the links and marker:

- update the text to reflect the **Open** command.
- insert a marker in **Open.rtf** and name it **open**.
- modify the **See also** section to refer to the **Save command** and the **New command**.
- select **Save.rtf** as the help file for the **Save command** and **save** as the marker.
- select **New.rtf** as the help file for the **New** command and **new** as the marker.

Figure 10.8 shows the **Open.rtf** file with these changes.

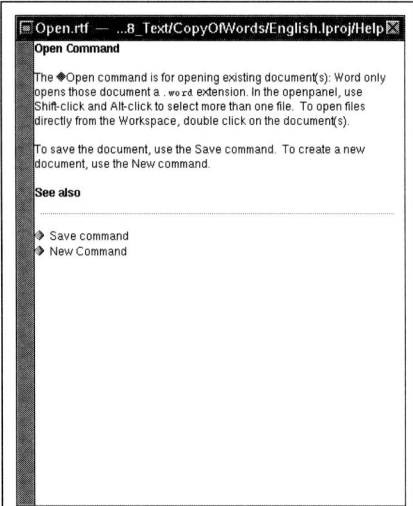

Figure 10.8 The **Open.rtf** file with the links and marker

In the **Save.rtf** file, highlight the entire text and then paste the text copied from the previous step. Follow these steps to update the links and marker:

- update the text to reflect the **Save** command.
- insert a marker in **Save.rtf** and name it **save**.
- modify the **See also** section to refer to the **New command** and the **Open command**.
- select **New.rtf** as the help file for the **New command** and **new** as the marker.
- select **Open.rtf** as the help file for the **Open** command and **open** as the marker.

Figure 10.9 illustrates the **Save.rtf** file with these changes.

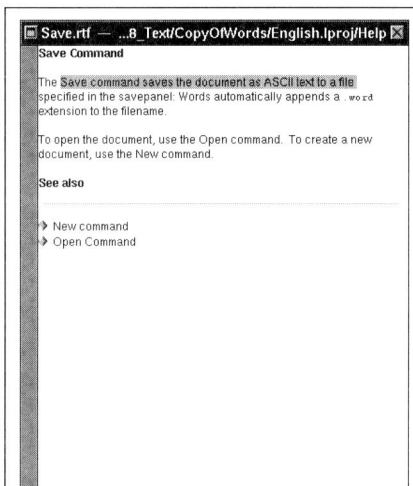

Figure 10.9 The **Save.rtf** file with the links and marker

Now that the help files are created, we can attach then to the user-interface controls. To attach a user-interface control to a help item, first select the control and then select the entry in the table of contents or the index. For the **New** menu option:

- select the menu option.
- select its corresponding help entry, **Creating a new document**, in the table of contents.
- click **Attach** in the Inspector to attach the help file to the menu option.

After creating the help files, attach them to the user-interface controls

Figure 10.10 illustrates this sequence.

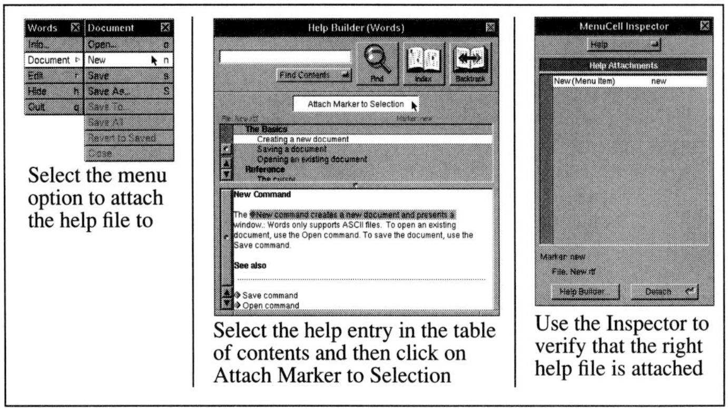

Figure 10.10 Attaching help to the **New** menu option

The on-line help system does not work in InterfaceBuilder's Test Mode

Now repeat this sequence for the **Open** and **Save** menu options. Build the application to verify on-line help facility works (the on-line help system does not work in InterfaceBuilder's **Test Mode**). Note that ProjectBuilder does not need to recompile the application because all of the changes (the help-related files) are stored in the *language*.**lproj** directory, and the application loads this information at runtime.

10.6 Troubleshooting

Here are some problems that can arise and their solutions:

- Changes made to the help files in Edit do not appear in the help files in InterfaceBuilder.
    - **Cause**: InterfaceBuilder only reads the help files in the **Help** directory when it first opens the **.nib** file and caches this information for quicker retrieval. However, InterfaceBuilder does not update this cache.
    - **Solution**: Save the **.nib** file, close it, and then reopen it to force InterfaceBuilder to read the latest version of the help files.
- We cannot select an entry in the table of contents in the HelpBuilder component of InterfaceBuilder.

- **Cause**: There is probably a marker in front of the link. This can be confusing since InterfaceBuilder does not display the markers in the table of contents or index.
- **Solution**: Open **TableOfContents.rtf** (or **Index.rtfd**, as appropriate), click **Format** ⇒ **Help** ⇒ **Display Markers** to display the offending marker. Remove it and save the file. To verify this change took effect, close the **.nib** file in InterfaceBuilder and then reopen it. As we mentioned in the preceding paragraph, changes made to the help files in Edit do not automatically propagate to InterfaceBuilder since InterfaceBuilder, when it first launches, caches the help information. Closing the file and reopening it forces InterfaceBuilder to read the latest information stored in the files.

- Selecting the **Help** menu option produces an error message.
    - **Cause**: By default, an application does not support help.
    - **Solution**: Use ProjectBuilder and InterfaceBuilder to build the help system.
- Although the application has a **Help** directory and contains all of the necessary files, clicking on the **Help** menu option still produces an error message.
    - **Cause**: Some of the components of the help system are probably missing.
    - **Solution**: Verify that the compressed help file, **/usr/lib/NextStep/Resources/English.lproj/Help.store**, exists. If it doesn't, copy it from another system into the appropriate directory.
- The **Help** submenu does not appear in the menus of Edit.
    - **Cause**: Edit is not in **Developer Mode**.
    - **Solution**: Click **Info** ⇒ **Preferences** to display the Preferences panel, select the **Developer Mode** radio button, click **OK**, and restart Edit.
- The **Help** menu options (**Insert Link**, **Insert Markers**, and **Show Markers**) are disabled.

- **Cause**: Edit will only enable the **Help** menu option if the current file is in Rich Text Format, and it has been saved.
- **Solution**: Make the current file Rich Text Format by using **Command-R** then save the file. Insert the link(s) and marker(s) as needed.

• Selecting many of the standard entries (such as **Click for Help**) in the **TableOfContents.rtf** file in Edit produces a **File Not Found** error message in the alert panel.
- **Cause**: Edit only searches the current directory for the help files whereas many of the standard help entries in the table of contents are in **/usr/lib/NextStep/Resources/English.lproj/Help.store**.
- **Solution**: There is no solution because this is a limitation of Edit and the help system.

• The text in the help files displays differently in the help panel than in Edit.
- **Cause**: NeXTSTEP assumes a particular window size for the help file: this window size is that of the **TableOfContents.rtf** or **Index.rtfd** file (these window sizes are identical). Thus, if the window size of a help file is different than the default help panel size, the text wrap will be different since NeXTSTEP resizes the window to match the help panel.
- **Solution**: Instead of creating a new help file, click **File ⇒ Duplicate** (**Command-d**) in the Workspace to duplicate the **TableOfContents.rtf** file (duplicating an RTF or RTFD file preserves its window size). Then update the text, links, and markers as needed.

• The help system does not work in InterfaceBuilder's **Test Mode**.
- **Cause**: This is a limitation of the help system.
- **Solution**: None.

10.7 Suggestions

The application now supports on-line help, although there are still some more features that can be added. Consider the following additions.

10.7.1 Adding the Help Entries to the Index

The newly added help entries are currently only accessible through the table of contents. Add the following entries to the **Index.rtfd** file to make them accessible through the index as well:

- Creating a new document
- Opening a document
- Saving a document.

10.7.2 Creating More Help Entries

Create help entries for the **Truncate** and **Prompt** defaults specified in the Preferences panel, and add these entries to the table of contents and to the index.

10.7.3 Adding Graphics to the Help Files

The help files currently only support text. Add graphics by using the Grab application in **/NextApps**. Grab can capture the contents of the screen (part or whole) or a window and save it to a file. For more info on how to use Grab, launch the application and click **Info** $\Rightarrow$ **Help**.

Grab an image of an openpanel, and save the contents to a file. Then drag this file into **Open.rtf** file; dragging a file into an RTF file automatically converts it into an RTFD file. We then need to modify the link in the **TableOfContents.rtf** file to use **Open.rtfd** instead of **Open.rtf**. Grab a picture of a savepanel, save it, and drag the file into **Save.rtf**. Update the link to use **Save.rtfd** instead of **Save.rtf**.

10.8 Summary

The on-line help system in NeXTSTEP is based on the book metaphor: there is a table of contents, an index, and the text body. All these files are stored in the application's **Help** directory.

To add on-line help to an application, use Edit to create the RTF help files. Afterwards, insert links and markers in these help files to cross-reference them. As the final step, use HelpBuilder in InterfaceBuilder to attach these help files to the appropriate user-interface objects.

Unfortunately, we must compile the application before we can test its on-line help system since it does not work from InterfaceBuilder's **Test Mode**.

10.9 Epilogue

Hurray! You have completed the first leg of your adventure into NeXTSTEP programming. At this point, you should feel comfortable with most of the basics of NeXTSTEP programming, and, as with any other skill, the more you practice, the better you will become. To familiarize yourself further with NeXTSTEP, read the bundled documentation on the classes we have covered: **Object**, **List**, **Application**, **Window**, **View**, **Control**, etc. Additionally, consider exploring the following topics and classes:

- **MenuCell**—the **Words** application currently does not disable the menu options appropriately. That is, the **Save** menu option is still enabled when there is no document to save. The **MenuCell** class provides methods for enabling and disabling menucells as needed.

- **Text**—the **Words** application currently only supports ASCII text. However, the **Text** class offers many methods for working with Rich Text Format as well.

- **SavePanel** and **OpenPanel**—these classes provide methods for customizing the accessory view, although we did not do so in our examples.

- **NXStringTable**—a NXstringtable associates a key with a value. Instead of hardcoding the text messages in an application, consider storing the text and its associated keys in an NXstringtable. This facilitates adapting the application to another language (also known as localization) because all the language-sensitive text is localized to one file. For more information on localization, consult **/NextLibrary/Documentation/NextDev/**

Concepts/Localization.rtfd, the **NXStringTable** class, the **NXBundle** class, and the **NXLocalizedString**() macro.

- **Services**—NeXTSTEP provides a powerful mechanism for applications to communicate with each other: the **Services** menu option. By simply adding this menu option to an application, the application can immediately communicate with other NeXTSTEP applications. For more information on how **Services** work, consult **/NextLibrary/Documentation/NextDev/Concepts/Services.rtf**.

Appendix E lists other resources that are available such as user groups, news forums, mailing lists, etc. Join a user group and meet other NeXTSTEP programmers. Study the examples in **/NextDeveloper/Examples/AppKit** and download examples from the Internet (consult Appendix E for instructions on downloading sample programs). Dissect these programs using the techniques presented in Appendix D. Many of the authors include an e-mail address for support and help.

Above all, good luck and have fun in becoming NeXTSTEP Grand Wizard!

Epilogue

Appendix A
A NeXTSTEP Tutorial

This appendix provides a crash course in NeXTSTEP and shows how to perform basic tasks such as logging in and launching applications. The intent is to familiarize ourselves with NeXTSTEP as quickly as possible. Therefore, we will concentrate on the features rather than the reasoning behind the features (this appendix also takes some liberties with the underlying UNIX operating system). Readers already familiar with how to use the user interface can easily skip this appendix.

Ready? Let's go!

1. Turn on the computer.
2. Type in the user ID and password at the login window (if the system has not been configured with a user account other than **me**, NeXTSTEP automatically logs us in and we can skip this step). Figure 1 shows the NeXTSTEP login window.

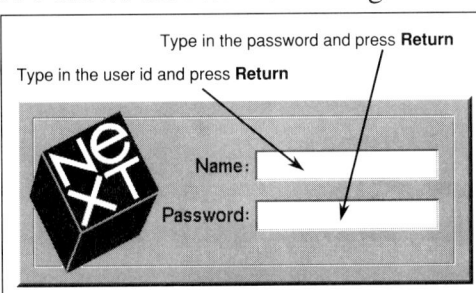

Figure A.1 The NeXTSTEP login window

3. After a few seconds, NeXTSTEP automatically launches the ***Workspace Manager*** (hereafter shortened to the Workspace), the application that allows us to perform most of our daily tasks such as launching applications, organizing files, etc. The

Workspace presents us with a *File Viewer*, a graphical representation of our filesystem. Figure 2 illustrates the initial screen after we are logged in.

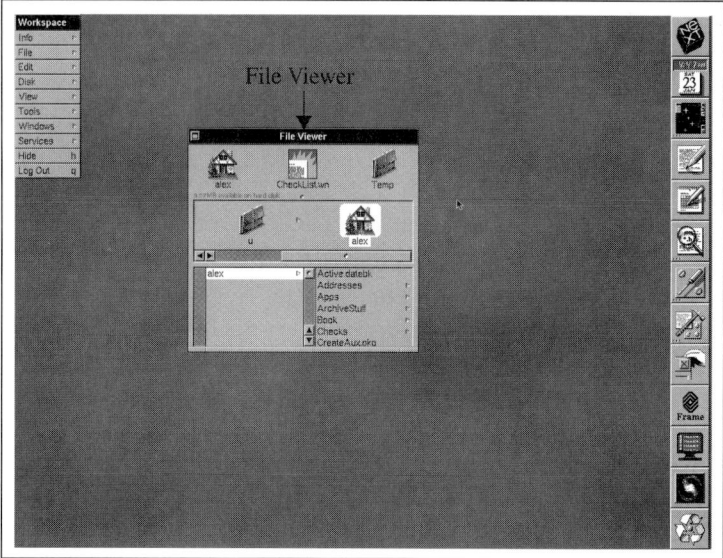

Figure A.2 The initial screen after logging in

4. Use the mouse (the device that looks like a soapbar or a round disk with two buttons attached to the back of the keyboard) to move the cursor around. The cursor should looks like a little arrowhead (▸).

5. NeXTSTEP uses small pictures called *icons*, to represent applications and files. To divide the screen into logical areas, NeXTSTEP defines *windows*, rectangular regions that can be moved as though they were sheets of papers. Windows can overlay each other, and the window on top will obscure a

window underneath it. To issue commands, we usually click one or more times on a window or an icon. Figure 3 illustrates a typical window and some icons.

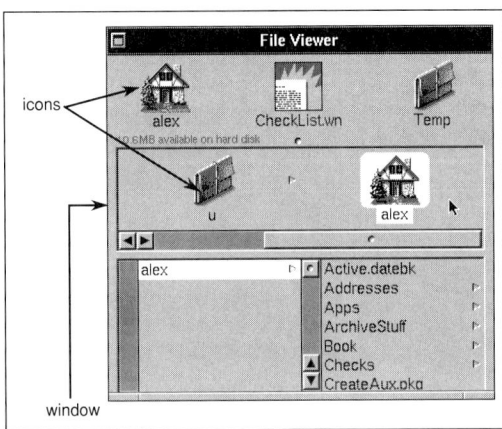

Figure A.3 NeXTSTEP windows and icons

6. Each application has a *Main Menu*, located at the top left edge of the screen. The top entry in the menu is the name of the application, and the other menu options are the commands we can issue. The little arrow ( ) indicates the menu has a submenu. For example, the **Window** menu option has a submenu. To display the submenu, position the cursor over the **Window** menu option and press the left mouse button (if nothing happens, press the right mouse button since NeXTSTEP may have been configured to use the right mouse button instead). Press-

ing a mouse button and releasing it is known as *clicking*. Figure 4 illustrates how to display a submenu by clicking on the parent menu.

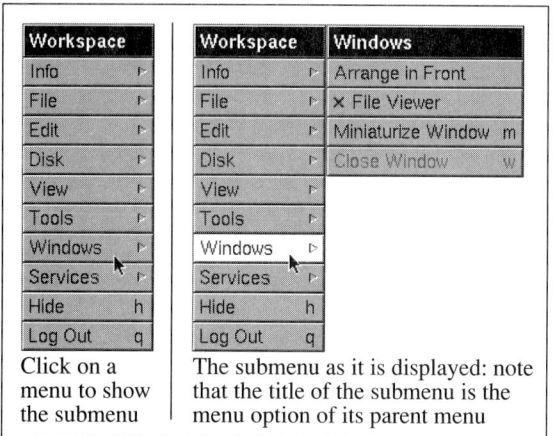

Figure A.4 Displaying a submenu

7. Notice that next to the menu option, **Miniaturize Window**, is a small **m**: this is the *keyboard alternative* for the menu option. Holding down the **Command** key and pressing the letter issues the command as though we had clicked on the menu option. A keyboard alternative provides an alternate way of issuing an often-used command because it is quicker to type a key than to move the cursor to the menu option and then click. Keyboard alternatives are case-sensitive: **Command-m** is different than **Command-M** (the latter requires us to hold down both the **Shift** and **Command** keys while pressing the **m** key).

8. Miniaturize the window by pressing **Command-m**; this miniaturizes the window (the File Viewer) into a small icon at the bottom of screen. Note that the **Miniaturize Window** menu option flashes to indicate that its associated menu option has been issued (we can just as easily miniaturize the window by

clicking on its *miniaturize button*, at the upper left edge of the window). Figure 5 illustrates what happens when we miniaturize a window.

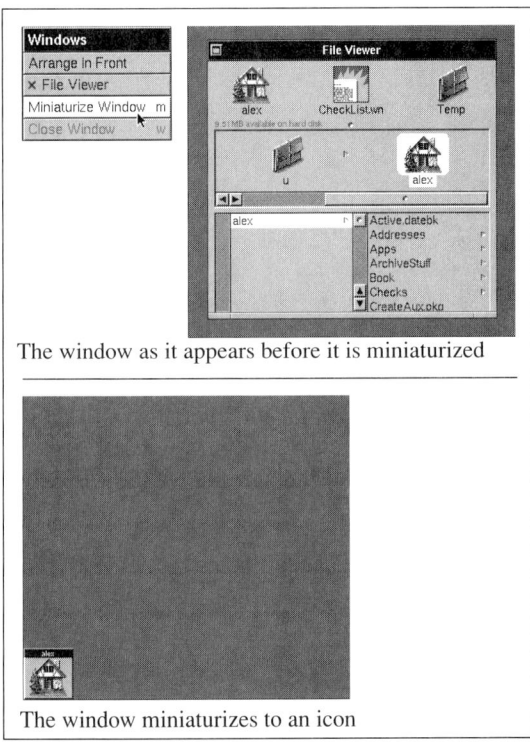

Figure A.5 Miniaturizing a window

9. To restore the window to its normal size, click twice in rapid succession on the icon: this is known as *double-clicking*.

10. Now click the small house icon to show the *folders* (folders can contain files and other folders) that are stored in our *home folder*. The home folder is also referred to as the *home directory*, and is symbolized by the tilde (~). We usually create files to store our data, and we use folders to organize the files. For example, we can create a folder called **Expenses** which contains expenses-related files. Ultimately, all the files (and folders) we create are stored in our home folder (each user has a different home folder). Another user cannot modify the contents (the files and folders) in our home directory and vice versa.

11. NeXTSTEP uses a small arrow ( ) to indicate that clicking on a folder reveals more information (namely, the files and the folders in the current folder). Click on the little computer icon (to select the top folder, also known as the ***root directory***). Then, click on the **NextDeveloper** folder, then **Examples**, **AppKit**, and finally **Lines**. There should be a file named **README.rtf** in the folder. Figure 6 illustrates an abbreviated sequence of the preceding steps.

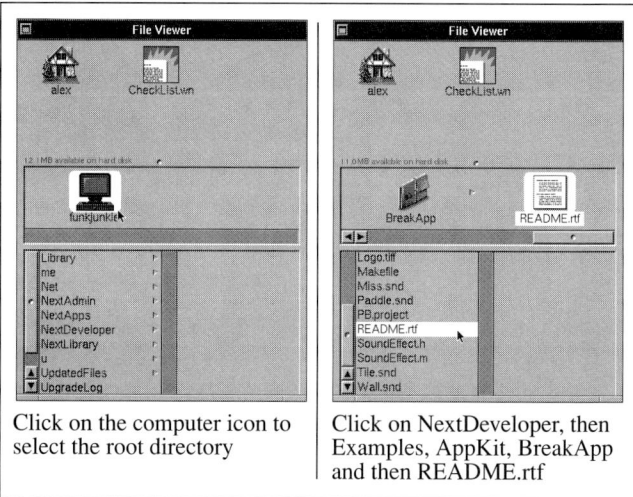

Figure A.6 Display the contents of a folder and selecting a file

12. To open a file, double-click on its icon; this launches the application that created it, which in this case is Edit (the Workspace uses the **.rtf** extension on the filename to determine which application to launch). The cursor may change to a small spinning disk ( ), which means the system is momentarily busy (this cursor is often referred to as the ***wait cursor***).

13. At this point, Edit (the application that created the **README.rtf** file) opens the files and displays them in a window. Note that Edit displays its Main Menu to inform us that it, instead of the Workspace, is now the ***active application***: the active application is the one that interprets all our mouse and keyboard actions.

14. Since the text is too large to fit in the window, NeXTSTEP produces a ***scrollbar.*** Position the cursor on the scrollbar, hold down the mouse button, and pull down downward: holding

down the mouse button and then moving the mouse is known as ***dragging***. Drag the scrollbar down to go to the bottom of the file, and drag it up to go to the top of the file. Dragging the scrollbar to see the contents of a file is known as ***scrolling***. Figure 7 illustrates how to use the scrollbar to scroll through the **README.rtf** file.

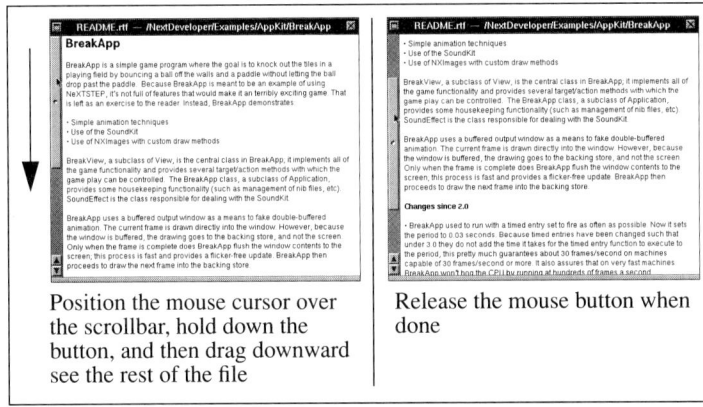

Figure A.7 Scrolling through the **README.rtf** file

15. We can achieve the same effect by ***pressing*** (holding down the left mouse button and releasing when done) the scroll buttons near the bottom left edge of the window. Experiment with scrolling through the file.

16. Note that the ***title bar*** (the small rectangular region at the top of the screen) for this window is black. This indicates that the window is the ***key window***: anything we type will be issued to this window.

17. The title bar contains the name of the file and the folder which contains the file (this folder itself can be contained in another folder still and so forth). The words are the names of the folders, and the slash (/) is a separator (much like a space in text). Therefore, **/NextDeveloper/Examples/AppKit/BreakApp/README.rtf** refers to the **README.rtf** file in the **BrekaApp** folder. **README.rtf** is the filename, and the **/**

NextDeveloper/Examples/AppKit/BreakApp refers to the *path*: the path is basically everything but the filename. Figure 8 illustrates the title bar along with the name in the title bar.

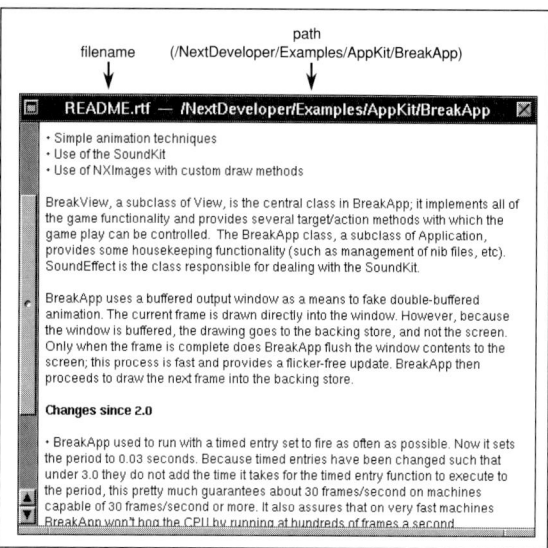

Figure A.8 The title bar contains the filename and the path

18. Rather than modify this document, create a new document by clicking on **Document** ⇒ **New**. This should create a new empty window.

19. Note that this new window becomes the key window (its title bar is black). Thus, anything we type will be issued to this window. Since the file has not been named, Edit uses **UNTITLED** as the name.

20. To insure that we do not modify the **README.rtf** file, close it by clicking on the *close button*, located at the right side of the window's title bar. Closing a window effectively dismisses the file until we open it again. Figure 9 illustrates how to close a window.

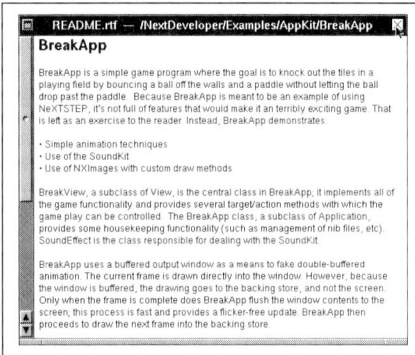

Figure A.9 To close a window, click on the close button, located in the upper right hand of the title bar

21. Type in some text in the new window such as: **NeXTSTEP is really cool!**

22. Note as soon as we type, the close button changes from a complete ☒ to a broken ☒. The latter indicates that the file has been modified since it was last saved. Since this file has not been saved, the close button will always display a ☒.

23. Create another document by pressing **Command-n**. Like most applications, Edit defines **Command-n** as the keyboard alternative for creating a new file.

24. In this new window, type: **This is a test of Edit**. The filename of this new file will be **UNTITLED1**.

25. Select the word **of** by first clicking anywhere on the word: clicking positions the blinking cursor. Now, double-click to highlight the entire word. Figure 10 illustrates how to select a word by double-clicking on it.

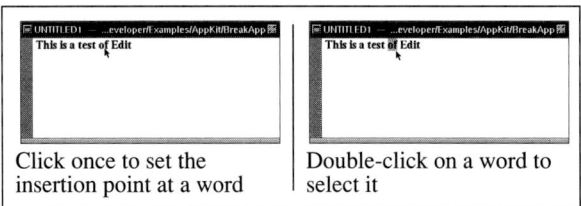

Figure A.10 Double-click a word to select it

26. Now, copy the word **of** with **Command-c**. Then, click at the end of the line and press **Command-v** to paste back the word. Note that Edit automatically inserts a space between the word **Edit** and **of** at the end of the line. Figure 11 illustrates copying and pasting.

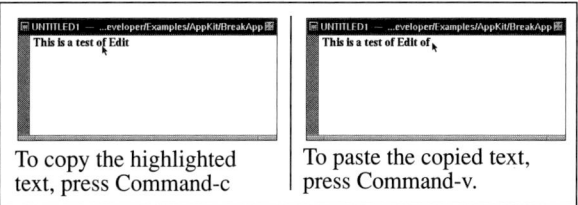

Figure A.11 Copying and pasting the text

27. At this point, the two windows are stacked on top of each other. To bring the **UNTITLED** file to the top, click on its window.

28. Move the **UNTITLED** window to separate it from the **UNTITLED1** window. To move a window, drag it by its title bar.

29. Quit Edit by clicking on **Quit**. Since we have not saved our changes yet, Edit produces an *alert panel*. An alert panel warns us that something about to happen requires our immediate attention; in this case, Edit is going to discard our changes. To insure that we do not ignore the alert panel, NeXTSTEP places the panel above all other windows and makes the alert panel the key window. Like most alert panels, this one has three buttons. The **Cancel** button cancels the **Quit** command

and returns us to Edit. The **Quit Anyway** button tells Edit to discard our changes. The **Review** button allows us to review files which have been modified. Note that the **Review** button contains a small arrow icon ( ) to indicate that this is the default action: when we press **Return**, it is equivalent to clicking on this button. Figure 12 illustrates the alert panel.

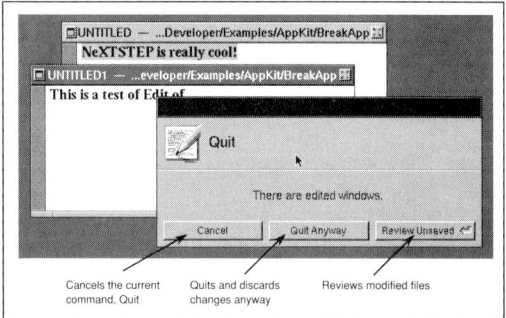

Figure A.12 To get our attention, NeXTSTEP places the alert panel above the other windows

30. Press **Return** to review the modified files. Edit then presents another alert panel to ask us what we wish to do with the current file (which should be **UNTITLED1** unless we have accidentally switched to another window).

31. Click **Don't Save** to discard the changes to **UNTITLED1**. Edit proceeds to place another alert panel. Click **Save** this time to save the **UNTITLED** document.

32. Since this file does not yet have a name, Edit places a *save-panel* to ask us for the filename. Figure 13 shows the savepanel presented by Edit.

Figure A.13 Edit displays a savepanel to ask us where to save the file

33. In the textfield with the blinking cursor, type **/junk/trash**. Since we are attempting to create a new folder, NeXTSTEP then prompts us again with another alert panel. Click **Create** to create the **trash** file in the **junk** folder. After saving our changes, Edit quits, and the Workspace again becomes the active application.

34. At this point, we may think that we want to get rid of our **junk** folder but we are not totally certain. Instead of deleting it (which is irrevocable), we can move it to the ***Recycler***. Recycling the file does not destroy it, but moves it to a special folder. We can always retrieve the recycled file(s) later.

35. To recycle a folder (or a file), select the folder and then drag it to the Recycler, the icon with the three intertwined arrows (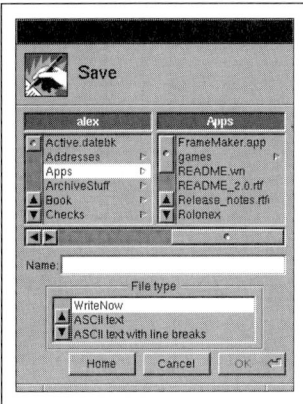). In this case, select the **/junk** folder by clicking on the

computer icon in the File Viewer to select the root directory. Select the **junk** folder and then drag it to the Recycler. Figure 14 illustrates how to recycle a folder.

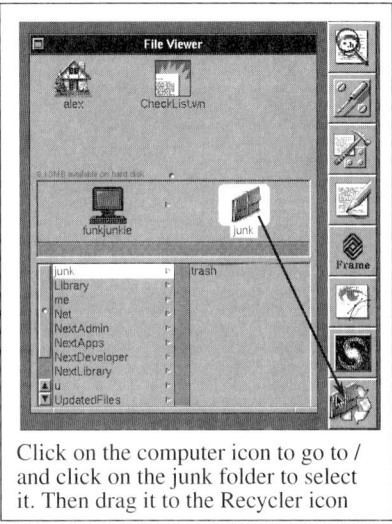

Figure caption (inside figure): Click on the computer icon to go to / and click on the junk folder to select it. Then drag it to the Recycler icon

Figure A.14 To recycle a folder, drag the folder to the Recycler icon

36. To see what is in the Recycler, double-click on its icon: this produces a small window (labeled **Recycler**) that shows the contents of the Recycler. The little sphere in the Recycler icon indicates that the Recycler contains recycled materials. Figure 15 shows how to display the contents of the Recycler.

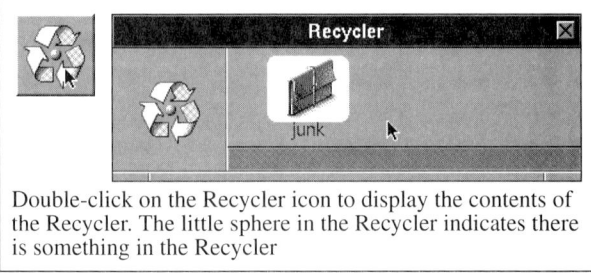

Figure caption (inside figure): Double-click on the Recycler icon to display the contents of the Recycler. The little sphere in the Recycler indicates there is something in the Recycler

Figure A.15 Displaying the contents of the Recycler

37. At this point, we can remove the file from the Recycler and place it back it our filesystem or empty the Recycler, which effectively destroys the file and recovers the disk space occupied by the file. Let's recover the file in another location.

38. Create a new folder in our home directory by first clicking on the home icon. Then press **Command-n**, which creates a new folder named **NewFolder** in the current folder.
39. Rename the folder to something a little more descriptive like **JunkContainer**. To rename the folder, select the text below the folder and then type over it. Press **Return** when finished. Figure 16 illustrates how to rename a folder.

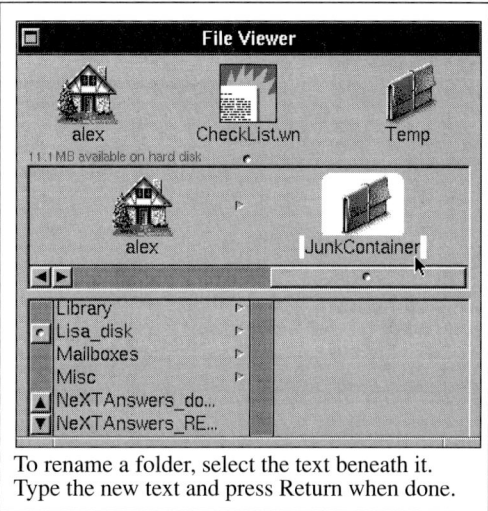

Figure A.16 Renaming the folder from **NewFolder** to **JunkContainer**

40. To move the **junk** folder from the Recycler to the **JunkContainer** folder, drag the **junk** folder and place it over the **JunkContainer** folder. The **JunkContainer** folder opens up to inform us that it is receiving the **junk** folder. Figure 17 illustrates how to retrieve a folder from the Recycler.

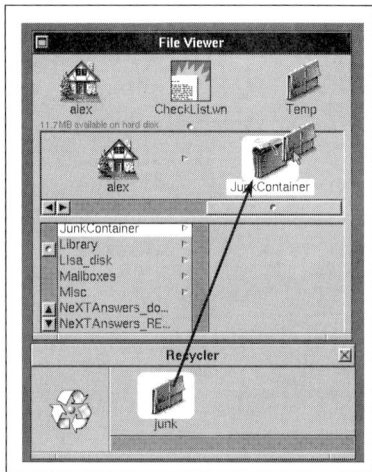

Figure A.17 Recovering the **junk** folder from the Recycler

41. Now log out by clicking **Log Out**. NeXTSTEP then presents an alert panel for verification because logging out terminates all applications that are running. Press **Return** to log out of NeXTSTEP. If we have any files that are modified, the owning application will allow us a chance to save the file(s).

Voilà! We have just completed the NeXTSTEP crash course. Of course, there are many more features of NeXTSTEP, and we have barely scratched the surface. However, this brief introduction provides enough background for us to use NeXTSTEP to effectively use the materials in this book. For more information on NeXTSTEP as a user's environment, consult the bundled *User's Guide* or the books listed in Appendix E.

Appendix B
Tools of the Trade

This appendix discusses additional tools to complement the ones we have already discussed. These tools include:

- Edit—a source code editor.
- Digital Librarian—a tool that can index and search documents based on a keyword.
- HeaderViewer—an application that can browse the header files of the various classes.
- Terminal—a VT100 terminal emulator.
- make—a command generator often used for project management.

This appendix does not list all the commands in each of these tools. Instead, it will cover the most commonly used features, offers tips, and points out the limitations of the tools.

B.1 Edit

Edit is a source code editor with some innovative features:

- an *implicit expansion dictionary* for expanding variable names, method names, and reserved words.
- a *customizable expansion dictionary* for typing in entire blocks of text with a few keystrokes.
- the ability to contract the listing so we can quickly determine the structure of an Objective-C application.

Edit has another powerful feature, the **Gdb** (GNU debugger) menu, which is covered in Appendix D.

B.1.1 Using the Implicit Expansion Dictionary

This feature allows us to type part of a word and then press the **ESC** key to complete the rest of the word. Edit can complete method names, variable names, and reserved words such as **for**,

Edit has can expand words

struct, etc. This feature reduces the number of keystrokes and the likelihood of syntax errors since Edit will only produce words that already exist in the current file. As we will see in the next section, we can create a dictionary to expand any word, whether it exists in the current file or not.

Word expansion is only available in Developer Mode

Before we can use this feature, however, we must switch Edit to **Developer Mode** (for more information on how to enable the **Developer Mode**, see Chapter 10). Then launch Edit by double-clicking on **/NextApps/Edit.app**. Open **~/Words/Document.m** (any other file would do, but we're using this particular file so we can compare results). Follow these steps to demonstrate the internal expansion dictionary:

- position the cursor at the blank line above the **@end** statement.
- type **str** and press **ESC**: Edit will then cycle through all of the keywords (in **Document.m**) that start with **str.** There is only one, **stream**. Figure B.1 illustrates this sequence.

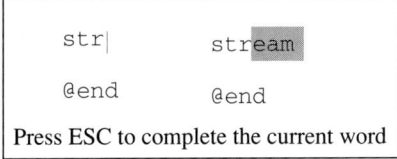

Figure B.1 Using the implicit Expansion Dictionary

> To display the number of a given line, position the cursor on the line and press **Command-l**, which produces a panel with a line number. To go to a line, type in the line number in the textfield of the panel and click **Select** or press **Return**.

Note that this feature has some limitations:

- the file must first be saved, i.e., if we are creating a new file, we must first save it, and then reopen it.
- the file must be a C or an Objective-C file (**.c**, **.h** or **.m**)
- Edit requires a minimum number of characters before it will complete the rest of the word. For example, typing **s** and then pressing **ESC** will not work, but typing **se** and then pressing **ESC** will complete to **self**.

B.1.2 Customizing the Expansion Dictionary

The implicit dictionary can only expand one word, and the word must already exist within the file. By creating an explicit expansion dictionary, we can extend this feature to type in an entire block of text. To create a key in the expansion dictionary, launch Edit and then click **Utilities** ⇒ **Expert** ⇒ **Expansion Dictionary** to display the expansion panel. For this example, we will create a dash (**-**) key to produce a template for an instance method that returns **self** since that is the most common occurrence.

Type **-** in the textfield of the Expansion Dictionary panel. Then click in the scrollview to type in the text that the **-** (followed by **ESC**) should expand to. Type in the following text (there is a space after the **-**):

Expanded text for the **-** key

```
- 
{
  return self;
}
```

The explicit expansion dictionary is more powerful than the implicit word expansion feature

Customizing the Expansion Dictionary

Click **Add** to add the key and its associated expansion to the Expansion Dictionary. Figure B.2 illustrates this entire sequence.

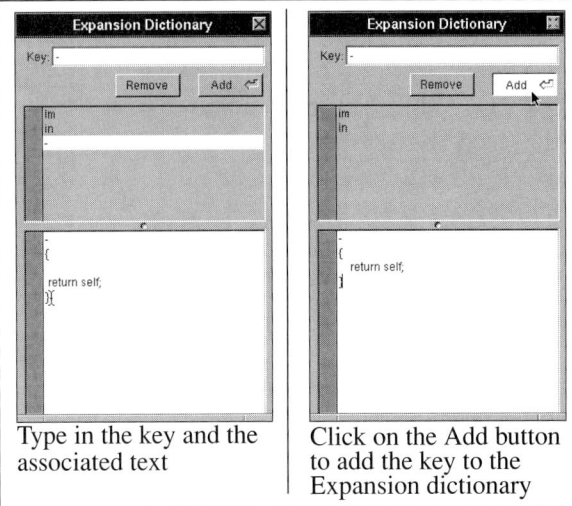

Figure B.2 Adding an entry to the Expansion Dictionary

> This information is stored in the **~/.editdict** file. However, instead of editing this file directly, use the panel provided by Edit.

To test this, open a new file, type **-**, and press **ESC**. Edit should create a template for an instance method and position the cursor at the end of the expanded text (after the **}**). Figure B.3 illustrates this sequence.

```
- |          -
            {
                    return self;
            } |
```
Type in the key (-) and press ESC to expand the text

Figure B.3 Using an entry from the Expansion Dictionary

With this technique, we can use the plus (**+**) as a key for a class method, **in** as the key for a header template, and **im** as the key for an implementation template, etc. For the class method, the key should be + and the expansion should be the following (there should be a space after the +):

Expanded text for the + key

```
+
{
  return self;
}
```

For the implementation template, the key should be **im** and the expansion should be the following:

Expanded text for the im key

```
#import <appkit/appkit.h>

@implementation :

{
}

@end
```

For the header template, we need to omit the class name from the **#import** statement since we cannot determine what the class name is. Therefore, the key should be **in** and the expansion should be the following:

Expanded text for the in key

```
#import ".h"

@interface :

{
}

@end
```

We can use this feature to eliminate a lot of tedious typing and reduce errors.

> One drawback of this feature is that the cursor will always be at the end of the expanded text; it would be more useful if we could specify where the cursor will be when Edit expands the text. For example, in the instance method template, we could save some keystrokes if the cursor would position itself immediately in front of the period in the **#import** statement.

B.1.3 Contracting and Expanding the Listing

Use Command-0 to contract the listing

When we first encounter a large implementation file, the number of lines in the file can be overwhelming. Edit offers a feature that allows us to condense either the entire file or a selected portion of it to help us manage the complexity. To demonstrate this feature, open **~/Words/Document.m** file. Now click on **Format ⇒ Structure ⇒ Contract All (Command-0)**. This condenses all of the statements in a method, leaving only the method name; Edit produces a small arrowhead to indicate that a method is contracted. By looking at the contracted listing, we can easily determine the structure of the program. Figure B.4 illustrates what a file with contracted methods looks like.

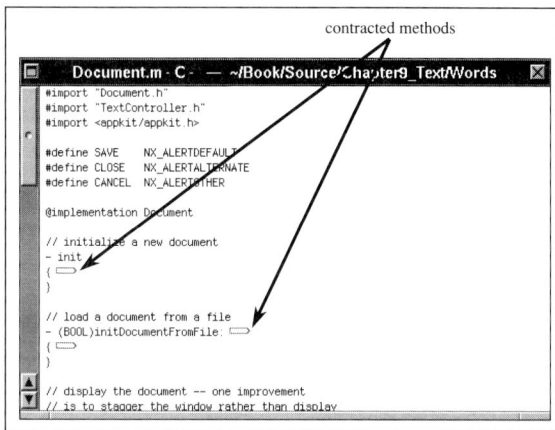

Figure B.4 Edit displays only the name of the method when the method is contracted

To display the contracted text, simply click on **Format** ⇒ **Structure** ⇒ **Expand All** (**Command-9**). Another useful feature is to be able to control what portion of text is contracted. For example, we may want to contract a particularly long method so that we can scroll through the file quicker. To contract the currently selected text, highlight the text and click **Format** ⇒ **Structure** ⇒ **Contract Sel**. To redisplay the contracted region, double-click on the arrowhead icon that represents the contracted text or click **Format** ⇒ **Structure** ⇒ **Expand Sel**.

Use Command-9 to expand the listing

B.2 Digital Librarian

Since the Digital Librarian (hereafter referred to as Librarian and often abbreviated as DL) can scan many documents quickly, it is indispensable for finding documentation on a particular topic. When we first launch Librarian, it displays a shelf with various folders (the shelf is a ***bookshelf***); Librarian refers to each folder in the bookshelf as a ***target***.

A target is a folder to be searched

Using Librarian to search a folder is quite straightforward; select one or more targets, type in the search string, and then press the

Search button. To add a target to the bookshelf, simply drag a folder from the Workspace and place it in an empty slot on the bookshelf.

Searching an indexed file is quicker than searching an unindexed file

Although Librarian can search any folder or file, it is typically used to *index* a folder and then search it. Indexing a folder is to build a table of the relevant search strings associated with the files in which they appear in. Searching an indexed folder is considerably quicker than searching an unindexed folder: the former action consists of reading only the index (stored in the **.index.store** file in the folder) to determine which files contain the search string while the latter consists of reading each file in the folder to determine which file contains the search string.

> Librarian intentionally ignores common articles and prepositions, such **a**, **an**, **the**, **of**, **with**, and other common words in building the index.

There are two ways of indexing a folder:

• using the **ixbuild** command like **ixbuild folder**.

- double-click on the target and then click on the **Set Up** button in the Target Inspector; an indexed target is labeled with a Roman numeral **I**. Figure B.5 illustrates this sequence.

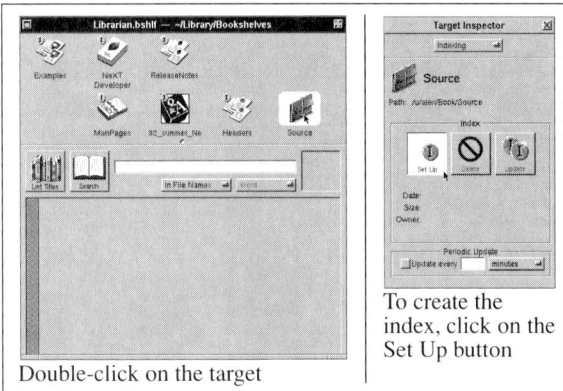

Figure B.5 Indexing an unindexed target in Librarian

> Since the indexing algorithm has changed in NeXTSTEP 3.0, the indices for targets indexed before 3.0 must be updated. To do so, select the target and then click on the **Update** button.

Ideally, the standard bookshelf in our home directory (**~/Library/Bookshelves/Librarian.bshlf**) should contain at least the following indexed targets (the order is not important):

- **NeXTDeveloper** (**/NextLibrary/Documentation/NeXTDev**)— this folder contains eight other folders:
    - **Assembler**—documentation on the assembler.
    - **Concepts**—documentation on general concepts such as drawing, the Application Kit, etc. This is the **Concepts** manual that was included with NeXTSTEP 1.0 and 2.0.
    - **DevTools**—documentation on the various development tools, such as IconBuilder, ProjectBuilder, InterfaceBuilder, Terminal, etc.
    - **Examples**—minimal source code for various examples including a small program that demonstrates Objective-C and some support files for the InterfaceBuilder tutorial in Chapter 8 of the **Concepts** manual.

- **GeneralRef**—general reference materials including all of the classes in the various kits (Application Kit, Common classes, 3DKit, DBKit, et al.), data formats, system bitmaps, etc.
- **OSSoftware**—documentation on the Mach operating system.
- **ReleaseNotes** (see the bullet marked **Developer RelNotes**)—release notes and last minute changes to the documentation. Note that even though this folder is in the **NeXTDeveloper** folder, it is not included in the index. To search the release notes, update the index (using **ixbuild** or the **Update** button in the Target Inspector) to include the release notes or add the release notes as another target on the shelf.
- **UserInterface**—guidelines on which objects to use in designing a NeXTSTEP-compliant user interface.

- **Developer RelNotes** (**/NextLibrary/Documentation/NextDev/ReleaseNotes**)—see the note above.
- **ManPages** (**/NextLibrary/Documentation/Unix/ManPages**)—the **man** pages for the UNIX utilities.
- **Headers** (**/NextDeveloper/Headers**)—header (**.h**) files for all of the UNIX functions and NeXTSTEP methods. Useful for determining the return type and parameters of a function or a method.
- **Examples** (**/NextDeveloper/Examples**)—bundled source code for various kits including the Application Kit, DBKit, et al. Useful when we need to search how a particular method is actually used in a working application.

> Another useful target is the quarterly **NeXTAnswers**, which contains commonly asked questions and their answers. For more information on how to obtain the NeXTAnswers from the archives, see Appendix E.

Librarian also supports a limited form of word expansion

B.2.1 Expanding the Search String

Librarian also supports a limited form of word expansion. That is, we can type in a word and then press **ESC** to cycle through all of the words stored in the index of the currently selected target(s) that start with that particular prefix. For example, select the **NeXTDev** target, type in **view**, and then press **ESC**. The following list contains the possible words which start with the **view** prefix:

- **view***angle*
- **view***er*
- **view***frame*
- **view***ful*
- **view***ing*
- **view***point*
- **view***sizechanged*

These seven words are contained in the index file (**.index.store**) of the **NeXTDev** folder.

B.2.2 Limitations of Digital Librarian

Even though Librarian is a powerful tool, it lacks some critical features including:

- multiple-word searches—we cannot specify more than one word as the search criteria. This can quite frustrating because many concepts are inherently multiple words such as content view. We can specify **content && view** as the search criteria but this returns all files that contain the word **content** and **view**. For example, assume that there is a hypothetical **document.rtf** file with the following text:

A hypothetical document.rtf file

```
We are content to simply view the file.
```

Librarian would consider this file to pass the **content && view** search criteria since the file contains the words **content** and **view**. Obviously, this is quite different then what we are searching for.

- case-sensitive searches—when we specify **window** as the search word, Librarian finds all occurrences of **window** and **Window**.

Unfortunately, this returns too many occurrences since at times we may be searching for **window** (as in the window object) and other times may be looking for **Window** (as in the class).

B.3 HeaderViewer

HeaderViewer is ideal for determining whether a class implements a method

HeaderViewer is not as well documented as the other tools in this appendix. In fact the only documentation seems to be the brief text in the Info panel. Although HeaderViewer has many uses, its ability to quickly determine whether a class implements a particular method makes it an indispensable tool in a dynamically-bound environment like Objective-C (an application crashes if an object receives a message and it or its superclasses does not implement the method).

Launching HeaderViewer produces a browser with a textfield. Figure B.6 illustrates the initial screen in HeaderViewer.

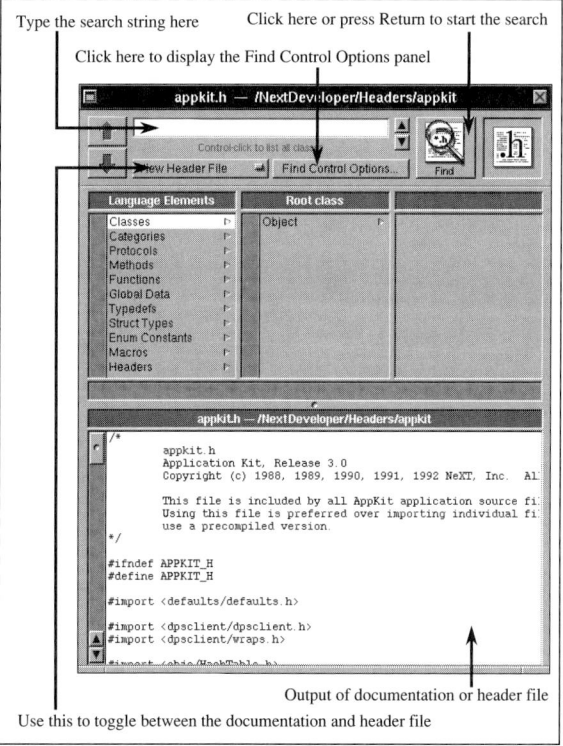

Figure B.6 The initial screen of HeaderViewer (the Browser view)

Upon start-up, HeaderViewer automatically prints the information for the selected precompiled header file. By default, HeaderViewer automatically opens **/NextDeveloper/Headers/ appkit/appkit.p**, the precompiled header file for the Application Kit (the unprecompiled version is **appkit.h**). If we use the **Open** command to open another precompiled header file such as **/NextDeveloper/Headers/dbkit/dbkit.p** (this contains all the header files related to DBKit), then HeaderViewer would display that file's contents instead.

HeaderViewer automatically opens appkit.p

> Note that HeaderViewer expects a precompiled header file and will quit abruptly if we open a regular header file. For example, assume we open **/NextDeveloper/Headers/dbkit.h**. HeaderViewer will produce a panel to ask if we want to precompile this file. If we close the panel, HeaderViewer will abruptly quit.

B.3.1 Language Elements

There are eleven different entries in the first column of the browser, which HeaderViewer refers to as *language elements*. The language elements are not sorted alphabetically, but the entries under each language element are alphabetized. The eleven language elements are:

There are eleven language elements

- **Classes**—shows a hierarchy of classes starting with the **Object** class. Using this, we can easily determine the inheritance path of any class. By default, this lists all the classes in a hierarchical fashion, starting with the **Object** class. To list all the classes in alphabetical order, **Control**-click on the **Object** class.
- **Categories**—lists all of the categories. As explained in Chapter 2, a category can be used to add methods to an existing class without subclassing.
- **Protocols**—lists all of the protocols. A protocol is a list of methods a class claims to implement. Protocols are a way to promote the reuse of a design.
- **Methods**—lists all of the methods in the various classes. This is probably the most used feature of HeaderViewer.

- **Functions**—lists all the functions including:
  - single C operators such as **PSstroke()**
  - **NX** functions such as **NXWriteDefault()**
  - UNIX system calls such as **malloc()**.
- **Global Data**—lists all of the global data such as **NXApp**.
- **Typedefs**—lists all of the type definitions such as **NXEvent**, the event record, and **BOOL**, the Boolean type.
- **Struct Types**—lists the **structs** from which the previous **Typedefs** are defined. For example, for the **NXEvent** type definition, there is a corresponding **_NXEvent struct**.
- **Enum Constants**—contains enumerated constants; many of these are used internally by the Application Kit and do not generally concern us.
- **Macros**— macros that deal mainly with advanced features such as byte swapping and determining the processor of a particular machine.
- **Headers**—lists the individual header files that make up the precompiled **appkit.p** file.

B.3.2 Using the Find Controls Options panel

The Find Control Options button limits the search

Using the Find Control Options panel (press the **Find Control Options** button to display the panel), we can specify which language element(s) HeaderViewer should display when it finds a match. That is, when we enter a search string, we can specify whether we want the methods that match that particular string, only the classes or any combination thereof. Figure B.7 shows the Find Control Options panel of HeaderViewer.

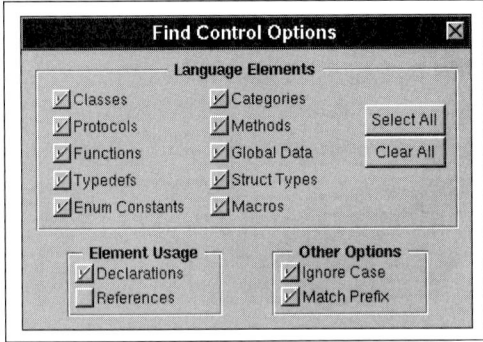

Figure B.7 The Find Control Options panel of HeaderViewer

> Note that the panel only contains ten of the eleven language elements. This is not an oversight; the last entry, **Headers**, lists all the header files that constitute the **appkit.h** file, the unprecompiled version of the **appkit.p** file. Since HeaderViewer automatically searches the entire **appkit.p** file by default, there is no point in specifying whether HeaderViewer should search the header files listed in the **Headers** entry or not.
>
> This panel is not the same as a Preferences panel since HeaderViewer does not preserve the settings between sessions. Additionally, any changes we make to the options take effect immediately rather than the next time the application is

Most of the selections in the panel are straightforward, although some do need further clarification:

- **Elements Usage**
    - **Declarations**—search for declarations that match the search string.
    - **References**—search for references that use the search string.
- **Other Options**

Using the Find Controls Options panel

- **Ignore Case**—ignore the case during searching. That is, **window** should match **Window**, **WINdow**, or any other permutation.
- **Match Prefix**—find words that start with the search string. For example, **window** should match **windowWillClose:**.

Toggle between the List view and the Browser view as needed

As an example, type **window** in the textfield and press **Return**. Assuming we have not changed the default settings—everything should be selected except for the **References** switchbutton—HeaderViewer returns with thirty-one occurrences. Note that HeaderViewer changes to another view, the List view, to display the information more effectively. To toggle between the two views, click **Header** ⇒ **Browse** (**Command-B**) and **Header** ⇒ **List** (**Command-L**). Figure B.8 shows the results of searching for **window**.

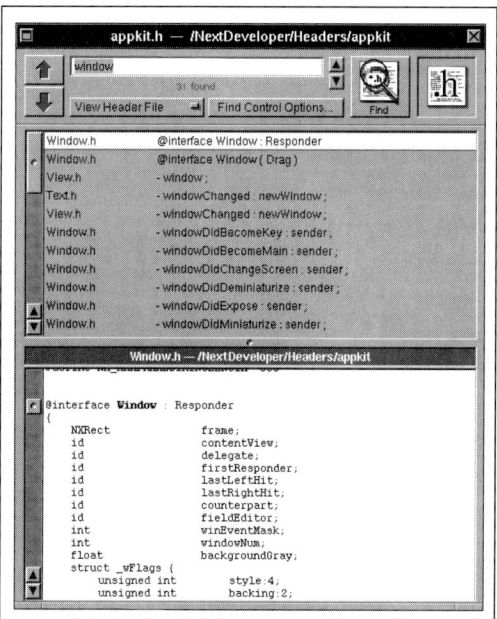

Figure B.8 The List view of HeaderViewer

Now, click on the **References** switchbutton to indicate that we also want references as well as declarations that contain **window**. This should return thirty-seven matches. The difference between a declaration and a reference is as follows: a declaration declares the variable specified by the search string while a reference uses the search string as a type, or more specifically, a class name. The following list contains declarations with the word **window** (recall that, by default, HeaderViewer ignores case):

Declarations with **window**

```
- @interface Window:Responder
- window;
- windowWillClose:sender;
```

This list contains references to the word **window**:

References to **window**

```
- @interface Panel:Window
- Window *_window;
```

Now click on the **Classes** button to indicate that we don't want classes that contain **window** and press **Return**. HeaderViewer should return thirty matches (the declaration for the **Window** class is removed). To narrow the search some more, click on the **Methods** button to indicate that we don't methods that start with **window** and press **Return**. HeaderViewer should return only one match, the **Drag** category for extending the **Window** class. Now click on the **Category** switchbutton to indicate that we don't want any categories that start with **window**. HeaderViewer should return zero matches. By looking at what buttons are still selected, we can conclude that those remaining language elements do not contain any references to **window**. That is, there are no **protocols**, **functions**, **typedefs**, **enumerated constants**, **global data**, **structs**, or **macros** that define anything with the word **window**.

B.3.3 HeaderViewer vs. Digital Librarian

Initially, HeaderViewer and Librarian may seem to overlap in functionality. That is, if we need to find documentation on a class, say **Window**, we can use either tool. In Librarian, we can type in **Window**, use the popuplist to specify that we are searching for filenames rather than text, and press **Return**. In HeaderViewer,

HeaderViewer and Librarian have different uses

we can type in **Window** (or **window**, depending on whether the **Ignore Case** button is selected or not) and then press **Return**. However, on closer inspection, the two tools are actually quite distinct.

> In our example, typing only **window** in Librarian returns six matches. Two of these include **UserInterface/ 01_VisualGuide/_Windows.rtfd** and **Concepts/Performance/ListingForNXWindowServerMemory.rtf**. To limit the search, append a **.rtf** extension to the search string (**window.rtf**) since the documentation for each class is the name of the class appended with a **.rtf** extension. Note that some classes, such as **Form**, have a **.rtfd** extension, but using **Form.rtf** would also match **Form.rtfd**.
>
> Unfortunately, this technique is not very useful when we are consulting the documentation for the development tools. For example, we know that there is a document called **Edit.rtfd** for the Edit application, but typing in **Edit.rtfd** returns only that particular file. There are many other associated documentation files for the Edit application such as **_UsingTemplates.rtfd**. How do we access these? The easiest way to do this is to take advantage of the fact that each development tool is stored under a separate folder under **DevTools**. For Edit, the folder name is **04_Edit**. Therefore, to find all the documentation related to Edit, use **DevTools/04_Edit** as the filename. To see the names of the other folders, use **DevTools** to list the containing folder, and scroll through the output.

Librarian is useful for finding general information

Librarian is useful for finding general documentation for a particular topic. For example, to determine how to use the **Window** class works or how a window displays itself to the screen, use Librarian. However, to determine whether the **Window** class implements a particular method (such as **setContentView**) or what the superclasses of **Window** are, or what methods start with **window**, use HeaderViewer.

HeaderViewer does not provide documentation to the C functions

Another limitation of HeaderViewer is that it does not have the documentation for the C functions. For example, if we specify

NXRunAlertPanel as the search string in HeaderViewer, we can view the header file in which **NXRunAlertPanel** is declared, but HeaderViewer cannot access the documentation. In this case, we have no choice but to use Librarian.

B.4 Terminal

While NeXTSTEP provides good mouse-driven tools for program development, there are occasions when it is more convenient to use the command-line interface to access various utilities like **vi** and **emacs**. The primary tool for issuing commands to the operating system is Terminal, a VT100 terminal emulator; the default shell is **csh**, the C shell. Instead of documenting the other tools that are available from the command-line interface such as **vi**, **emacs**, and **make**—these UNIX utilities are already documented by other sources—we will concentrate instead on features which Terminal provides but other terminal emulators lack:

- copying text
- interacting with the Workspace
- interacting with HeaderViewer
- interacting with Librarian.

Terminal has some special features that other terminal emulators lack

B.4.1 Copying Text

NeXTSTEP provides us the following interface for copying text: highlight the text, use **Command-c** to copy the text, and then use **Command-v** to paste the text in the destination. However, there are two drawbacks to this technique:

- Terminal converts all tabs to spaces, which can be disastrous when we are working with **Makefile**s (for more information on **Makefile**s, see "The make Utility" on page 470.). That is, if we highlight text from a **Makefile** in Terminal, paste it into a **Makefile** window in Edit, save the file, and then try to use the **Makefile**, **make** will produces some fairly terse error messages (**Must be a separator on line** *n*).
- the amount of text we want to paste may be larger than the screen. Thus, we would have to highlight the text, use

Command-c to copy the text, **Command-v** to paste the text (the pasteboard can only hold one copy of a buffer at a time), and then repeat these two steps. However, this sequence is tedious, not to mention error-prone.

Use cat to list an entire file to stdout

The easiest way to preserve tabs while copying text from Terminal is to use the **copy** command, which copies *stdout* to the pasteboard. In UNIX, **stdout** specifies where the output of a command is displayed. In most cases, **stdout** for a given command defaults to the screen. The command that is actually issued when we use **Command-c** is **copy**. Thus, what we want to do is list the contents of a file to **stdout** and then send the output to **copy**. Using the output of one command as input to another command is referred to as *piping*: piping is symbolized by the vertical bar (|), which is also referred to as a pipe.

To list the contents of a file to **stdout**, use the **cat** command. To redirect the output, use | and then specify the command to pipe to, which in this case is **copy**. Thus, these two commands copy the contents of a file to the pasteboard:

Copying the contents of a file to the pasteboard

```
% cat file | copy
```

> Don't confuse the **copy** command with the **cp** command. The former is unique to NeXTSTEP and is used to copy the contents of a file for pasting with **Command-v.** The latter is a UNIX command used for copying file(s) in the filesystem.

To paste the text, use **Command-v** as normal. To place part of the file on the pasteboard, use another command, *sed* (which stands for stream editor). Like **cat**, **sed**'s **stdout** is the screen. Let's us use **sed** to print part of a file, lines **1** through **10**:

Printing lines **1** through **10** to stdout with **sed**

```
% sed -n '1,10p' file
```

The parameters to **sed** actually makes more sense backwards: **'1,10p'** tells **sed** that we are interested in lines **1** through **10** and that **sed** should print (the **p** following the **10** means to print) the results of the expression to **stdout**. The **-n** flag is an additional flag needed when we are using the **p** command (not entirely true, but close enough for our discussion). The '' around the numbers are a safeguard, in case the shell tries to expand the expression.

Therefore, to copy lines **1** through **10** to the pasteboard, use:

Copying lines **1** through **10** to the pasteboard

```
% sed -n '1,10p' file | copy
```

Using this technique, we can copy a large range of text with a single command. For example, to copy lines **50** through **900**, we can use:

Copying lines **50** through **900** to the pasteboard

```
% sed -n '50,900p' file | copy
```

Of course, all these examples assume that we know what line numbers we are interested in. How do we find out what the line number of a given line is? There are several ways:

- open the file in Edit, use **Command-l** to bring up the Line panel.
- use **sed** with the = parameter, which prints the line number at the start of each line as shown in the following fragment:

Printing line numbers in the output

```
% sed = 'p' file
```

By not specifying any line numbers to the **p** command, we are telling **sed** we are interested in the entire file.

B.4.2 Messaging the Workspace

One of the most useful features Terminal offers is the ability to paste the path of the currently selected folder (in the File Viewer) into the current shell. This feature is useful if we need to quickly change to a given directory (via the **cd** command) on the command-line interface. To use this feature, perform the following steps:

- launch Terminal and open a new shell by clicking **Shell** ⇒ **New** (**Command-n**).
- type **cd** followed by a space.
- select the desired folder in the File Viewer. For this example, select **/me/Mailboxes**.
- drag this folder into the Terminal shell, and Terminal automatically prints the directory, which is **/me/Mailboxes**.
- press **Return** to execute the command as normal.

Figure B.9 illustrates this sequence.

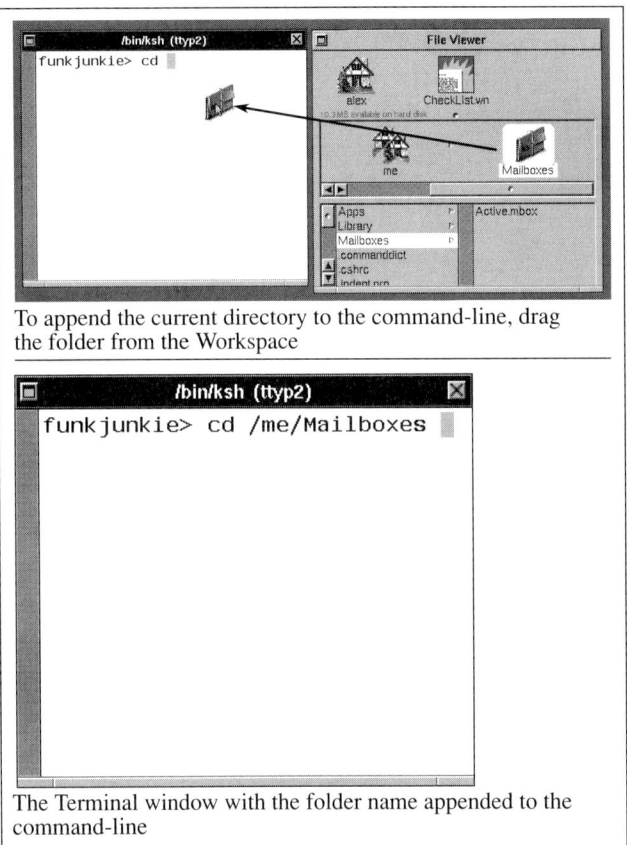

Figure B.9 Appending the current directory in Terminal by dragging from the Workspace

B.4.3 Messaging HeaderViewer

To access HeaderViewer from Terminal, simply highlight some text and click **Services** ⇒ **HeaderViewer** ⇒ **Find in appkit.h** (**Command-?** is the keyboard alternative). This launches HeaderViewer and displays the documentation pertaining to the highlighted text. Note that if the word can be interpreted as a class name or a method, HeaderViewer will choose the latter. For example, if we highlight the word **window**, HeaderViewer will display the documentation for the **View** class, since this class defines a **window** method. Using this technique, we can easily determine if a class implements a particular method.

> Use Command-? to message HeaderViewer

Note that Terminal is the only application that can message HeaderViewer with **Command-?**. Most applications use this as the keyboard alternative for the Help facility. For more information on the on-line help facility, see Chapter 10.

B.4.4 Messaging Digital Librarian

Use Command-F to message Librarian

To use the Digital Librarian to search its currently selected target(s), highlight the desired word and then click **Services** ⇒ **Digital Librarian** ⇒ **Search** (**Command-F**). This is the equivalent of typing in some text and then clicking the **Search** button.

B.5 The make Utility

make is a commands generator

The *make* utility is a command generator that allows us to automate many tasks that occur during the development cycle. A project usually includes many files, and in the course of development, we modify the files, compile them and we then—more often than not—repeat this cycle. However, since we rarely modify *all* the files in a project, it would be unproductive to recompile and relink every single file. Instead, NeXTSTEP should only compile those files that have changed since the previous compilation.

B.5.1 The Makefile

ProjectBuilder automatically generates and updates the Makefile

Like most development environments, NeXTSTEP uses **make** to maintain the relationships between the files associated with a project; we typically create this information and record it in a *Makefile* (NeXTSTEP names this file **Makefile**, although it could be almost anything). Although ProjectBuilder produces and maintains the **Makefile** for us, learning the basic terminology and mechanics of **make** will shed some light on the development cycle.

Assuming that we didn't have ProjectBuilder, we would invoke **make** as follows:

```
% make program
```

This tells **make** to produce the program specified by **program**; **program** is dependent on other files, and we will refer to these files as *prerequisites*, which may also depend on other prerequisites. An executable (application) is built from object files, and object files are built from source files. If the source file has changed, then **make** should first compile the source file to produce the object file and then link the new object file to the existing object file(s) to produce the executable. Thus, a source file is a prerequisite of an object file, which is, in turn, a prerequisite of the executable.

For example, the **PopUp** application from Chapter 8 has two source files, **PopUp_main.m** and **TargetObject.m**. In a perfect world, we could have typed the following commands once and produced the executable:

```
% cc -c -g -o PopUp_main.o PopUp_main.m
% cc -c -g -o TargetObject.o TargetObject.m
% cc -g -o PopUp PopUp_main.o TargetObject.o -lNeXT_s
```

However, it is more likely that we will repeat this many (many!) times before we get the executable working properly. This is where **make** and the associated **Makefile** can streamline the process and save us a great deal of time and frustration. A **Makefile** is composed of *stanzas*, and each stanza is composed of two parts: one *dependency line* and one or more associated *commands line(s)*, the commands that **make** should execute if the prerequisites are more recent than the *target*.

> Do not confuse the commands line in a **Makefile** with the command-line in Terminal, where we issue commands to the operating system.

A sample dependency line looks like:

```
PopUp_main.o: PopUp_main.m
```

The file(s) on the right on the colon are the prerequisites and the file specified on the left is the target. Thus, **PopUp_main.m** is a

A source file is a prerequisite for an object file, which is a prerequisite for an executable

Using make can streamline the development process

An object file depends on a source file

prerequisite of the target **PopUp_main.o**. Another way to state this relationship is to say that the **PopUp_main.o** object file *depends* on the **PopUp_main.m** source file. The commands line for this dependency is the command we would normally type to compile the target, **PopUp_main.m** (recall that we need to use the **-c** flag to tell the C compiler that we don't want to link the source file but only to compile it):

```
cc -c -g -o PopUp_main.o PopUp_main.m
```

Together, these two lines read:

```
PopUp_main.o: PopUp_main.m
    cc -c -g -o PopUp_main.o PopUp_main.m
```

In English, this basically reads: if the **PopUp_main.m** source file is more recent than the **PopUp_main.o** object file, then compile **PopUp_main.m** (without linking) to produce an updated **PopUp_main.o** file.

> How does **make** determine if one file is more recent than another? NeXTSTEP timestamps each file to reflect the last time we updated it. To see the time on the file, use the **ls -l** command or select the file in the Workspace and then click **Tools ⇒ Inspector**.

Each commands line must start with a tab

Notice that the commands line is indented while the dependency line is not. This is probably the source of most of the errors in **make** so we will emphasize it: **EACH COMMANDS LINE MUST START WITH A TAB**. If a commands line does not start with a tab, then **make** will complain with the following descriptive error message with *n* is the line number on which the error occurred (for more error messages and how to correct them, see "Error Messages in make" on page 480.):

```
Make: Makefile: Must be a separator on line n.
Stop.
```

> An easy way to determine if an indented line contains spaces or tabs is to use the **cat** command:
>
> ```
> % cat -t -v -e Makefile
> ```
>
> The flags and their meanings are as follows:
>
> - **-t** and **-v** show tabs as **^I** (the ^ indicates a **Control** letter: the tab character and the **Control-i** are equivalent)
> - **-e** places **$** at the end of each line, which is useful when dealing with long commands lines.

The dependency line and commands line for the **TargetObject** class are also similar (recall that a class is actually an object file):

```
TargetObject.o: TargetObject.m
    cc -c -g -o TargetObject.o TargetObject.m
```

With the object-source dependencies in place, now establish the executable-source dependency.

```
PopUp: PopUp_main.o TargetObject.o
    cc -g -o PopUp PopUp_main.o TargetObject.o
-lNeXT_s
```

This deceptively simple line exemplifies the power of **make**. **make** recursively determines the dependencies and executes the associated commands before producing the current target. Thus the English equivalent of the aforementioned dependency is as follows: if either the **PopUp_main.o** or **TargetObject.o** file is newer than the **PopUp** executable, **make** should link both **PopUp_main.o** and **TargetObject.o** to form the new executable. However, recall from the previous discussion that the **PopUp_main.o** and **TargetObject.o** files depend on **PopUp_main.m** and **TargetObject.m** respectively.

By issuing **make PopUp**, we can be certain that NeXTSTEP will:

- compile only those source file(s) that are more recent than their respective object file(s).

- relink the object file(s) to produce the executable if the object file(s) are more recent than the executable.

make goes one step further and provides another convenient feature: if a target is not specified, then **make** defaults to the first target. Thus, by placing the **PopUp** target as the first target, we can simply type **make** rather than **make PopUp** to produce the executable.

B.5.2 Removing Files: make clean

Another common task is removing unwanted files to recover disk space

Another common task we have to perform is to remove the object files and executable of a given project to recover disk space. A common convention is to specify a **clean** target without any prerequisites (note that we still need the colon to specify that **clean** is a target). For example, the **clean** target for the **PopUp** executable would be as follows:

```
clean:
    rm *.o *.~ PopUp
```

make treats a nonexisting target as an out-of-date target

make treats a nonexisting target as an out-of-date target. Thus, assuming there is no file named **clean** in the current directory, typing **make clean** would remove the following files:

- all of the object files; the ***.o** means to match all filenames that end with **.o**, which is the suffix for object files. Therefore, the expression ***.o** means all object files.
- all files that end with **~**; most editors create backup files and append a **~** to the filename.
- the **PopUp** executable itself.

B.5.3 Installing the Application: make install

Strip the debugging information before installing the application

Another common task is to install the executable in a predetermined installation directory (usually **~/Apps**) after it has been tested. However, we should **strip** the debugging information before copying the application to the installation directory because as much as 90% of the executable's size is taken up by the debugging info. The **install** target for **PopUp** would be as follows:

```
install: PopUp
   strip PopUp
   cp PopUp ${HOME}/Apps
   rm PopUp
```

The **install** target first checks the **PopUp** target—and recompiles it as explained earlier, if necessary—then copies the executable to **~/Apps**. Afterwards, the executable is deleted from the current directory. Note that due to the way **make** works, we have to use **{$HOME}**, rather than **~**, to specify our home directory.

> Why didn't we simply move the executable (with **mv**) rather than copy it (with **cp**) and then remove it (with **rm**)? The **mv** command would fail if the source directory and destination directories are on different filesystems. On the other hand, the **cp** command can cross filesystems, if the installation directory and our home directory should happen to be on different filesystems.

B.5.4 Deinstalling the Application: make deinstall

Once we have installed the application, we may eventually want to deinstall it to recover the disk space. The **deinstall** target would be:

```
deinstall:
   rm -rf ${HOME}/Apps/PopUp
```

Table B.1 summarizes the four most common **make** targets and their meanings.

Command	Meaning
make	produces the latest executable
make clean	removes all of the temporary files, including object files, backup files, and executable
make install	strips the executable and installs it in the installation directory, usually ~/Apps
make deinstall	removes the executable from the installation directory

Table B.1 Common **make** targets and their meanings

B.5.5 Makefiles for the Applications

This section lists all the **Makefile**s for the applications which we built without the aid of ProjectBuilder and InterfaceBuilder (the applications which we built with ProjectBuilder already have pre-generated **Makefile**s). The first **Makefile** is for the **Sample** application from Chapter 2. In **make**, # at the start of the line indicates that the line is a comment.

Makefile for **Sample**

```
# Makefile for Sample application

Sample: Sample.m
  cc -g -o Sample Sample.m -lNeXT_s

install: Sample
  strip Sample
  cp Sample ${HOME}/Apps
  rm Sample

deinstall:
  rm -rf ${HOME}/Apps/Sample

clean:
```

```
    rm -rf *.o Sample *~
```

The next **Makefile** is for the **ShapeArea** application from Chapter 3. Note that the **Makefile** is only usable during the third pass of implementation because it assumes that all the classes are present.

Makefile for ShapeArea

```
# Makefile for ShapeArea application

ShapeArea: ShapeArea_main.o AbstractShape.o Rectangle.o Square.o
    cc -g -o ShapeArea ShapeArea_main.o AbstractShape.o Rectangle.o Square.o -lNeXT_s

ShapeArea_main.o: ShapeArea_main.m
    cc -c -g -o ShapeArea_main.o ShapeArea_main.m

AbstractShape.o: AbstractShape.m
    cc -c -g -o AbstractShape.o AbstractShape.m

Rectangle.o: Rectangle.m
    cc -c -g -o Rectangle.o Rectangle.m

Square.o: Square.m
    cc -c -g -o Square.o Square.m

install: ShapeArea
    strip ShapeArea
    cp ShapeArea ${HOME}/Apps
    rm ShapeArea

deinstall:
    rm -rf ${HOME}/Apps/ShapeArea

clean:
    rm -rf *.o ShapeArea *~
```

The next **Makefile** is for the **AppKitDemo** application from Chapter 4. Note that since **AppKitDemo** includes only one source file, we don't need to create an object file: we can compile and link the source file to form the executable.

Makefile for AppKitDemo

```
# Makefile for AppKitDemo application

AppKitDemo: AppKitDemo.m
  cc -g -o AppKitDemo AppKitDemo.m -lNeXT_s

install: AppKitDemo
  strip AppKitDemo
  cp AppKitDemo ${HOME}/Apps
  rm AppKitDemo

deinstall:
  rm -rf ${HOME}/Apps/AppKitDemo

clean:
    rm -rf *.o AppKitDemo *~
```

The only application in Chapter 5 was built using InterfaceBuilder and ProjectBuilder. Thus, the application already has a **Makefile**. Chapter 6 has two applications that we build from scratch: **ControlDemo** and **DelegateDemo**. Notice that since **ControlDemo** only contains one source file (as is the case with **AppKitDemo**), we can compile and link the source file to produce the executable without first producing an object file.

Makefile for ControlDemo

```
# Makefile for ControlDemo

ControlDemo: ControlDemo.m
  cc -g -o ControlDemo ControlDemo.m -lNeXT_s

install: ControlDemo
  strip ControlDemo
  cp ControlDemo ${HOME}/Apps
  rm ControlDemo

deinstall:
```

```
   rm -rf ${HOME}/Apps/ControlDemo

clean:
   rm -rf *.o ControlDemo *~
```

Makefile for DelegateDemo

```
# Makefile for DelegateDemo

DelegateDemo: DelegateDemo_main.o WindowDelegate.o
   cc -o DelegateDemo DelegateDemo_main.o WindowDelegate.o -lNeXT_s

WindowDelegate.o: WindowDelegate.m
   cc -c -g -o WindowDelegate.o WindowDelegate.m

DelegateDemo_main.o: DelegateDemo_main.m
   cc -c -g -o DelegateDemo_main.o DelegateDemo_main.m

install: DelegateDemo
   strip DelegateDemo
   cp DelegateDemo ${HOME}/Apps
   rm DelegateDemo

deinstall:
   rm -rf ${HOME}/Apps/DelegateDemo

clean:
   rm -rf *.o DelegateDemo *~
```

The next **Makefile** is for the **PopUp** application from Chapter 8.

```
# Makefile for PopUp

PopUp: PopUp_main.o TargetObject.o
   cc -g -o PopUp PopUp_main.o TargetObject.o -lNeXT_s

PopUp_main.o: PopUp_main.m
   cc -c -g -o PopUp_main.o PopUp_main.m
```

```
TargetObject.o: TargetObject.m
  cc -c -g -o TargetObject.o TargetObject.m

install: PopUp
  strip PopUp
  cp PopUp ${HOME}/Apps
  rm PopUp

deinstall:
  rm -rf ${HOME}/Apps/PopUp

clean:
    rm -rf *.o PopUp *~
```

The last **Makefile** is for the **Scroll** application from Chapter 9.

```
# Makefile for Scroll

Scroll: Scroll.m
  cc -g -o Scroll Scroll.m -lNeXT_s

install: Scroll
  strip Scroll
  cp Scroll ${HOME}/Apps
  rm Scroll

deinstall:
  rm -rf ${HOME}/Apps/Scroll

clean:
    rm -rf *.o Scroll *~
```

B.5.6 Error Messages in make

This section lists some of the common error messages that **make** produces, their causes, and their solutions.

- **Make: Makefile: Must be a separator on line *n*. Stop.**
  - **Cause**: The two most common causes are:
  - a target (in this case, **clean**) is missing a colon.
  ```
  # clean is missing a colon
  clean
      rm -rf ${HOME}/Apps/PopUp
  ```

- the command line does not start with a tab (this could have happened if we pasted the text from Terminal. For more information on this limitation, see "Copying Text" on page 465.):
  ```
  clean:
  rm -rf ${HOME}/Apps/PopUp
  ```
  - **Solution**: Verify that each target has a colon and that each commands line start with a tab. Use **cat -t -v -e file** to list the file; tabs will appear as **^I**.
- **Make: Don't know how to make target.**
  - **Cause**: We specified a nonexisting target.
  - **Solution**: Verify that the target is spelled properly and that there is a stanza in the **Makefile** for the target.
- **'target' is up to date.**
  - **Cause**: The dependencies the target depends on have not changed since the last time we have made the target. In short, **make** does not need to do anything.
  - **Solution**: None needed.

Error Messages in make

Appendix C
Common NeXTSTEP Mistakes

This appendix lists common errors a programmer usually encounters when first learning to program in Objective-C and NeXTSTEP. Some of these mistakes will cause the application to crash, and many will produce warnings during compilation. The warnings can be ignored, but they may cause subtle errors later. Even if we choose not to modify the source code to remove the warnings, we should at least determine the nature of the warnings. Each mistake is listed in the following format: the symptom, the cause(s) of the error message or warning, and the solution(s).

C.1 Runtime Errors

Runtime errors are errors which will cause the application to crash during execution. The list of errors includes the following:

- The application crashes with an error message similar to the following: *anObject* **does not recognize selector** *selector.*
  - **Cause**: The application sent an invalid message to a particular object. The actions that may have caused this include:
    - sending an instance method to a class object—the following code fragment produces an error because it is trying to use an instance method to initialize a class object.

      ```
      theWindow = [Window init];
      ```
    - misspelling the method name—remember that the colon is an integral part of the method name. The following code fragment is trying to make a window the key window. However, the method is **makeKeyAndOrderFront:** (notice the colon) instead of **makeKeyAndOrderFront**.

      ```
      [theWindow makeKeyAndOrderFront];
      ```
  - **Solution**: If the receiver is an instance, make sure that the selector is an instance method. If the receiver is a class object, make sure the selector is a class method. To quickly

determine whether a method is a class method or an instance method, highlight the word and click **Services** ⇒ **HeaderViewer** ⇒ **Find in appkit.h** to message HeaderViewer. For more information on HeaderViewer, see Appendix B.

- The application crashes with a message like **objc: FREED(id): message free sent to freed object=0xbe970**.
  - **Cause**: The application is sending a message to an object that has already been freed. For example, in Chapter 9, in its **free** method, the document frees its **window** outlet. The document can safely do this since the window did not attempt to free itself. However, if we used InterfaceBuilder to set the window to automatically free itself when it is closed, then trying to free the window again **Document**'s **free** method would crash the application. This occurs because the application continues to message the window although it has already been freed.
  - **Solution**: Do not send a message to a freed object. For more information on this, see Chapter 9.
- The application crashes with a **Bus error** message.
  - One common mistake is that the application is working with uninitialized pointers. Consider the following code fragment (an excerpted version of **showSavePanel:** from Chapter 9).

Excerpted listing of **showSavePanel:**

```
- showSavePanel:sender
{
   const char *wordType = FILE_EXTENSION;
   const char *fullPathName, *title;
   id document = [[NXApp mainWindow] delegate];
   id savePanel = [SavePanel new];

   // make sure there is a document first
   if (document)
      {
      // if document has not been saved
      // then present savepanel to get filename
      title = [[document window] title];
      if (strcmp(title, UNTITLED) == 0)
```

If the **(if document)** statement is removed, the application may crash at the **strcmp()** statement because **title** may be an uninitialized pointer. How can this happen? If there is no main window, **[NXApp mainWindow]** will return **nil**. Thus, **[[document window] title]** will also return **nil** because there is no window to return a title.

Additionally, if a method does not allocate enough memory for a string, the application will crash inexplicably. For example, consider the **mouseDown:** method from Chapter 7:

Excerpted listing for **mouseDown:**

```
- mouseDown:(NXEvent *)theEvent
{
   char buffer[30];

   // round co-ordinates to 1 digit
   // after decimal point
   // print co-ordinates in window co-ordinates
   sprintf(buffer, "%.1f", theEvent->location.x);
     .
     .
     .
```

The method allocates thirty bytes for the **buffer** string. However, recall that in C, a string terminates with a null terminator (**\0**). The null terminator takes up a byte in storage so there is only room for twenty-nine characters. The application will crash at the **sprintf** statement if it needs more than twenty-nine characters to convert **theEvent->location.x** from a **float** to a string.

- **Solution**: Verify that a string is initialized before accessing it and that the memory allocated for a string is large enough to contain the string and the null terminator.

> Note that NeXTSTEP does not redirect **Bus error** messages to the Console window. If we launch the application by double-clicking on it or using the **open** command, we will never see these error messages. The only way to see these messages is to launch the application from the command-line as follows:
>
> ```
> $ Words.debug/Words &
> ```

C.2 Warnings

These are warnings produced by the compiler during compilation. They may mask more serious problems elsewhere in the application.

- The compiler produces the following warning: **local declaration of '*variable*' hides instance variable**.
  - **Cause**: A method is declaring a local variable with the same name as an instance variable. The following code fragment illustrates a hypothetical **SampleObject** class which defines an **area** instance variable and a method which defines an **area** local variable (the lines in bold indicates where the compiler would produce the warning). Note that the compiler issues the warning on the lines where the method accesses the variable, not where the variable is defined. Objective-C applies the same scoping rules to methods that C applies to functions; that is, if two variables of the same name exist, the function (method) uses the one that is defined closest. In short, **printArea** would print **20** since **printArea** declares **area** locally: the method would ignore the value of the instance variable **area**.

Listing for SampleObject.h

```
#import <appkit/appkit.h>
```

```
@interface SampleObject:Object
{
   int area;
}

- printArea;

@end
```

Listing for **SampleObject.m**

```
#import "SampleObject.h"

@implementation SampleObject

- printArea
{
 int height = 5, width = 4;
 int area;
 area = height * width;
 printf("Area is %d\n", area);
 return self;
}

@end
```

- **Solution**: Rename the local variable or the instance variable so that they no longer match.
- The compiler produces the following warning: **return of integer from pointer lacks a cast**.
  - **Cause**: A method declared as returning an **int** is returning a pointer instead. Objective-C implements objects using pointers. Hence, returning **self** is the same as returning a pointer. The following code (taken from the **SampleObject** class from above) would produce the warning:

Mismatched return type

```
- (int)printArea
{
```

```
        int height = 5, width = 4;
        int area;
        area = height * width;
        printf("Area is %d\n", area);
        return self;
}
```

- **Solution**: Make sure the declaration type and the return type of the method match.

> Note that returning a **BOOL** value in a method that is declared to return an **int** will not produce an error message. Even though this is not encouraged, it can happen. For an example of this, see "Opening Files from the Workspace" on page 402.

- The compiler produces the following warning: **conflicting types for** *method*. **Previous declaration of** *method*.
    - **Cause**: The method declaration in the header file does not match the method implementation in the implementation file. The following code would produce a **Previous declaration of -(int)printArea** warning message because the method is originally defined to return an **int** in the header file and is declared to return an object (**self**) in the implementation file.

Listing for SampleObject.h

```
#import <appkit/appkit.h>

@interface SampleObject:Object

{
  int area;
}

- (int)printArea;

@end
```

Listing for **SampleObject.m**

```
#import "SampleObject.h"

@implementation SampleObject

- printArea
{
 int height = 5, width = 4;
 int area;
 area = height * width;
 printf("Area is %d\n", area);
 return self;
}

@end
```

- **Solution**: Verify that the method declaration in the header file matches the declaration in the implementation file.
- The application does not send its delegate any of the delegate methods.
    - **Cause**: The application has probably not set the **delegate** outlet to the other object.
    - **Solution**: In InterfaceBuilder, connect from the object to its delegate, select **delegate**, and click **Connect**.
- Sending a message to an object does not do anything.
    - **Cause**: The object has probably not been initialized and is probably **nil**; sending a **nil** object an message does nothing except return **nil**.
    - **Solution**: Make sure that the object is initialized before messaging it.
- InterfaceBuilder does not display all the outlets declared in the header file of a class.
    - **Cause**: For InterfaceBuilder to recognize a variable as an outlet, the variable must be:
        - of type **id**.
        - declared on a separate line.

- **Solution**: Declare each outlet as type **id** on a separate line. For more information on how declaring outlets, see "Troubleshooting" on page 205 in Chapter 6.

Appendix D
Debugging

In a perfect world, we would be able to write programs, and they would work on the first try. However, a more realistic view is that our application will probably have bugs just waiting to spring on us at the most inopportune time. Debugging is a difficult skill to learn. However, NeXTSTEP applications, because they are object-oriented and event-driven, pose even more challenging problems. Unlike Appendix C, which focuses on syntax errors during the compilation stage, this appendix concentrates on tracing through the code and on isolating bugs in the application when it is executing. NeXTSTEP provides **gdb** (the Gnu debugger) for debugging applications; we cover how to use **gdb** from the command-line and from the **Gdb** panel in Edit.

Since NeXTSTEP is an event-driven and object-oriented environment, it poses some unusual challenges for debugging

Before we can effectively debug a program, however, we must first learn how to trace the control flow of the application. Recall from Chapter 2 that a NeXTSTEP application is composed of many files. How, then, do we know where—what file, much less what method—to start tracing?

Before we can debug a program, we must be able to trace it

D.1 Tracing the Program

A program is a series of instructions executing in a particular order. The order of the instructions is just as important as the instructions themselves. As we will shortly discover, however, one of the most difficult things about learning NeXTSTEP is to determine this order. This difficulty is inherent in NeXTSTEP because it is an event-driven and object-oriented environment. In the following sections, we explore how to first trace a non-event-driven application and then an event-driven one.

One of the main challenges in tracing a NeXTSTEP application is determining when objects are created and initialized

D.1.1 Tracing a Non-Event Driven Application

In a non-event-driven environment, it is fairly easy to trace the program. Invariably, the structure of the program is similar to the **ShapeArea** application from Chapter 3 (recall that **ShapeArea** is an Objective-C application which does not follow the event processing loop that is inherent in a NeXTSTEP application):

Excerpted listing of **ShapeArea_main.m**

```
/* skeleton of ShapeArea */
void createObjects(void)
{
}

void run(void)
{
  // stay in loop until Q is pressed
}

BOOL readInput(void)
{
}

void calculateAreas(void)
{
}


void freeAll(void)
{
}

void main(void)
{
  createObjects();
  run();
  calculateAreas();
  freeAll();
  exit(0);
}
```

To trace the flow of the application, look at **main()**, the starting point of program execution, and then continue from the first function call to the last. In order, they are **createObjects()**, **run()**, **calculateAreas()**, **freeAll()**, and **exit()**. This order provides us with an overview of what the application is trying to do.

> **For a non-event driven program, look at main() to determine the flow of control**

D.1.2 Tracing an Event-Driven Program

Now consider the **main()** function of an event-driven program in NeXTSTEP (this is from the **Words** application in Chapter 9):

The **main()** function of **Words**

```
/*
Generated by the NeXT Project Builder
*/

#import <appkit/Application.h>

void main(int argc, char *argv[])
{
  [Application new];
  if ([NXApp loadNibSection:"Words.nib"
    owner:NXApp withNames:NO])
      [NXApp run];
  [NXApp free];
  exit(0);
}
```

All we can determine from looking at **main()** is that if **NXApp** successfully loads the main **.nib** file (**Words.nib**), **NXApp** proceeds to the event loop to wait for incoming events. This program structure is inherent in an event-driven environment; the application waits for incoming events and then dispatches them to the appropriate objects. However, even before an application receives its first event, it has already gone through an initialization phase. In NeXTSTEP, an application does not create and initialize its objects in the **main()** function. The objects are created and initialized in either the **.nib** file or in one of the following methods:

> **In a NeXTSTEP program, all main() does is load the main .nib file and then enter the event loop**

- the designated initializer method for the class (such as **initFrame:** for a view)
- **awakeFromNib**
- **appDidInit:**
- **setOutletName:**
- **initialize** (the class method).

However, the two main challenges are determining in which method the application can safely initialize the objects (they may not be defined yet) and when the application will receive messages. The order in which the objects are created and initialized is as follows (note that many of these steps are intertwined; for example, while loading in the **.nib** file, **NXApp** will send the application a **set***OutletName***:** message for each outlet):

- in the main **.nib** file, the appropriate objects are created and initialized. The main **.nib** file is named *application***.nib** and is loaded in **main()**.
- as the application is loading in the **.nib** file, it can initialize an outlet specified by *outletName* in **set***OutletName***:** (recall that an outlet is ultimately an object). Avoid using methods of this type because they cannot safely reference another outlet, since it is impossible to determine the order in which the outlets are initialized. Use **awakeFromNib** instead since the application is assured that it will not receive the **awakeFromNib** message until all the objects and outlets are defined. Additionally, using **awakeFromNib** localizes all of the initialization to one method instead of multiple **set***OutletName***:** methods.
- in the designated initializer method of the class; for example, in the **Shapes** area from Chapter 7, **SquareView** implements the **initFrame:** method (via inheritance from **ShapeView**) to initialize the squareview's instance variables. Note that **Shapes** will still work even if **ShapeView** does not implement **initFrame:**. However, the instance wouldn't be initialized with the desired values. The **initFrame:** method is as follows:

Initializing instance variables in **initFrame:**

```
- initFrame:(NXRect *)frameRect
```

```
{
  [super initFrame:frameRect];
  angle = 360;
  xScale = 1;
  yScale = 1;
  x = 50;
  y = 50;
  return self;
}
```

- in **awakeFromNib**, the application can create and/or initialize objects (which may or not be outlets). For example, in the **Money** application from Chapter 9, **awakeFromNib** reads the defaults database to determine what state to set the **truncateSwitch** (a button) to:

Initializing outlets in **awakeFromNib**

```
- awakeFromNib
{
  const char *appName = [NXApp appName];
  const char *truncateFlag;

  truncateFlag =
    NXGetDefaultValue(appName, "Truncate");
  // make sure truncateFlag is not NULL before
  // comparing it
  if (truncateFlag)
    {
    if (strcasecmp(truncateFlag, "YES") == 0)
      [truncateSwitch setState:ON];
    else
      [truncateSwitch setState:OFF];
    }
  return self;
}
```

Note that **set*OutletName*:** or **awakeFromNib** are not needed to create the outlets (they are created when the class is parsed in InterfaceBuilder): these methods are only needed to *further* initialize outlets. However, we still have to make the connections in InterfaceBuilder to first establish what is an outlet. In short, if we don't make the connection in InterfaceBuilder to establish

set*OutletName*: and awakeFromNib are used to further initialize outlets

- the outlet, it will be **nil**. At this point, where we initialize the outlet is moot because sending a message to a **nil** object does nothing but return **nil**.
- in **appDidInit:**, the application can perform any final initialization before it receives its first event. For example, the **Words** application in Chapter 9 uses **awakeFromNib** in the **TextController** class to create an openpanel and savepanel. However, **TextController** can just as easily create these objects in **appDidInit:**.

Creating and initializing objects in **appDidInit:**

```
- appDidInit:sender
{
  // NXapp's delegate automatically receives
  // this message before the application
  // receives its first event
  id savePanel = [SavePanel new];
  id openPanel = [OpenPanel new];
  // by default, an openpanel only allows
  // one file to be opened
  [openPanel allowMultipleFiles:YES];
  return self;
}
```

However, **appDidInit:** has two main limitations:

- it is a delegate method of **Application**. Thus, the object implementing the method must be set as the delegate of **NXApp** before it will receive the message. In the aforementioned example, **appDidInit:** is implemented by a textcontroller, which is a delegate of **NXApp**.

NXApp's delegate receives an appDidInit: message only once

- it is impossible to perform repeated initialization since **NXApp**'s delegate receives this message only once (**appDidInit:** works in the aforementioned example because **Words** only has to create and initialize the savepanel and openpanel once). Consider if we wish the scrollview in each document to support horizontal scrolling (the scrollview provided by InterfaceBuilder only supports vertical scrolling). We can use **[scrollView setHorizScrollerRequired:YES]** to add support for horizontal scrolling, but we couldn't use this statement in **appDidInit:**. Why? Because NeXTSTEP only sends the **appDidInit:** message once before the application receives its first event. Recall that the **.nib** file containing the scrollview (**Document.nib**) is loaded only *after* we click on **Document ⇒ New**. By this time, **NXApp**'s delegate will have *already* received the **appDidInit:** message because clicking on a menu option generates events. Thus, the application has no choice but to implement **awakeFromNib** or **setScrollView:** (in the same class that is loading the **.nib** file for the document object) to further initialize the scrollview.

> The **appDidInit:** method will appear in the Connections Inspector in InterfaceBuilder, even though it is not a control-action related method. Why? Because, like most delegate methods (another example is **windowWillClose:**), **appDidInit:** has a single colon and the parameter is **sender**. InterfaceBuilder treats all such methods as action-related, even though they may not be.

- in **initialize**, the application can perform other forms of initialization which are not related to instances. For example, the **Money** application from Chapter 8 used **initialize** to register its defaults.

Registering defaults in **initialize**

```
+ initialize
{
  // make sure that self is a PrefsController
  // class before setting class initialization:
  // this prevents subclasses from performing
  // reinitialization
  if (self == [PrefsController class])
    {
    const char *appName = [NXApp appName];

    static NXDefaultsVector theDefaults =
      {
        {"Truncate", "NO"},
        {"Prompt", "NO"},
```

```
        {NULL, NULL}
    };

    NXRegisterDefaults(appName, theDefaults);
    }
  return self;
}
```

D.1.3 Implicit and Explicit Message Sending

Implicit message sending is more difficult to trace than explicit message sending

Another challenge in tracing the program flow is, quite often, there is no explicit reference to the method in question in any of the implementation files (while debugging, we don't want to search through the header files because they only declare the methods). Consider the **awakeFromNib** method. Even if we search every implementation file in the project directory, we would discover that no object sends an **awakeFromNib** message.

This is one of those many cases where **NXApp** sends the object a message if the object implements the method. That is, if the class implements the method, its instance will receive the message; if not, the instance will never receive the message. We refer to this as a case of *implicit message sending*. Implicit message sending is different than *explicit message sending*, where an object explicitly messages another object or itself. One such example is **ShapeView**'s **scale:** method from Chapter 7. Among other things, the shapeview sends a message to its **sender** to determine what the selected cell is.

An example of explicit message sending

```
- scale:sender
{
  // sender is a matrix: thus, obtain
  // cell by asking the matrix
  // for the selected cell
  id cell = [sender selectedCell];
  int tag = [cell tag];

  switch(tag)
```

```
  {
  case 0:
    xScale = [cell floatValue];
    break;
  case 1:
    yScale = [cell floatValue];
    break;
  }
  // display view with updated values
  [self display];
  return self;
}
```

Although explicit message sending is easier to debug (we can simply search the appropriate file to determine what objects are messaging each other), it is more troublesome in many cases. Consider the **awakeFromNib** method. If an object had to explicitly send itself an **awakeFromNib** message, where would it do it from? By implementing this method (and others) as implicit methods, **NXApp** will message the object at the appropriate time; all we have to do is implement the method.

Implicit message sending is more powerful than explicit message sending

> There are cases where **NXApp** sends a message implicitly and explicitly. Consider the **display** method. In the **Shapes** application in Chapter 7, moving any of the sliders explicitly sends the custom view a **display** message (the **display** message then implicitly sends a **drawSelf::** message). However, if we move the window which contains both the circleview and the squareview, NeXTSTEP implicitly sends a **display** message to the window, which in turns implicitly sends its subviews—the circleview and squareview are included in the window's subviews—a **display** message.

The **awakeFromNib** is not the only example of implicit message sending. Some other examples include **appDidInit:**, **initialize**, **freeObjects** (in **ShapeArea** from Chapter 2), and the event-related methods from Chapter 7 such as **mouseDown:** and **mouseUp:**. Consider the **freeObjects** method of the **List** class,

There are many examples of implicit message sending in NeXTSTEP

referenced in the **freeAll()** function from **ShapeArea** in Chapter 3:

The freeAll() function with List's freeObjects method

```
void freeAll(void)
{
  // free the objects in the list
  // freeObjects sends a free message
  // to each object in the list
  [theList freeObjects];
  // free the list itself
  [theList free];
}
```

The freeObjects method implicitly sends a free message to the list's contents

The **freeObjects** method implicitly sends a **free** message to each object in the list. Again, it would be difficult to conclude this from simply looking at the code because there is no association between the **freeObjects** method and the **free** method of its contents (the **free** methods are implemented in **Rectangle.m** and **Square.m** because the list initially stores rectangles and squares).

mouseUp: and mouseDown: are two more examples of implicit messages

Now consider the **mouseDown:** and **mouseUp:** methods. Again, **NXApp** implicitly sends a view these messages if we click down and release the mouse button in a view's boundary. This frees the application from having to determine when a **mouseDown:** or **mouseUp:** event occurs. The application only needs to implement what should happen when it receives one of these events.

All delegate methods are sent implicitly

Finally, all the delegate methods are implicitly sent. The object's delegate—if one exists—will receive a message if it implements a method of the same name. One such example is the **windowWillClose:** method as illustrated in Chapter 6. The windowdelegate object uses this method to display an alert panel when a window is about to close.

In summary, from a debugging viewpoint, there are two types of messages in NeXTSTEP: implicit and explicit. Implicit messages are automatically sent by **NXApp** in response to predetermined occurrences such as:

• a **.nib** file finishes loading (**awakeFromNib**)

- the object is initialized in its designated initializer method such as **initFrame:** for a view.
- an outlet is set *while* a **.nib** file is loading (**set***OutletName***:**)
- before an application receives its first events (**appDidInit:**)
- mouse-events (**mouseDown:**, **mouseUp:**, etc.)
- delegate methods (**windowWillClose:**, etc.).

Implicit messages free the application from having to determine when the object should be messaged: the application only has to implement the method, and **NXApp** will automatically message the application at the appropriate time. However, implicit message sending makes it more difficult to debug since we can never find any reference to the method name (aside from where it is implemented, of course) in any of the implementation files.

With implicit messages, NXApp sends the object the message if the object implements the method

Explicit message sending is when an object specifically sends itself or another object a message such as **[self erase]**. We can find at least two occurrences of **erase** in the implementation files: the statement where the message is initiated (as shown) and the location the method is actually implemented. This association allows us to determine which object sent the message and which object received the message, thereby facilitating the debugging process.

Explicit messages are easier to debug

D.1.4 Reverse-engineering an Application

At this point, we have determined where to look to determine how objects are initialized. However, we have yet to learn how to dissect a NeXTSTEP application so that we can understand it. To do so, follow these steps (this discussion assumes that we have the source code):

- launch ProjectBuilder and open the project file: it will be named **PB.project**.
- look under the **Classes** entry and **Interfaces** entries to determine the names of all the classes and **.nib** files in the project.
- double-click on the main **.nib** file in InterfaceBuilder; the name of this file is *application***.nib**.

- use the Connections Inspector in InterfaceBuilder to determine all of the connections. Start with the **File's Owner** icon (**NXApp**) and determine if it has a delegate. If **NXApp** has a delegate:
    - determine what object is the delegate.
    - open its implementation file and search for **appDidInit:** and/or **initialize** (since the method names consist of lower and uppercase letters, set the Find Panel in Edit to ignore case when searching). If these two methods are present, they will contain some of the initialization code.
- determine what other instances are available in the main **.nib** file. Use the Class Inspector to determine if a given instance's class defines outlet(s). If so, open its implementation file and search for **set***OutletName***:** to determine if the class further initializes the outlets.
- determine what actions a given class defines and what actions triggers these methods. This produces some of the messages the objects send to each other in the event loop. From this, we can produce an (incomplete) message diagram.
- if the application contains multiple interface files, search through all of the implementation files for **loadNib** (we only search for **loadNib** because the method can start with **loadNibSection** or **loadNibFile**). Instead of opening the files and using the Find panel to search each individual file in Edit, click on **Tools** ⇒ **Finder** in the Workspace to bring up the Finder. This tool can recursively search the files and subfolders for a given string. To do so:
    - drag the project folder from the File Viewer to the shelf in the Finder panel.
    - select the second option, **Find items with Contents that match**, in the popuplist.
    - select the project folder as the target to be searched.
    - type the text string in the textfield and click **OK**.

Reverse-engineering an Application

Figure D.1 illustrates searching the **Money** folder from Chapter 8 for **loadNib**.

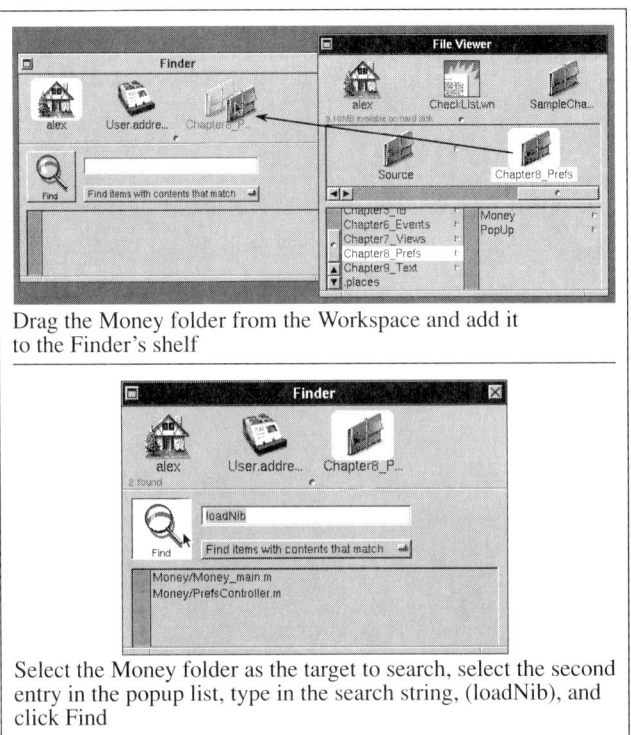

Select the Money folder as the target to search, select the second entry in the popup list, type in the search string, (loadNib), and click Find

Figure D.1 Searching an entire folder for a given string

- open all the implementation files except the main program (we don't need to search this because we know that it has already loaded its **.nib** file). Find all occurrences of **awakeFromNib** to determine what initialization the objects perform.

By following these steps, we can determine the following information about an application:

- what the classes are (this provides us with the CRC cards, although without the responsibilities)
- how and when the objects are initialized (this fills in the responsibilities in the CRC cards)
- what messages the objects send to each other: this includes the collaborators, a message diagram, and the class summary tables.

With this framework, we can gain more insight about how the application works. At this point, we will progress to debugging, that inescapable session when we need to isolate the reasons why our program doesn't work or, even more troubling, why it does!.

D.2 Debugging with gdb

Bundled with the NeXTSTEP environment is the powerful GNU debugger, **gdb**. The version of **gdb** in NeXTSTEP has been enhanced so it can understand Objective-C syntax, which greatly facilitates debugging.

gdb understands Objective-C syntax

In this section, we provide step-by-step instructions on how to debug a given application (the **Money** application from Chapter 8). This tutorial highlights some of **gdb**'s major features including:

- setting breakpoints
- printing and altering the values of variables
- single-stepping a method or function
- continuing after a breakpoint is encountered.

> **gdb** uses lowercase commands. However, Edit labels the interface to these commands with the first letter capitalized. Therefore, when we refer to the graphical interface, we will use Edit's capitalization convention, but when we refer to **gdb** on the command-line, we will leave the commands in lowercase.

D.2.1 Compiling for Debugging

Before we can effectively trace and debug an application, it must contain debugging information. To compile an application with debugging information, do one of the following:

- in ProjectBuilder, specify **debug** in the **Args** field of the Build accessory view. Figure D.2 illustrates this.

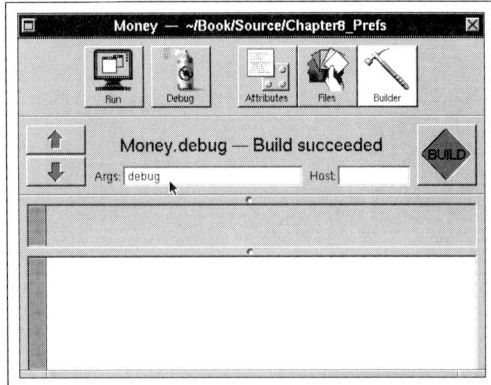

Figure D.2 Including debugging information in ProjectBuilder

- on the command-line, specify the **-g** option to **cc**. Note that each object file and the resulting executable needs debugging information before we can effectively debug the executable.

Edit provides a graphical interface to **gdb** through the **Gdb** menu option. However, the **Gdb** menu option does not appear until we are debugging and Edit is in **Developer Mode** (for more information on how to enable **Developer Mode** in Edit, see Chapter 10).

Before proceeding, compile the **Money** application from Chapter 8 with debugging information. Afterwards, start the debugging process by clicking on the **Debug** button. Clicking on this button does the following:

- Terminal launches and opens a window to run **gdb** (this will be referred to as the *gdb shell window*).
- Edit launches with a **Gdb** menu option, located above the **Print...** menu option.

Figure D.3 illustrates what happens when we click on the **Debug** button.

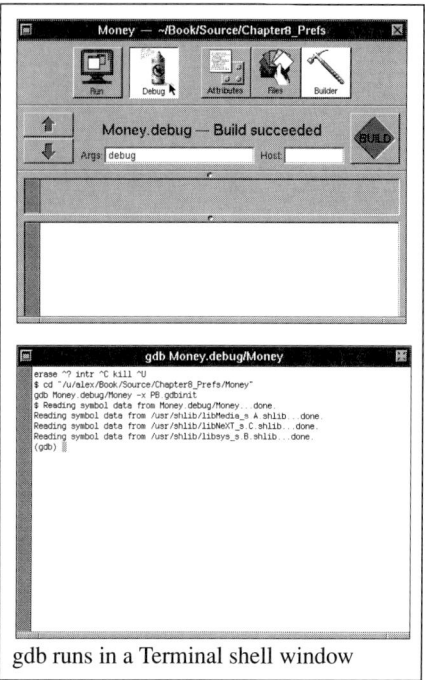

gdb runs in a Terminal shell window

Figure D.3 Clicking on the **Debug** button in ProjectBuilder produces a gdb shell window

The **gdb** shell window displays the application's output and can accept **gdb** commands. However, instead of typing these commands, we will issue them using the Gdb panel. To display this panel, click **Gdb** in Edit. Figure D.4 shows the Gdb panel.

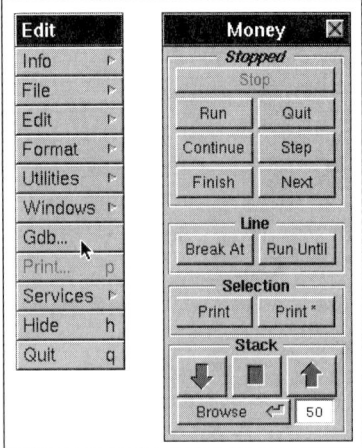

Figure D.4 The Gdb panel in Edit

We will use all of the buttons in our examples except for the three immediately under the word **Stack**. These allows us to examine the stack frames, which we are not interested in. We are primarily interested in examining two methods from the **Money** application:

- **displayPrefsPanel:**—in this method, the prefscontroller loads in its **.nib** file (which initializes all the outlets) and sets itself as the owner of the **.nib** file. We will verify that an uninitialized outlet is **nil** and find out what **nil** really is.

- **convert:**—we will modify some variables to determine their effects on the application and then continue execution.

> An application does not execute more slowly if it has debugging information because NeXTSTEP automatically strips out the application's debugging information before executing the application. Thus, applications are usually stripped for storage-related issues rather than performance-related ones. For small applications, the debugging information may constitute 90% of the application's size.

gdb handles control to us when it encounters a breakpoint

D.2.2 Setting BreakPoints

To debug an application, we must be able interrupt it at a desired point of execution and then examine its state. To halt an application, we need to set *breakpoints* at the appropriate places. When **gdb** (or any debugger, for that matter) encounters a breakpoint, it temporarily halts the program execution and turns over the control to us. We can then print out variables, *single-step* (execute one program statement at a time), and, of course, continue execution.

To set a breakpoint at out first location, **displayPrefsPanel:**, perform the following steps:

- in ProjectBuilder, switch to the Files accessory view, and open the source file (**PrefsController.m**) where the breakpoint should be set. To open **PrefsController.m**, double-click on it under the **Classes** entry.

- position the cursor at the start of the method (**displayPrefsPanel:**) and then click **Break At**. At this point, **gdb** issues a message in the **gdb** shell window to tell us the line number and the file where the breakpoint is set. The address **0x4794** (it is in hexadecimal) will be different, although the line number and filename should be the same:

Setting a breakpoint

```
Breakpoint 1 at 0x4794: file PrefsController.m:88
```

Now set another breakpoint at **convert:**. To do so, first open **MoneyConverter.m** because it contains the **convert:** method. Position the cursor at the start of **convert:** and click **Break At**. The **gdb** shell window responds with:

```
Breakpoint 2 at 0x4498: file MoneyConverter.m:11
```

At this point, verify that the breakpoint is set at the appropriate place by using the **info break** command in the **gdb** shell window (the Gdb panel does not provide this command).

Displaying the breakpoints

```
(gdb) info break
     Enb    Address    Where
  #1   y    0x00004794  in -[PrefsController
displayPrefsPanel:] at PrefsController.m:88
  #2   y    0x00004498  in -[MoneyConverter convert:]
at MoneyConverter.m:11
```

The output is as follows:

- the breakpoint number
- the status of the breakpoint, i.e., whether it is enabled or not; **gdb** will not stop at disabled breakpoints
- the address (in hexadecimal; for our purposes, we can ignore this)
- the type of method, instance or a class
- the name of the method
- the source file with the line number.

> If we use the **b** command in the **gdb** shell window to set a breakpoint, the line number will two greater than the line numbers shown (the breakpoint for **displayPrefsPanel:** would be at line 90 instead of line 88; see the listing in the next section). The **b** command sets the line number to the first statement inside the method after the opening bracket ({) at line 89, whereas we are setting the breakpoint at the method name. Our debugging session will not be affected by this.

D.2.3 Running the Application

Now start the application by clicking **Run** in the Gdb panel. The application will launch, although we need to double-click on its icon to make it the active application. To trigger the first breakpoint (**displayPrefsPanel:**), click **Info** ⇒ **Preferences**, which sends a **displayPrefsPanel:** message to the prefscontroller. This triggers the breakpoint, and the application will immediately

When the application triggers a breakpoint, NeXTSTEP displays the wait cursor

freeze. The spinning cursor (☸) should appear, telling us that the application is in a wait state. To facilitate discussions, we are listing **displayPrefsPanel:** with italicized line numbers.

Listing for displayPrefsPanel: in PrefsController.m

```
88  - displayPrefsPanel:sender
89  {
90    if (!prefsPanel)
91    {
92      [NXApp loadNibSection:"Prefs.nib"
93        owner:self withNames:NO];
94      [switchView switchToView:truncateSwitch];
95    }
96    [prefsPanel makeKeyAndOrderFront:nil];
97    return self;
98  }
```

At this point, switch over to Edit to start examining the method.

D.2.4 Printing Variables

To print a variable, highlight it and then click Print

At this point, line 89 of **displayPrefsPanel:** should be highlighted. This is the *next* line to execute. The first thing we want to know is what is the receiver of this message, i.e., what is **self**. To print a variable, highlight the word (by double-clicking on it) and then click **Print**. To see what the receiver is, highlight **self** and then click **Print** to show:

Displaying self

```
$1 = (struct PrefsController *) 0xc703c
```

The **$1** is a mnemonic for the current **gdb** variable. If we are using the command-line interface to **gdb**, we can use **$1** in place of **self**. The **(struct PrefsController *)** tells us that **self** is an instance of **PrefsController**.

> An object is ultimately a C pointer to a **struct** and the parenthesis and asterisk (*****) is used to *typecast* the pointer to the appropriate type (class). Without this typecast, the output would be meaningless.

Recall that each prefscontroller has five outlets (**prefsPanel**, **switchView**, **promptSwitch**, **truncateSwitch**, and **popUpButton**). At this point, the prefscontroller has not yet loaded its interface file, so the outlets should be **nil** (uninitialized). To verify this, use the **Print*** to print the contents of **self** (the prefscontroller):

The Print* button prints the contents of an object

Displaying **self** (the prefscontroller) and its outlets

```
$2 = {
  isa = 0x8028,
  prefsPanel = 0x0,
  switchView = 0x0,
  promptSwitch = 0x0,
  truncateSwitch = 0x0,
  popUpButton = 0x0
}
```

As previously mentioned, an object is ultimately a pointer in memory. The value **0x0** indicates that the pointer is not pointing to anything. In other words, a **nil** object is a pointer with a value

A nil object is a pointer with a value of 0x0

of **0x0**. This explains why sending a message to a **nil** object does nothing since the object is pointing to nothing.

> The asterisk (*) in the **Print*** button refers to the deference operator in C. That is, **Print*** means to print the contents of the memory the pointer is pointing to while the **Print** button prints the address of the pointer itself.
>
> The asterisk (*) is the most confusing operator in C since it can be used for different purposes:
>
> - dereferencing a pointer such as ***(self)**
> - declaring a variable as a pointer such as **char *string**
> - multiplying arithmetic values such as **x = 3 * 2**
> - typecasting such as **(struct * PrefsController)self**.

At this point, it would be meaningless to examine these outlets further since they are not yet initialized. To initialize them, we need to step through the code, which is the topic of the next section.

D.2.5 Single-Stepping

There are two commands for single-stepping: **Next** and **Step**. Each command executes one program statement and then proceeds to the next line. However, if the statement is a method invocation or function call, **Step** enters the method or function and allows us to trace each statement in the method or function. With **Next**, the function or method executes and then returns immediately to the next program statement.

Step traces through the method while Next simply returns after executing the method

The highlighted line is the next line to execute

At this point, click on the **Next** button to proceed to line 90, the **if (!prefsPanel)** statement. If the **if** statement is true, the method will enter the block to load the **.nib** file. Click **Next** once more to enter the block (since the **if** is true). Note that even though the **loadNibSection:** line is highlighted (line 92), **gdb** has not yet executed the line. Click **Next** again and the prefscontroller will load the **.nib** file (we will verify that the outlets are initialized momentarily).

> Double-clicking on another line will highlight the line but it not alter where **gdb** is currently executing.

At this point, we are at line 94. Since we want to trace through the **switchToView:** method, click **Step** to enter the method; **gdb** will open **SwitchView.m** and display the cursor at line 35 in the **switchToView:** method (this is the first executable statement in the method; all lines before this are simply declarations). An excerpted listing of **SwitchView.m** with line numbers is as follows:

Excerpted listing of **switchToView:** in **SwitchView.m**

```
30    - switchToView:newView
31    {
32      NXRect rect;
33
34      // remove the old view
35      [accessoryView removeFromSuperview];
36
37      // add the new subview
38      accessoryView = newView;
39      [self addSubview:accessoryView];
.
.
.
57      return self;
58    }
```

Now click **Step** to trace through the **removeFromSuperView** method. Instead of placing us in the **removeFromSuperView** method, **gdb** skips the blank lines and returns to line 38 of **switchView.m**. Is this a bug in **gdb** that prevents us from tracing through some methods and not others? Not exactly. We can only step through a method (or function) if the code was compiled with debugging information. The **removeFromSuperView** method is

We cannot single-step through the AppKit's methods since the AppKit does not have debugging information

part of the Application Kit, and this has been stripped of debugging information for disk space considerations (among other reasons).

Since we are not interested in tracing through the rest of **switchToView:**, finish it and return to the calling method (**displayPrefsPanel:**) by clicking **Finish**. **gdb** will complete this method to return to line 95 (line 94 sent a **switchToView:** message). Since **switchToView:** returns **self**, **gdb** prints out this information in the gdb shell window.

gdb displaying a returned value

```
Value returned is $3 = (struct SwitchView *) 0xc8038
```

As far as the **switchToView:** method is concerned, **self** is the switchview while in **displayPrefsPanel:**, **self** is the prefscontroller. At this point, we are ready to examine the outlets since they should be initialized.

D.2.6 Browsing Objects

To examine an object, use the Object Browser

To examine an object (recall that an outlet is an object), use the Object Browser. To display this, click on **Browse** in the Gdb panel. This shows the class of the receiver (**PrefsController**) and a host of other things. To see what **self** is, click on that entry in the browser. Figured D.5 illustrates the Gdb panel showing **self** and its contents.

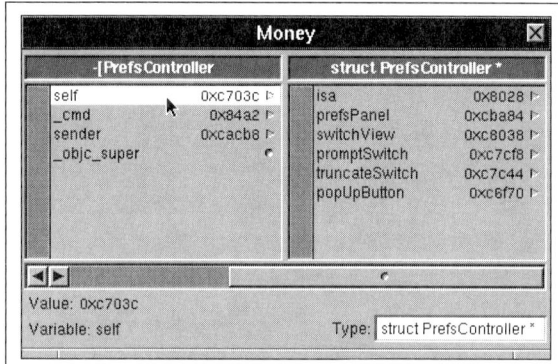

Figure D.5 Click on **self** to display its contents

Note that the outlets are no longer **nil** (**0x0**), since they have been initialized when the prefscontroller loaded the **.nib** file and made itself the owner of the **.nib** file (line 92 and 93 of **displayPrefsPanel:**). To determine the class of an outlet, click on the outlet.

To determine the class of an outlet, click on the outlet

First, click on **popUpButton**. This displays another column that tells us that **popUpButton** is an instance of **PopUpList**. Since **popUpList** is a button (which is ultimately a view, and a view is always inside a window), it has a **window** outlet for the window that contains it. Write down this hex value (in our example, it is **0xcba84**). Now, click on **switchView** to display its information. The Browser tells us that **switchView** is an instance of **View**. Compare the value of its **window** outlet to the previous **window** value; it should be identical since the same window contains both

Two objects that have the same hex address are actually the same object

the button (the trigger button for the popuplist) and the switch-view. Figure D.6 illustrates this.

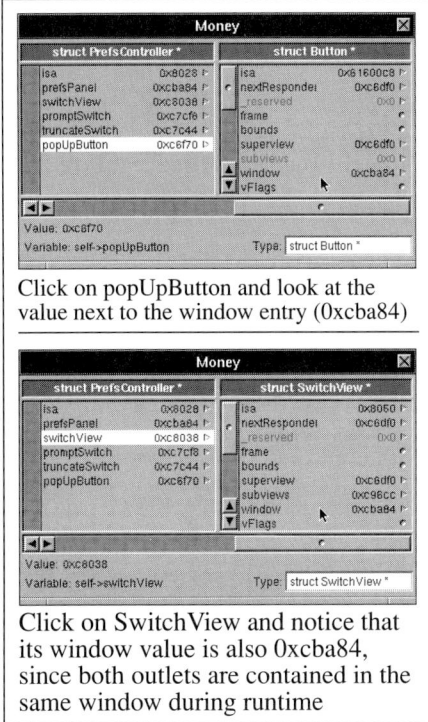

Click on popUpButton and look at the value next to the window entry (0xcba84)

Click on SwitchView and notice that its window value is also 0xcba84, since both outlets are contained in the same window during runtime

Figure D.6 The value of **popUpButton**'s and **switchView**'s **window** outlets should be identical since they refer to the same window

Now scroll down through **switchView** and look at the value for its **accessoryView** outlet. This value (**0xc7c44**) should match the value for **truncateSwitch** since the first accessory view for the switchview is the truncate switchbutton. Figure D.7 illustrates this.

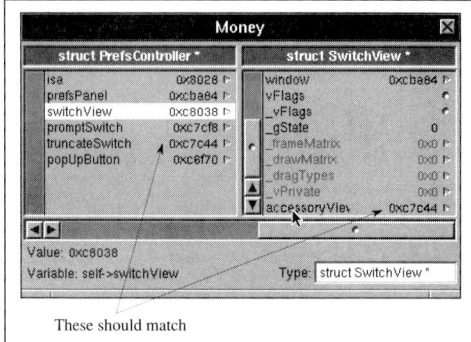

Figure D.7 Comparing the value of **switchView**'s **accessoryView** outlet against **truncateSwitch**

There are four types of entries in the Object Browser:

- entries with a small arrow ( ) such as the **switchView** outlet indicate that there is more information to be displayed.
- disabled entries, which represent **nil** objects. For example, since **popUpButton** does not have any subviews, its **subviews** outlet is **0x0** and grayed out.
- entries with values immediately next to the field name such as the case with **promptSwitch**'s **tag**. These entries represent simple scalar values like **int**s and **float**s.
- entries with a dimple ( ), which indicate that the variable is a **struct**, like **promptSwitch**'s **frame**, or an array (we will see an example of this shortly). The **frame** variable is a **struct** that contains two other **struct**s, **origin** and **size**. The **origin struct** contains two **float**s, **x** and **y**, and the **size struct** contains two **float**s,

width and **height**. To examine these values, simply click on them.

> Recall that an object is actually a pointer to a **struct**. Thus, an object's instance variable is simply a field in the **struct**. Therefore, to print the value of an object's instance variable, we must print the value of the **struct**'s corresponding field. For example, to print the value of the **popUpButton** outlet, use:
>
> ```
> (gdb) p *$1.popUpButton
> ```
> **$1** is a mnemonic for **self** from the first step. Thus, this command basically dereferences the pointer to arrive at the **struct** and then print out the value of the **popUpButton** field of the **struct**.

D.2.7 Continuing the Execution

Exit the **displayPrefsPanel:** by clicking **Finish**; **gdb** then completes the method and prints:

gdb exiting **displayPrefsPanel:**

```
Value returned is $4 = (struct PrefsController *) 0xc703c
```

However, the Gdb panel still indicates that our application is stopped and we still cannot interact with our **Money** application. So we click **Finish** again. At this point, **gdb** prints out a fairly cryptic message:

Tracing an AppKit method

```
0x605dd7e in -[Application sendAction:to:from:] ()
```

To continue execution, click Continue

Try as we might, we cannot seem to get out of this method. What is happening? **gdb** is tracing through methods in the Application Kit (the one above is an event-dispatch message to **NXApp**, the application object), and the output is gibberish to us since we do not have the source to the Application Kit. To have our program continue as normal, click **Continue**.

Now that we have a feel for setting breakpoints and continuing, we will explore how to modify variables.

D.2.8 Setting Variables

By setting variables and then continuing, we can experiment with our application or fix one bug and then continue without first recompiling. This feature is a great time-saver since the compilation and linking process can be fairly time-consuming. Before we can modify a variable, however, we must trigger a breakpoint. In our case, we set one at **convert:**. To trigger it, click on the first field (**American dollars**), type **1**, and press **Return** to send a **convert:** message to the moneyconverter.

gdb allows us to modify variables during execution

Excerpted listing of **convert:** in MoneyConverter.m

```
11  - convert:sender
12  {
13    int index, loop;
14    unsigned int right,left = 10;
15    float entry, value, dollar_equiv;
16    id cell;
17
18    // Array contains the conversion of rates
19    // of other currencies to dollars
20    static float rate[MAXIMUM] =
21      {1.00, 135.0, 0.50, 1.67, 6.00, 14.5};
22
23    // Determine which field of the form
24    // was the last to be edited
25    index = [theForm selectedIndex];
26
27    // Calculate equivalent of foreign currency
28    // at edited field to dollar equivalent
29    entry = [theForm floatValueAt:index];
30    dollar_equiv = entry / rate[index];
```

Setting Variables

```
60    return self;
61  }
```

Using the Object Browser, click on **rate** to display the **rate** array. Figured D.8 illustrates this.

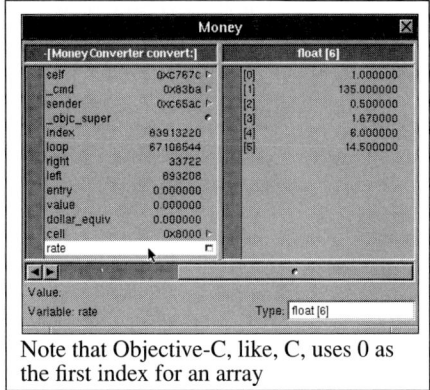

Note that Objective-C, like, C, uses 0 as the first index for an array

Figure D.8 Checking the values of the **rate** array in the moneyconverter

Now assume that a dollar is actually worth 7 francs (rather than 6, which is presently the case in the application). Thus, we want to change the fifth field, **francs**, to **7**. To change a variable, use the **set** command in **gdb** shell window. To set **rate[4]** (since C uses **0** as the starting index for an array, **rate[4]** is actually the fifth field) to 7, use:

Setting a variable during execution

```
(gdb) set rate[4]=7
```

Now click **Continue** to continue the execution. The **francs** field should now display **7.000000** instead of **6.000000** since we have changed the value of **rate[4]**.

We can also send messages to objects to query their values

We can also send messages to the objects to query them. For example, we can query what value is at a given field of **moneyForm**. To do so, trigger the breakpoint again by clicking the **Convert** button. In the **gdb** shell window, type:

Messaging an object to print one of its values

```
(gdb) p/f [moneyForm FloatValueAt:3]
```

This should return the value in the fourth field of **moneyForm** (**1.670000**, assuming that **1.000000** is in the first field). The **/f** parameter specifies that **print** (abbreviated as **p**) should print the output as a floating point number, similar to **%f** in a **printf()** function call.

D.3 Suggestions

So far, we have covered the most common commands in **gdb**. To explore **gdb** further, try the following exercises in **gdb**.

- explore the **switchToView:** method and verify that the **sender** of the message is the matrix that contains the popuplist entries. To do so, send a **class** message to **sender** and print the result with the **p** command.
- verify that the popuplist is the target of the trigger button by sending **popUpButton** a **target** message.
- use the Object Browser to see how **switchView**'s **accessoryView** outlet updates when we use the popuplist to toggle between the accessory views (**promptSwitch** and **truncateSwitch**). The **accessoryView** outlet should match the **id** of the outlet that is being displayed in the switchview.
- set a breakpoint at **awakeFromNib** in **PrefsController.m** and verify that the prefscontroller receives an **awakeFromNib** message after loading its **.nib** file.

D.4 Summary

In this appendix, we covered some techniques for tracing NeXTSTEP applications. The two main challenges are isolating where the objects are created and when implicit messages are sent since these do not explicitly appear in the source code. For example, **NXApp** automatically sends an **awakeFromNib** message to the object if it implements the method.

For debugging applications, NeXTSTEP provides **gdb,** a powerful Objective-C debugger that offers a host of commands. In this appendix, we covered some of the major commands including setting breakpoints, continuing the execution, printing, and altering variables. Edit provides an interface to most of these commands through the Gdb panel, although we still need to use the **gdb** shell window for some commands such as **set** (for setting a variable to a specified value).

Appendix E Resources

This appendix lists other sources of information that cover NeXTSTEP. Keep in mind that NeXTSTEP is a fairly new but very dynamic technology, and its community is one of the most active in the industry. Consequently, there is a great number of sources to look to for help. These include, but are not limited to:

- books
- periodicals
- newsgroups (on Usenet and Internet)
- the quarterly NeXTAnswers
- product catalogues
- prefabricated objects
- free source code and tutorials from the archives
- users groups
- conventions
- and, of course, the bundled on-line documentation and source code.

E.1 Bundled Documentation and Source Code

The on-line documentation contains a wealth of information and should be the first source for any questions. Note that this appendix lists only the on-line documentation that pertains to the topics covered in this book such as the Application Kit and Objective-C. It does not list other topics such as the other kits (DBKit, Sound Kit, PhoneKit and Indexing Kit), Mach, et al.

Most of the documentation is stored under **/NextLibrary/ Documentation**. The easiest way to consult this documentation is to use the Digital Librarian (for more information on Digital Librarian and the contents of these folders, see Appendix C). The folders that pertain to the topics in this book include:

- **Concepts**
- **DevTools**
- **Examples**
- **GeneralRef**
- **UserInterface**.

Note that Addison-Wesley Publishing Company has published the entire bundled documentation for NeXTSTEP. Some of them are listed in the next section.

The bundled source code is another source of inspiration and information. These examples are stored under **/NextDeveloper/Examples/AppKit** and **/NextDeveloper/Examples/PostScript**. Each AppKit example includes a **README.rtf** which explains what the example illustrates.

E.2 Books

As of this writing, there are few books that is specifically written on NeXTSTEP. However, since NeXTSTEP is composed of many diverse topics (object-oriented design and programming, Objective-C, PostScript, UNIX, etc), the list of reference book is still quite extensive.

E.2.1 NeXTSTEP

These books concentrate on using and programming in the NeXTSTEP environment.

NeXTSTEP Programming: Step One: Object-Oriented Applications by Michael K. Mahoney and Simson L. Garfinkel (ISBN 0-387-97884-4). Springer Verlag, 1992. A reference for NeXTSTEP programming with a wealth of information.

NeXTSTEP General Reference Volume 1 by NeXT Inc. (ISBN 0-201-62220-3). Addison-Wesley, 1992. Includes documentation on the Application Kit and all of the NeXTSTEP functions, such as **NXWriteDefault**().

NeXTSTEP Programming Interface Summary by NeXT Inc. (ISBN 0-201-63253-5). Addison-Wesley, 1992. Lists all of the methods and their return types in NeXTSTEP. This book does not explain what the methods and functions do.

NeXTSTEP Development Tools and Techniques by NeXT Inc. (ISBN 0-201-63249-7). Addison-Wesley, 1992. Includes documentation on how to use the various development tools such as **gdb**, Yap, etc.

E.2.2 Object-Oriented Design and Technology

Object-Oriented Design with Applications (ISBN 0-8053-0091-0) by Grady Booch. The Benjamin/Cummings Publishing Company, 1991. Extremely detailed and considered by many software engineers to be the premier reference on object-oriented design.

Designing Object-Oriented Software (ISBN 0-13-629825-7) by Rebecca Wirfs-Brock, Brian Wilkerson and Lauren Wiener. Prentice Hall, 1990. This book discusses issues involved in formulating an object-oriented design such as how to delegate responsibilities, what pitfalls to avoid, etc.

Object-Oriented Information Systems (ISBN 0-471-54364-0) by David Taylor. John Wiley & Sons Inc., 1992. This book explores the benefits of object-oriented technology and object-oriented databases. Dr. Taylor's prose is a work of art. Highly recommended.

E.2.3 Object-Oriented Programming and Objective-C

There has been very little documentation on this language but hopefully, that will change as more people are introduced to NeXTSTEP.

Object-Oriented Programming: An Evolutionary Approach, 2nd Edition (ISBN 0-201-54834-8) by Brad J. Cox and Andrew J. Novobilski. Addison-Wesley, 1991. Dr. Cox is the creator of Objective-C and founder of StepStone Inc. In this book, he discusses the merits of using an evolutionary approach rather than a revolutionary approach to reap the rewards of object-oriented programming.

Objective-C: Object Oriented Programming Techniques (ISBN 0-201-50828-1) by Lewis J. Pinson and Richard S. Wiener. Addison-Wesley, 1991. This book discusses the differences between Objective-C in NeXTSTEP and Objective-C as implemented by StepStone Inc. Includes some mini-tutorials in NeXTSTEP.

An Introduction to Object-Oriented Programming (ISBN 0-201-54709-0) by Timothy Budd. Addison-Wesley, 1991. This introduces object-oriented programming concepts and illustrates these ideas in four different object-oriented languages: Smalltalk, Objective-C, C++, and Object Pascal.

E.2.4 PostScript

These books concentrate on PostScript, the device-independent language that gives NeXTSTEP its powerful imaging capability. Display PostScript (PostScript with extensions for interactive imaging) is also covered.

PostScript Language: Tutorial and Cookbook (ISBN 0-201-10179-3). Adobe Systems Incorporated, 1992. As the inventor of PostScript and Display PostScript, Adobe's references are the most authoritative source of information for these languages. Each of Adobe's books sports a different color cover and each is nicknamed after the color. This is the "Blue Book" and introduces PostScript with many examples and tutorials.

Programming the Display PostScript with NeXTSTEP (ISBN 0-201-58135-3). Adobe Systems Incorporated, 1992. Also known as the "Purple Book," this covers Display PostScript as it is specifically implemented in NeXTSTEP and includes many optimization techniques.

Learning PostScript: A Visual Approach (ISBN 0-938-151-12-6) by Ross Smit. PeachPit Press, 1990. An excellent introduction to PostScript. The author uses the unusual approach of showing the

PostScript code on one page and displaying the results on the opposite page. Highly recommended.

Thinking in PostScript (ISBN 0-201-52372-8) by Glenn Reid. Addison-Wesley, 1990. This PostScript book is specifically aimed at programmers already familiar with other languages who need to unlearn certain concepts before programming effectively in PostScript.

E.2.5 C

Since Objective-C is ultimately based on C, having a solid foundation in C is a prerequisite for debugging in and mastering Objective-C.

The C Programming Language ISBN (0-13-110362-8), 2nd Edition by Brian Kernighan and Dennis Ritchie. Prentice-Hall, 1988. The authors are the creators of the C language and, as such, this book is widely regarded as *the* C reference manual: it is often referred to as the "C bible" or "K&R." Amazingly concise, although it may be too terse for beginners.

Practical C Programming (ISBN 0-937175-65-X) by Steve Oualline. O'Reilly and Associates, 1991. Written in a light style with many amusing anecdotes, this text is an introductory C textbook that emphasizes writing human-readable code.

Microsoft C Programming for the PC, Revised Edition (ISBN 0-672-22661-8) by Robert LaFore. The Waite Group, 1989. Although this book concentrates on a different compiler in a different operating system (MS-DOS), the author's explanations are so clear that this book deserves to be mentioned here. Highly recommended.

E.2.6 UNIX

Since NeXTSTEP is currently built on Mach and UNIX, it is essential that a NeXTSTEP programmer become familiar with the UNIX terminology and system calls. Some of these books are geared toward using UNIX and some are geared toward the internals of UNIX.

C on the UNIX System (ISBN 0-937175-23-4) by David Curry. O'Reilly and Associates, 1989. This book concentrates on BSD 4.2 (although it also mentions SystemV) and it is aimed at intermediate C programmers who wish to become UNIX programmers.

Design and Implementation of the 4.3 BSD UNIX Operating System (ISBN 0-201-06196-1) by Samuel J. Leffler, Marshall Kirk McKusick, Michael J. Karel and John S. Quartermain. Addison-Wesley. Some of the authors are the key developers of the BSD implementation and this book is considered the definitive book on BSD UNIX.

E.2.7 User-Interface Design

TOG on Interface (ISBN 0-201-60842-1) by Bruce "Tog" Togzinni. Addison-Wesley, 1992. A light hearted and very useful book on user-interface design techniques.

E.2.8 Miscellaneous

Managing Projects with make (ISBN 0-937175-18-8) by Andrew Oram and Steve Talbott. O'Reilly and Associates, 1991. This is about the only concise and readable reference to this otherwise-cryptic tool. Highly recommended.

Learning GNU Emacs (ISBN 0-937175-84-6) by Debra Caerson and Bill Rosenblatt. O'Reilly and Associates, 1991. The authors do a wonderful job of explaining this ubiquitous editor (emacs is bundled with NeXTSTEP). While emacs is undeniably less user-friendly than Edit, it contains many more features; Emacs can do everything that ProjectBuilder and Edit are capable of including editing, compiling, debugging, etc. Highly recommended.

The vi Editor (ISBN 0-93175-67-6) by Linda Lamb. O'Reilly and Associates, 1990. A no-nonsense book on the ubiquitous UNIX line editor. Highly recommended.

E.3 Magazines and Journals

There are three major magazines available at newsstands and there are many others available either through Internet or directly from the publisher.

NeXTWorld
A bi-monthly marketing-oriented magazine available at most newsstands. The articles are primarily about how NeXTSTEP is used and its impact on the industry. It also contains interviews with key figures and products reviews. For more information, contact NeXTWorld at:

> NeXTWorld
> 501 2nd Street
> San Francisco, CA 94107

NeXT User's Journal (formerly BuzzNUG)
A valuable source of technical information with topics ranging from system administration to image processing. This journal is produced on a sporadic schedule and the current issue, as well as back issues, are freely available from the Internet archives (see the following section for more information on the Internet archives). For more information, contact:

> Jon Bennett
> jdb@dkstar.UUCP

Object-Based Computing
A monthly magazine that concentrates on object-oriented technology; the publisher also offers electronic distribution via e-mail.

> Object-Based Computing
> Geordie Korper
> Phone: (312) 951-7462 or (800) 394-4487

NeXTWorld Extra
A monthly supplement to NeXTWorld that contains the latest developments in the NeXT community. For more information, contact:

> NeXTWorld

501 2nd Street
San Francisco, CA 94107

NeXTWatch Journal
A monthly magazine that concentrates on product reviews. For more information, contact:
NeXTwatch Journal (Product Reviews)
Skylee Press
Phone: (415) 474-7803

AppWrapper
A monthly catalog that lists new product releases and includes short articles. The publisher also offers electronic distribution. For more information, contact:
AppWrapper
Paget Press
Phone: (206) 448-0845

E.4 Internet Archives

The *Internet* is basically a global network that consists of thousands of computers. Connecting to the Internet gives you access to a wide variety of services, including e-mail and *anonymous ftp* (file transfer protocol). For more information about the Internet, consult your system administrator or user group(s).

There are dozens of NeXT-related archives (computers which serve as repositories) but the most important ones are **sonata.cc.purdue.edu** (at Purdue) and **cs.orst.edu** (at Oregon State University). Both of these sites have a bewildering number of sample programs and documentation. There are two different ways of *downloading* (copying data from their machine to yours) from these machines: **anonymous ftp** and the mail server (only **sonata** offers the mail server).

The following section explains how to use **anonymous ftp** and the mail server at **sonata.cc.purdue.edu** to obtain the source code for the examples in this book. Since the reply time for the e-mail server is variable (from a few hours to several days), use it only if your site is not on the Internet. Unfortunately, there are currently no NeXTSTEP interfaces for either **anonymous ftp** or for the mail server.

E.4.1 Using anonymous ftp

For **anonymous ftp**, the remote site has created a login ID, **anonymous**, that anyone can use. Use your login ID as the password. This is a courteous gesture to the system administrators, since they want to track who is downloading from their site. The following section shows a sample **anonymous ftp** session, which downloads the **AlexNeXTSTEPSource.tar.Z** file to the current folder (this file contains the source code examples from this book).

Sample anonymous ftp session

```
% ftp sonata.cc.purdue.edu
Connected to sonata.cc.purdue.edu.
220 sonata.cc.purdue.edu FTP server (Version 5.1
(NeXT 1.0) Tue Jul 21, 1992) ready.
Name (sonata.cc.purdue.edu:alex): anonymous
331 Guest login ok, send ident as password.
Password: (Type in your login ID as the password)
230 Guest login ok, access restrictions apply.
Remote system type is UNIX.
ftp> cd pub/next/submissions
200 PORT command successful.
ftp> binary (The file is in binary)
200 Type set to I. (Binary and image are synonymous)
ftp> get AlexNeXTSTEPBook.tar.Z
200 PORT command successful.
150 Opening BINARY mode data connection for
AlexNeXTSTEPSource.tar.Z (49262 bytes).
226 Transfer complete.
49262 bytes received in 2.6 seconds (18 Kbytes/s)
ftp> quit (Quit ftp)
221 Goodbye.
%
```

At this point, the **AlexNeXTSTEPSource.tar.Z** is on your machine in the current directory. However, it is **compress**ed and **tar**red. See "Unpacking the Data" on page 533 to see how to un**compress** and un**tar** the data.

E.4.2 Using the Mail Server

To contact the mail server at **sonata**, use the Mail application and send a message to **archive-server@sonata.cc.purdue.edu** with commands. The mail server understands many commands, but we are only interested in the following:

- **help**—unlike the other commands, this one should be entered on the subject line of the mail request. This asks the mail server to mail the help file with the commands and their uses.
- **index** *directory*—lists the contents of the folder specified by *folder*. We typically request the index to find out what programs are available and then follow-up with another message to download for the program(s).
- **path** *machine*—specifies a different destination e-mail address to send the file(s) to. For example, **john@nomachine.edu** can mail a request and have the files sent to **jane@nomachine.edu**.
- **size limit**—many sites impose a limit on the size of mail messages. Since the files at the archives tend to be quite large, specify the limit imposed at your site. If the mail message is larger that your site's limit, it will never arrive at your site.
- **send** *file*—send the file specified by *file*. Note that the **send** command expects only one parameter, although each mail request can include as many **send** commands as needed.

To request the mail server to send the **AlexNeXTSTEPSource.tar.Z** file from the **pub/next/submissions** directory and to request an index of this directory, perform the following steps.

1. Start the Mail application.
2. Use **Command-n** to get a new mail window.
3. Address the mail message to **archive-server@sonata.cc.purdue.edu**
4. Type the following in the mail body:
   ```
   path userid@address
   index pub/next/submissions
   send pub/next/submissions/AlexNeXTTEPSource.tar.Z
   ```
5. Click on the **NeXTMail** button to make it non-NeXTMail, since the mail server cannot understand NeXTMail format.

6. Click **Deliver** to deliver the mail message.

After a few hours to several days, the mail server should process the mail message and mail to you a message, which is the encoded form of the requested file. Since standard UNIX mail cannot process binary data, the mail server has to convert it to ASCII (using **uuencode**) before sending it to you. Therefore, you have to convert the data back to binary using **uudecode**:

1. Highlight the mail message from the line that starts with **begin** (that is, do not copy the mail header) to the last line (the one with **end**).
2. Use **Command-c** to copy the highlighted text.
3. Launch Edit and open a new document. Make sure that it is an ASCII document and not Rich Text Format.
4. Use **Command-v** to paste the text and then save the file as /**tmp/tempfile** (or anything else).
5. Launch Terminal and type:
    ```
    % uudecode /tmp/tempfile
    ```
6. This creates **AlexNeXTTEPSource.tar.Z** in /**tmp** by decoding the data in /**tmp/tempfile**.

However, the data will still be **compress**ed and **tar**red. To convert it to a usable format, see the next section.

> If **uudecode** complains with a **Short file** message, it means you probably did not copy the entire last line (with the **end** statement). Copy the entire text of the mail message (without the mail headers) including the **end** line and try again.

E.4.3 Unpacking the Data

Since the **AlexNeXTSTEPSource.tar.Z** file is **compress**ed and **tar**red, use the following command to untar and uncompress it.

```
% zcat AlexNeXTSTEPBookSource.tar.Z | tar -xvf -
```

This command uncompresses the file to **stdout** and then pipes it to **tar** to extract the individual files that constitute the **tar**red file.

E.5 NeXTAnswers

Another source of valuable information is the **NeXTAnswers**, a directory containing commonly asked questions collected by the NeXT support staff.

The **NeXTAnswers** file is distributed quarterly as a **compress**ed **tar**red file via the Internet; the file usually resides under **/pub/next/submissions** at the Internet archive sites. The name of the file is **NeXTAnswers** followed by the date which it was released. After downloading the file, un**tar** and un**compress** it to create a directory.

Afterwards, add the directory as another target to your bookshelf in Digital Librarian. Search the target as normal.

E.6 Newsgroups

Short of having an account with NeXT Inc. or having a resident NeXTSTEP expert, posting a question to the newsgroups is about the fastest way of receiving an answer. There are five major newsgroups that deal primarily with NeXTSTEP and a few additional ones that deal with broader topics such as object-oriented programming, PostScript, etc. For more information on how to set up a newsfeed and subscribe to newsgroups, contact your system administrator or user group.

The best program for reading news is *NewsGrazer*, an amazing newsreader program with many, many features. Since NewsGrazer is a public domain program, the easiest way to obtain it is to ask someone who already has it like members of your local user group(s) or look for it at the Internet archive sites. The following forums are related to the topics discussed in this book.

- **comp.sys.next.programmer**—concentrates on programming-related issues such as how to use the savepanel, how to use the Application Kit, etc.
- **comp.sys.next.misc**—discusses miscellaneous issues, everything from the future of NeXTSTEP to various NeXT sightings in the media.

- **comp.sys.next.advocacy**—concentrates on the merits of NeXTSTEP; often degenerates into mud-slinging and name calling.
- **comp.sys.next.marketplace**—lists used hardware and software for sale. A bargain hunter's paradise.
- **comp.sys.next.software**—focuses on how to use various third-party software packages.
- **comp.sys.next.hardware**—discusses how to use various hardware such as scanners, printers, etc.
- **comp.sys.lang.objective-c**—discusses Objective-C including uses, limitations, and design.
- **comp.sys.lang.postscript**—discusses PostScript including uses, limitation, and design.

E.7 Users Groups

User groups are another great resource. They often offer discounts on software and hardware since they can purchase in bulk. Most members are quite helpful and can be indispensable for answering questions such as how to set up modems (for hooking up to the Internet), where to purchase the cheapest disks, etc. As of this writing, there are more than 400 user groups, and many more are formed daily. Most user groups meet once a month.

Special thanks to Conrad Geiger of NeXT for providing this list. For more information on how to form a user group, contact Conrad Geiger at:

>Conrad Geiger
>Manager, International NeXT User Groups
>NeXT Computer, Inc.
>2445 Carillon Point
>Kirkland, Washington 98033 USA
>FAX: (206) 827-6360

Also, e-mail to: **user_groups@next.com** or call (800) 848-6398.

UNITED STATES

Alabama

BANGED-UP (Birmingham Alabama NeXT Group for Educators, Users, Programmers)
Robert Buster
Phone: (205) 942-2314

NANCUG North Alabama NeXT User Group
Daniel L. Green
Phone: (205) 772-8561 or (205) 730-1770
Russell George
Phone: (205) 837-2027

Alaska

LUGNUTS (Arctic Circle NeXT User Group)
Greg Johnson
Phone: (907) 474-7538 or (907) 474-5676

Anchorage NeXT User Group
Marty Fossum
Phone: (907) 561-5111 or (907) 564-4566

Arizona

Phang (Phoenix NeXT User Group)
Gary Frederick, President
Phone: (602) 869-0316
Jim Ames
Phone: (602) 965-2906

Tucson NeXT User Group
David Koski
Phone: (602) 629-0962

Motorola NeXT Group (Arizona chapter)
Ray Doskocil, Director
Phone: (602) 897 5096

StrataNUG (Phoenix Chapter)
Noah Davids
Phone: (602) 852-3108

Arizona Corporate Computer Society
Bob Padua
Phone: (602) 545-7421
Jon Ayers
Phone: (602) 491-1014

Arkansas

Arkansas NeXT User Group
Tim Neudecker
e-mail: ten@engr.uark.edu

ARKNUG
Caruth Alexander
Phone: (501) 521-3124

California

BANG (Bay Area NeXT User Group)
P.O. Box 1731
Palo Alto, CA 94302
Phone: (415) 327-BANG

Berkeley NeXT User Group
Bernt Wahl
Phone: (510) 644-0139

BMUG
Rick Reynolds
Phone: (415) 978-3385

Orange County NeXT Group
Phone: (714) 938-8850

Santa Barbara NeXT User Group
Fabian E. Schonholz, President
Phone: (805) 968-3101

Nuggets
Gary Novak, President
Phone: (213) 343-2400

CaJUN (Caltech and JPL Users of NeXT)
Ernest N. Prabhakar, President
Phone: (818) 356-8379

UC Riverside NeXT User Group
Paul Lowe, President
Phone: (714) 787-3883

SlugNUG (Santa Cruz NeXT Users' Group)
Doug MacIntire
Phone: (408) 423-2870

SNuG (San Diego NeXT User Group)
Nicholas MacConnell, President
Phone: (619) 481-7535 or (619) 565-9738
SNUG BBS: (619) 456-2522 (24 hours)

Carl Lowenstein (SNuG Developers Group)
e-mail: clowenstein@UCSD.EDU

Santa Barbara Business NeXT User Group
Geofrey Wyatt
e-mail: 0003302040@mcimail.com
Phone: (805) 963-5904

SLACNUG (SLAC NeXT User Group)
Dennis Wisinski
Phone: (415) 926-3335

cc:NeXT users
Brent Gilmore
Phone: (619) 594-7579

SCaN (Southern California NeXT Group)
Michael Mahoney, Professor and Chair
Phone: (310) 985-1550
e-mail: mahoney@csulb.edu
Bob Desharnais, Vice-President

Phone: (213) 343-2056
e-mail: bob@biol1next.calstatela.edu

CP-NUG (Cal Poly NeXT User Group)
Mont Rothstein, President
Phone: (805) 543-8795 (h)

FogNUG (NeXT User Group)
Peter Preuss
e-mail: preuss@futon.sfsu.edu
Dr. Lawrence S. Kroll
Phone: (415) 338-2539 (w) or (415) 386-0243 (h)
UC, Irvine NeXTclub
John Gulas
Phone: (714) 786-3733

Black Box Club (University of Southern California)
Tyson Hartman, President
Phone: (213) 749-1096

Gold-NUG (UC, Davis)
Wayne Jackson, President
Phone: (916) 756-1540

Sacramento NeXT User Group
Scott Collard
Phone: (916) 443-7413

Canon NeXT User Group
Subrata Sircar
Phone: (415) 852-2000 Ext. 234
e-mail: ssircar@canon.com

NOCCC NeXT SIG
(North Orange County Computer Club)
Don J. Davis
Phone: (714) 870-4424

CSuNeXT (Cal State Northridge)
Nader Nafissi
Phone: (310) 838-2680

Naval Postgraduate NeXT User Group
Bradley M. Polk
Phone: (408) 646-2354

TRW NeXT User Group
Mark R. Thomsen
Phone: (310) 812-7353

ESL NeXT User Group
Denis Lynch
Phone: (408) 743-6318

Amdahl NeXT User Group
Joel Ledain
Phone: (408) 737-5709

NASA NeXT User Group
Juan Urista
Phone: (818) 306-6191

LLNL NeXT User Group
Erik Sowa
Phone: (510) 422-2415

Oracle NeXT User Group
Michael B. Parker
Phone: (415) 506-6278

El Segundo NeXT User Group
Phil Rorex
Phone: (310) 643 5111

Alain Pinel NeXT User Group
Mark Richards
Phone: (408) 356-0715

Sonoma County NeXT User Group
e-mail: poff@vax.sonoma.edu

Val Verde NeXT User Group
Darrell Lynn

Phone: (714) 940-6100 Ext. 240
e-mail : dlynn@mail.valverde.edu

Humboldt NeXT User Group
Phone: (707) 826-3218

Novell NeXT Users (California Chapter)
e-mail: jscherer@novell.com

LANUG
Penny Ragland
Phone: (310) 363-1891

SMNL (Santa Monica NeXT Legal Group)
Rosario Perry
Phone: (310) 394-9831

Colorado

rmNUG (Rocky Mountain NeXT Users Group)
Barbara Dyker
Phone: (303) 443-2665

CSU NeXT User Group
Matthew Moran / Robert LaBelle
Phone: (303) 223-5513

Connecticut

Elm City NUG
Nathan Janette, Coordinator
Phone: (203) 432-5065 (days)

UCONN NeXT User Group
David Ferrero
Phone: (203) 429-4695

CTNUG (Southern Connecticut NeXT User Group)
Tom Affinito
Phone: (203) 221-4616
Chuck Herrick
Phone (203) 846-0383

Delaware

University of Delaware NeXT User Group
Chris Pyrros
Phone: (302) 239-1868 (h) or (302) 738-7551 (w)

District of Columbia

WaNUG (Washington area NeXT Group)
Hugh O'Neill, President
Phone: (410) 224-3116 (after 8 p.m EST)

Naval Research Labs NeXT User Group
John Michopoulos
Richard Pitre
Phone: (202) 767-2165 or 2189

Florida

Miami NeXT User Group
Marshall Gilula
Phone:(305) 854-8954

Gainesville NeXT Users Group (GNUG)
e-mail: statman@stat.ufl.edu

North Florida NeXT User Group
Harald W. Kegelmann
Phone: (904) 644-4720

Southern Florida NeXT User Group
Oscar Brooks
Phone: (407) 633-5790 or (407) 867-4430

Palm Beach NeXT User Group
Robb Aley Allan
Phone: (407) 832-401

Georgia

BuzzNUG (Georgia Tech NeXT User Group)

Bert Lindgren, Buzznug meeting coordinator
Phone: (404) 841-6220

Atlanta NeXT User Group
Ram Madabushi
Phone: (404) 621-3126

Hawaii

Hawaii NeXT Group
Eric Uyeda, Chair
Phone: (808) 225-3830 (pager number)

Idaho

Boise State University NeXT Group
Phone: (208) 385-1172

Illinois

Argonne NeXT User Group
Mark Henderson
Phone: (708) 972-5963

ChiNUG (Chicago NeXT User Group)
J.H. Yoon
Phone: (708) 332-1340

SSNUG (South Side NeXT Users Group)
Paul Woods
Phone: (708) 361-6800

IHNUG (AT&T NeXT User Group)
Felix Lugo
Phone: (708) 713-4374

The Loop Group (Downtown Chicago group)
Edward (Ted) Shelton, President
Phone: (312) 951-7462

Motorola NeXT Group (Illinois chapter)

Ernie Chan, Director
Phone: (708) 576 7266

University of Chicago NeXT User Group
Marianne Guntow
Phone: (312) 702-7500

IlliNUG
Steven Hinkle
Phone: (217) 333-6120

Champaign-Urbana NeXT Users Group
Philip M. Johnson
Phone: (217) 398-0700 Ext. 160
Joe Kaiping Ext. 172

Illinois Institute of Technology NUG
Robert Von Borstel
Phone: (312) 567-5962

Knox NUG
Dennis M. Schneiderl
Phone: (309) 343-0112 Ext. 420

Indiana

Notre Dame NeXT User Group
Bruce Williams
Phone: (219) 239-6588

THaNG (Terre Haute Area NeXT Group)
Bill Blackert
Phone: (812) 877-9030

Indiana University NeXT Users Group
Mike Basinger
Phone: (812) 336-0714

Iowa

NUGI (University of Iowa NeXT Group)

Maury Leysens
Phone: (319) 354-5990

ISNUG (Iowa State NeXT User Group)
David Swanlund
Phone: (515) 296-2565 (h) or (515) 294-3130 (w)

Kansas

Kansas City NeXT User Group
Meg Grice
Phone: (816) 235-5212

Kentucky

Kentucky NeXT User Group, Inc.
Neil Greene
Phone: (606) 254-4060 or (606) 254-0899

Louisiana

LaNG
John Rettenmayer
Phone: (318) 342-1125

LSU NeXT User Group
Richard Miller
Phone: (504) 388-8690

Louisiana Tech NeXT User Group
Pat Bronson
Phone: (318) 255-0868

TuNG (Tulane NeXT User Group)
Matt Hopkins
Phone: (504) 865-5727 or (504) 897-9861

Maine

Maine NeXT Users Group

Malcolm M. Sanders
Phone (207) 288-4202

Maryland

MDnug (Maryland NeXT Users Group)
Bruce Verner
Phone (301) 637-5737

MENUS (Maryland Educational NeXT Users' Society)
Jeff Kight
Phone: (202) 885-2281

Johns Hopkins University NeXT User Group
Lee Watkins, Jr.
Phone: (410) 516-8096
Sue Harrison
Phone: (410) 747-7062 (w)

ARMY NeXT User Group
Thomas B. Bahder
Phone:. (301) 394-2042

City of Baltimore NeXT User Group
Tim Krus
Phone: (301) 396-4952

Massachusetts

The Boston Computer Society NeXT Users Group (#1)
Shawn Broderick
Phone: (617) 252-2090
Charles Perkins
(617) 523-1570

StrataNUG (Stratus NeXT User Group)
Eric Williams
Stratus Computer
Phone:(508) 460-2915

NUHU (NeXT Users of Harvard University)
David Joerg, Vice-President

Phone: (617) 493-3418
Tony Roth, Vice-President
Phone: (617) 493-7962

Boston University Club-NeXT (ACM)
Robert La Ferla
Phone: (617) 252-0088

NeXT Developers' Association
Charles Perkins
Phone: (617) 891-5555

WHOINUG (Woods Hole Oceanographic)
Institution NeXT User Group
Nathan Ulrich
Phone: (508) 457-2000 Ext. 3267

WMassNUG
Eric Mohr
Phone: (413) 367-9669

Michigan

Michigan State University NeXT User Group
Eric Byrne
Phone: (517) 353-4973 or (517) 882-2281
Mark Sullivan
Phone: (517) 353-9122 (w) or (517) 355-7653 (h)

MiNUG (University of Michigan NeXT Group)
Glen Gersten
Phone: (313) 353-9209

KaNu (Kalamazoo Next Users)
Jon E. Ferguson
Phone: (616) 387-0938 (w) or (616) 342-1483 (h)

Grand Valley NeXT User Group
Dr. Carl Erickson
Phone: (616) 895-2309

Minnesota

Minnesota NeXT User Group
Rodger McBride, President
e-mail: rmcbride@is.com
Mike Tie, Secretary
Phone: (507) 663-4067
e-mail: mtie@carleton.edu

Mayo Clinic NeXT User Group
Geoff Brunkhorst
Phone: (507) 284-1805

Twin Cities NeXT Publishing User Group
Dave Garbe
Phone: (612) 888-2645 Ext. 131

Mississippi

Mississippi NeXT User Group
Randy Bowie
Phone: (601) 232-7281

Missouri

St. Louis NeXT User Group
John Bartley
Phone: (314) 928-6913

Kansas City NeXT User Group
Meg Grice
Phone: (816) 235-5212

Montana

Big Sky NeXT User Group
Phone: (406) 587-7164

Nebraska

NANU (Nebraska Area NeXT User Group)

Hubert Hickman
Phone: (402) 397-8624

Nevada

Nevada NeXT Users Group
Karl Kraft
Phone: (702) 792-6799

UNR-NUG
Steven Foster
Phone: (702) 784-4292 (w)

New Hampshire

D.A.N.U.G. Dartmouth NeXT Users Group
Pete Schmitt
Phone: (603) 646-2085

New Hampshire NeXT User Group
Phone: (603) 743-4987

New Jersey

Princeton NeXT User Group
Jeffrey R. Blum
Phone: (609) 258-8394

Edward Lau
Phone: (609) 258-7707

New Jersey NeXT Group
Dr. Ted H. Szatrowski
Phone: (908) 418-1934
BBS #: (201) 622-5526 using login: guest
Joe Ryan
Phone: (609) 737-5582

AT&T User Group (New Jersey Chapter)
Dave Kallman
Phone: (908) 615-2989

SINS (Stevens Inst. NeXT Society)
Phone: (201) 216-3555

New Mexico

ANuG (Albuquerque chapter)
Mark Williams
Phone: (505) 265-2720 (h)

ANuG (Las Cruces chapter)
Gregory Burd
Phone: (505) 521-7010

Los Alamos NeXT Users Group
Chris Zoeller
Phone: (505) 662-9497 (h)

New York

GUN (Gotham Users of NeXT)
Paul Murphy, President
Phone: (718) 260-9848

NY NeXT Financial Services (NYFSNUG)
Eric Bergerson and Jon Roman
e-mail: jon@object.com and eb@object.com

Long Island NeXT Users Society (LINUS)
Mike McMahon
Phone: (516) 877-7805

Columbia NeXT User Group
Mara Helmuth
Phone: (212) 864-2667

Up-State New York NeXT User Group
Dr. Anthony G. Holland
Skidmore College
Phone: (518) 584-5000 Ext. 2606

UnNUG (Rochester & Upstate New York)

Eric Brown
Phone (716) 288-2786

FuNK (The Finger Lakes NeXT Users Group)
Jiro Nakamura
Phone: (607) 277-1440

RPI NeXT User Group
c/o Garance Alistair Drosehn
e-mail: gad@eclipse.its.rpi.edu

Syracuse University NeXT User Group (SUNG)
Dave Rebnord
Phone: (315) 443-1585

STONYBROOK NeXT User Group
William T. Jie / Peter Brink
Phone: (516) 632-3096

North Carolina

Triangle Area Users of the NeXT Group
Pranav Patel
Phone: (919) 677-8000

CHaNG (Charlotte area NeXT User Group)
David Silla
Phone: (704) 786-1185
Roberto E. Arrocha
Phone: (704) 554-9673

Ohio

CONE (Central Ohio NeXT Enthusiasts)
Jeff Schluep
Phone: (614) 292-4843

CWRUnug (Case Western Reserve University)
Mike Neuman
Phone: (216) 754-2051

SONG (Southern Ohio NeXT Group)

Tyler Gingrich
Phone: (513) 579-0455

Cleveland NeXT User Group
Louis J. (Jim) Kiraly
Phone: (216) 433-6023

Dublin, Ohio NeXT User Group
Gene Levine
Phone: (614) 761-5045

Oklahoma

Tulsa NeXT User Group
Charles Mather
Phone: (918) 588-5255

Oregon

Portland NeXT User Group
Lance Charlish
Phone: (503) 234-5644

Reed NeXT User Group
Jon Bieley
Phone: (503) 774-8647

JuriNUG
Gregory Miller
Phone: (503) 222-3613

PSU NeXT User Group
Pitak Chenkosol
e-mail: pitakc@eecs.ee.pdx.edu

Mid Valley Next Users Group
John Sechrest, President
Phone: (503) 737-5562

University of Oregon NeXT User Group
Audun Runde
Phone: (503) 346-1714

Pennsylvania

IBUG (Interface Builder User Group)
David Andeson
Phone (814) 332-2390

Carnegie Mellon Computer Club - NeXT SIG
Frank Tropschuh, Chair
Phone: (412) 268-5325
Bill Bumgarner
e-mail:bbum+@cmu.edu

PhANG (Philadelphia)
Noam Arzt
Phone: (215) 898-3029 (voice)
Shumon Huque
Phone: (215) 898-0588 or (215) 387-2494

Philadelphia NeXT SIG
Jason Ehrlich
BBS: (215) 635-2341
Phone: (215) 782-1328

PennNUG
Michael Mellinger
Phone: (814) 861-6594

Gettysburg NeXT User Group
Kit Beall
Phone: (717) 337-6932 or (717) 337-7124

University of Pennsylvania NeXT User Group
Peter J. Rucki
Phone: (412) 463-6377

Duquesne NeXT User Group
Lynda Barner West
Phone: (412) 434-6200

Lancaster NeXT User Group
Beth Katz
Phone: (717) 299-5987

Allentown NeXT User Group
Dan Stahlnecker
Phone: (215) 866-2881

Puerto Rico

Puerto Rico NeXT User Group
Dr. Francisco Tome
Phone: (809) 798-4464 (w) or (809) 257-8223 (h)

Rhode Island

Brown NeXT User Group
Ronald Antony
Phone: (401) 521-2829

South Carolina

University of South Carolina NeXT Users Group
Tim Mousseau
Phone: (803) 777-8047

Tennessee

East Tennessee NeXT User Group
John Wooten
Phone:(615) 576-9495

Nashville NeXT User Group
William Swats
Phone: (615) 665-1640

Texas

Austin NeXT User Group
Bill Dodd
Phone: (512) 331-9932

University of Texas NeXT User Group
Gary Terrell
Phone: (512) 471-0321

DaNG (Dallas Area NeXT Group)
Chris Bradley, Program Director
Phone: (214) 830-2273 M-F 8-5
Troy Whitsett
Phone: (214) 680-2060
Charlie Lindahl
Phone: (817) 794-5922

hAng (Houston Area Next Group)
John R. Glover, President
Phone: (713) 743-4430

Texas A&M NeXT User Group
Walter Daugherity, Faculty Advisor
Scott Beaudreau
Phone: (409) 846-5525

Trinity University NeXT User Group
Gregory Gerard
Phone: (512) 737-4648

SFA NeXT User Group
Joe McWilliams
Phone: (409) 568-1702

LoNG (Logical Objectives NeXT Group)
Vince Jordan
Phone: (713) 364-4125

iNG! (Angleton NeXT User Group)
Mike Bischoff
Fax: (409) 848-6000

UTSANUG - San Antonio NeXT User Group
Daniel Shelton
Phone: (512) 691-5594 (w)

Utah

Salt Lake NeXT Users Group
Kris Magnusson, Chair
Phone: (801) 355-6351

Robert Perkins, President
Phone: (801) 373-4394

Novell NeXT User Group (Utah Chapter)
James Grant
Phone: (801) 429-3268

Logan NeXT User Group
David Farrelly
Phone: (801) 750-1608

Virginia

McLain NeXT User Group
Ryon Packer
Phone: (703) 883-1355

VaTNUG (NeXT Users Group at VPI&SU)
Tim Buck
Phone: (703) 951-0655 (h) or (703) 231-4159 (o)

Hampton, Virginia NeXT User Group
Al Thompson, Director
Phone: (804) 728-3629

CVNUG, Central Virginia NeXT User Group
Jim De Arras
Phone: (804) 784-3127

University of Virginia NeXT Group
Stelios Makrinos
Phone: (804) 982-6279

Washington

Puget Sound NeXT Users Group
Peggy Thompson
Phone: (206) 448-0845

University of Washington NeXT User Group
Bill Barker
University of Washington

David Adler
Phone: (206) 543-0716

Washington State University NeXT Group
Jay P. Weidner, DVM
Phone: (509) 335-0812 or (509) 335-0711
Joe Gerkman
Phone: (509) 334-9594

Washington Islands NeXT Enthusiasts
Irving Wolfe
Phone: (206) 463-9399 x101
Fax: (206) 463-9399 Ext. 116

Wisconsin

MadNUG
Kim Simmons, President
Phone: (608) 263-0807
Don Thomson, MadNUG Technical Wizard
Phone: (608) 262-0138

Viterbo NeXT User Group
William Jensen
Phone: (608) 791-0250

Milwaukee NeXT User Group
Alberto Ricart
Phone: (414) 377-6039

Wyoming

WoNUG
John Perry Barlow
Phone: (307) 367-2466

ARGENTINA

Argentina NeXT User Group
Gaston Groisman
Phone: (941) 22664

AUSTRALIA

Victoria

OzNUG (Australian NeXT User Group)
Melbourne Chapter
Paul Davis, Chair
Phone: (61) 3 344-5397

OzNUG (Australian NeXT User Group)
Victoria Chapter
Brett Adam, chair
Phone: (61) 3 696 2490

OzNUG (Australian NeXT User Group)
La Trobe Chapter
Nicole Kaiyan
e-mail: nicolek@latcs1.lat.oz.au

OzNUG (Australian NeXT User Group)
Perth Chapter
Kevin McIsaac
e-mail: kevin@pyrmania.pyramid.com.au

Sydney

NoiSE! (NeXT Sydney Enthusiasts!)
John E. Venema
Telephone: (61) 2 930 9000

AUSTRIA

NUGat (NeXT User Group Austria)
Martin Laubach, coordinator
Phone: (43) 58801/8135-8138

Salzburg NeXT User Group
Bernhard Nocker
Phone: (43) 662-8044-6750

BELGIUM

Belgium NeXT User Group
Raf Schietekat
Phone: (32) 3-7763039

BERMUDA

Bermuda NeXT User Group
Richard Zuile
Phone: (809) 295-8777

BRAZIL

Brasilia NeXT User Group
Samuel Rocha de Oliveira
e-mail: SAMOLIVE@BRUNB.BITNET

CANADA

Alberta

NeXT User Club of Calgary
Vince Demarco, Coordinator
Phone: (403) 274-4002

NeXT/Edmonton Owners Network (NEON)
George Carmichael, chair
Phone: (403) 492-2462
Peter Karbaliotis, President
Phone: (403) 492-0197 (w) or (403) 481-4955 (h)

British Columbia

Simon Fraser Universty NeXT Users Group
Rory Gibson, Chair
Phone: (604) 922-5643

V-NUS, UBC Chapter

Robert Wong Jr.
Phone: (604) 322-6918

Vancouver NeXT Users Society (V-NUS)
Bob Bajwa
Phone: (604) 822-2928

Victoria NeXT User Group
Wayne Henriques
Phone: (604) 926-8826

Manitoba

Manitoba NeXT User Group
Richard Tilley
Phone: (204) 474-9738 (h) or (204) 474-9249 (w)

Nova Scotia

Nova Scotia NeXT Society (NS2)
Christopher Majka
Phone: (902) 425-3725

Nova Scotia NeXT User Group
Todd Rose
Phone: (902) 835-1028

Ontario

TANG (Toronto Area NeXT Group)
Phone: (416) 365-1899

Ottawa NeXT User Group
Hayward (K.H.) Lam, President
Phone: (613) 763-3663 (h) or (613) 233-8225 (w)
U. of Guelph NeXT User Group (UGNUG)
Phone: (519) 824-4120, Ext. 4521 or Ext. 4520

University of Western Ontario NeXT Group
Phone: (519) 858-0817

Ontario NeXT User Group

Kevin Ford / ComputerActive
Phone: (613) 225-4842

MacNUG
Pascal Gaudette
Phone: (416) 525-9140 Ext. 3184 (w)
(416) 525-1329 (h)

Sudbury NeXT User Group
Andre Roberge
Phone: (705) 675-1151 Ext. 2234

YUNUG
Steve Azmier
Phone: (705) 736-5376 Ext. 44693

Newfoundland

Newfoundland NeXT User Group
Tim Seifert
e-mail: tseifert@morgan.ucs.mun.ca

Quebec

Montreal NeXT Section of Club Macintosh
Robert Paulhus, President
Phone: (514) 939-0382

McGill University NeXT Group
Peter Deutsch
Phone: (514) 398-3709

Concordia University NUG
Stefanos Kiakas
e-mail: stefanos@concour.cs.concordia.ca

Saskatchewan

Saskatchewan NeXT User Group
Mishkin Berteig

Phone: (306) 343-6692
e-mail: gruber@abraham.usask.ca

Yukon Territory

NUGYT (NeXT User Group Yukon Territory)
Richard Lawrence
Phone: (403) 668-6280 (h) or (403) 668-7502 (w)

COMMONWEALTH OF INDEPENDENT STATES

Moscow NeXT User Group
Sevrioukov Vladimir Anatoljevich
Phone: (095) 200-25-68
Sergei E. Morozov
Phone: (095) 299-96-35

The 2nd Moscow NeXT User Group
Oleg S. Batsukov
Phone: (007 095) 576 4481

GlasNug
Steve Sarich
Phone: 011-7095-255-9698

DENMARK

Denmark NeXT User Group
Brian Mayoh
e-mail: bmayoh@daimi.aau.dk

DKNUG
Karsten Thygesen
Phone : (45) -98124259

DKNUG
Karsten Thygesen
Phone : (45) -98124259

BaNiA - Danish Users Group
e-mail: herring@pd.dth.dk

FINLAND

Finland Users of NeXT
Timo Vendelin
Phone: +358-0-456 1 (switchboard)
+358-0-456 5953 (direct)
+358-0-809 1287 (h)

FRANCE

FaNG - French area NeXT Group
Thierry Charles
Phone: (33) 67 64 07 97

French NeXT User Group
e-mail: eric@cubx.oleane.com

French NeXT Group
Hubert Delahaye
Phone: (33) 49 63 82 07

NaNG - North area NeXT Group
Christophe Janot
Phone: (33) 33 80 00 23

Nice NeXT User Group
Kjartan Emilsson
Phone: (33) 93 52 98 36

Paris NeXT User Group
Frederic Pralong
Phone: (33) 40 60 78 36

GERMANY

Hannover NeXT User Group
Martin Ortlepp
Phone: (49) 511 421278

BeNG - Berlin NeXT User Group
Matthias Klose
Phone: (49) 30-7722456

Users Groups

NoGeNUG (North German NeXT Group)
Gerhard Moeller
Phone: (49) 441 75520

Black Forest NeXT User Club
Heinz Conrad
Phone: (49) 7442-7654

German NeXT User Group
Marcus Bruggemann
FAX: 0231 75892-90

NeKSt (NeXT Klub Stuttgart)
Michael Haeuptle
Phone: (49) 07154/16442

Heidelberg NeXT User Group
Gregor Hoffleit
Phone: (49) 6221 56-2771

Germany e.V. (Friends of NeXT User Group)
Ulrich Becker
Phone: (49) 040-2706479

NugRNK (NeXT Group Rhein-Neckar)
c/o Christian Schleich
Phone: (49) 6202 74071

sBANG (small Baltic Area NeXT Group)
Arne Schroeder
Phone: (49) 431-81243

GENEUS (German NeXT User Societies)
Mathias Pruestel
e-mail: mp@augur.han.de

NeXTusern der Ruhr-University Bochum
Martin Lades
Phone: (49) 234/700 79 94

MUC-NUG (Munchner NeXT User Group)

Boris Baermichl
Phone: (49) 89-580 29 53

NUK (NeXT Usergroup Karlsruhe)
Bernd Wild
Phone: (49) 721-9654-310

GREECE

Greek NeXT User Group
Ioannis Koutselas
e-mail: iok@theseas.ntua.gr

HONG KONG

Hong Kong NeXT User Group
Bill Schell
Phone: (852) 666 8412 (w) or (852) 666 5506 (h)
Hong Kong NeXT User Club
Edwin Tam / Jardine Office Systems
Phone: (852) 565-2011

HUNGARY

Budapest NeXT User Group
Dr. Laszlo Kovacs
Phone: (361) 129-7861

INDIA

Bombay NeXT User Group
Mr P. K. Kapur
Phone: (91) 22-208-6620

IRELAND

Dublin NeXT User Group
Kevin Mc Donnell
Phone : +353-1-325028

ISRAEL

YIN (Israel NeXT User Group)
c/o Shmuel Browns
Phone: +972.2.610785

ITALY

Italian Next User Group
Gianfranco Pocecai, Coordinator
Phone : (39) 2-7575244

BoNG (Bologna Next User Group)
Arrigo Benedettii, Coordinator
Phone: (39) 59 224929 (h) or (39) 59 216688 (w)

JAPAN

Japan NeXT User Society
Kazunori Shioya, Chairman
Phone: (81) 3-3357-9361 Ext. 3117

Osaka University NeXT Users Group
Mr. Ogihara, Chairman
e-mail: ogihara@rd.ecip.osaka-u.ac.jp

KOREA

Korea NeXT User Group
Soonam Kahng
Phone: (82) 02-516-1231

KUWAIT

Kuwait NeXT User Group
Nader al-Twaijri
Phone: (96) 5 246-3068

MALAYSIA

MALAYSIAN NeXT User Group
Thomas Lee
Phone : 603-791 6888

MEXICO

Mexico NeXT Group
Aurelio Sanchez, President
David Trevino, Vice-President
Phone: (83) 58-20-00 Ext. 4071 or Ext. 4073

Usuarios de NeXT en Mexico
Hugo Villegas
Phone: (83) 35 19 14 or 35 19 15

Ciudad de Mexico NeXT User Group
Pablo De Urquijo
Phone: (83) 525 5561316

NETHERLANDS

Netherlands NeXT User Group
Francisco de Urquijo
e-mail: urquijo@seri.philips.nl

NoW (NeXT One World)
Diederic Vlamings
Phone: (31) 20 686 9502

NORWAY

Norges NeXT Brukergruppe
Thor-Lee Legvold
Phone: 05/27 69 45

POLAND

Warsaw NeXT User Group

Janusz Motoszko/Darek Piotrowski
e-mail: jasio@frodo.nask.org.pl

PORTUGAL

LisboNUG (Lisbon NEXT User Group)
Amaro Rica da Silva
Phone: (351)-1-802045 Ext 1619

PUERTO RICO

Puerto Rico NeXT User Group
Dr. Francisco Tome
Phone: (809) 798-4464 (w) or (809) 257-8223 (h)

SAUDI ARABIA

Saudi Arabia NeXT User Group
Isam S Ayoubi
e-mail: ayoubi@cs.tamu.edu

SINGAPORE

Singapore NeXT User Group
Kelvin Tan
Phone: 2787888

SNG (Singapore NeXT Group)
Paul Wang
Phone: (65) 288-4184 (h)
(65) 479-1525 Ext. 6280 (h)

SLOVENIA

Slovenia NeXT User Group
Igor Tavcar
Phone: (38) 61 272 146 or (38) 61 213-661

SOUTH AFRICA

South Africa NeXT Group
Robert Stacey
Phone: (011) 716-5429

SPAIN

Madrid (UAM NeXT Group)
Javier Poves
Phone: (34) 1 397 45 73

Bilbao NeXT User Group
Marisa Fernandez
Phone: (34) 4-464.77.00 Ext. 2536

SWEDEN

SnAG (Svenska NeXT-AnvandarGruppen)
Bjorn Backlund
Phone: (46) 8 612 89 95
Fax: (46) 8 612 89 96

SWITZERLAND

Swiss NeXT User Group
Florian Gutzwiller
Phone: (41) 61 312 20 50

NiCE (NeXT User Group)
Marcel Waldvogel, President
George Fankhauser, Vice-President
Phone: (41) 1 312 10 32 (George)
(41) 1 311 89 03 (Marcel)

Suisse Romande's NeXT Users' Club
Daniel Allgoewer
Phone and Fax: (41) 21 25 80 07

TAIWAN

TwNUG (Taiwan NeXT User Group)
Tony Guo
Phone: 886-7-711-4540 (Taiwan)
(213) 470-9685 (US)

NCTU-Nug (NCTU NeXT Group)
Joshua Hou / Applied Arts
Phone: 886-35-712121 Ext. 4410

UNITED KINGDOM

UK NeXT User Group
Paul Beaumont
Phone: (44) 844-28332

UK NeXT Users Bulletin Board Service
BBS number: (44) 602-455444
BBS high speed number: (44) 602-455497 / 844-28660

SWaN   (South West area NeXTs)
c/o Scott McIntyre
e-mail: S.A.McIntyre@durham.ac.uk

GNaSH (Group for NeXT-users at Sheffield)
Malcolm Crawford
Phone: (44) 742 768555 Ext. 5577

UK NeXT User Newsletter
Nigel Metheringham
Phone: (44) 904-432374

Belfast NeXT User Group
Ron Perrott
Phone: (44) 232-245133
Fax: (44) 232-331232
Answering machine: (44) 232-663755

CompuServe's NeXT User Forum UK Sysop
Paul Lynch
Phone: (44) 0494 671501

York NeXT User Group
Ian Stephenson
Phone: (44) 904-430000 Ext. 2381
e-mail: ian@ohm.york.ac.uk

UOENUG
Paul Chernett
Phone: (44) 206-872048

YUGOSLAVIA (Slovenia, Macedonia)

Slovenia NeXT User Group
Igor Tavcar
Phone: (38) 61 272-146 or (38) 61 213-661

Macedonia NeXT User Group
Mr. Kotevski Cane
Telephone: (38) 91 42 28 22

ZIMBABWE

Zimbabwe NeXT User Group
Gary Nelson
e-mail: nelson@mango.apc.org

E.8 Special Interest Groups Mailing Lists

While members of user groups tend to meet fact-to-face to cover various topics, special interest groups (*SIG*'s) discuss their specialized topics via electronic-mail. To subscribe to a particular **SIG**, simply mail a short message to the listed e-mail address. Although there are dozens of SIG's, there are only a couple that pertain directly to programming. Due to the nature of the **SIG** (and temperament of its existing members), would-be-members are advised to already be a little familiar with the topic of the **SIG** before joining, i.e., don't join a **SIG** and then ask what the **SIG** is about.

> Note that most of these sites use programs to parse the incoming mail messages, and most of these programs are not equipped to process NeXTMail. Therefore, when mailing a request, make sure that the request is non-NeXTMail by clicking the NeXTMail button in the Mail application.

- Developer SIG mailing list—discusses programming-related questions. Most programmers post their questions on this mailing as well as the Usenet newsgroups, comp.sys.next.programmer. To join, e-mail to next-prog-request@cpac.washington.edu.
- GNU Objective C and C++ list—discusses the Objective-C project embarked by the Free Software Foundation, the makers of the C compiler which the bundled compiler is based on. Most of the discussions are very advanced. To join, e-mail to gnu-objc-request@prep.ai.mit.edu
- NeXT Managers SIG—offers quick solutions to critical problems related to administrative procedures such as printer failures, etc. To join, e-mail to next-managers-request@stolaf.edu.

E.9 Bulletin Boards

Bulletin boards are electronic meeting places much like mailing lists. However, discussions on bulletin boards can happen in real-time like a phone call, although both (or more parties) are typing rather than talking.

NeXT Users Forum on CompuServe
Phone: (800) 848-8199

NeXT Users Bulletin Board on Portal
e-mail: next_sig@portal.com

UK NeXT Users Bulletin Board Service
BBS number: (44) 602-455444
BBS high speed number: (44) 602-455497 / 844-28660

New Jersey NeXT Bulletin Board Service
BB number: (201) 622-5526 (using login: guest)

E.10 Associations

ANDI (Association of NeXT Developers International) can offer its members (corporate and individual) various benefits including an Internet e-mail account, discounts on software and hardware purchases. For more information, contact:

>Bill Strehl, Executive Editor
>ANDI
>9921 Woodburn Road
>Silver Springs, MD 20901-2730
>(301) 681-0613
>bill@andi.org (Internet)
>73130.3135@compuserve.com (Compuserve)

E.11 Conventions

Another way to keep up with the many developments in the NeXT community is to attend conventions. These offer a glimpse of latest developments in the hardware and software market; they are a great way to meet the people in the industry. While attending all of the conventions would be totally impractical, NeXT Inc. promotes its products the most at the following three conventions:

- **NeXTWorld Expo**—this exposition is entirely devoted to the NeXT market and draws developers and users from all over the world. A great way to meet many of the key people in the NeXT community.
- **UNIX Expo**—since the NeXT market is somewhat tied to the UNIX market, NeXT often has hospitality suites at these conventions.
- **OOPSLA**—NeXT also often has hospitality suites at the OOPSLA conference since NeXT is a key player in the dynamic object-oriented market.

Conventions

Appendix F
Porting to NeXTSTEP/Intel

This appendix reprints a document which issues involved in porting an application from NeXTSTEP to NeXTSTEP/Intel. The article is originally titled, "Building Portable NeXTSTEP Applications".

© 1992 NeXT Computer, Inc. All rights reserved. "Building Portable NeXTSTEP Applications" reprinted with permission. All information in this document is subject to change without notice.

The operating system, client processes, development tools, and software libraries that NeXTSTEP comprises are standard for all computers on which NeXTSTEP runs. This means that, in general, when you port your NeXTSTEP application to a new computer, you won't have to redesign your code to achieve expected behavior. All the pieces are there, and as they work on one machine, so will they work on every other.

If you use "good" programming practices, avoid hard-wired data values, and follow the NeXTSTEP user interface guidelines, then your application will probably be portable. It will run properly on all configurations of a given architecture and should need only to be recompiled to run on a new architecture. But few applications are perfect; yours might fall prey to the differences between computers, requiring a bit of fine-tuning before it will work with a new configuration or on a new architecture. It's anticipated that all such necessary changes will be of the type that generalize your code—you should rarely need to "special-case" your code to adapt to a particular computer.

This paper describes some of the differences between computers that can run NeXTSTEP and suggests ways to avoid configuration- or architecture-specific code that could make your application non-portable. It's divided into two parts:

• The first part discusses differences between hardware configurations, such as differences in screen size and color capability, or between types of keyboards.

- The second part deals with differences in data representation between computer architectures. Almost all problems that arise in this arena can be cured by adhering to the tenets of good programming.

Except as they relate to porting your application, this paper doesn't describe the new or modified features introduced by NeXTSTEP Release 3. General features of Release 3 are described in the Release Notes (**/NextLibrary/Documentation/ NextDev/ReleaseNotes**) and in *NeXTSTEP Development Tools and Techniques*.

F.1 Hardware Considerations

Every computer on which NeXTSTEP runs will certainly possess the three hardware pieces that have come to be regarded as obligatory: a screen, a keyboard, and a mouse. However, the attributes of these devices aren't the same on all computers. The sound capabilities of computers also vary widely. The following sections describe the facilities that allow your application to query a computer for the attributes of its hardware devices, and warn against assumptions about the computer's configuration that can make your application less portable.

F.1.1 The Screen

Not all screens are the same size, nor do they provide the same color support. Therefore, a portable application shouldn't depend on a particular screen size or color capability.

The greatest impact of a screen's size is in the placement of windows. For example, a window designed to appear at the edge of a very large screen might not appear on a smaller screen at all. To guarantee that windows appear on-screen in an appropriate manner, your application should always place them relative to the edges of the screen, rather than in absolute positions. InterfaceBuilder's Size Inspector can be used to set the position of a window relative to the edges of a screen, so when the window is displayed, it automatically appears in the proper place. If a window or panel must have a minimum size, try to keep it at a reasonable value (Computer screens are usually at least 640 × 480 pixels). Non-resizable windows and panels should be given similar consideration about their sizes.

The **Window** class guarantees that windows are displayed in such a way that the user can manipulate them. If a window's position would result in its title bar being off-screen, the window will move itself enough so that the title bar does appear. Similarly, if a window is so tall that its resize bar would be below the bottom of the screen, the window will change its height to show the resize bar. All of **Window**'s placement and movement methods perform this forcing to the screen, so if you need a standard window that's not visible, you should use the **orderOut:** method to remove it from the screen list, rather than trying to position the window out of the screen's bounds.

To handle the different color capabilities of screens, your application should use the **NXImage** class for bitmapped images. **NXImage** automatically uses the most appropriate image representation for a given screen. You should also make use of the **View** method **shouldDrawColor**. This method lets application choose appropriate grayscale equivalents of colors (to avoid dithering on a grayscale screen, for example).

If you need more control over screen information than that provided by the above facilities, you can use the **NXScreen** structure, which represents the attributes of a screen. This structure is declared in **appkit/screens.h**. The Application Kit's **Application** and **Window** classes provide methods that return the **NXScreen** structures that represent the screens that are available to your application.

For more information on using the **Application**, **Window**, **View**, and **NXImage** classes in handling different screen configurations, see the specifications of those classes in **/NextLibrary/ Documentation/NextDev/GeneralRef/02_ApplicationKit**. For more information on using Interface Builder, see *NeXTSTEP Development Tools and Techniques*.

F.1.2 The Mouse

All mice have at least one button—some have two. If your application was designed for a NeXT Computer, you may have used the second button that all NeXT mice have. This obviously subverts portability to a configuration that has a one-button mouse.

You should never depend on having a two-button mouse; the NeXT user interface guidelines urge you to ignore the second button on a NeXT mouse. However, a slightly less strict reading of the rule has it that at the very least, you must make sure that all second-button operations can be performed through some other method. For example, if you use the second button to create a "special" selection, you might provide a menu item that acts on the current selection to turn it into such a selection, or use the **Shift** or **Alternate** key to signal this behavior on a mouse click.

If your application needs to know the type of mouse (or other pointing device, such as a tablet) that's attached to the computer, the **NXEventSystemInfo**() function can be used. This function describes the computer's input devices, including the type of mouse (see **/NextLibrary/Documentation/NextDev/ReleaseNotes/EventStatusDriver.rtf** and the header file **bsd/dev/ev_types.h** for more information). Unfortunately, NeXTSTEP doesn't provide any functions or methods through which you can specifically query for the number of mouse buttons.

F.1.3 The Keyboard

The keyboard, like the mouse, can't be queried for its attributes. However, you generally don't need to know how a keyboard is laid out—for example, whether it has a number pad as well as number keys. What you do need to know is what character was generated when the user pressed a key.

The **NXEventData** structure, defined in **dpsclient/event.h**, describes a keyboard event in its **key** substructure. The description is twofold:

- The *key code* describes the key that was pressed.
- The *character code* describes the character that was generated.

These two attributes, which sound similar, aren't necessarily the same. For example, the "**1**" key that's typically found in the top row of the keyboard generates the same character code as the "**1**" in the number pad, but they have two different key codes, since they are, physically, two different keys.

A keyboard event's key code is described in a single field, **key.keyCode**. The event's character code is a combination of two fields in the **key** substructure: **key.charSet**, which identifies a set of characters (such as ASCII or Symbol), and **key.charCode**, which indicates the character in the set. For portability, you should never use the **keyCode** field since, by its nature, it's keyboard-dependent. For example, the key code for the letter "**a**" on one keyboard might be different from that on another. However, when the user presses "**a**", the same character code (in other words, the same **charSet** and **charCode** combination) will be generated regardless of the type of keyboard.

The set of character codes doesn't necessarily distinguish all key codes; as demonstrated in the number pad example above, there may be two key codes that are represented by the same character code. Thus, by using only character codes you may lose some keyboard-specific precision, but you gain portability. There are keyboard-independent ways to get certain information, though. For example, you can check for a key on the numeric keypad by masking the event record's **flags** field with the **NX_NUMERICPADMASK** mask.

As with the mouse, the **NXEventSystemInfo**() function can be used to determine what type of keyboard is attached to the computer (see the online release note **/NextLibrary/Documentation/NextDev/ReleaseNotes/EventStatusDriver.rtf** and the header file **bsd/dev/ev_types.h** for more information). If your application requires keyboard-specific information (as some terminal emulators do, for example), contact NeXT Developer Support.

F.1.4 Sound

The sound capabilities of different computers vary considerably. You can't assume that a particular computer will be able to play a sound created on another computer. If NeXTSTEP's sound software can't play a sound, the function or method will simply return an error code; the inability to play a sound should never cause your application to crash.

For information about determining the sound capabilities of a host machine at run time, see the online release notes.

F.2 Data Representation Considerations

Beyond concern with a computer's configuration, you must consider platform-specific differences when recompiling your application for a new architecture. One of the most fundamental differences between computer architectures is how data is represented. These differences fall into four arenas: datum size, byte alignment, byte order, and argument passing. The following paragraphs describe these properties and suggest ways to avoid the simple problems that arise from their differences. More complicated situations are examined in "External Data" and "Internal Data," below.

Certain NeXTSTEP kits require special consideration; the Indexing Kit, for example, maps file-based data directly into memory, which causes problems when the in-memory representations of data vary among computer architectures. If a kit has its own idiomatic portability issues, there will be a notice in the introduction to that kit's reference material, and the specific methods and functions requiring special care will have notes about how to use them in a portable manner.

F.2.1 Datum Size

Datum sizes, or the amounts of memory that are devoted to single items of the various data types, aren't the same for all computers. Although almost every computer represents (as examples) a **char** in one byte, a **short** in two, and **int**s and **float**s in four, these sizes aren't mandated. Thus, you should never assume how much memory is needed to store the data that you allocate. In other words, you should never use hard-wired values in a call to a memory allocation function (such as **malloc()**); instead, use the **sizeof()** function to programmatically discover the size of a datum. This also applies to structures and unions, since different alignment restrictions (see below) can force them to be different sizes on different machines.

F.2.2 Byte Alignment

Some computers demand that the starting address (the first byte) of a value fall on a particular boundary. For example, a computer that uses *natural boundaries* expects the address of a value be divisible by the number of bytes that it takes to represent the value: the address of a two-byte value must be divisible by two, the address of a four-byte value must be divisible by four, and so on. In general, this isn't a concern to the programmer because the compiler and C allocation routines guarantee that all memory allocations, whether static or dynamic, will be on appropriate boundaries. However, there are two situations in which the compiler and C functions can't help you:

- By casting the data type of a pointer, you can write data into an illegal location. This is explained further in the section "Internal Data," below; briefly, you can avoid this error by never casting a data pointer to which you're writing data.
- If you redefine the memory allocation functions, you're on your own. Most visible of these—and most typically reimplemented—is **malloc()** (and **realloc()**, and so on), but also included are the zone-allocation functions that make up the **NXZone** facility.

F.2.3 Byte Order

A datum of a type that can't be represented in a single byte is given as a series of consecutive bytes. If the most significant byte is given first, then the computer is said to be "big-endian"; if the least significant byte is first, then it's a "little-endian" machine.

Byte order is only a concern when you're reading or writing "external" data. The data that your application creates and uses whiles it's running will by nature be ordered correctly.

If you use the data-reading and -writing mechanisms described in the section "External Data," below, your application may never need to know whether its running on a big- or little-endian machine. However, there are some situations in which this determination is essential. For this, the C preprocessor macros **__BIG_ENDIAN__** and **__LITTLE_ENDIAN__** can be examined:

```
#ifdef __BIG_ENDIAN__
/* do something for big-endian data */
#else
/* do something for little-endian data */
#endif
```

F.2.4 Datum Format

Like alignment restrictions, the form that a data type is given on one architecture may vary from that given on another. The general rule with regard to the internal format of any datum is: Never rely on it. *Always* use field names for structures and unions, and don't assume that you can pick apart a **float**'s mantissa and exponent directly (there are library functions to do this).

The format of structure bitfields is particularly variable from architecture to architecture. You should use bitfields only for data items that will remain entirely internal. If a structure is going to be written to or read from a file, you should avoid using bitfields unless absolutely necessary.

F.2.5 Argument Passing

The data that you pass as arguments to a function must be put somewhere so the function can retrieve it. Some computers place argument data (contiguously) on the stack, while others put arguments in CPU registers, for which there is no notion of contiguity. As long as a function always refers to its arguments symbolically, the difference between the stack and register approaches is inconsequential. However, a function that steps through its arguments by incrementing (or decrementing) a data pointer—thus assuming that the arguments are being passed on the stack—won't be portable.

Functions that take a determinate number of arguments should never need to use the data-pointer approach. But if you're designing a function that takes a variable number of arguments—a function in the style of **printf**(), for example—you may be tempted to read the arguments by setting and moving a data pointer. The correct approach to reading an indeterminate number of arguments is to use the **stdarg** macros provided by the standard C library. These macros are included in your program by importing the file **stdarg.h**; they're described under **varargs** in section 3 of the UNIX manual.

F.2.6 External Data

The problems of external data—data that's read from an external source—arise primarily from differences in byte-order: Data written on a little-endian machine will be swapped when it's read on a big-endian machine (and vice versa). All NeXTSTEP data-communication mechanisms (such as those provided by the Application Kit's pasteboard and data link objects, and the distributed objects paradigm) automatically transform data that's transmitted between applications to the correct byte-order; thus, inter-application communication is taken care of.

What you need to be concerned with is data that your application reads and writes directly. The rule is simple: If you're reading and writing multi-byte data, you should *always* use typed streams. The typed stream functions recognize the byte-order differences between machines and can identify the sort of machine on which a particular stream of data was written. Typed streams are comprehensively described in Chapter 3, "Common Classes and Functions," of the *NeXTSTEP General Reference* (/**NextLibrary/Documentation/NextDev/GeneralRef/03_Common**); the typed stream functions are declared in the header file **objc/typedstream.h**.

Note: Previous versions of NeXTSTEP documentation for the **NXRead()** and **NXWrite()** functions give an example which ignores this portability issue, and uses these functions to store a multi-byte structure. That example should not be considered a proper use for **NXRead() and NXWrite()**.

Given typed streams as the rule, then, you should be aware that there are a few exceptions:

- One-byte data (such as ASCII strings) can be written and read through any of the usual C functions, such as **read**() and **write**(). Writing ASCII through a typed stream isn't wrong, but it is somewhat inefficient. Of course, this slackening of the typed stream rule depends on the immutability of one-byte data on different machines (in other words, you must be sure that one-byte data on one machine isn't going to be two-byte data on another).
- Bitfields in a structure, even when written through a typed stream, will be improperly represented. The use of bitfields in a file format is strongly discouraged.
- File formats that already exist and that weren't written through typed streams can't be read through typed streams.

The following sections describe solutions to the bitfield and existing file format problems.

F.2.6.1 Reading and Writing Structure Bitfields

Structure bitfields can help you conserve memory when your application is running. However, they're a poor choice with regard to storing data in a file, since neither the compiler nor typed streams resolve the order of contiguous bitfields to match the endian-ness of the computer. If you don't do anything to correct this situation, a series of bitfields that are written on a big-endian machine will be ordered differently when read on a little-endian machine, and vice-versa. The best solution to this problem is to avoid it altogether. If, for efficiency or compatibility reasons, your application must be able to read and write structure bitfields, you have two general options: modify the routines that read and write the structure, or redefine the structure itself.

• **Approach 1: Modify the Read and Write Routines**
By modifying the routines that read and write particular structures, you can change the way the structure is represented externally. Thus, you can make sure that the external representation is portable. For example, consider the following class declaration:

```
@interface Dog : Mammal
  {
    char *name;
    short age;
  struct _dogFlags
      {
      unsigned int canWalk:1;
      unsigned int canTalk:1;
      unsigned int whiskerCount:10;
      unsigned int PAD:20;
      } dogFlags;
  }

/* ... */

@end
```

The **name** and **age** instance variables will be written and read correctly by the typed stream functions, but the bitfields won't be. To write the object and ensure its portability, you can define the **write:** method to "expand" the bitfields into full-byte values and then write the expanded data:

```
- write:(NXTypedStream *stream)
   {
     [super write:stream];

     /*
     Create vars for the "expanded" bitfield data
     */
     unsigned char canWalkHolder =
       dogFlags.canWalk;
     unsigned char canTalkHolder =
       dogFlags.canTalk;
     unsigned int whiskerCountHolder =
       dogFlags.whiskerCount;
```

```
        /* Write the data. */
        NXWriteTypes(stream, "*sCCI", name, &age,
          &canWalkHolder,&canTalkHolder,
          &whiskerCountHolder);
        return self;
}
```

You would, of course, have to create an analogous **read:** method. Note that the data type of the variables that hold the expanded bitfield data must be big enough to represent the values that the bitfields contain.

By writing expanded bitfield data, the external representation of an object or structure may waste some space (compared to the internal representation), but unless you're writing thousands of items the waste is insignificant. Also, this is the only approach that's guaranteed to be portable with regard to bitfield layout, whatever machine the application is run on.

• Approach 2: Redefine the Structure

A quicker but less elegant (and discouraged) solution is to redefine the structure to accommodate the endian-ness of the machine. This means predicating the order of the bitfields according to the machine's byte order:

```
@interface Dog : Mammal
    {
    char *name;
    short age;
    struct _dogFlags
        {
        #ifdef __BIG_ENDIAN__
           unsigned int canWalk:1;
           unsigned int canTalk:1;
           unsigned int whiskerCount:10;
           unsigned int PAD:20;
        #else
           unsigned int PAD:20;
           unsigned int whiskerCount:10;
           unsigned int canTalk:1;
           unsigned int canWalk:1;
        #endif
```

```
        } dogFlags;
    }

    /* ... */
@end
```

This approach works transparently when used in the following manner:

- The bitfield structure is always read or written with the typed streams mechanism.
- The bitfield structure is designed so that its total size in bits is equal to one of the standard unsigned integer types: 8 (**unsigned char**), 16 (**unsigned short int**), 32 (**unsigned int** and **unsigned long int**). This involves using pad fields to fill out the structure, and never using zero-width fields to force alignment.
- A multi-byte bitfield structure is treated as its size-equivalent integral type when reading or writing it, instead of as an array of **char**s. This allows the typed streams mechanism to perform byte-swapping if needed.

For example, the **dogFlags** bitfield structure above is 32 bits, and would be written with this function call in Dog's **write:** method:

```
/*
The proper way to write a bitfield
structure. Since dogFlags is written as an
unsigned int, NXWriteTypes() swaps it
automatically if needed.
*/
NXWriteTypes(stream, "*sI", &name,
    &age, &dogFlags);
```

If you don't use typed streams, you need to use the byte-swapping functions described later in this paper to swap the structure before writing and after reading it. In either case, you should always make sure that your bitfields are of a total size in bits equal to one of the standard unsigned integer types.

Although reversing the bitfield declaration is a quick way to solve the bitfield problem, you should be warned that it may not be a permanent solution: some future architecture may define a new way of representing bitfields, and you may have to revisit your code to add another branch to the endian predicate. In general, you should use the first approach (modifying the archival routines) rather than reversing bitfields.

F.2.6.2 Reading Existing Files

If your application defines its own (non-ASCII) file format, but doesn't use typed streams to read and write these files, you may have to rewrite the file-reading and -writing routines to accommodate the endian-ness of the machine that your application is running on. NeXTSTEP provides a suite of byte-swapping functions that convert individual data items. These functions come in two varieties, those that always swap, and those that only swap if needed.

An "always-swap" function takes a datum of a particular type, swaps the order of the bytes it comprises, and returns the swapped datum. There are six such functions, one for each multi-byte data type:

- **NXSwapShort()**
- **NXSwapInt()**
- **NXSwapLong()**
- **NXSwapLongLong()**
- **NXSwapFloat()**
- **NXSwapDouble()**

Each function takes a single argument and returns a single value. The value that you pass as the argument can be used to store the value that's returned, as shown in the following example:

```
/* Swap the order of the bytes in a given int.*/
givenInt = NXSwapInt(givenInt);
```

The second set of functions (called *predicated* functions) also take single data items of a particular type, but they're defined to swap the byte order only if the endian-ness indicated in the function name doesn't match the endian-ness of the machine the code is being compiled for. Determining the endian-ness of data is up to you (as explained in a later section). There are four groups of these functions:

- **NXSwapBigTypeToHost()**
- **NXSwapLittleTypeToHost()**
- **NXSwapHostTypeToBig()**
- **NXSwapHostTypeToLittle()**

where **Type** is one of the six multi-byte data types (there are 24 of these function in all). **NXSwapBigIntToHost()**, for example, would swap on a little-endian (**i386 family**) machine, but would do nothing on a big-endian (**MC68000** family) machine.

- **How to Use the Byte-Swapping Functions**

Regardless of which set of byte-swapping functions you use, you must determine the endian-ness of the data that you want to convert. To use the always-swap functions, you must also know the endian-ness of the host computer; you would use these functions only if the format of the given data and that of the host aren't the same. The predicated functions determine the host format for you and swap if the format indicated by the function's name doesn't match that of the host.

In the following example of the always-swap functions, it's been determined (by one of the methods given in the next section) that the data being read is in big-endian format. The bytes are swapped if the host is little-endian:

```
#define COUNT 1024
int buf[COUNT];
int byteCount, itemCount;

/*
aStream is open to a file that contains
big-endian integer data.
*/

byteCount = NXRead(aStream, (void *)buf,
    sizeof(buf)))
```

590   **External Data**

```
    itemCount = byteCount / sizeof(int);

#ifdef __LITTLE_ENDIAN__

/* Swap if this is a little-endian machine. */
while (itemCount--) {
    buf[itemCount] = NXSwapInt(buf[itemCount]);
}

#endif
```

The same effect can be achieved more cleanly by using a predicated function:

```
#define COUNT 1024
int buf[COUNT];
int byteCount, itemCount;

/*
aStream is open to a file that contains
big-endian integer data. */

byteCount = NXRead(aStream, (void *)buf,
    sizeof(buf));
itemCount = byteCount / sizeof(int);

while (itemCount--) {
    buf[itemCount] = NXSwapBigIntToHost
      (buf[itemCount]);
}
```

As you can see, using a predicated function rids your code of an unsightly **#ifdef** query.

• How to Determine Endian-ness of External Data

As mentioned above, you need to know the endian-ness of a datum whether you're using the always-swap functions or the predicated functions. You can't simply ask a datum for its byte-order, so how do you determine which format it's in?

One approach is to assume that files created by a certain application are of one endian-ness. For example, if you're reading existing data that was written by a NeXTSTEP application prior to the release of NeXTSTEP 3.1, you can be sure that it's in big-endian format. This is because NeXTSTEP, until now, only ran on NeXT Computers, and all existing NeXT Computers are big-endian. However, if you accept the guarantee that a file format is always of one endian-ness and not the other, then you must stick with that endian-ness when you write the data back to a file (so it can be read again). Thus, for example, you would use the **NXSwapBigTypeToHost()** functions to swap data that you've just read, and convert it back through the **NXSwapHostTypeToBig()** functions just before you write it. For applications running on a host with an endian-ness opposite that of the file format being used, this results in a performance penalty for both reading and writing that file format.

You don't have to adhere to the assumed-big-endian rule if your application inserts a "magic number" in the files that it writes. Magic numbers are used to confirm the identity, format, or version of a file, and can also be used to determine whether the file as it lies on disk is in the same or the opposite endian-ness as the host machine. For example:

```
/*
MY_MAGIC is the first long int in the file.
If the value read from the file doesn't match,
swap it and try again. The magic number
shouldn't be byte-symmetric; for example, it
shouldn't be 0x50404050, as swapping results
in the same number.
*/
#define MY_MAGIC 0x50ab40cd
#define COUNT 1024

BOOL fileNeedsSwapping;
long int magicNumber;
int buf[COUNT];
int byteCount, itemCount;

/* Assuming the file is opened onto aStream */

byteCount = NXRead(aStream, &magicNumber,
    sizeof(magicNumber));
```

592 External Data

```
        if (sizeof(magicNumber) != byteCount)
           /* error */

        if (MY_MAGIC == magicNumber)
           fileNeedSwapping = NO;
        else
           {
           magicNumber = NXSwapLong(magicNumber);
           if (MY_MAGIC == magicNumber)
             fileNeedsSwapping = YES;
           else /* bad file? */
           }

    /* Now read the rest of the data. */
    byteCount = NXRead(aStream, (void *)buf,
        sizeof(buf));
    itemCount = byteCount / sizeof(int);

    if (fileNeedsSwapping)
           {
           while (itemCount--)
             buf[itemCount] =
               NXSwapInt(buf[itemCount]);
           }
```

Checking for endian-ness mismatch allows the routine to work for hosts of either endian-ness reading the file. This approach permits maximum performance in all possible cases: writing an entire file is always at normal speed regardless of host endian-ness, but reading is only slower when there's an endian-ness mismatch between the file format and the host. The only complication is that if an application writes into an existing file, it must remember the original endian-ness of that file and alter its output accordingly.

Since magic numbers are used to store several kinds of information, care should be taken in choosing a number for a particular version of a file format. Magic numbers should also never be byte-symmetric or mirror images of other magic numbers. If your application will be reading files created by other applications, you'll need to check what magic numbers they use. You should choose a magic number far from the range for file formats you intend to support. When file formats are revised, their magic numbers are often merely incremented instead of re-assigned; if you've chosen a magic number 1 greater than the file format's, you could come into conflict with that format's magic number when it's updated.

F.2.7 Internal Data

Internal data—data that your application creates and uses while it's running—shouldn't be a problem as long as you adhere to a few principles:

- Always refer to the elements in a data structure by name. Because of possible byte-alignment padding, the distance between contiguous elements in a data structure (in other words, the elements in a **struct**, or the instance variables in an object) may be different on different computers. You should never try to access these elements by moving a pointer inside the structure.
- Be scrupulous about pointer types: use character pointers to point to characters, integer pointers to point to integers, and so on. For example, if you've allocated an integer array and then read the elements of the array through a character pointer, the data that you read may differ as the computer is big-endian or little-endian. If you must manipulate data of an unknown type through a pointer, use a pointer to **void** instead of a pointer to **char**.
- Never write the "wrong" type of data by recasting a pointer. As a demonstration, the following code will break an application running on a computer that expects data on natural boundaries:

```
/*
Create a character array and a pointer to
the array.
*/
char buffer[6];
char *bufptr = buffer;

/*
Write a character into the array and
increment the pointer.
*/
```

```
      *bufptr++ = 'd';

      /*
      Write an integer into the array;
      THE PROGRAM WILL CRASH.
      */
      *((int *)bufptr) = 10;
```

The example is trying to use the character array as a data structure. A better approach is to create a **struct** to store the data:

```
      /*
      Create a struct that contains a character
      and an integer.
      */
      struct shoeSize
          {
          char width;
          int length;
          } aShoe;

      aShoe.width = 'd';
      aShoe.length = 10;
```

F.2.8 Memory-mapped Data

NeXTSTEP's Mach operating system allows files to be mapped directly into the address space of a process, turning external data directly into internal data. For performance reasons, you may want or need your application to access file-based data by mapping the file. If you do this, there are two things you should do to make your file format portable:

- Always use a magic number to record the endian-ness of the file's data.
- To skirt your way around alignment restrictions, always pad data elements so they lie on natural alignment boundaries.

The first point has been well covered in the previous section. The second, however, deserves some explanation. As an example, let's assume you have the following structure declaration for use with mapped files:

```
typedef struct _mappedFile
    {
    unsigned long int magicNumber;
    unsigned long int numRecords;
    addressRecord addresses[0];
    } mappedFile;

mappedFile *myFile;
/* a pointer should align on a 32-bit boundary */
```

The idea is that the application will map a file into **myFile**, directly accessing the file's data in memory (swapping each datum upon access if needed). In order to avoid any alignment restriction problems, the as-yet-undefined **addressRecord** type should declare all of its fields on the most natural alignment boundaries. For example, 32-bit **int**s should lie on 4-byte boundaries, 64-bit **double**s should be on 8-byte boundaries, and so on. When using character arrays, it's best to declare them in multiples of 4 or 8 bytes, to avoid having to keep track of running offsets. Bitfields should be avoided altogether if possible, as using them requires detailed knowledge of how the compiler lays them out—which may differ between processor architectures.

Here, then, is the **addressRecord** type:

```
typedef _addressRecord
    {
    char lastName[32];  /* multiple of 4 chars */
    char firstName[32];
    char street[32];
    char city[32];

    char state[2];
    char PAD[2];/* forces alignment to */
              /* unsigned long int */

    struct _phone
      {
      unsigned long int area;/* kept apart to */
                       allow convenient */
      unsigned long int prefix;
                       /* access to each part */
```

```
            unsigned long int phone;
        } phone;
    } addressRecord;
```

Note the use of the **PAD** field after **state**, which forces the next structure field to be aligned on a natural **unsigned long int** (32-bit) boundary. The phone number is stored in separate **long int**s, even though each could fit into a **short int**. Although groups of two **short int**s would each make 32 bits, keeping all fields (and the entire structure) on 32-bit boundaries guarantees that there will be no alignment restriction problems when this file is memory-mapped on some new architecture. The phone number could also be stored as an array of characters, or as a single **unsigned long int**; the form chosen depends on space considerations and on how the data will be used.

Note also that the entire structure fits into a multiple of 4 bytes, so that the following structure will begin on a natural boundary for most basic datum sizes. If this structure contained any **double**s, it would be better declared as fitting into a multiple of 8 bytes. Keeping alignment at its most general at every level of declaration within a mapped file guarantees that the file format will be maximally portable.

Index

Symbols
\# (comment in make) 476
\#import 32
\#include 32
$ (gdb variable) 510
% (C shell prompt) xxix
% (PostScript comment) 228
* (dereferencing operator) 512
- (instance method declaration) 36
+ (factory method declaration) 36
. (hidden file prefix) 280
.app (application package) 146
.eps (Encapsulated PostScript) 146
.h (Objective-C interface file) 31
.index.store (Digital Librarian index file) 454
.lproj (language project file) 146
.m (Objective-C implementation file) 33
.NeXTDefaults.D 280
.NeXTDefaults.L 280
.nib (NeXTSTEP InterfaceBuilder) file 128, 147, 289, 296, 326, 334
.project (ProjectBuilder file) 126, 353
.psw (wraps file) 234
.rtfd (Rich Text Format Directory) 418, 427
.snd (sound file) 146
.tiff (tag image file format) 146
: (as part of a method name) 25
@end 32, 33
@implementation 33
@interface 32
\0 (null terminator) 340
~ (home directory) 435
~/.editdict (Edit word expansion dictionary) 450
~/.NeXT 279
~/Library/Bookshelves/Librarian.bshlf (Digital Librarian bookshelf file) 455

Numerics
0x0 (nil) 511
3DKit 2
75040.3647@compuserve.com xxxii

A
abstract data types 23
abstract superclass 20
abstraction 13
accessoryView 306
active application 436
addEntry: 170
addSubview: 213
alert panel 179
alloc 35, 47, 282, 351
allowMultipleFiles: 358
alpha channel 223
anonymous ftp 530
app:openFile:type: 402, 404
appAcceptsAnotherFile: 402, 404
appDidInit: 174, 199, 201, 202, 203, 292, 402, 494, 496
appkit.p (precompiled header file for the entire Application Kit) 461
Apple Desktop Bus 412
Application class 175, 292
Application Kit 4
application.tiff 405
AppWrapper 530
arc 227
archive-server@sonata.cc.purdue.edu (mail server id at sonata) 532
automatic garbage collection 46
awakeFromNib 203, 286, 293, 306, 387, 494, 495, 498, 499, 521

B
base coordinate system 210
bezeled line 330
big-endian 581
bitmaps 146
bookshelf 453
Boolean 78
breakpoint 508, 509
Button class 152, 154–158
BuzzNUG 529

C
C++ 21
calculateAreas() 87
Cancel (button in an alert panel) 179
cat (showing the contents of a file) 473
cc 29, 74, 85, 505
Cell class 154
character code 578
CircleView class 248
class 10
    allocating 10, 44
    freeing 185, 397
class object 35
clicking (a mouse button) 434
client 3
client-server model 3
clip path 217
clipview 346
Close (button in an alert panel) 179
close button 439
code reusability 10
colon (as part of a method name) 25
colors
    portable usage of 577
Command key 434
Command-c (for copying text) 465

Command-click (in Edit to edit an existing link) 414
command-line environment 150
Command-v (for pasting text) 465
common errors 483
compiling files 85
composite object 15, 184
compositing 223
Console 145, 277
const (keyword) 354
content view 159
Continue (Gdb panel) 519, 520
Control class 152–172
ControlDemo 156, 158, 159, 164, 167, 170, 171
controller object 175
convert: 184, 196, 304, 307, 331, 332, 333
convertPoint:fromView: 221
convertPoint:toView: 221
convertPointFromSuperView: 221
convertPointToSuperView: 221
copy (for copying to the pasteboard) 466
copying text (using Command-c) 440
cp (copying a file) 475
creating a new folder 444
cs.orst.edu (archive site) 530
cursor
   help 411
   standard 411
customizable expansion dictionary 447
CustomView class 254

D

Dallas Cowboys Cheerleaders xxxiv
DBKit 2
debugging 504–522
defaults
   search order 284
defaults database 280, 286
defineps 235
delayedFree: 396, 397
delegate 201, 496
delegation 149, 172–180, 198, 201
dependency (in make) 472
dependency line (in make) 471
designated initializer method 35
Developer Mode (in Edit) 505
Digital Librarian 447, 453–458, 463, 470
   Menu
      Search (Command-F) 470
directory (for obtaining the directory from a savepanel) 358
dirty (modified window) 362
display
   ShapeView class 499
   SwitchView class 329
   View class 159, 216

Window class 218
Display PostScript 4, 223
displaying menus 433
displayPrefsPanel: 306, 325, 326
Document class 368, 397
document view 347
document.tiff 404
double-clicking (a mouse button) 435
downloading 530
dragging 437
draw: 217
drawcircle() 271
drawSelf:: 216, 217, 218, 223, 499
   SwitchView class 306, 329
dread 280–281, 286, 323
dwrite 287, 288
dynamic binding 21, 40, 87, 94, 193

E

early binding 40
Edit 447, 447–453
   Menu
      Contract All (Command-0) 452
      Contract Sel 453
      Expand All (Command-9) 453
      Expand Sel 453
      Expansion Dictionary 449
      Insert Link 414
      Insert Marker 416
      Line Range (Command-l) 448
      Make Rich Text (Command-R) 414
      Show Markers 414, 416
Encapsulated PostScript 128
encapsulation 9, 291
endps 235
English.lproj 146
Enter key xxx
EPS 128, 146
errors
   allocating enough memory for strings 485
   anObject does not recognize selector 483
   Bus error 484
   conflicting types for method. Previous declaration of method 488
   displaying outlets in InterfaceBuilder 489
   local declaration of 'variable' hides instance variable 486
   message free sent to freed object 484
   return of integer from pointer lacks a cast 487
   sending messages to an object 489
   with delegate methods 489
   with uninitialized pointers 484
ESC key (for word expansion) 448, 456
event 150
event loop 150, 352
event queue 152, 153
event-driven environment 149, 151

exit(0) 185
explicit message sending 498

F

factory method 35
file extensions 353
file package 146
File Viewer 432
File's Owner 130, 290, 292, 311
filename (for obtaining the filename from a
        savepanel) 352
filenames (for obtaining filenames from an
        openpanel) 358
files
   hidden 280
Finish (Gdb panel) 518
flipped coordinate system 338
floatValueAt: 170, 196
focusing 217
folders 435
font
   selecting a font 240
Form class 168–172
frame rectangle 212, 345, 350
free 46, 88, 397, 500
Free Software Foundation 5
freeAll() 88
freeObjects 88, 499
fullPathName 361
function 8
function prototyping 77

G

-g (debugging option for cc) 505
gdb (GNU debugger) 491
Gdb panel 491, 507
gdb shell window 506
getSel:: 339
getSubstring:start:length: 340
GLOBAL 401
Grab (application) 427
graphics state 216

H

HeaderViewer 447, 458–465, 469
   Menu
        Browse (Command-B) 462
        Find in appkit.h (Command-?) 469
        List (Command-L) 462
Help.store 417, 418, 425
Hide 153
hide: 153
home directory 435
home folder 435
hypertext 411, 417

I

icons 432
id 23
implementation file 31
implicit expansion dictionary 447
implicit message sending 498
importing header files 76
improving launch time 290
Index.rtfd 418
Info Panel 334
inheritance 13
init 282, 351
initDocumentFromFile: 373
initFrame:
   Button class 155
   Form class 170
   ShapeView class 494
   Slider class 162
   TextField class 166
initFrame:text:alignment: 338
initialize (a factory method to initialize the class) 282,
        306, 324, 494, 497
instance drawing 237–241
instance method 35
instance variable 8, 486
instances 10
   initialization 45
instantiation 10, 44
interface file 31
InterfaceBuilder 6, 149
   adding a keyboard alternative 375
   adding a scrollview 380
   adding actions 189
   adding an icon to a control 194
   Construction Mode 141
   creating a new module 311
   creating entries in a popuplist 312
   cutting an object 374
   editing the text in the menu option 137
   editing the title of a textfield 137
   enabling a menu option 335
   File Window 130
   instantiating a class 190
   Main Menu 132
   Main Window 132
   making a connection 138, 193
   Menu
        Cut (Command-x) 374
        Group (Command-g) 257
        Make Column (Command-C) 257
        Make Row (Command-R) 259
        New Empty 311
        Revert to Saved (Command-u) 198
        Test Interface (Command-r) 141
   Palettes Window 131
   parsing a class 200
   selecting an object 137
   setting a window's delegate 198

600   Index

setting a window's minimum size 198
setting the class of the File's Owner 311
subclassing 187
Test Interface 141
Test Mode 141, 424
unparsing a class 194
Internet 530
isa 36
ISDN 2
isDocEdited: 362
ixbuild 454, 456
IXKit 2

J

JAMZ SQUAD xxxiii

K

key code 578
key window 343, 437
keyboard alternative 434

L

Language
  compiled 222
  hybrid 22
  interpreted 222
  page description 224
  pure object-oriented language 22
  stack based 224
language elements (in HeaderViewer) 459
last-in-first-out 225
late binding 40
launching applications 431
lazy loading 295
libraries 128
LIFO 225
linking files 85
links 413–415
List class 78
little-endian 581
loadNibSection:owner:withNames: 292
local coordinate system 215
local variable 486
localization 146
lockFocus 239
logging in 431
login window 431
loose coupling 94
ls (list files) 280, 472

M

Mach 2
  messaging 151–152
magic numbers 591
mail server (at sonata) 530

main window 343, 369
main() 185
make 143, 447, 470–481
Makefile 123, 465, 470
makeKeyAndOrderFront: 159
malloc() 47
manageability 289
markers 415–417
Matrix class 168, 298, 302
  creating in InterfaceBuilder 254
memory leak 49, 283, 367
MenuCell class 298
message 15
message dispatch table 36
message sending 17
method names 25
methods 8
miniaturizing a window 434
modal 352
modal loop 179
MoneyConverter class 184, 291, 305, 307
Mouse events 218
  detecting number of clicks 275–276
  mouseDown: 249
  mouseUp: 249

N

name (of a default) 280
natural boundaries 581
new 351
newDocument: 388
NewsGrazer 534
Next (Gdb panel) 512
NeXTSTEP486 575
NeXTWatch Journal 530
NeXTWorld 529
NeXTWorld Expo 573
NeXTWorld Extra 529
nil 175, 203, 294, 295, 326, 396, 507, 517
notifyAncestorWhenFrameChanged: 350
NULL 354, 361
null terminator 47, 340
NX_ALERTALTERNATE 179
NX_ALERTDEFAULT 179
NX_ALERTOTHER 179
NX_FREE() 47
NX_FREEBUFFER 355, 361
NX_MALLOC() 47
NXApp 151, 175, 282, 290, 352, 396, 397, 402, 494,
    498, 499, 500, 518
NXAttachPopUpList() 302
NXCloseMemory() 355, 361
NXCoord 211
NXDefaultsVector 284
NXDefaultsVector struct 284

NXEvent 219
　->location 219
　->type 219
NXEventData 578
NXEventSystemInfo() 578
NXFont 401
NXFontSize 401
NXGetDefaultValue() 286, 287, 332
NXGetNamedObject() 292
NXHelpPanel class 411
NXMapFile() 361
NXOpenMemory() 355
NXPoint 211
NXRead() 584
NXRect 158
NXRegisterDefaults() 284, 285
NXRunAlertPanel() 179, 352
NXSaveToFile() 355
NXSelPt 340
NXSetRect() 158, 163
NXSize 211
NXSwapBigTypeToHost() 589
NXSwapDouble() 588
NXSwapFloat() 588
NXSwapHostTypeToBig() 589
NXSwapHostTypeToLittle() 589
NXSwapInt() 588
NXSwapLittleTypeToHost() 589
NXSwapLong() 588
NXSwapLongLong() 588
NXSwapShort() 588
NXUpdateDefault() 287, 332
NXWrite() 584

O

object 8
Object Browser 514
Object-Based Computing 529
Objective-C 5, 21
object-oriented programming 7
　abstraction 13
　encapsulation 9
　polymorphism 18
　reusability 7
OOPSLA 573
openFile:ok: 402
OpenPanel class 175, 357–361
　instantiating 388
　opening multiple files 388
outlets 188, 200, 201, 511
　initialization 292–296
　　　setOutletName: 293
overriding a method 16
owner (of a .nib file) 292
owner (of a default) 280

P

Paste (menu option) 345
pasteboard 341
pasteboard server (pbs) 341, 342
pasting text (using Command-v) 440
path 438
PB.project (project file) 126
performClick: 156, 171, 182, 192
pointer 511
polymorphism 18, 21, 40
PopUp 327
PopUpList class 298–300, 302, 308, 327
　determining the selection 327
　tag 327
portability considerations
　argument passing 582
　byte order 581, 583
　byte swapping functions 588, 589
　data alignment 581, 594
　datum format 582
　datum size 580
　determining endian of external data 590
　external data 583
　general 575
　internal data 593
　keyboard support 578
　memory mapped I/O 594
　mouse support 578
　non-ASCII data files 588
　screen control 577
　sound support 580
　use of bitfields 584
　use of color 577
　use of pointers 593
　window sizing 577
PostScript 209
　closepath 227
　comments 228
　creating shadows 229
　device-independence 222
　displaying a string 240
　drawing a circle 227
　executing 225
　extensions 223
　fill 226
　interfacing to Objective-C 232–237
　interprocess communication with the Window
　　　Server 233
　operands 224
　operators 224
　optimizing drawing 234
　popping 224
　pushing 224
　resolution-independence 222
　rlineto 226
　rotating 229
　scaling 229
　setgray 226
　setting gray level 226, 227

special effects 229
stack based language 224
syntax errors 277
POTS 2
Preferences (application) 412
Preferences panel 288
PrefsController class 281, 290, 303, 304, 306
PrefsController subsystem 308
Print (Gdb panel) 510
printf() 145
printPSCode: 274
printSelection: 302
procedural programming 8
procedure 8
project file (PB.project) 126
ProjectBuilder 5
   adding header files via dragging 311
   Attributes accessory view 129
   Build accessory view 129
   Build button 143
   Builder button 143
   Command-double-clicking 194
   Debug button 129, 144, 505
   Files accessory view 127
   installing an application 406
   Menu
       Add Help Directory 418
   Run button 129, 144
prototyping 123
PSgsave 217
PSnewinstance() 238
PSrestore() 217
PSselectfont() 240
PSsetinstance(NO) 238
PSsetinstance(YES) 238
PSshow() 240
pswraps 234

R

readInput() 79, 86
readText: 361
receiver 17, 153
Recycler 280, 442–443
registration table 284, 285, 286, 287, 325
Release Notes 576
RenderMan 2
responder chain 344
Responder class 152
restoring the window 435
Return key xxx, 171
reusability 289
root class 20
root directory 436
rotate 229
RTF 401
run 151

Run (Gdb panel) 509
run() 79
runModal 352, 358
runModalForDirectory: file: 353
runModalForDirectory:file:types: 360

S

Save (button in an alert panel) 179
saveDocumentToFile: 355, 373
SavePanel class 175, 351–354, 442
   instantiating 388
scale 230, 231
scrollbar 436
searching (multiple files for a string) 502
sed (stream editor) 466
selectedCell 302
selectedIndex 170, 196
selector 18, 24
self 41, 510, 514, 515
sendAction:to: 153
sender 153, 190
server 3
set (gdb command to set a variable) 520
setDocEdited: 363
setDocView: 347
setEditable: 166
setFloatingPointFormat:left:right 332, 333
setFloatValue: 333
setHorizScrollerRequired: 496
setMaxValue: 162
setMinValue: 162
setOutletName: 293, 494
setRequiredFileType: 353, 354
setSel:: 339
setting a target 138
setTitle: 155
setTruncate: 306
ShapeView 247
Shift-Tab key 169, 182
showAccessoryView: 306, 327
showError: 373
showOpenPanel: 372
showSavePanel: 354, 372
SIG (special interest group) 571
single operators 232
single-stepping 508
sizeToFit 170
Slider class 152, 161–164
Smalltalk 21, 22
smartPrintPSCode: 274
sonata.cc.purdue.edu (archive site) 530
sprintf() 240
SquareView 247
standard help entries 417
stanza (in make) 471

static (keyword) 354
static binding 40
static typing 23
stdarg 583
stderr 145
stdout 145, 466
Step (gdb command) 512
strcasecmp() 287, 325
stream 354, 355
subclass 13
subproject 128
subsystem 184, 308
subview 159
super 42
superclass 13
superview 158, 214
switch button 297
switchToView: 327
SwitchView class 303, 304, 306

T

tab (in make) 472
Tab key 169, 182
TableOfContents.rtf 418
tabs (preserving during cut and paste) 466
takeFloatValue: 168
takeFloatValueFrom: 168
target 153
　querying the target 327
　setting the target 167, 171, 302
target (in make) 471
target-action 149, 153
TargetObject class 298
targets (searching targets in Digital Librarian) 453
Terminal 447, 465–470
　Menu
　　　New (Command-n) 468
terminate: 149, 151
Text class 175, 337
　alignment 339
　ASCII 401
　clipped 346
　delegate 362
　initializing 338
　instantiating 338
　Rich Text Format 401
textDidGetKeys:isEmpty: 362, 363, 369, 373
textfield 297
TextField class 165–168
TIFF 128
tight coupling 94
Tim Heap xxxii
title bar 437
tracing (a program) 491–504
tracing (without debugging information) 513
transparency 223

truncate 306, 332
typecast 23
typed streams 583

U

unified imaging model 209
union 275
Unix Expo 573
uudecode 533
uuencode 533

V

value (of a default) 280
varargs 583
View class 152, 209
　adding a subview 213
　bounds rectangle 272
　clipped 216
　converting coordinates 220
　coordinate system 215
　creating 212
　determining the window 214
　determining the superview 214
　drawing order 214
　focusing 217
　graphics state 216
　hierarchy 214
　initializing 212
　instantiating in InterfaceBuilder 253
　lockFocus 278
　printing support 274
VT100 447

W

wait cursor 436
warning messages 486
window 214
Window class 175, 368
Window Server 3
windowWillClose: 174, 175, 179, 333, 373, 500
windowWillResize:toSize: 173
wizzywig 209
word expansion (in Digital Librarian) 456
word expansion (in Edit) 447
Words 364
Workspace 5, 431, 468
　Menu
　　　Duplicate (Command-d) 419
　　　Empty Recycler 280
　　　Finder 502
　　　Inspector 472
　　　Open as Folder 147
　　　Open as Folder (Command-O) 418
　　　Update Viewers (Command-u) 419
Workspace Manager 5
wraps file 234
writeText: 355

WYSIWYG 209

Y
Yap 225